Rome- [illegible]

To Clifford
c̄ love & deep
respect
As ever
Leo & Anita

signed by Angell

I
£35

The Psychoanalytic Core

The Psychoanalytic Core

Essays in Honor of
Leo Rangell, M.D.

edited by

Harold P. Blum, M.D.
Edward M. Weinshel, M.D.
F. Robert Rodman, M.D.

International Universities Press, Inc.
Madison Connecticut

Library of Congress Cataloging-in-Publication Data

The Psychoanalytic core/edited by Harold P. Blum,
Edward M. Weinshel, F. Robert Rodman.
p. cm.
"In honor of Leo Rangell"—Pref.
Includes bibliographical references.
ISBN 0-8236-4409-X
1. Psychoanalysis. I. Blum, Harold P., 1929- . II. Weinshel, Edward M. III. Rodman, F. Robert (Francis Robert), 1934- . IV. Rangell, Leo.
RC506.P7763 1989
616.89' 17—dc20 89-36104
CIP

Manufactured in the United States of America

CONTENTS

CONTRIBUTORS

JACOB A. ARLOW, M.D.
Clinical Professor of Psychiatry and Training Analyst, Psychoanalytic Institute, New York University Medical Center; Training Analyst, New York Psychoanalytic Institute; Past President, American Psychoanalytic Association; Former Editor-in-Chief of The *Psychoanalytic Quarterly*.

HAROLD P. BLUM, M.D.
Clinical Professor of Psychiatry and Training Analyst, Psychoanalytic Institute, New York University Medical Center; Executive Director, Sigmund Freud Archives; Past Editor, *Journal of the American Psychoanalytic Association*.

CHARLES BRENNER, M.D.
Training and Supervising Analyst, New York Psychoanalytic Institute; Past President, American Psychoanalytic Association.

JANINE CHASSEGUET-SMIRGEL, Ph.D.
Training Analyst, Paris Psychoanalytic Society; Professor, University College, London, Freud Chair (1982–1983).

R. HORACIO ETCHEGOYEN, M.D.
Vice President, International Psychoanalytical Association.

BARBARA FIELDS, M.S.W.
Private practice, New York, NY; Task force member, Education for Careers in Infancy, National Center for Clinical Infant Programs, Washington, D.C.

ELEANOR GALENSON, M.D.
Clinical Professor of Psychiatry, Mount Sinai School of Medicine; Vice President and Member, New York Psychoanalytic Society.

JULES GLENN, M.D.
Clinical Professor of Psychiatry, New York University Medical Center; Training and Supervising Analyst, Psychoanalytic Institute, New York University Medical Center.

LEÓN GRINBERG, M.D.
Former Vice President, International Psycho-Analytical Association. Member, Argentine Psychoanalytic Association.

MARJORIE HARLEY, Ph.D.
Former Member of Columbia Center for Psychoanalytic Training and Research; Past Faculty Member, Baltimore-Washington Psychoanalytic Institute; Adjunct Professor of Psychoanalytic Psychology, John Hopkins University.

MILTON E. JUCOVY, M.D.
Training and Supervising Analyst, The New York Psychoanalytic Institute; Visiting Staff Psychiatrist, North Shore University Hospital, Manhasset, New York; Past President, New York and Long Island Psychoanalytic Societies.

OTTO F. KERNBERG, M.D.
Associate Chairman and Medical Director, New York Hospital-Cornell Medical Center, Westchester Division; Professor of Psychiatry, Cornell University Medical College; Training and Supervising Analyst, Columbia University Center for Psychoanalytic Training and Research.

PEARL H. M. KING, B.A. Hons.
Training Psychoanalyst, Past President, and now Honorary Archivist, British Psychoanalytical Society; Former Hon. Secretary, International Psychoanalytical Association.

SERGE LEBOVICI, M.D.
Emeritus Professor of Child and Adolescent Psychiatry, University Paris-North; Member, Paris Psycho-analytical Society; President-Elect, World Association For Infant Psychiatry and Allied Disciplines; Former President, International Psychoanalytical Association.

ADAM LIMENTANI, M.D., FRCPsych
Training Analyst, British Psychoanalytic Society; Honorary Consultant Psychotherapist, Portman Clinic, London; Past President, International Psychoanalytic Association.

RAFAEL MOSES, M.D.
Erik H. Erikson Scholar in Residence, Austen Riggs Center; Training and Supervising Analyst, Israel Psychoanalytic Institute; Past Sigmund Freud Professor of Psychoanalysis, Hebrew University, Jerusalem; Past President, Israel Psychoanalytic Society.

F. ROBERT RODMAN, M.D.
Member, Los Angeles Psychoanalytic Society and Institute; Member, Center for Advanced Psychoanalytic Studies, Princeton, New Jersey.

LEONARD SHENGOLD, M.D.
Clinical Professor of Psychiatry and Training Analyst, Psychoanalytic Institute, New York University Medical Center.

ROBERT J. STOLLER, M.D.
Professor of Psychiatry, U.C.L.A. School of Medicine.

NIKOLAAS TREURNIET, M.D.
Psychoanalyst, private practice; Training and Supervising Analyst, Dutch Psychoanalytical Society and Institute.

HEIMAN VAN DAM, M.D.
Training and Supervising Psychoanalyst, Adult and Child Psychoanalysis, Los Angeles Psychoanalytic Society and Institute; Supervising Psychoanalyst, Child Psychoanalysis, Southern California Psychoanalytic Institute; Associate Clinical Professor, Departments of Psychiatry and of Pediatrics, U.C.L.A. School of Medicine; Contributing Editor, *Arbeits Hefte Kinderpsychoanalyse.*

ROBERT S. WALLERSTEIN, M.D.
Professor of Psychiatry, University of California at San Francisco, School of Medicine; President, International Psycho-Analytical Association.

EDWARD M. WEINSHEL, M.D.
Training and Supervising Analyst, San Francisco Psychoanalytic Institute; Clinical Professor, Department of Psychiatry, University of California School of Medicine, San Francisco; Secretary, International Psychoanalytic Association; Former North-American Editor of *The International Journal* and *International Review of Psychoanalysis;* Former Chairman Board on Professional Standards, American Psychoanalytic Association.

Clifford Yorke, FRCPsych, DPM
Medical Director, The Anna Freud Centre, London; Fellow, Royal College of Medicine, London; Training Analyst, British Psychoanalytical Society; Editor, Internation Psychoanalytic Library.

1

IN HONOR OF LEO RANGELL, M.D.

Harold P. Blum, M.D.

The editors take pride and pleasure in this celebratory volume honoring Leo Rangell. He is one of those rare personalities whose brilliant achievements set him apart from his colleagues and peers. With extraordinary and extensive contributions to all areas of psychoanalysis, he is one of the most distinguished and admired analysts of our time. This book extends congratulations to Leo Rangell, now 75 years old, from all the authors in the volume, as well as from the entire psychoanalytic and mental health community. As an original scholar, researcher, author, lecturer, teacher, and administrator, Dr. Rangell is permanently imprinted upon the entire field. His unusual analytic skills have enriched the understanding of theory and technique, but they have also been applied to important interests outside the classical psychoanalytic situation. Dr. Rangell provided central perspectives of both microscopic and macroscopic views of the analytic and intrapsychic processes; he also enlarged our vision of group process, political process, and social regulation. His profound and prolific work resulted in many classics of the psychoanalytic literature. The power of his intellect; the force of his ideas; his personal integrity, genuine charm and wit; his generosity of unstinting service to students, institutes, and major psychoanalytic institutions—all have continuously rewarded his science, his profession, and his colleagues.

While he helped to preserve and protect the core of psychoanalytic discoveries, Leo Rangell has also been an intrepid explorer who advanced the frontiers of psychoanalysis. In all of his creative endeavors and his analytic accomplishments, he has always stood up for his convictions, candidly expressed his accord or dissent, and refused any compromise of integrity. Surveying the administrative concerns with which he was regularly entrusted as twice president of the American Psychoanalytic Association, twice president of the International Psycho-Analytical Association, and three-time president of the Los Angeles Psychoanalytic Society, Dr. Rangell analyzed the threats of irrational infiltration of judgment and decision by regressive transference, political process, social pressure, and other irrational forces. With all of his work, Dr. Rangell has sought to further the development of psychoanalysis and to expand its explanatory power. He has aimed at a comprehensive theory of the personality, which includes all the metapsychological points of view and a balanced view of normality, pathogenesis, and psychopathology. Leo Rangell's own original formulations and additions, combined with respect for all that is valuable in the work of Freud and the past pioneers, have represented a remarkable synthesis of the past, present, and future of psychoanalysis. His work demonstrates a unique ability for synthesis an integration, yet possesses its own novel gestalt.

While aware of the ubiquity of unconscious infantile conflict and attitudes, disrupting and corrupting tendencies in the human condition, Rangell has also attended to ego mastery, commitment and conviction, friendship, and the mature process of moral judgment. He has always managed to preserve an overview that takes into account the intrapsychic and the interpersonal, the biological and the psychological, the individual and the group, past and present, fantasy and reality, regressive and progressive tendencies, and developmental thrust.

Rangell stimulates analytic curiosity, and he also stimulates our curiosity about Leo Rangell himself. He is not a native of California but was born and reared in Brooklyn, New York. A first-born son, he was a superlative student. He graduated from Columbia University in 1933 with Phi Beta Kappa honors. He received his M.D. degree at the University of Chicago School of Medicine, and his medical school recently gave him the very rare honor of a distinguished service award. He began training in psychiatry and then also in neurology at the New York State Psychiatric Institute and at Montefiore Hospital. Drawn to psychoanalysis during his medical, neurological, and psychiatric education, Rangell started his candidacy at the New York Psychoanalytic Institute and completed his training at the Los Angeles Psychoanalytic Institute after World War II. During the War, he served in the United States Airforce with distinction and was promoted to Major, a harbinger of his rapid ascent to the highest offices in psychoanalytic organizations. He continues to be a leader and consultant in national and international psychoanalysis and is currently clinical professor of psychiatry at the University of California in Los Angeles as well as in San Francisco. He has been visiting professor, consultant, lecturer, and discussant, not only at analytic institutions and conferences, but also at the leading universities of the world. From the Turner Professorship at Columbia University to his recent Lectureship of the Freud Chair in Israel, Rangell has delivered numerous Freud and other highly distinguished lectures and has received many prizes. He has served on the Board of the Center for Advanced Psychoanalytic Studies in Princeton and Aspen, was a Fellow at the Center for Advanced Study in the Behavioral Sciences at Stanford, California, and a Guggenheim Foundation Fellow for "The Unconscious Roots of the Decision-Making Process." In 1981 he received the *Journal of the American Psychoanalytic Association* Prize and in 1985 the Heinz Hartmann Award of the New York Psychoanalytic Institute. Dr. Rangell may be the only individual to have been twice awarded the Clinical Essay Prize of the British Psychoanalytical Society for "The Analysis of a Doll Phobia" in 1952 and "The Psychology of Poise" in 1954. He received awards and citations throughout his career in a most remarkable and illustrious series of achievements, contributions, and recognition of outstanding service.

Leo Rangell has also rendered most distinguished service to scholarly journals in the field. I would particularly like to mention his long association with the *Journal of the American Psychoanalytic Association*. I had the personal gratification and great reward of being associated with Leo Rangell during my years of editorship and having him as a special consultant to the *Journal*. It is one thing to be an author and quite another to be able to empathize with the reader and the audience. To be a concerned and caring critic, able at the same time to explain the most arcane and recondite subject matter, to grasp the essence and essentials of another author's contribution, to place someone else's work in the context of ongoing developments in psychoanalysis, and to vigorously and logically present and evaluate a paper's ideas, strengths, and problems—all with grace and wit—is very rarely found in any reader or referee. I can say, without qualification, that Rangell's reports to the editor were as unfailingly illuminating as they were exquisitely insightful and thoroughly impartial. His reports enormously furthered the editorial process and the reciprocal analytic education, which is one of the finest rewards of *Journal* participation. Leo Rangell would not be seduced or intimidated by what was popular or trendy, by glossy repetition of time-honored positions, or by empty expeditions and pretentious investigations without scientific yield. He searches for valid innovation and constructive advance without yielding to pretentious presentations which, upon closer inspection, have nothing to say that is really challenging or significant. Searching for and alert to new ideas and propositions, ever interested in the ongoing growth of the field, Rangell evaluated with an analytic attitude and without prejudgment. His genuine convictions have sometimes led him to isolated, passionately held positions, but never to rigid adherence or monolithic dogmatism.

In surveying the decades of Leo Rangell's brilliant contributions, one is struck by his bridging of clinical and theoretical concepts and of different perspectives and models. Combining many current dichotomies, the biological-structural coexists with the hermeneutic, and drive theory with a complex theory of affect and motivation. Shifting between microscopic detail and macroscopic overviews, Rangell succeeds in establishing new links and a new organization. This architecture is readily discerned in his work on psychic trauma, which integrated the metapsychological points of view and the various clinical components of trauma. His work on trauma is related to his renowned studies of anxiety. From disparate components of the danger situation and anxiety response, Rangell achieved a comprehensive solution to the different theories of traumatic anxiety and of signal anxiety.

Studies of the signal function of anxiety led to formulations concerning the signal function of other affects and their role in conflict and defense. Rangell expanded the psychoanalytic conceptualization of affects and placed affect theory in close relation to the classical concepts of conflict and defense, but also at the frontiers of contemporary psychoanalytic studies of ego development and object relations. With respect to developmental studies, Rangell has been described as a cryptic child analyst. He has given major papers at conferences on infant psychiatry, adolescent psychiatry, and psychoanalytic developmental theory. His studies have ranged from an early paper on the infantile roots of poise to a recent investigation of the "Biopsychological Base of Infancy." His work on "The Role of Early Psychic Functioning in Psychoanalysis" (1961) paralleled his interest in "Reconstruction and Theory Formation." "Beyond and Between the No and Yes" (1963), written in honor of René Spitz, advanced formulations of early infantile communication and demonstrated the close relationship between infant observation and psychoanalytic reconstruction. Object relations interests were already evident in his paper "On the Role of the Parent in the Oedipus Complex" (1955), foreshadowing his later contributions to the object concept, and psychoanalytic theories of the self, the object, and reality. His extensive work on the individual in the family was balanced with an appreciation of the importance of society and culture in "The Human Core" (1967), and considerations of morality and values in "The Compromise of Integrity" (1974, 1980). But Rangell also explicates and illuminates the role of the individual within the group and the effect of the group and its dynamics upon the individual. The relationship between the leader and the led, the interidentification within the group, and the maintenance of a differentiated self or self-constancy as a resistance to regressive engulfment by the group are all presented with masterful clarity, e.g., in *The Mind of Watergate* (1980). Here the compromise of integrity was explored in the individual, the leader, the power elite, and mass society.

One of the most difficult areas of psychoanalytic theory concerns the paradox between a strict psychic determinism and an active ego which, when faced with conflict, can choose and decide among different alternatives. The problem of evaluation and judgment leading to choice and decision has been a thorny issue even before Hartmann's work on ego autonomy and intentionality. Leo Rangell's investigations of these issues uniquely bridged between determinism and ego autonomy, and between psychoanalysis, academic psychology, and philosophy. Rangell's "Decision-Making Process" (1971) is the foundation for a series of studies culminating in "The Executive Functions of the Ego: An Extension of the Concept of Ego Autonomy" (1986). These studies offer an expanded view of autonomy and responsibility, determinism and will. Indecision, he deduced, does not always spring from intersystemic conflict or the polarization of drives, but can result from disturbances in the ego's decision-making function. Unconscious structural conflict typically may result in compromise formations and instinctual polarities in ambivalence. But with signal anxiety, the ego must choose and decide between competing alternatives. Choice is added to oppositional conflict. Extending his formulations in "Unconscious Choice: An Extension of Psychoanalytic Theory" (1987), Rangell underscores the importance of unconscious decision. A theory of action emerges, consistent with structural theory and the metapsychological points of view. Because so much of the mental life is unconscious, man has less control over his behavior than he realizes, but he is also more responsible for his thoughts and actions than he cares to acknowledge.

Leo Rangell's style tends to both narrow and expand as his writing proceeds toward an increasingly clear focus. There is always more to be understood than is directly expressed because of the compression of several intersecting analytic thoughts. Many a paragraph can easily be the nucleus of another paper, packed with ideas without being prolix or pretentious. He is always himself, an individual who can be passionately devoted to his own interests and views, defending his position with candor and integrity, but always retaining scientific skepticism and attunement with the views of others. His vast knowledge of the literature is apparent in his attributions and citations of colleagues as it is in his panel introductions and discussions.

At 75, Leo Rangell is actively contributing and creative, surveying the human condition, and working at the frontiers of the science of man. He is forever learning, fascinated by new observations and experience, a perennial student of human nature. Given his monumental scholarly accomplishments, Leo Rangell is, at the same time, a dear and devoted friend, a wonderful raconteur, a witty and wise counselor, a great humorist who narrates, creates, and appreciates jokes. His marvelous imitations can be satirically side-splitting, but they also represent higher levels of trial identification and empathy.

Leo Rangell's fabulous achievements have been almost entirely independent with few exceptions, for example, the classic paper on tics that he co-authored with Margaret Mahler in the auspicious beginning of his career. He is at the same time inseparable from his lovely life partner, his wife, Anita. Anita and Leo are a composite whole so that one cannot imagine one without the other. Ever gracious, thoughtful, and considerate, Anita has been an alter ego and steadfast support for Leo throughout the years. Devoted to her family and friends, Anita has also pursued her own interests in art appreciation and aesthetics.

Leo Rangell has continued the legacy of the great structural theorists and ego psychologists, following after Freud, who so enriched and expanded psychoanalytic thought. He has represented total composite psychoanalysis and is represented within every area and every aspect of psychoanalysis. He has preserved what is enduring in classical psychoanalysis while adding steady contributions of his own. Leo Rangell's magnificent scientific work, his humanity, integrity, and genuine concern, have profoundly influenced and inspired the authors of this Festschrift and their psychoanalytic colleagues throughout the world. This Festschrift celebrates the "complete psychoanalyst and humanist."

2

PERSONAL MEMOIR

Jacob A. Arlow, M.D.

There are some people who at first contact transmit a sense of vibrant vitality that marks them off from all others. This was my experience when I first met Leo Rangell. We were both assistant residents in neurology at Montefiore Hospital. I was an old married man of three years' standing, and Leo was newly wed. He projected a sense of intellectual vigor and friendly curiosity. I knew immediately that I had just made a special friend.

Brief though they were, the days at Montefiore took on mythic proportions. The learning process was intense and challenging. The colleagues and teachers were colorful and demanding. Among the attendings, Moses Keschner was outstanding. He was a master clinician, an exacting teacher with a special interest in neurological manifestations of abnormal involuntary movements. Many residents, including ourselves, found themselves chagrined when Keschner demonstrated a fine tremor or some extrapyramidal sign we had missed. Accordingly, I could understand Leo's excitement when he told me that he had just admitted a young woman who exhibited a variety of unusual, abnormal, involuntary movements that would surely delight and challenge our mentor. We went over the case together and had no small difficulty in trying to localize or even understand the nature of the patient's lesions. Fortunately, Nathaniel Root, who was chief resident at the time, came to our aid and demonstrated to us beyond doubt that we were dealing with a hysterical woman.

Now we had a plan in mind. We would present the case to Dr.

Keschner as a straightforward neurological problem and see what he would do with it. Leo Rangell would not present even a hint of the richly hysterical fantasy life that he was able to elicit from the patient once the diagnosis of hysteria had been made. At the clinical conference, he presented the case in a most straightforward, organically minded fashion. Keschner listened impassively, not a question, not a comment. Nor did he say a word while the patient's bizarre "neurological" findings were being demonstrated. As soon as the presentation was over, Keschner paused for a moment, looked over at Leo, and said, "Okay, Rangell, now give us the dirt."

Leo has a great gift of mimicry and could be very entertaining giving funny imitations of public figures and characters we knew around the hospital. In fact, as part of the graduation show, the house staff put on at the end of the year, Leo and I, together with two other colleagues, played the characters of four members of the attending staff, whom we commonly referred to as "the Four Manics of Montefiore." Leo gave a bravura imitation of Nathan Savitsky, one of the most brilliant, most colorful, and most unpredictable of our teachers.

Only later did I come to appreciate how important such a gift could be in our professional work. To be able to give an accurate imitation means to be an accurate observer. Leo could capture the cadence and intonation typical for the speech disorders of the various neurological conditions. When you observed his imitation, it was possible not only to diagnose the condition but to identify the precise patient whom we had seen on the wards. I recognized later as well how this ability of Leo's entailed one of the most important qualities of the gifted psychoanalyst. To recreate a condition or a character one has to be able to empathize with the patient and his condition. This is a quality he possesses to the highest degree. It is clearly reflected in his clinical work, especially in such studies as "The Psychology of Poise: With a Special Elaboration on the Psychic Significance of the Snout or Perioral Region" (1954). To this day, Leo often greets me with an imitation of a lovable, but seriously defective, hydrocephalic little boy whose care we shared as residents.

Whatever Leo does, he does wholeheartedly, that is to say,

with intensity, joyousness, and ebullience, a sense of excitement that he generates in others. One night, for example, I heard an insistent tooting of an automobile horn beneath my window at the hospital. I looked out and there was Leo in his brand new Chevrolet. "Get someone to cover you and come down. We'll go for a ride," he called out. Here, I felt, was a man much to be envied. He had this beautiful bride, Anita, his own apartment near the hospital, no mean accomplishment for any assistant resident in the late 1930s, and now this car. It was a joyous ride. His enthusiasm and pleasure were absolutely infectious. We drove through southern Westchester and back again to the hospital, and I returned feeling quite elated.

There is an ironic postscript to this story. Some while later, while Leo was serving as a psychiatric resident at Grasslands Hospital, one of the patients, in a suicidal attempt, stole the car and wrecked it. If I recall correctly, Leo confronted the situation with surprising equanimity, much more concerned about the fate of the patient than about the car.

In those days, most of the residents in neurology at Montefiore and at other leading hospitals eventually turned to psychoanalytic training. That was the exciting thing to do. To be sure, this was most disappointing to some of our most eminent teachers. Among them was Professor Sachs, a man keenly interested in heredodegenerative diseases, whose name figures in the eponyme for Tay-Sachs Disease. He offered us both fellowships for research in this area, but we chose instead to go on to psychoanalytic training. Since that time, of course, the study of genetic abnormalities has been a subject of major interest in medicine in general and neurology in particular. It makes me think of our little hydrocephalic patient, who today could have been helped by surgery.

Leo and I met again some months later when we were both residents at the New York State Psychiatric Institute. By this time, we were close friends and had both decided to begin our training in psychoanalysis. To this new enterprise, Leo dedicated the same wholehearted interest and enthusiasm that was characteristic of him in other activities. It was a dedication that persists to this very day. Whether traveling together on the subway to our analytic hours or walking along Central Park West after classes at the Institute, there was this constant, intense discussion of every aspect of psychoanalytic theory and practice. By now we had begun to establish both our families and our practices, but the all-consuming interest in psychoanalysis never abated. It was striking how frequently we came to similar conclusions about the many issues in psychoanalysis that were being debated at the time and since.

But world events were soon to overtake us. It was at his home on a Sunday afternoon, his new daughter in her basket and my new son in his basket, that we listened to Winston Churchill, promising even to make a pact with the devil in order to crush Hitler. It was not long thereafter that our country was at war and, if I remember correctly, some time at the beginning of the new year, Leo flew out of New York City to enter the service of his country. My colleagues in the study group, David Beres, Charles Brenner, and Martin Wangh, all felt that, had Leo remained in New York, he would have been the fifth member of our group. As it was, after Leo settled in California, we felt that he was our West Coast participant.

Upon completing military service, Leo settled in Los Angeles, where he finished his psychoanalytic training and established his career. I have always felt that his deracination from the East Coast and New York City has never been complete, that he has never really fully settled in to the special ambiance of southern California. I recall on one occasion discussing with him the special problems of transference and countertransference when conducting analyses in the glamorous atmosphere of Hollywood. Leo started to say, "When in reality," then he paused and added, "or what goes for reality in Los Angeles." As he demonstrated in both word and action, his integrity was not to be compromised.

With all the ebullience and zest for living so characteristic of him, one can nevertheless detect a certain inner sadness and loneliness. It is a very specific kind of quality that I have found to be characteristic of unusual men with exceptional talent. Perhaps it stems from a feeling of not being able to share fully the depth of one's understanding, or a concern about being so different, or anxiety about evoking the hostile envy of others. It is an ineffable quality, hard to discuss. Nonetheless, it is a quality one cannot fail to perceive.

All this discussion would be faulted indeed without mentioning Anita. In fact, Leo would not be Leo without Anita. She has been part of every decision, every position, every experience in Leo's life, hovering over him continuously and tidying up the details of his forgetfulness and delaying. It would not be beyond Leo, who notoriously leaves the preparation of speeches, reports, etc., to the last moment, to put a manuscript aside in a briefcase and to find Anita carrying the briefcase he had forgotten to take along. Many times while we were walking the streets of Manhattan, deeply engaged in some psychoanalytic discussion, Leo would dart unthinkingly into the perilous New York traffic, only to be safely retrieved by Anita's watchful concern.

Neither time nor distance can dim the luster of the memories we share.

3

LEO RANGELL AND THE INTEGRITY OF PSYCHOANALYSIS

F. Robert Rodman, M.D.

An examination of Leo Rangell's published work, now well beyond 250 articles and two books, calls forth numerous, fitting, descriptive words, but one, the word *integrity,** stands above and includes all the rest. In its several meanings, it applies both to the work and the man, and, insofar as it describes the work, it may be applied to Rangell's labor on behalf of the theory and practice of psychoanalysis, and to the relationship of the ego to the superego, where the battle for integrity is continuously fought. This site had been regarded as off limits to the neutral and nonjudgmental psychoanalyst until Rangell showed that his or her point of view is required there too. By adding problems of integrity to the list of legitimate psychoanalytic concerns, he made a more integrated theory and practice possible.

Rangell's work on "the compromise of integrity" appeared in the '70s and coincided with the American ethical crisis known as Watergate. Long before this, however, his contributions were laying the necessary groundwork, and long thereafter Rangell would

*The Oxford English Dictionary (1971) lists the following definitions of *integrity:* "(1) The condition of having no part or element taken away or wanting; undivided or unbroken state; material wholeness, completeness, entirety; (2) the condition of not being marred or violated; unimpaired or uncorrupted condition; original perfect state; soundness; (3) In moral sense (a) unimpaired moral state; freedom from moral corruption; innocence, sinlessness (b) soundness of moral principle; the character of uncorrupted virtue especially in relation to truth and fair dealing; uprightness, honesty, sincerity." The word *integrity* comes from the Latin *integritas,* meaning wholeness, entireness, completeness, integrity, chastity, purity. Another related word of the same origin is *integer.*

venture further into the realm of human responsibility by bringing the will into the heart of psychoanalytic thought, and, along with it, an understanding of action within the structural theory.

His first paper, on "Cerebral Air Embolism," appeared when he was 29, in 1942, and in the following year he and Margaret Mahler published their paper on Gilles de la Tourette's disease. A mass of detail throughout this 24-page study yields a vivid impression of the young patient.

By 1950, his first truly analytic paper appeared in *The Psychoanalytic Study of the Child,* "A Treatment of Nightmares in a Seven-Year-Old Boy." Rangell recounts treatment by correspondence, in which he combines education of the parents with suggestions for interventions, on the model of Freud's treatment of Little Hans. He writes to friends in New York, the city of his childhood, from Los Angeles, his new home. Bringing together the disparate is to be another of his hallmarks. This paper shows a fine analytic mind already in being, just at the end of his training, but there is no hint that by 1955, at the age of 42, Rangell will demonstrate his sense of having a role to play in psychoanalytic history by undertaking the effort to unify Freud's two theories of anxiety.

In that five-year span, a burst of contributions established him as one of the leading psychoanalysts in the world. His doll phobia paper (1952a; republished recently in Sholevar, 1987) and long a staple in institute curricula, presents such a multiplicity of observations, meanings, and conclusions, that the stamp of human reality is on every page. His paper on the macroscopic point of view (1952b) shows how he can make us see the previously invisible, add it to what we already know, and then make a new whole out of the two of them. Yes, he says, as analyst-microscopists, we have shown the world what can be seen deeply, but we must stand away sometimes, too, to see the large picture. His paper on the interchangeability of phallus and female genital (1953) is another of his contributions to the study of opposites. His unceasing attention to the relationship of opposites will one day lead him to write: "The capacity of the analyst to represent subtly and consistently a fusion of opposites becomes for the patient, unconsciously if not overtly, a model for the resolution of conflict" (1986a).

In 1954, a committee of the American Psychoanalytic Association had been unable to arrive at a consensus on a definition of psychoanalysis. Rangell makes the following bold attempt: "Psychoanalysis is a method of therapy whereby conditions are brought about favorable for the development of a transference neurosis, in which the past is restored in the present, *in order that,* through a systematic interpretive attack on the resistances which oppose it, there occurs a resolution of that neurosis (transference *and* infantile) *to the end* of bringing about structural changes in the mental apparatus of the patient to make the latter capable of optimum adaptation to life" (1954a, pp. 739–740).

This definition, ignoring questions of whether the couch is used or how frequent the sessions are, shibboleths that defined psychoanalysis for the public and, to a certain extent, for a proportion of psychoanalysts themselves, will stand the test of time. A 1981 essay on the same subject, which measures the progression of his viewpoint, provides him with an opportunity to reaffirm, in the light of a quarter century of added experience, the importance of the individual parts. This second attempt to discuss the same subject contains a defense of reconstruction in the therapeutic process, with which to argue against a contemporary trend toward transference interpretation to the exclusion of the ultimate analysis of the infantile neurosis. Rangell is never swept away by the appeal of purity of method, which is one of the attractive elements in a simplified focus on transference. In every case, he chooses the ethical over the aesthetic, and often has to face unpopular consequences as a result.

In his paper on poise (1954b), he says that the state of poise

> is in its essence an integrative and sometimes a defensive function of the ego, constituting a state of anticipation of and readiness for incoming stimuli. It comes into play only in a social or interpersonal situation. The event feared and warded off is the cutting off of the stream of narcissistic supplies and the substitution for it of a state of shame; and unpoise is such a state of traumatic shame. The aim in poise is to hold on to and maintain the source of narcissistic supply, to belong, to be anchored to a larger and firm unit (person or group). The organs especially cathected for this holding on or contact function and through which these functions are mainly

> mediated are (1) the perioral or snout region; (2) the postural system and (3) the hand [p. 331].

Rangell captures the delicate teetering and overlap between the psychological and the physical, man in search of ground (1955c). Again, he is attentive to phenomenological reality within the confines of an exposition of causes and connections. The mind, the body, and, in this case, the group as well are centers of concern and will continue to be so throughout his career.

In his unpublished "A Tertiary Gain of Symptoms" (1954c), Rangell shows how chronic symptoms may become so much a part of a personal synthesis that effective treatment poses a threat to individual integrity. Long-suffering patients may yet be afraid to dispense with the limitations imposed by symptoms, lest they lose part of their very identity.

"The Role of the Parent in the Oedipus Complex" (1955a) once more shows us the other side of an equation, here the contribution of the parent which dovetails with the natural tendency of the child. Rangell's perception of the true dimensions of the importance of the Oedipus complex enlarges upon Freud's teachings about its fundamental role in human life. In 1971, at the Vienna Congress of the International Psychoanalytical Association, Rangell's discussion (1972) of the role of aggression in the oedipal myth and the Oedipus complex underscores the clinical finding that it is never completely resolved and is reactivated in typical situations and crises within the life cycle. This never-ending role, with powerful elements of aggression always present, is part of a more complete appreciation of the complexity of what Freud had first identified. He had used the word *resolution* for the events that lead into latency. Rangell speaks for only a "conditional resolution," and therefore only a conditional latency, even in healthy individuals.

Finally, in May 1954, four years after his first analytic paper, Rangell makes his initial attempt to unify the psychoanalytic theory of anxiety (1955b). This and related papers comprise the central focus of Rangell's theoretical concern and as such are the sturdy point of anchorage for numerous other contributions. In this most fundamental area of anxiety, Rangell forges a platform of conceptualizations on which psychoanalysis as a whole may rest and from which it may expand.

The two anxiety papers (1955b, 1968c) are accompanied by a number of others that address what he has named "the intrapsychic process." The anxiety signal is the point of maximum significance within the intrapsychic process. He identifies two kinds of conflicts within the structural model, oppositional conflicts which Freud conceptualized, and choice or dilemma conflicts, in which the ego must choose between conflicting alternatives. Rangell's discovery that the unconscious ego faces the need for choices makes the phenomenon of will basic to analytic theory. This supplements the resolution of intersystemic intrapsychic conflict through compromise formation. Rangell's expansion and integration of psychic functions revise and expand our view of the ego and make room for an adequate consideration of the ethical element in human life.

Freud's 1926 paper on anxiety concludes with his famous comment *non liquet*. He was not able to bring together two distinct ideas about anxiety, the first of which was that anxiety was "brought about as the direct effect of a traumatic factor whenever the ego was overwhelmed by undischarged instinctual excitation" (quoted by Rangell, 1955b, pp. 390–391); and the second of which conceptualized anxiety as a signal actively produced by the ego when it was threatened with a potential for trauma. In the first instance,

> A situation analogous to the trauma of birth is established in the id and an automatic reaction of anxiety ensues. . . . This mechanism is considered to be operative in the actual neuroses, while signal anxiety remains typical for the psychoneuroses. Two sources of anxiety are considered to exist, one involuntary, automatic, and experienced passively, and the other actively produced by the ego as a signal. The former hypothesis "possesses less interest for us now than it once did," *but* "we shall have to distinguish different cases" [quoted by Rangell, 1955b, p. 391].

> [I]nstead of a result of the traumatic state, anxiety was now seen as a signal of its approach. The anxiety reaction was no longer automatic, a direct transformation of libido, or physical-toxic in origin. It now had a psychological meaning, was a function of the

> ego, where it resided, and was produced and used by the latter in controlled amounts to serve as a signal of the approach of danger, which was an impending or potential traumatic state [Rangell, 1968c, p. 373].

Rangell's 1955 effort to unify these two theories "concentrated chiefly on the influence and applicability of the second theory on the first," and, in 1968, he attempted "to add . . . the effects and relevance of some of the formulations of the first theory to that of the second" (1968c, p. 378).

> A comprehensive psychoanalytic theory of anxiety, which applies to all instances of anxiety, combines elements of Freud's two historical theories of anxiety. The anxiety reaction is always set in motion by an existing traumatic state, either one which has invaded the ego involuntarily and from outside of its control (as in Freud's first theory); or one which has been brought about by the ego under its control in a minimal and experimental way (from Freud's second theory). This constitutes a twofold origin, in agreement with Freud's persistent idea. Both origins then converge in setting off a single common and unitary mechanism. The reaction is always a signal of the anticipation of danger (from the second theory). The danger is that of the traumatic state getting worse and out of control (first theory), or that the trauma which was sampled tentatively will come on in full force (second theory). The reaction always results automatically and involuntarily (as in the first theory), and is then *used* by the ego in an active way (from the second). The reaction, which is experienced by the ego (second theory), has both id (first theory) and ego (second theory) components. The reaction itself is both a psychological (from second theory) and a somatic one (from first theory).
>
> . . . With this combined unitary explanatory theory the small but definite kink at the heart of psychoanalytic theory may be smoothed out, and Freud's *"non liquet,"* I submit, can be changed to *"liquet"* [1968c, pp. 401–402].

Rangell's efforts in this area have not generally been noted or discussed in the literature. The theory of anxiety comprehends the border between mind and body, and Freud's theories exemplified the effect of Cartesian duality on the Western cast of mind. Rangell's effort is reparative, to bring mind and body closer together at their conceptual dividing point. By achieving this, he laid down a path for the future integration of the findings of neuroscience with psychoanalysis. His contributions make it unnecessary for investigators of biological aspects of behavior to turn away from the field of psychoanalysis as we know it. Present-day psychiatric thinkers, in search of legitimizing historical roots, seek to make a psychoanalytic basis for conceptualizations of what they call panic disorder by going back to the beginnings of Freudian thought, where they find the congenial concept of actual neurosis and the "Project for a Scientific Psychology" (1895). Rangell has provided a thoroughly modern alternative that facilitates the investigation of anxiety from any direction without the danger of losing a comprehensive grasp of all aspects of the subject. With the rearrangement of psychological professions taking place in the world—psychiatry returning to the body of medicine, psychoanalysis moving toward a more nonmedically based training — Rangell's ideas lay down a basis for a development of thought which moves in an opposite direction: toward unification. This is equally true of his conceptualizations on the subject of will and intention, where mechanisms and meanings are encompassed in a single unitary point of view.

Freud's conclusion left the way open for someone like Rangell to do the required work of integration. Freud was not willing to sacrifice an idea that he believed to have merit (the first theory of anxiety) for the sake of a spurious completeness. Although this is, I believe, the only place where he actually uses the words *non liquet,* his retention of earlier notions, even in the face of succeeding ones which would appear to have superseded them, is well-known to students of his work. It is significant, I think, that Rangell was drawn to the task. The prospect of such a piece of work must have resonated with his own disposition toward integration, so opposite to the spirit of eclecticism, which does not strain toward internal consistency but contents itself with a celebration of diversity.

There are a number of corollaries to these observations. Rangell's rootedness in the world of physical reality demands a theory that gives it a proper place. This will eventually put him in opposition to those who would reshape psychoanalytic thinking by cutting its conceptual ties to the physical world. Furthermore, Rangell will not sacrifice ideas with a powerful base in lived reality (such as Freud's first, physical, theory of anxiety) for the sake of spurious completeness (the second theory alone). This will eventually put him in opposition to theoreticians who would "unify" psychoanalytic thinking into a purely clinical theory by cutting away all metapsychological thought. Rangell will insist, instead, that, difficult though it may sometimes be, unwieldly to the seeker after simplicity, we must retain elements of mind and body or we will never achieve an integrated overview of human psychological functioning.

Rangell's grasp of the innumerable elements of a complex but unitary theory of the mind is rare. Just as in his intrapsychic process Rangell conceptualizes the inherent instability of mental function, so too in the realm of psychoanalytic theory there is an instability that tends in the direction of change, primarily loss of the complete, complex picture. Theories that *pars pro toto* represent one aspect for the whole are not the only models for destructive change masquerading as the liberating new. Rangell's point of view is similar to that of an Old Testament prophet who is protecting the achievement of man's internal unity via a conception of a single god, as opposed to an unlimited range of gods. The epoch-making achievement was an unstable one that required renewal and reinforcement. The sternness of the spirit of the Old Testament, with its emphasis on the quality of inescapable reality about right and wrong, and only vague reference to an afterlife, was succeeded by the charity and forgiveness of the New. Kohut's addition of kindness as treatment, a shortcut of relief in the direction of forgiveness, with its initial accompanying theory that self psychology was simply to be added onto traditional psychoanalytic thought, is a New Testament kind of mythology being added onto an Old. The result is an eclectic, nonintegrated point of view, with a less stringent philosophical and professional superego function, more useful in the practice of psychotherapy than psychoanalysis, or in those moments of psychoanalysis that veer into psychotherapy. Rangell, as we shall eventually see, achieved *liquet* for a more inclusive and coherent theory. He did this by making room for man's will. "Guilty man," to use Kohut's phraseology, and "tragic man" are clearly in view when problems of intention and purpose are accessible to analysis, though Rangell never becomes philosophical. He bears down on a subject as a scientist, leaving philosophical conclusions to others. His appeal is purely to reason.

Rangell's outline of steps in the intrapsychic process, one of the major scientific efforts of his career, first appeared in his article "The Scope of Intrapsychic Conflict" (1963a). It was repeated in "The Intrapsychic Process and Its Analysis" (1969a) and in "Choice-Conflict and the Decision-Making Function of the Ego" (1969b). Reference is made to this fundamental conceptualization in every paper having to do with decision-making, will, and the executive functions of the ego, for it is only within a grasp of the intrapsychic process that human choice takes on a meaning that is truly psychoanalytic.

> In a typical and model situation, the ego, having permitted a small amount of instinctual discharge to take place experimentally. . . , experiences a reactive response from the superego, and from other judging aspects of the ego itself, in accordance with the latter's evaluation of the nature of the discharge and its permissibility to these internal censors. This evaluation is accomplished by an internal scanning process in which the ego screens the present partial gratification through its filter of past memories, to see whether or not any past traumatic memory is revived, associatively connected with the experimental discharge. On the basis of the response received, the ego experiences either a feeling of safety and security, or a signal of anxiety, indicating the danger of punishment or disapproval by the superego, and/or of the external world. In the latter case, a tentative, experimental and signal conflict has been followed by the signal of anxiety.
>
> Following the experience of anxiety the ego is confronted with a choice of what to do next, whether to permit further discharge, or how not to, or how to effect a compromise or some other adaptive response. Possessed now of an awareness of cause and expected effect, of impulse and anticipated punishment, the ego is confronted with an internal intrasystemic decision-dilemma as to what to do next, which path to choose, how to find a way out. What is important here is that another type of conflict is being recognized and introduced at this point from the usual type en-

> visaged in the conventional use of the term "intrapsychic conflict." As a result of the estimate of danger accompanying the presence of signal anxiety, the ego is "in conflict" as to what to do next. To the traditional meaning of psychoanalytic conflict as an opposition between forces, as exemplified in the classic oppositional ego-id conflict, is added a second meaning of conflict as a "choice," a "decision-dilemma" type of intrapsychic conflict, a crucial type of intrasystemic conflict within the ego. This is now a competition between alternatives, a dilemma over which a decision must be made. . . .
>
> From this point on, a myriad of possibilities unfold as to possible outcomes . . . the unstable internal state continues striving towards a point of internal stability, either with or without resort to symptom formation. Further choices are involved along the way, of types of defence, action or inaction, choice of symptom, etc. The history of previous internal "solutions" lays down facilitating pathways which guide future choices, to the point of making the latter appear at times to be automatic. All of these result in predictability and become incorporated into enduring and structured character traits [1969b, p. 600].

Rangell's preoccupation with the intrapsychic process takes form as a style of writing which is often compelling, in spite of its theoretical complexity and depth. Nowhere is this more apparent than in his paper "Structural Problems in Intrapsychic Conflict" (1963b), where he devotes an extensive first section to proving that only the ego can have intrasystemic conflicts. He argues quietly, forcefully, and relentlessly. His conclusions seem inevitable.

We then have the sort of experience we have had many times while reading Freud's dialectical treatises. He begins to reflect deeply on the evidence available through clinical experience, and soon retracts his earlier conclusion: "We must assume some concern with order and consistency to exist within the superego; from this it follows that there is, at least to a certain degree, an organizing and synthesizing function within the superego and the ability to exercise a choice in order to effect this; therefore the superego *can* suffer internal intrasystemic conflicts when such cohesiveness and uniformity are either disrupted or nonexistent (1963b, p. 128).

In spite of his strenuous effort to comprehend the ego, Rangell the theoretician is also the practical psychoanalyst, and, deeper than that, the practical physician, whose grasp of reality is rooted in the experience of physical being. In a recent interview, he stated: "New contributions as well as extensions of old ones have to be judged by the emotional resonance of truth" (1988). His own far-reaching psychoanalytic thinking is thus always balanced by a function of the emotions, a "resonance." He frequently reminds his readers that the final test of an idea is in the clinical realm. Rangell's own struggle to arrive at cogent, coherent, integrated theories of human psychological function takes place in the area between his logical powers on the one hand and emotional resonance on the other. His study of reality is guided by the correcting effect of intellect and feeling acting on each other.

In a way that could be viewed as the working through of his ideas, Rangell's contributions continue to pursue the implications of his findings to their logical conclusions. The 1970s are centered on the decision-making process and its ethical implications, with the 1980s demonstrating a renewal of fundamental concepts through the medium of response to those who would alter what is, to Rangell, irreplaceably psychoanalytic about psychoanalysis. His tone, as the '80s progress, becomes quiet and direct. His papers on "A Core Process of Psychoanalytic Treatment" (1987a) and "The Executive Functions of the Ego" (1986b) are simple, factual, and convincing.

Rangell's expanded study of the ego's decision-making function was accompanied, in the 1970s, by an explicit focus on the relationship between the ego and superego. Pursuing the implications of one piece of insight after another, he was to find himself observing the contemporary sociopolitical scene through psychoanalytic eyes (1980) and generalizing his findings into the previously unexplored territory of unconscious ethical problems, what might be called the pathology of everyday morals.

"The Decision-Making Process" (1971a) is a clinical and theoretical paper in which Rangell continues the work that will one day become a true psychoanalytic theory of action. "The delineation of a psychoanalytic decision theory serves as a link between motivation (Rapaport, 1960) and action, and is en route to a psychoanalytic theory of action, which, as Hartmann (1947) pointed out, we do not yet have" (p. 435).

Connecting decision-making to his study of the intrapsychic process, Rangell says: "Psychoanalysis adds the level of unconscious mental functioning, with its scanning for memories of previous psychic traumata, by which the utility of anticipated decisions are judged. The scope and accuracy of predictions are thus enormously amplified by bringing into play previous experience and the entire sweep of the genetic past" (p. 439).

Focusing on the applicability of his ideas to the clinical situation, this paper generalizes its significance to man's ability to bear the responsibility for his decisions. "The delineation of an intrapsychic choice conflict spells out a moment in intrapsychic life in which the human psyche is confronted with the opportunity, and the necessity, to exercise its own directive potentials and to determine its own active course" (p. 440). "Correct interpretation is not enough" (p. 443). Describing the clinical experience he uses to illustrate the ideas, he says: "When the patient, continuing to fail to choose, instead constantly bombarded the analyst with the physical evidences of his mounting anxiety, to the point of almost a hypochondriacal orgy, the technique was now to interpret to him that it was his own failure to choose, again and still, which determined this inner state. The manifest 'I can't' meant the latent 'I won't' " (p. 444). "The analyst must . . . adopt and maintain a . . . vigilant analytic attitude and vigorously pursue the phenomena of inaction" (p. 447). Rangell tells us that "many psychosomatic symptoms which at the height of his anxiety I had assured him, with some trepidation on my part, were reversible have indeed reversed themselves" (p. 446). In the midst of the exertion of his own psychoanalytic will in the service of making way for the assertion of the patient's, Rangell provides reassurance. In spite of the power and thrust of his theoretical contributions, he never abandons the human provision of support for the laboring patient, and he demonstrates his belief that interpretation is never enough in psychoanalysis.

Rangell's (1971b) review of Robert Waelder's book *Progress and Revolution* is a fitting prologue to his own attempt to stake out psychoanalytic territory in the world of ethics and morality. Waelder had undertaken a sweeping view of world history, the study of which appealed to Rangell's alert concerns with the behavior of men in groups. The Watergate scandal in the United States, coming in the aftermath of the Vietnam war, with its public crisis of the morality of nations and of individuals, provided the immediate illustrative material for his reflections, which moved through his Vienna paper on aggressive aspects of the Oedipus complex, to his 1973 paper, delivered at the Paris Congress (published in 1974), in which he coined the term "the syndrome of the compromise of integrity." The effort required to bring the patient described in his "decision-making" paper to the point of action, together with voluminous clinical experience, underlines the multiplicity of solutions to conflict available to man. Among them, visible to all, was the compromise of integrity.

The area of morality and ethics had been studiously placed outside the role of psychoanalysis as therapy, first by Freud (at least in his written pronouncements, although it was always clear that Freud chose his patients from among those he could respect), and later by a variety of writers, the most important of which was Heinz Hartmann (1960). Psychoanalysis, it seemed, partly to avoid a reputation for imposing moral systems on patients, partly to maintain its objective status among sciences, must stay away from problems of morality and ethics. The analyst, by implication, was too vulnerable in the analysis of a patient's own moral views to remain safely scientific. Yet the times pressed for opinion in this matter (just as they always had) and Rangell's preparatory work led straight into this area.

He measures the distance psychoanalysis has traveled by writing that "the relation between the analysis of the Rat Man or the Wolf Man to a psychoanalysis of today is as the relationship of the first electric bulb to Times Square or Piccadilly—or to Edison's first gramophone to a modern sound studio" (1974, p. 3). He reviews the phenomena of psychoanalytic splits, with their evidence of struggles among analysts to cope with the pressures of membership in groups and the stresses of understanding themselves and their patients, and he concludes: "over the rubble, psychoanalysis still stands, like a colossus, ravaged and gouged but always there, to the relief even of those who attack it" (p. 7). In fact, Rangell's work was in no small measure responsible, at the time the paper was given, and even more so at the present time, for that survival.

Compromises of integrity, which he conceptualizes as taking place between the ego and the superego, analogous and of equal importance to the traditional analytic grasp of compromises which take place between ego and id, "are as ubiquitous in unconscious mentation as are the ingredients which will result in neuroses" (p. 7). They are "on a par with neurosis in human affairs" (1976, p. 37).

In addition, "there is another 'borderline' than what we commonly mean by that term," he says. "Clinical and life experiences show that there is a grey area, a 'borderline' between neuroses and Cs of I (compromises of integrity), as common as that between neurosis and psychosis. A psychic act to resolve intrapsychic conflicts can be a combination or a vacillation between the two" (p. 8). "Narcissism unbridled is the enemy of integrity" and instinctual pressures are "to neuroses as ego interests are to the compromises of integrity" (p. 8). "Analysis aims at turning out an honest man" (p. 10). "The scientific attitude of psychoanalysis is carried to the patient by a caring human. The capacity to achieve the proper blend between the two is one of the most difficult but necessary goals for training to impart" (p. 11).

The Watergate background, the study of which was eventually issued in a book *The Mind of Watergate* (1980), forms the link between the intrapsychic and man's behavior as a social being. Taking the instance of public failure to rebuke Richard Nixon, Rangell states: "The syndrome . . . is accepted by the population because it satisfies both sides of the unconscious of the latter" (p. 9). This extension of psychoanalytic understanding to the influence of the social environment in the life of man, via the relationship of ego to superego, completes Rangell's overarching view. Beginning deep in the intrapsychic process, man's inevitable making of choices is now seen to affect and be continuously affected by events in daily life, from experience on a small scale, such as that of family life, to membership in groups of any number. Rangell's inclusion of problems of integrity parallels Freud's foray into the same field with *Group Psychology and the Analysis of the Ego* (1921) on which he builds.

Rangell is very much aware of the difficulties of approaching this field. He reassures that his comments do not constitute "a crusade nor a call for the imposition of morality from cosmic heights," but a scientific attitude toward morals—"the same attitude psychoanalysis always has—but one which includes a more complete range of psychic forces." He knows that the "scientific study of the superego elicits more resistance than that of the id. There is greater resistance, . . . individually and collectively, to insight into a moral break than to an instinctual breakthrough." He reminds us that the "psychoanalyst is not without a value system," that "Freud separated himself from transient, culture-bound neurosogenic values, not from the timeless values of civilized man," that "neutrality does not include an abandonment of values nor of the role they play in the determination of final pathways in mental behavior" (p. 57). Generally speaking, Rangell turns our attention to the study of the superego in a new and comprehensive fashion. This is a chapter of psychoanalytic history which has only begun to be written. It does not lead into that genre of psychobiography in which the lives of public figures are treated as data in the same way that a patient's free associations are. Rangell's Watergate book (1980) showed us how to take a point of view without invading the privacy of those involved. His experience at the Center for Advanced Study in the Behavioral Sciences at Stanford had taught him "the unswerving necessity to keep a footing at all times in a solidly anchored psychoanalytic position" (1967, p. 173). Learning from others in nonpsychoanalytic fields of social science, and teaching them in turn, reinforced the scope of his formulations and adds the social to the biological as two arms of the human psychoanalytic core, exactly parallel to the id and the superego articulating with the ego. This full sweep of human affairs provides the student of human life with all the subject matter that is necessary for a coherent and integrated view of man.

Rangell had commented, throughout his career, on aspects of theory and technique, but, beginning in 1981, he wrote a long series of papers in response to the numerous challenges to traditional psychoanalytic thinking which had begun to preoccupy a steadily advancing proportion of practicing psychoanalysts. At the same time, his own theory of action within the structural point of view was taking further shape.

The stress in 1981 is on transference interpretation as a means to an end, not an end in itself. In this he opposed, among others, Merton Gill, whose emphasis had come to rest strictly on here-and-now phenomena in analysis. Strachey's 1934 paper on the mutative effect on transference interpretation had by then come to seem an unchallengeable given to many more analysts than the followers of Melanie Klein. Rangell reiterates the importance of the past as a vital component of interpretation, the present as it tells us about the past, the past as it has continued into the present, the importance therefore of analytic efforts at reconstruction of the past, including the infantile neurosis.

By pointing out that the stresses on patients are not limited to the time of the original traumas, but continue throughout life, he revises our view of the magnitude of the task facing the analyst, whose interpretations are the equivalent of shining a flashlight into the Grand Canyon. This point of view, which again stresses the continuation of the past into the present, provides support for any analyst in his daily undertaking, and, by extension, support for patients who may thereby grasp the magnitude of the task which confronts them. This idea of lifelong response to trauma is an example of an appraisal of truth which probably yields an orientation to reality which lessens the frustration of psychoanalytic work.

"The Self in Psychoanalytic Theory" (1982a) was stimulated by numerous theories emphasizing personal wholeness (Kohut, Gedo, Schafer, G. Klein), presumably intended to counteract what was regarded as a dangerous analytic tendency toward viewing a person as a collection of parts. Chief among these theories was that of Heinz Kohut with his self psychology. Rangell reminds his readers that the "whole was where Freud started; the person or self existed prior to the advent of psychoanalysis. It was Freud's breakthrough to dissect the whole into its parts, to assign to each a coherent role. While we have learned that analogizing to somatic processes has its limitations, the organism does not perform its functions, somatic or mental, as a unit without parts" (p. 869). What is lost by "an abandonment of our knowledge of internal structure" is "the explanatory reach amassed by total psychoanalytic theory, explanations of dreams, symptoms and character traits as compromise formations, the analysis of anxiety, conflicts and their derivatives, the understanding of a phobia, an obsession, the structure of depression" (pp. 869–870).

Rangell is concerned with the phenomenon of a "group swell approaching cultist proportions clamoring for a new paradigm and feeling it has found one" (p. 870), without acknowledgment of arguments and criticisms advanced against its claims. Systematically, he approaches the basic claims to new ideas in self psychology, from Kohut's separate developmental line for narcissism, to his implied claim that the importance of the analyst's empathy is a discovery of self psychology, to structural deficiency as the sole explanation for the problems of patients with what he calls narcissistic personality disorders.

Rangell offers "the observation that many analysts do not credit their own experiences but yield belief in their perceptions to a respected but unconsciously exalted authority figure" (p. 872), a phenomenon possibly related to Kohut's injunction against the analysis of idealization. This simple observation is strong support for the individual analyst laboring in his consulting room to understand the phenomena before him in his own way. This atmosphere, removed from the bubble of the group, is where reason is likely to reign. What he terms "my own piecemeal struggling with theory" (1988) is the spirit behind his contributions. Rangell likes to draw the contrast between a personal charisma and a charisma of ideas, believing that it was the latter, and not the former, which distinguished Freud.

Criticizing the shift of emphasis from the analysis of conflict to the healing of defects in development, Rangell sees a movement toward an existential mode of treatment, "no longer for what the patient suffers but for what he is" (p. 877). There is an accompanying shift away from precise definition and thought into generalities and vagueness. "Obscurity of language and imperviousness to criticism . . . turn out not to elicit rational critique, but . . . to enhance an image of invincibility and of a durability of self which is identified with and vicariously joined" (p. 884). Clearly, Rangell's reflections on group behavior, part of his study of compromises of integrity, are finding application here.

In the same year "Transference to Theory" (1982b) extends the subject. "It is the indefensible arguments, not the compromises which can be agreed upon, which are invariably the glue which binds such a new group together" (p. 31). Rangell is referring to groups that hold views on the nature of psychoanalysis that are fundamentally different from long-accepted ones, such as deficiency as a replacement for unconscious conflict, and empathy as treatment instead of interpretation. "The need to merge with the group may activate latent ambivalence to theory, after which the two then act together in mutual union" (p. 34); "the dynamic of this repeated phenomenon is a repression of the Oedipus complex in theory, and an acting out of it in group life" (p. 38). "To be more specific as to what is avoided and defended against, it is not the impulse side of the oedipal drama, but the castration anxiety apposite to it which is focally subject to repression and defense" (p. 40); "a significant segment of those who espouse new theories combines an exuberant declaration of a new selfhood with a calumny and opposition to the role of the oedipal process as virulent as existed against analysis as a whole in the early days of psychoanalysis and has existed in the extra-analytic world since then" (p. 45). Rangell is careful to make it plain that "the type of transference displacements I am describing can be to any theory, old or new" (p. 48).

The following year, in "Defense and Resistance in Psychoanalysis and Life" (1983), Rangell continues his examination: "a common motivation in the followers of these theories is the feeling that scientific decomposition of the mental apparatus is somehow accompanied by a psychological fragmentation of the person or personality or, in the latest theory, of the self" (p. 155). "The interest to maintain wholeness of the organism does not preclude separateness and harmony between internal parts" (p. 159). "The road to healthy integration in analysis is differentiation and reintegration, by destratification of clinical aggregates and their resynthesis into more stable and adaptive wholes" (p. 161).

Rangell's understanding of the paradigm hunger of the present psychoanalytic scene bears comparison to the conditions of the early days of psychoanalysis when individuals split themselves off one by one. With Anna Freud's death and that of so many pioneers of the second generation, psychoanalysis now lacks a generally accepted, deeply wise, and anointed leader (repugnant though anointing may be to the scientific mind) whom all or the majority may respect, and from whom may come nurturance for individual scientific courage. There is a wildness about the multiplicity of viewpoints, with the most fundamental elements in psychoanalysis sometimes discarded. Rangell, in the eye of the hurricane, is the quintessential observer. His thought is formed out of experience gained as a clinician and from the unique viewpoint of his elected positions in international, national, and local organizations. He appeals unswervingly to reason, which is what is likely to remain after the dying away of emotional overtones in new theories and groups.

"The Object in Psychoanalytic Theory" (1985b) is a continuation of the themes of these years, now with a moving, because so accurate, description of the bewildering nature of interchanges between individuals and their objects. He shows us precisely how a thorough awareness of the parts of the whole yields a convincing portrait of the reality of human relationships. "Just as the individual does not initiate action with his whole self, psychic or somatic, but with special parts performing their particular functions, so does the subject not necessarily react to the whole object but to specific traits, components, functions or aspects of behavior of the latter" (p. 303). "The coexistence of the concept of an integrated whole, along with a harmony of internal components, in the case of both subject and object, is a *sine qua non* of any psychoanalytic theory which would claim completeness and relevance to the phenomenon being observed" (p. 306).

In the following, Rangell begins to transcend a merely psychoanalytic focus and to describe the problem and the wonder of reality itself. His workmanlike effort to describe reality through the medium of internally consistent theory gives rise to a natural and convincing eloquence.

The subject acts and reacts with these various and changing forces

> of the object. And the object reciprocates as a self to the same subject as object. To relate to another personality or "character" is to invest in and be influenced by the modes of his particular intrapsychic relations. Parts of each are acting and reacting and determining the outcomes. This is the case even though the ego, by a process not unlike the secondary revision of dreams, covers the parts at the end with an integument to make it a whole, integrating them, like the dream, into as plausible and acceptable a final unity as it can achieve with the parts that have gone into making it [p. 304].
>
> Grossman (1982) has described the self as fantasy; he might say this of the object as well. What this can more accurately apply to, however, is the representation of the self and object, not the actual entity of either. That such a representation might be more fantasy than memory is the case when the internalized version, called up on the mental screen for direct attention, which takes place on the unconscious as well as the conscious level, is elaborated by the ego, acted upon by instinctual and superego derivatives, into a more subjective and personalized creative product. To the extent, however, that the primary perception of objects *de novo* is already universally acted upon and individually distorted during the process between external perception and internal registration, the characterization of these inner representations at any stage as fantasy formations has a general validity for the storage not only of memories, but of self and object concepts [p. 322].
>
> The universality of subjective distortion should not lead us to lose sight of the fact that the object existed prior to its encounter with the subject self, and continues to exist, however changed, after the interaction has ceased [p. 324].
>
> The person does not change when he becomes an object in the sense of an intrapsychic unity within another self, except insofar as every person is shaped, probably not to an inconsiderable degree, by his awareness of the roles he occupies in the mental lives of others [p. 325].

Rangell, in complete control of his complex subject, is describing man struggling with confusion in the realm of relationships, and essentially misrepresenting reality by adding an "integument to make it whole." Man works toward the illusion of unity in the face of fragmentation, an idea of which one possible corollary is that theories that make "the whole person" their banner may well be theoretical rationalizations unconsciously intended to facilitate the development of an illusion of wholeness. This may help to explain the messianic element observable in some of the group phenomena. It also exposes Rangell's own struggle, and that of all analysts, for integration and integrity in their personal version of psychoanalytic theory. It is a struggle to be honest about the potential for rationalization in one's own theory, to be open to reasonable criticism, and to reshape it in accordance with all data that seem solidly based. This willingness is the hallmark of rationally arrived-at theory and differentiates it from that which ignores criticism and/or denatures its findings with a language of defiance. Rangell's version of psychoanalytic theory, with its continuous review for internal consistency, accord with phenomenological data, connectedness to biological and social reality, and applicability to psychoanalysis as a therapeutic procedure, has, by this point in his career, taken on a unitary form which bears comparison to the work of his predecessor, Otto Fenichel, in *The Psychoanalytic Theory of Neurosis* (1945).

Rangell continues with a focus on technique:

> Contrary to the opinions of many, Freud did not eliminate reality but enlarged it [p. 327].
>
> It is not amiss to interpret to a patient from convincing evidence that a parent was rejecting or helpful or seductive and not only that the patient felt that. To interpret reality is part of the psychoanalytic method. Failure to do so, in fact, can lead to antitherapeutic results. . . .
>
> The "real" as well as the distorted exist in life and in analysis. Both, not one, are also reflected in the transference. The "real relationship" described by Greenson (1972), and the transference distortions in every analysis can, in a sense, both be thought of as transference phenomena. The capacity to observe and interact realistically, and not to distort, has not been typically recognized as also transferred from early figures to the analyst. There is a carry-over of the normal and appropriate as well as the pathological and distorted from previous modes and capacities in life to the transference. Perception of the real and distortion by the subjective can both be displaced to new objects [p. 328].

Freud's (1905) seminal insight, so often quoted, that "the finding

> of an object is in fact a refinding of it" (p. 222), can be misapplied and overdone. Not every human contact in life is to reestablish a perceptual identity with a mnemic image. The human mind is also always open to presentations as well as representations, i.e., to fresh perceptions and new experiences (Loewald, 1960). That is why psychoanalysis has the possibility of effecting change [p. 329].
>
> Winnicott (1953) felt there can only be "good-enough mothering." Perhaps, as with initial registration of outer perceptions, analysis can provide only "good-enough" approximation to reality, inner and outer, of self and object [p. 330].

Rangell's introduction of the phrase "good enough" bears comparison to the place in his "Structural Problems" paper (1963b) in which he lets clinical experience override the rigors of theoretical logic, or where, in "The Decision-Making Process" (1971a), he assures a patient his symptoms are reversible in the heat of the effort to stick to the analysis of his failure to act on his newly acquired insights. These three instances (others are scattered throughout his writings) show a temperate and unperfectionistic attitude, which is easily overlooked, because the sense of passionate conviction and the pursuit of logical lines of thought to their conclusions are so evident throughout his work.

In "On the Theory of Theory in Psychoanalysis and the Relation of Theory to Psychoanalytic Therapy" (1985a), he continues: "there is a large, if latent, irrational substructure behind the opposition to theory in psychoanalysis—this includes the theory of both understanding and therapy—the very kind of unconscious distortion toward which psychoanalysis itself is directed" (pp. 73–74); "what is most defended against in the alternative theories and encircled by a wide swathe of avoidance is the oedipal phase, more specifically anxiety over castration danger which is the negative side of the oedipal coin" (p. 79); "openness to new theory can mean a closure to unacceptable aspects of the old" (p. 79).

He quotes Meissner (1981) who, "discussing the seeming conflict between hermeneutics and metapsychology, shows how much each needs the other: 'Without the one we are left with sterile abstractions; without the other, disembodied significances' " (p. 86). And finally, "total psychoanalytic theory to me is a composite which achieves diversity within unity" (p. 86).

The results of a lifetime of thought about psychoanalysis are evident in Rangell's comments in honor of an old friend, Charles Brenner. In "The Enduring Armature of Psychoanalytic Theory and Method" (1986a), he writes:

> One's basic character before training needs to contain at least the potential for the relentless incorruptibility, resistance to seduction, and tolerance for frustration necessary to maintain the life of an analyst. The high priority of the value of truth had best bring with it ego satisfactions as well as superego peace if it is to last [p. 91].
>
> The capacity of the analyst to represent subtly and consistently a fusion of opposites becomes for the patient, unconsciously if not overtly, a model for the resolution of conflict. No two analysts do this in the same way, perhaps not even similarly. Each has his or her individual style, and there is room for differences. But these characteristics, in a broad way, are held in common [p. 92].
>
> I venture to say from experience that the patient's choice of analyst is not a random one, that the status and nature of the patient's deep desire to know may exert an influence on that initial decision [p. 92].
>
> [He quotes Blum (1983)] "What stimulates trust in the patient for the analyst are the nonmoralizing and nonintrusive aspects of the analyst's neutral, uninvolved stance" [p. 94].
>
> Analysis is not directed to what a person is, but what he suffers [p. 98].
>
> It is the latent and unconscious operations around anxiety that determine the motives and directions for the analytic path. . . .
>
> The basic anxieties are still those related to separation and castration, not anxiety over madness and death, as claimed in recent revisions (Green, 1975) purportedly based on new clinical experience. . . .
>
> From my cumulative clinical experience, castration anxiety is the most overlooked of the insights to come from analysis [p. 99].

These quotations show the aphoristic element in Rangell's recent writing. In the light of his unceasing effort to define and redefine the elements of psychoanalysis, they reduce to essential terms what he has learned, and what he has to teach us about the fundamental and the irreplaceable in the psychology of man.

"The Executive Functions of the Ego" (1986b) and "Action Theory within the Structural View" (1987b) summarize and unify numerous papers that lead inevitably to a synthesis. Rangell has made scores of contributions to diverse psychoanalytic subjects, which, though of great intrinsic interest, are peripheral to this main thrust of theoretical development. The relevant papers, which have appeared throughout his career, include, besides the primarily theoretical contributions to ego psychology, a number that have to do with psychoanalysis as therapy. His papers on acting out (1968b), the termination of analysis (1966, 1982c), and the postanalytic phase (1980–1981) all refer to the subject of action and, in particular, to an assessment of action as normal or abnormal.

In his recent attempts to bring together diverse observation and theory into a unitary view, Rangell detaches the word *will* from its constant companion, *free* (as he had previously [1959] detached *conversion* from *hysteria*), and reasons toward a new configuration which, while retaining determinism, makes a place for will. He sees will as itself determined to varying extents, more so in the state of neurosis, less and less with the progress of a successful analysis. As conflicts rise to the psychoanalytic surface and are analyzed to resolution, the anxiety signal occurs less and less often, and the sense of safety is enhanced. The store of conscious memories grows, and the capacity for free choice increases. This strengthened capacity for free choice is not limited to the conscious state, however, but also occurs unconsciously and automatically, according to the principles of secondary process reasoning. The action of the unconscious will carries with it a sense of responsibility which is often not easily accepted. Yet it is inescapable that to choose is to bear responsibility for choice. Decision is the prelude to action, and therefore to responsibility for action, i.e., for the implementation of decision. These are the executive functions of the ego.

With the introduction of choice, decision, purpose, intention, and increased responsibility goes a new dimension within the structural point of view. Rangell contends that psychoanalysis does not require a new theory, out of synchrony with the accumulated knowledge of decades of psychoanalytic thought, to encompass man's necessity for choice. A world of human responsibility, which is vastly enlarged in comparison with the already vastly enlarged world that Freud marked out, becomes visible as Rangell's new concepts are understood and appreciated. He does not say so, but it is quite clear that what, in other terms, we know as tragic elements in human life are now there for psychoanalytic consideration in new and deepened conceptual terms. Theoretical efforts to achieve the same end must now be compared to Rangell's synthesis. Psychoanalysts must ask themselves how important Rangell's achieved continuity actually is. They must consider whether exciting encounters with new conceptions that shoulder aside previously won knowledge are worthwhile in the long run, when compared to terms and ideas that preserve what we know and strive for consistency with that knowledge. One of the underlying themes of such comparative reflection has to do with the role of newness itself. There is an appeal to the new which may supply the energy for renewed effort. In itself, such an effort in the conduct of psychoanalytic treatment may yield results that seem to confirm the content of the theory behind it. Yet new theories eventually become old. And in the end, the bones and sinews of the theory itself will survive. Its content, relieved of its emotional tenor, will tell us of its ultimate weight.

Rangell's conceptualization of will and of compromises of integrity carries him into territory that is, I believe, familiar to the followers of Melanie Klein. The great reach and intensity of his thought, rooted in the theory of anxiety, now begins to touch another powerful psychoanalytic theory, centered in its own version of anxiety theory, in a way which promises to give meaning to the phrase "total composite psychoanalytic theory." I am referring to the Kleinian view of depressive anxiety as a response to the perception of injury to the good mother and her later equivalents. The unbearable nature of that anxiety may lead to the employment of a manic defense. These conceptions overlap with Rangell's observation that unconscious choice and therefore responsibility are not only not easily acknowledged, but may be stubbornly ignored. Compromises of integrity, in Kleinian terms, may sometimes be regarded as instances of the manic defense. The Kleinian idea would emphasize the unbearably harsh superego, in contrast to Rangell's implication of a defectively permissive superego, but the way is open, nonetheless, for a dialogue in this area.

Rangell seems to have begun as a young man by grasping, all at once, the Freudian and post-Freudian legacy, and then to have slowly filtered it through the medium of his life and work. As a result, he has been able to produce an expanded, immensely strengthened restatement that can serve as a new baseline for total psychoanalytic theory and practice. Psychoanalysts of every stripe, be they adherents to the continuous line of growth that originated with Freud, or of theoretical schools that feature a radical departure, may be grateful for the orientation Rangell has so generously provided.

REFERENCES

Blum, H. (1983), The psychoanalytic process and analytic influence. *Internat. J. Psycho-Anal.*, 64:17–33.

Fenichel, O. (1945), *The Psychoanalytic Theory of Neurosis.* New York: Norton.

Freud, S. (1895), Project for a scientific psychology. *Standard Edition*, 1:283–397. London: Hogarth Press, 1959.

——— (1905), Three essays on the theory of sexuality. *Standard Edition*, 7:125–243. London: Hogarth Press, 1953.

——— (1921), Group psychology and the analysis of the ego. *Standard Edition*, 18:67–143. London: Hogarth Press, 1955.

——— (1926), Inhibitions, symptoms and anxiety. *Standard Edition*, 20:77–175. London: Hogarth Press, 1959.

Green, A. (1975), The analyst, symbolization and absence in the analytic setting. *Internat. J. Psycho-Anal.*, 56:1–22.

Greenson, R. R. (1972), Beyond transference and interpretation. In: *Explorations in Psychoanalysis.* New York: International Universities Press, 1978, pp. 441–450.

Grossman, W. I. (1982), The self as fantasy: Fantasy as theory. *J. Amer. Psychoanal. Assn.*, 30:919–937.

Hartmann, H. (1947), On rational and irrational action. In: *Essays on Ego Psychology.* New York: International Universities Press, 1964, pp. 37–68.

——— (1960), *Psychoanalysis and Moral Values.* New York: International Universities Press.

Loewald, H. W. (1960), On the therapeutic action of psychoanalysis. *Internat. J. Psycho-Anal.*, 41:1–18.

Meissner, W. W. (1981), Metapsychology—Who needs it? *J. Amer. Psychoanal. Assn.*, 29:921–938.

Oxford English Dictionary (compact edition) (1971), New York: Oxford University Press.

Rangell, L. (1942), Cerebral air embolism. *J. Nerv. & Ment. Dis.*, 96:542–555.

——— (1950), A treatment of nightmares in a seven-year-old boy. *The Psychoanalytic Study of the Child*, 5:358–390. New York: International Universities Press.

——— (1952a), The analysis of a doll phobia. *Internat. J. Psycho-Anal.*, 33:43–53.

——— (1952b), Macroscopic transmission and the macroscopic point of view. *J. Hillside Hosp.*, 1:228–233.

——— (1953), The interchangeability of phallus and female genital. *J. Amer. Psychoanal. Assn.*, 1:504–509.

——— (1954a), Similarities and differences between psychoanalysis and dynamic psychotherapy. *J. Amer. Psychoanal. Assn.*, 2:734–744.

——— (1954b), The psychology of poise. *Internat. J. Psycho-Anal.*, 35:313–333.

——— (1954c), A tertiary gain of symptoms. Read at the Meeting of the American Psychoanalytic Association, New York, December 3.

——— (1955a), The role of the parent in the Oedipus complex. *Bull. Menn. Clin.*, 19:9–15.

——— (1955b), On the psychoanalytic theory of anxiety: A statement of a unitary theory. *J. Amer. Psychoanal. Assn.*, 3:389–414.

——— (1955c), The quest for ground in human motivation. Address to the first Western Divisional Meeting of the American Psychiatric Association and the West Coast Psychoanalytic Societies, October 29.

——— (1959), The nature of conversion. *J. Amer. Psychoanal. Assn.*, 7:632–662.

——— (1963a), The scope of intrapsychic conflict—Microscopic and macroscopic considerations. *The Psychoanalytic Study of the Child*, 18:75–102. New York: International Universities Press.

——— (1963b), Structural problems in intrapsychic conflict. *The Psychoanalytic Study of the Child*, 18:103–138. New York: International Universities Press.

——— (1966), An overview of the ending of an analysis. In: *Psychoanalysis in the Americas*, ed. R. E. Litman. New York: International Universities Press, pp. 141–165.

——— (1967), Psychoanalysis, affects, and the "human core"—On the

relationship of psychoanalysis to the behavioral sciences. *Psychoanal. Quart.*, 36:172–202.
——— (1968a), The psychoanalytic process. *Internat. J. Psycho-Anal.*, 49:19–26.
——— (1968b), A point of view on acting out. *Internat. J. Psycho-Anal.*, 49:195–201.
——— (1968c), A further attempt to resolve the "problem of anxiety." *J. Amer. Psychoanal. Assn.*, 16:371–404.
——— (1969a), The intrapsychic process and its analysis—A recent line of thought and its current implications. *Internat. J. Psycho-Anal.*, 50:65–77.
——— (1969b), Choice-conflict and the decision-making function of the ego—A psychoanalytic contribution to decision theory. *Internat. J. Psycho-Anal.*, 50:599–602.
——— (1971a), The decision-making process. A contribution from psychoanalysis. *The Psychoanalytic Study of the Child*, 26:425–452. New York: Quadrangle.
——— (1971b), Toward a cool look at burning issues. Book review essay on: Waelder, R., *Progress and Revolution. Psychoanal. Quart.*, 40:663–677.
——— (1972), Aggression, Oedipus and historical perspective. *Internat. J. Psycho-Anal.*, 53:3–22.
——— (1973), On the cacophony of human relations. *Psychoanal. Quart.*, 42:325–348.
——— (1974), A psychoanalytic perspective leading currently to the syndrome of the compromise of integrity. *Internat. J. Psycho-Anal.*, 55:2–12.
——— (1976), Lessons from Watergate. *Psychoanal. Quart.*, 45:37–61.
——— (1980), *The Mind of Watergate: An Exploration of the Compromise of Integrity*. New York: Norton.
——— (1980–1981), Some notes on the postanalytic phase. *Internat. J. Psychoanal. Psychother.*, 8:165–170.
——— (1981), Psychoanalysis and dynamic psychotherapy. Similarities and differences twenty-five years later. *Psychoanal. Quart.*, 50:665–693.
——— (1982a), The self in psychoanalytic theory. *J. Amer. Psychoanal. Assn.*, 30:863–892.
——— (1982b), Transference to theory: The relationship of psychoanalytic education to the analyst's relationship to psychoanalysis. *Annual Psychoanal.*, 19:29–56.
——— (1982c), Some thoughts on termination. *Psychoanal. Inq.*, 2:367–392.
——— (1983), Defense and resistance in psychoanalysis and life. *J. Amer. Psychoanal. Assn.* 31 (Suppl.): 147–174.

——— (1985a), On the theory of theory in psychoanalysis and the relationship of theory to psychoanalytic therapy. *J. Amer. Psychoanal. Assn.*, 33:167–185.

——— (1985b), The object in psychoanalytic theory. *J. Amer. Psychoanal. Assn.*, 33:301–334.

——— (1986a), The enduring armature of psychoanalytic theory and method. In: *Psychoanalysis, the Science of Mental Conflict*, ed. A. D. Richards & M. Willick. Hillsdale, NJ: Analytic Press, pp. 89–106.

——— (1986b), The executive functions of the ego. An extension of the concept of ego autonomy. *The Psychoanalytic Study of the Child*, 41:1–37. New Haven, CT: Yale University Press.

——— (1987a), A core process in psychoanalytic treatment. *Psychoanal. Quart.*, 56:222–249.

——— (1987b), Action theory within the structural view. Read at the 35th International Psychoanalytic Congress, Montreal, July 27.

——— (1988), Interview with Leo Rangell. *Los Angeles Psychoanal. Bull.* (in press).

——— Mahler, M. S. (1943), A psychoanalytic study of "maladie des tics" (Gilles de la Tourette's disease). *Psychoanal. Quart.*, 17:579–603.

Rapaport, D. (1960), On the psychoanalytic theory of motivation. In: *Nebraska Symposium on Motivation*, ed. M. R. Jones. Lincoln: University of Nebraska Press, pp. 173–247.

Sholevar, C. P., ed. (1987), *Psychoanalytic Case Studies*. New York: International Universities Press.

Strachey, J. (1934), The nature of the therapeutic action of psycho-analysis. *Internat. J. Psycho-Anal.*, 15:197–223.

Winnicott, D. W. (1953), Transitional objects and transitional phenomena. In: *Collected Papers: Through Paediatrics to Psycho-Analysis*. New York: Basic Books, 1975, pp. 229–242.

4

ON INCONSOLABILITY*

EDWARD M. WEINSHEL, M.D.

At the first class on the morning of my very first day of my first year in college, the professor arrived promptly, walked briskly to the blackboard, and wrote the following:

> I am Dr. Jones.
> This is Biology IA.
> Biology is the study of life.
> Life is one god-damned thing after the other.

This was my first "scientific" encounter with the problem of inconsolability. One cannot separate the question of inconsolability from that of consolability, and there is a sufficient abundance of "one god-damned thing after the other" to guarantee, for all of us, an equally abundant supply of situations that will call for attempts at comfort and consolation. I am referring to one of those ubiquitous and hardly infrequent states of unpleasure with which all of us must cope throughout life. These states come about as a consequence of pain, loss, frustration, rejection, and a host of comparable commonplace experiences. These states of unpleasure differ in their subjective and objective manifestations and in their severity and duration; they invariably involve blows to the individual's sense of self-esteem together with some degree of anxiety

*Earlier versions of this paper were presented as the Freud Anniversary Lecture of the Psychoanalytic Association of New York, at the Cleveland Psychoanalytic Society, and as a keynote address at an International Colloquium of the Anna Freud Centre. I am most grateful to the many helpful criticisms and suggestions that came from these previous presentations.

and some element of the depressive affect; each person appears to utilize his or her own somewhat idiosyncratic pattern of obtaining relief from this unpleasurable state, i.e., to obtain consolation.

With some individuals, a good deal of that process depends on the comfort and solace one can receive from another person; however, some individuals seem to depend more on themselves as a source of comfort and consolation. They can and wish to be consoled, but they insist on doing the work by themselves. In this presentation I will focus on those individuals who at least consciously do not wish to be comforted and consoled, and, in fact, many of them will take a vigorous stand against any attempts to alleviate their distress or misery. I do not believe there is a discreet entity such as "inconsolability," and, similarly, I do not believe that any one individual is *always* inconsolable. It is more reasonable to adhere to the position that, on different occasions, a given person will be consolable via external or internal means, or more likely a combination thereof, and that, in different circumstances, that same person will become "inconsolable." However, there are individuals who will more or less habitually react to that particular mood by not permitting consolation or solace.

There is no one set clinical picture of inconsolability; yet certain familiar characteristics appear with some regularity. To some extent, that clinical picture is determined and colored by the event that has triggered this particular affective state. Not infrequently the inconsolable individual is capable of hiding or disguising his mood and misery to the point that no one is aware that something is very much amiss; more often the reverse is true, and the inconsolability will manifest an intrusive, invasive element which can be a conspicuous hallmark of the phenomenon, endowing the mood with a contagious quality which impinges on everyone in the immediate environment. These persons invariably demonstrate a variety of depressive affects; they tend to be withdrawn, ruminative, occupied with their thoughts and their unhappiness, and, even though they do not want to give up their unhappiness, they do not "enjoy" that unpleasure. Yet they are often quite candid in admitting to "hang on" to their misery.

Various manifestations of aggression are commonplace. These

individuals are often irritable, especially if others, however kindly and discreetly, attempt to interfere with their privacy and their brooding. The disconsolate person appears to have a knack for stimulating sympathetic friends and relatives to try to alleviate his or her unhappiness by some form of humor. Invariably, these attempts fall flat or will evoke a hostile rejoinder. To accept the solace of humor would be tantamount to accepting comfort, something that the inconsolable one experiences as surrender and defeat. Some feel these gestures are an intrusion or an attack; others will react as if the consoler is trying to "seduce" them into surrendering their disconsolate state. Most patients with whom I have worked describe quite freely a definite feeling of stubbornness and of resolute determination around not giving up their misery.

I cannot claim that this more or less composite description is comprehensive or applicable to *all* inconsolable patients. The characteristics to which I have pointed and have emphasized are the ones that impressed me most in the patients I have treated in analysis. The bulk of this chapter consists of a presentation of case material in which inconsolability is an issue that came up early and frequently.

CLINICAL MATERIAL

Case 1

Mrs. D. was in her mid-30s when she came to see me, explicitly requesting analysis. She had been referred by a psychiatrist friend whose analysis I had completed about a year earlier. Later she "confessed" that the "real" reason that she selected me as her analyst was the specific wording of an interpretation that I had made to her friend and which he had related to her.

Her appearance was striking and arresting. Although by no means beautiful by conventional standards, she displayed what had to be called a "commanding presence." She was tall, slim, and, although tense and taut, extremely poised, almost to the point of aloofness. Her manner of speech was striking. Mrs. D. spoke in a low voice, carefully choosing her words with an unselfconscious an unpretentious precision. She explained that she had been considering analysis for a number of years because of her concern over the failure of two relatively brief marriages and increasing difficulties and distress in the relationship with Tom, a man with whom she had been living the past three years. Mrs. D. was uncomfortable with her 13-year-old son, but she had considerable trouble in articulating the basis and nature of that discomfort. She told me about her career as a professional actress (which suddenly seemed to make understandable her "presence"); how she had abandoned that promising career because of increasing anxiety over the possibility of making a serious error in a performance because the "whole script might suddenly drop out of my mind"; and how she had turned to teaching social sciences to junior college students. Mrs. D. described an active, diversified social life with many friends and interests but which provided her with "little comfort when I needed it"—her first reference to the inconsolability. She also described transient periods of "moodiness when I'm not really depressed, but when I'm not really happy either and when I'd just as soon be left alone until I feel more like myself."

Mrs. D. came from a wealthy East Coast family, the youngest of three sisters. Her father was a successful physician, a handsome and glamorous figure who died of a cerebral accident when the patient was 14.

Mrs. D. painted her mother with an altogether different brush. It is difficult to recall anything positive that she could find to say about her mother. The latter was portrayed as a good-looking, vain, self-centered woman who had come from a well-to-do family that had always been preoccupied with materialistic and superficial issues; the patient felt, unequivocally, that her mother's activities and interests reflected much more these values than concern for husband, children, and home. The care of her daughters fell into the hands of a number of nurses and housekeepers whom the patient conceded were all warm and loving. Mrs. D.

complained that her mother was strict, opinionated, overly concerned with good manners and proper protocol, finicky about the cleanliness and appearance of her children. However, my patient's chief criticisms of her mother centered around a whole complex of problems in trying to talk with her mother. Mrs. D.'s own terse and global summary of the trouble, "We just never talked," was a bit hyperbolic, but it accurately reflected how she felt about this aspect of the relationship with her mother. According to the patient, her mother would frequently insist, "Darling, we just have to have a nice long chat together"; but somehow these talks rarely eventuated. Or, if the almost formally scheduled talk did take place, the mother would appear disinterested and distracted, "Not there," as the patient put it, and could precipitously break off the already desultory interchange with an embarrassingly lame excuse. Often the patient had great difficulty in understanding what the mother was saying. At these moments, Mrs. D. would become hesitant and uncertain as to what she should say lest she say the wrong thing or, in turn, be misunderstood. The patient's response to some remark of the mother's might well evoke a curt "I don't know where you got that—it certainly isn't what *I* said." My patient would then counter with the protest that it was the mother who had been unclear, and that it was not the patient's fault that the mother had not understood. Such ripostes would infuriate the mother, who then accused the daughter of being stubborn and inattentive. These painful dramas invariably ended up in screaming fiascos punctuated by mutual accusations and the patient in despair and tears.

After these traumatic events, Mrs. D. would feel depleted, sad, and "disconnected." She would retreat to her room sometimes to cry, sometimes to mope, sometimes to try and make sense out of what appeared to her to be inexplicable. For the following two or three days, the patient would be removed and be morose, quite unapproachable by other members of the household, and feeling apprehensive about another flare-up with her mother. Except for the not terribly reassuring and relatively short-lived thought that "It wasn't just my fault," she found it impossible to comfort herself. What I have presented represents a composite of eruptions that took place as far back as the patient's sixth or seventh year and continued until late adolescence. Obviously the form and the sophistication of her own thinking and reasoning varied throughout the years, but the overall structure and sequence of the event remained constant.

Mrs. D. was reasonably successful in school, had a coterie of good friends, but was preoccupied with her acting activities which began around six. She was determined to become a famous actress and started her dramatic training at age seven and continued until she was in college, at which time she dropped out of the theater world for the reasons given above. She then married a young and already successful lawyer whom she had known for many years. The marriage was stormy from the start and ended in divorce after the birth of her son when the patient was in her early 20s. The patient remarried several years later, but this marriage also collapsed. About three years before she came for analysis, she met a divorced man with three children with whom she felt comfortable rather than "truly in love." Although their relationship has not been without its problems and pressures, Mrs. D. was quite satisfied with it and did not feel any great urge to remarry.

The major traumatic event in her life was her father's death from a massive stroke when she was 14. Mrs. D. recalled being extremely disturbed, and her description of a feeling of strangeness and "fogginess" suggested an episode of mild derealization. The events following her father's death were, to her, even more disturbing than his death itself. Soon it was revealed that the father had squandered almost all of his money, and, even though it was apparent that the bulk of the losses was the consequence of imprudent investments, the whispered allegations that a good deal of the family fortune had gone to support a series of mistresses and bookies were the items that stuck in her mind and caused her the greater distress.

The father's financial irresponsibility did not, however, lead to any alteration in the patient's standard of living. His family banded together to provide the survivors with a more than sufficient income to maintain their security and comfort. Four years later, the mother married a crotchety but conspicuously wealthy bachelor with whom the patient battled until his death when Mrs. D. was 23. The mother then became a wealthy widow who was able to offer all of her daughters considerable sums of money each year. The patient felt humiliated by her dependence on this maternal dole, and, at the same time, was not unaware of how much she coveted that money, how competitive she was with her sisters as to who was going to get the larger share of it, and how apprehensive she was lest mother remarry and have a new stepfather dissipate this fortune, as her father had done years before.

My first encounter with Mrs. D.'s inconsolability took place within the first months of the analysis. In a number of sessions, she related a series of ostensibly unconnected failures: her marriages, her career as an actress, the virtual estrangement from her sisters, the current coldness in the relationship with Tom, some difficulties she was experiencing in her teaching. Then, without making any connection to these extra-analytic disappointments, Mrs. D. began alluding to her concerns about her performance in the analysis. She made reference to her not infrequent lateness, to the fear that she was talking too much about petty issues, to her preoccupation that she might not be able to express herself clearly, and so forth. I told her that just as she felt that she had failed to do as well as she had expected in various aspects of her life outside of the analysis, she was now concerned that she might also fail to do well in the analytic work.

Her split-second response was an irate demand that I explain how I had come to *that* conclusion. She insisted that I had not really understood what she had been saying, and she complained that my "playing with words" was both unfair and confusing. She went on, as her anger gathered momentum, to let me know that she was not going to accept in a docile fashion ideas that I wanted to foist onto her. *She* was only doing what was expected of her, to say what came to mind. She was clearly deflated and discouraged, sad and hurt—and then silent.

I confess that I did not feel so good either. After a relatively brief wait, I told Mrs. D. that I did not understand all that was going on at this time and that it was not clear to me why this misunderstanding had arisen. I suggested that perhaps she had been disappointed by what I had said and that she was therefore afraid she might not be able to depend on me to help her understand what was going on. She made no reply and spent the rest of the session quiet except for a bit of muted crying, apparently oblivious of my presence. In the following session, after a period of silence, I opined that perhaps her silence and her tension were related to what had happened here in the previous hour. She suggested that it had not been necessary for me to have gone to medical school to have reached *that* conclusion. I said that she felt that it was necessary for her to remain angry and silent because she was concerned that she might become less *vigilant*—and with that word, I did luck out—and say something that *I* might not understand or for which, in some way, *I* might fault her. Somewhat to my surprise, she agreed and said that she was, indeed, quite vigilant. She added that what had happened on the previous Thursday had, indirectly, led to a quarrel with Tom. She had withdrawn from him during the entire weekend, staying by herself most of the time in spite of his apologies and entreaties. She added that for her to have in any way made up with him at that time was scary and unthinkable. Then Mrs. D. observed that there were a few times when she had tried to *console* herself with pleasant thoughts, but those thoughts would "slip away" before they could have any effect on her mood; from there, Mrs. D. launched another prolonged attack on Tom. I suggested that in this instance, at least, it was important for her to sustain her angry and disconsolate feelings in regard to Tom in order for her to sustain comparable feelings toward me.

The rest of the week was ostensibly a carbon copy of the session except that on one of those days she began to tell me more about some of her difficulties with Tom that would lead to these inconsolable moods, and once she ventured to elaborate on her frustrations around jogging and how on one recent occasion that frustration had precipitated a comparable reaction. She was still very wary, very vigilant, and very distant; but it was also evident that she was less miserable and withdrawn. Exactly what had produced these admittedly slight changes was not clear, but my own impression was that it was related to my use of the word *vigilant*. I permit myself all this detail because what took place during this first example of Mrs. D.'s inconsolability in the analysis was in general the model of similar events during the first three years of the analysis. A significant number of these episodes was triggered by some "misunderstanding" between us, be it apparent or real; but her reaction to widely diverse factors could produce the same sequence and so on.

At the same time, it became both necessary and productive to examine the inconsolability as a significant and central resistance in the analysis; as we were able to do so, we were able to learn more about the inconsolability and its constituents. The disconsolate states consequent to the "misunderstandings" served as an externalized vehicle for keeping her distance from Tom and hiding her feelings, both positive and negative, toward me. She had an uncannily acute ear for the cliché-tainted interpretation, and she experienced such lapses as evidence of my not really listening to her. Mrs. D. wanted to be special, the sole object of my interest and attention, and the cliché represented something that I could say to *any* patient. It was in the midst of trying to cope with such feelings that the patient would experience the hopelessness and what she had labeled the "disconnection" from me. It also became apparent that one of the significant determinants of being overwhelmed by the rush of these thoughts and feelings was the need to hide from both me and herself derivatives of various fantasies and their component wishes. One of the first of these to emerge for analytic scrutiny was her wish, in the period of inconsolability, to get close to or to regain the love of an object that had been lost either in reality or intrapsychically.

This was a pattern that, in different degrees and in different guises, I observed in all of my inconsolable patients. Mrs. D. could describe quite clearly the problem of not being able "to soothe myself." This is what she alluded to in what I mentioned earlier when she tried to console herself with "pleasant thoughts," which would, however, "slip away." As we were able to explore this more thoroughly, Mrs. D. was able to explain how she would plumb her mind for the reservoir of "good memories"; but feelings of guilt or uneasiness or actual contrary "bad memories" would intrude, and the "good memories" would disappear from consciousness.

A particular variant of the above deserves special comment. As stated above, in the first episode of inconsolability within the analysis Mrs. D. had alleged that my "playing with words was unfair." I had recognized that although my patient was almost obsessive in her precise and punctilious choice of words, it was also true that she never really "played" with words. For her, it was all work, and very hard work at that, and it *was* true in a sense that it was "unfair," because it was something that she would have liked to do, tried to do, but never really could do so in the fashion that she envied in others. The same was true for other kinds of play or in her sexual life. Although she would find herself indulging in daydreams, Mrs. D. never felt altogether comfortable in doing so; she could never rid herself of the suspicion that she was doing something forbidden. The main exception to this had been the acting. While rehearsing or performing, she could simultaneously abandon herself to fantasies of being great and being admired, and it was only in mid-adolescence that she began to feel uncomfortable with these gratifying fantasies. It was this conflict that eventually manifested itself in the intrusive thought, "The whole script might drop out of my mind." This interfered with both her fantasies and her acting and brought her theatrical career to an unhappy end. All of these phenomena are, of course, highly overdetermined; therefore I will focus only on those elements that are particularly relevant to the inconsolability.

In the third year of the analysis, Mrs. D. began her session by rather breezily telling me of how she had crossed the street to my office against the red light. In some detail, she described the situation, by no means minimizing the fact that her little prank was not an altogether innocuous one. In what probably was not my wisest intervention in the analysis, I asked her if she had any ideas about why she would take any chances at all; there was therefore some justification for the blast that followed. Mrs. D. was furious. I recognized immediately that my question was, at least in part, motivated by my irritation with the teasing and provocative nature of her recital; what I had missed was that the teasing also contained a genuine playful quality. This was exactly the point on which she focused her barrage. She accused me of being a wet blanket and a spoilsport, and she went on to harangue me for not wanting her to play, to have fun, to fool around. She added her conviction that I enjoyed spoiling her fun and depriving her of play.

Before withdrawing into an angry silence, she pointed out that I was behaving like her mother who could never tolerate anyone playing or having any fun, not even her husband whom she claimed to have loved very much. Mrs. D. started to tell me about an early memory but thought better of it, and, with ill-concealed disgust and discouragement, said, "Ah—what's the use," and became withdrawn and silent for the rest of that session. The next two weeks were very difficult for her, both in and out of the analysis. Mrs. D. was obviously angry with me but offered no explanation for those feelings. She was being very circumspect and very vigilant but made little effort to hide the fact that she was withholding something from me. This could be interpreted to her, and Mrs. D. explained that on the day of the red-light incident she had started to tell me about the earliest clear memory she had in regard to her father, one she assumed was from the age of five or six. She recalled the family at dinner with the father being unusually ebullient and garrulous. She could not remember the substance of the conversation, but, at one point, her mother suddenly interrupted him and, quite sternly, said, "Not in front of the children, Larry." The patient conjectured that the mother's rebuke had been in response to his using "bad words."

As we discussed this memory, over a period of many months, Mrs. D.'s initial emphasis was on how awful her mother had been. Her mother also was described as a spoilsport and wet blanket, and the patient railed about her mother's inability to let her father have a good time. She also told of many examples of her mother's behaving in a similar fashion with her sisters and herself and of how the mother never seemed to permit herself to be relaxed or playful. She repeated many of the vignettes of her mother's reluctance to talk with her, her mother's lack of spontaneity, and her mother's insistence on the correct words. One day, in this context, Mrs. D. complained that her mother always had to be "so *real*."

Then, in the midst of one of her exasperated harangues, she stopped short and wondered why her mother was like this. Almost as soon as the patient asked herself this question, her whole demeanor and focus shifted, and an altogether different set of observations began to emerge. She recalled that her mother had not always been this way. There had been a time, probably before the patient was five, when the mother had been more relaxed and playful. Further, the patient had to recognize that, although her fundamental portrayal of her mother was *essentially* correct, it was also exaggerated and even a bit distorted. Mrs. D. was chagrined to realize that all along there had been times when the mother had even been fun and that there had been occasions when they had been able to laugh together. From here the patient was able to realize that a certain aspect of her mother's behavior had been in reaction to the father's irresponsibility and infidelity and that the mother's killjoy approach to life must have been determined, at least in part, by the need to bring some semblance of order and control into what was a chaotic household. Mrs. D. could now look back on the "Not in front of the children" memory with a much more sympathetic eye and acknowledge that her father's behavior was more than a little inappropriate. After the first burst of enthusiasm for her new insight and her remorse over the scapegoating of her mother had waned a bit, the patient was able to arrive at a considerably more balanced image of her mother; but it took another 18 months of analysis before my patient was able to recognize how a significant portion of her own perceptual and mnemonic distortion of mother's character was the product of the vicissitudes of her oedipal conflicts.

In the analysis a more immediate fallout from the revised understanding of her mother was a much greater availability of what took place in her periods of inconsolability. Again this touched on Mrs. D.'s attempts to console herself, not just with "good" and happy thoughts but with more elaborate fantasies as well. She experienced these fantasies as a form of "playing with words," something that was forbidden not only because of content but because they were fantasies, i.e., not real. These potentially healing, soothing fantasies reflected, in addition to her wish for self-consolation, the wish for a daring and dangerous defiance of her mother (a part of which involved an identification with the misbehaving father). It will not come as a surprise that Mrs. D. revealed that both the fantasies and the reaction to them often involved masturbation. The patient's efforts to use fantasy, what was not real, as a means of combatting her misery would invariably be short-lived; the various repressive processes that contributed to the transience of those fantasies also contributed to the patient's inconsolability by interfering with the self-consoling mechanisms.

One of the principal reasons for her vigilance, her stubborn refusal to "give in" to any gesture or offer of consolation, was the fear that such efforts on the part of others represented an implicit or actual promise that would not be honored. This reaction derived, at different times in different proportions, from her fear of disappointment and its subsequent depressive feeling, her humiliation at the expectation of being pleased and then being ungratified, and her anxious concern in regard to the rage that often accompanied such disappointments. Although Mrs. D. was hypersensitive to almost any type of promise, three groups were particularly prominent: those related to her mother's promises to have talks with her; those related to her father's implied promises of approval and admiration; and those related to her nursemaids' less implicit promises of the rewards she would receive in the future if she was a good girl in the present.

I have already discussed the impact of the mother's unfulfilled promises around the prospect of "nice, little chats." Mrs. D.'s father was a prolific promiser and an equally profligate promise-breaker. The patient learned to tolerate his habitual promising since his failure to carry out these seriously undertaken vows was such a commonplace in the household and he was so indiscriminate in his choice of victims that, after a while, the patient just accepted these numerous derelictions.

More complex and insidious were the unspoken promises from her father that the patient brought up later in the analysis. These emerged first in the transference when Mrs. D. accused me of violating certain "promises." In her list of complaints, she included such items as my being late, the phone ringing, or changing my appointment schedule. She "knew," of course, that I had not in fact ever made promises about these issues, but, at the same time, she "felt" that she was quite justified in drawing such inferences from my behavior and some of the things that I had said. Further discussion disclosed what she called her "crush" on me and her conviction that I must entertain comparable feelings about her. Thus she could interpret my listening to her, tolerating her bouts of inconsolability, being "nice" to her as incontrovertible evidence of my being in love with her; therefore all of this was also evidence of my promising her that I would never be late, never permit the phone to ring, never change the hour of our meeting. I do not believe that this "unilateral contract" phenomenon is rare or limited to patients with inconsolability, and I have not found that it represents a significant defect in reality testing. With Mrs. D. it became an important element in the transference neurosis and replicated comparable experiences with her father.

When Mrs. D. was about five or six, her interest in acting manifested itself in her amateur performances around the home. She was not unaware of her wish to show off for her father and to gain his attention and admiration. He became a most appreciative audience and an enthusiastic admirer, praising her skill and her beauty. All of this was both exceedingly gratifying and exciting to the patient, and she chose to interpret his response as evidence of his love for her and also as evidence of a promise that when she grew up he would abandon the mother and marry his daughter. This somewhat illusory conclusion already had its basis in the previous phases of development, which I will relate below.

The third area of concern about promises, those centering around experiences with her nursemaids, also entered the analysis via the transference and the patient's persistent uneasiness over the basic rule—to say whatever came to mind. She could not convince herself that I really meant that she could say what came to mind with impunity and retained many reservations about "letting myself go." As the analysis proceeded, Mrs. D. justified her suspicions and her caution with an impressive piece of casuistry. She conceded that it was true that I did not blame her, hold her *culpable*, for the secrets she revealed, but, she argued, I did hold her *responsible* for that material. Thus she concluded, with more than a trace of triumph, my implied offer of impunity was not genuine, and I had, in effect, broken my promise to her.

Eventually these same issues entered into her associations regarding her nursemaids and various derivatives from her anal phase of development. The nursemaids would urge her to busy herself with her toys and were complimentary when she occupied herself with these games, but they were irritated and critical when she left her toys in disarray, when she had made a mess. Further, the nursemaids would encourage her obediently to move her bowels; but then they would be annoyed and unhappy with her at those times when she might make a mess of it. For Mrs. D., this apparent inconsistency represented another betrayal and another example of broken promises. These very useful analytic data and the memories the data contained helped to demonstrate her sensitivity to apparently broken promises, but it also made more evident a certain "hunger" for promises and an uncanny capacity for eliciting them from significant others; in turn, she could then utilize them as defenses against a variety of forbidden wishes.

The latter became clearer as the analytic work progressed. During that period in the analysis when Mrs. D. recognized that her oedipal aspirations were not going to be gratified, her frustration and depression were comingled with indignation and rancor. Gradually we were able to reconstruct specific interactions with her nursemaids that, around the age of three or four, became somewhat elaborate bedtime rituals. She would ask the nursemaid if she had been a good girl, and the latter would invariably respond that indeed she had. The patient then would inquire about the specific ways in which she had been good, and the nursemaid would enumerate all of the virtuous acts her charge had carried out that day. Most of these centered on being clean and neat and obedient. Then my patient would carefully interrogate her nursemaid about the rewards she might anticipate for such exemplary behavior, and the nursemaid would reply to the effect, "When you grow up, you will have all the things you want." The patient would then cross-examine her nursemaid with some species of "Are you sure?" and the answer was always an unconditional affirmative. This "game" would, over a period of many months, be enacted almost every night before the patient went to bed. The elaborations could become quite complicated, and, for the patient, the whole event was a source of satisfaction and reassurance.

What was for the nursemaid only an innocent game was for Mrs. D. a serious and sacred vow, a promissory note that she expected to be redeemed at some future date, a contract that was to be fulfilled at her bidding. Further, it was the confidence in this fulfillment that—for her at least—gave substance and reality to her father's multiple promises, and at the same time these expectations intensified the pain and bitterness of her disappointments when those promises were not honored. This whole panoply of fantasies and feelings resurfaced in adolescence, at the time of her father's death, when her marriages dissolved in disappointment, and in the transference. In less dramatic fashion, derivatives of these traumas played a not insignificant (if not always entirely conscious) role in many of her episodes of inconsolability.

Any attempt to console carries with it at least the implicit promise that solace and succor will be forthcoming. For my patient no such attempt was to be trusted. Such gestures merely loomed up as insincere or completely treacherous maneuvers to trick her, to lull her into a sense of security, which would prove to be false or insubstantial. She was frightened by these however ostensibly warm approaches that she was certain would lead to traumatic disappointment, humiliation, and despair, and, as a consequence, she had no recourse but to repel the offer of consolation and to withdraw into herself.

I wish to say a few words about those instances of inconsolability that presented themselves around her tendency to come late for the analytic sessions. This tendency manifested itself shortly after the beginning of the analysis and persisted for a large portion of it. My attempts to deal with this problem as a resistance based on anal phase conflicts were accepted readily, maybe too readily, by the patient, and while Mrs. D. began to control her tardiness outside of the analysis much more effectively, there was no change within the analysis. If anything, her lateness and the feelings of despair connected with the lateness—and the resultant disconsolateness—became much more marked.

One day, while talking about these issues, Mrs. D. started to say that something was unconscious, but, instead, she stated that it was "unconscionable." She was embarrassed; then, after a brief silence, she confessed that she used to steal. From here the patient was able to reveal how much the analysis and the analyst meant to her and how *eager* she was to come to the session each day. She was concerned that this would make me both uncomfortable and angry and could lead to my terminating the analysis. I will only summarize that which is somewhat apparent but which took a number of years to unravel. Beneath Mrs. D.'s eagerness were not only her budding positive feelings for the analyst but a variety of incorporative and competitive fantasies—and underlying these more specific wishes were the more proximal derivative of her oral incorporative impulses and the more general feelings of greed.

These tendencies and wishes played a significant part in her inconsolability. Not only did they contribute to the feelings of badness and unworthiness that made it difficult for her to accept some form of consolation, but there was frequently the conscious apprehension that, if others observed that she *was* consoled and *was* satisfied, they would also recognize the illicit basis on which she had obtained that gratification and consolation—her greediness would be exposed, and she would be punished.

Summary. In this lengthy description of Mrs. D. and her analysis, I have not attempted to give a comprehensive picture of her pathology or of her analysis; I have focused, rather, on the problems of her inconsolability, how those problems manifested themselves in the analysis, and what understanding we achieved about the inconsolability and its genesis and meaning. I should also point out that Mrs. D., like most of us, was also *capable* of letting others console her, and she was also *capable* of consoling herself. When, for whatever concatenation of circumstances at the moment, neither self-consolation nor consolation from others was possible, her inconsolability became evident. In my discussion of Mrs. D. I have presented analytic material that bears on her difficulty in permitting others to offer her solace (i.e., her fear of promises being broken, her fear that her feelings of greed might be exposed, and her fear that, in her case, at least, via breaks in verbal communication, contacts with others could lead to further loss of love or even loss of object—what Mrs. D. called "disconnected") and I have also presented material that bears on the patient's difficulty in providing solace for herself (i.e., the problem she had in making use of her reservoir of "good" memories, an issue related to the concept of what has been called the "loving" superego, and her problem in making use of fantasy, play, and illusion). I do not pretend that these factors are by any means the only or the necessary ones in the evolution of inconsolability, and I recognize that these factors cannot really be seen as isolated and independent; they are all interdependent. In a more general sense *anything* that interferes with an individual's ability to obtain solace from others and *anything* that interferes with the individual's ability to provide solace for himself must contribute to the vulnerability to and the tendency toward the state of inconsolability.

Case 2

Mrs. K., a 30-year-old married mother of two, presented numerous episodes of inconsolability both in the analysis and at home. She was preoccupied with her role as a woman, her feelings that women were treated unfairly, and her angry competitiveness with men. One day, she spoke of her concern that she was not as "logical" as I was, and she went on to say that this inferiority in being logical was one of the reasons women were not treated as well as men. Driving to her hour, Mrs. K. had tried to "console" herself by thinking about her relatively new baby and how "good" she felt about being a mother.

These consoling thoughts were not sustained for a very long time. They were replaced by thoughts about her baby. She recalled that when she first became pregnant, she had the fantasy that when the pregnancy was over, her body would be quite different; she had been very disappointed when, after her baby was born, her body was "still the same." Her concern about the analysis was that it could not change her body. Then she said (not for the first time) that her mother had promised her repeatedly that when she grew up, she would be altogether changed; but since she had not changed, her mother had broken her promise. She could not accept any compliment her husband offered about her body. She felt that he was lying, and the thought made her feel worse. She wanted to "crawl away and die" and she felt "unapproachable."

In the session Mrs. K.'s mood became worse. She was sad, angry, and very soft-spoken; but she continued to speak. Her five-year-old daughter had announced her intention to marry her uncle, and she had been openly seductive with him. My patient was concerned with how the daughter might be spared the humiliation of an oedipal disappointment, and she recalled her own, comparable, disappointments. Mrs. K. wanted me to help her advise the uncle on how to deal with his niece; she wanted to know some way that he could "go along with the 'make-believe' without really making her believe that she could marry him." This led to her concern that her feelings toward me were so much more intense than mine toward her. She wanted so much from me; it made her feel greedy and ashamed.

DISCUSSION

This clinical material throws some light on the role of penis envy (or other "loss") in inconsolability. The feelings of loss and deprivation per se do not cause the inconsolability; they produce an internal situation that necessitates consolation. The other factors (here her feelings of greed, her concern about broken promises) interfere with the process of restitution and reparation and lead to the inconsolable state.

The best known examples of inconsolability, and the situation to which the word is most frequently applied, are those related to the loss of a beloved person: parent, close friend, lover, spouse, or child; this is more strikingly so in the latter two instances. In my own work I have had the opportunity of analyzing a number of patients who have suffered the loss of a child or who have undergone abortions, and in these cases (especially when a child died), a significant, protracted period of inconsolability was observed. Without suggesting that other factors were not also operative, I have been impressed with a particular set of data that emerged in these analyses. These patients were burdened with a specific form of guilt and the fantasy that the loss of the child (or fetus) was their fault. This conviction was derived from oedipal guilt, and the fantasy that the dead child was the consequence of the product of an incestuous union. These women saw themselves as guilty of the crime of infanticide and their disconsolate state as evidence of a well-deserved punishment.

Although there are many more variants that could be described, I will mention only one final group that, for want of more precise criteria, I have labeled unconsolables. These are patients whose inconsolability was so intractable and so unrelenting that I have separated them from those with inconsolability. As far as I can tell, the factors that produce the painful state that requires consolation and those that interfere with the process of consolation are the same as in those whose inconsolability is less severe and of shorter duration; but either these elements are quantitatively greater or other factors must be operative. These patients not only seem to suffer more and for a longer period of time, but they produce more archaic material which at times suggests a psychotic substratum. Also, these patients frequently are not able to tolerate the pain and pressure of their disconsolation by withdrawal, rumination, or brooding alone, and, often in desperation, they may resort to various forms of action: drinking and drug taking; compulsive, repetitive masturbation, which may be free of any accompanying fantasies; bouts of eating, often in extreme amounts and in bizarre patterns; head-banging and hair-pulling, self-mutilation, and so forth. I do not feel comfortable in offering any kind of precise formulation, but it would appear that these manifestations are evidence of regressive processes in which the more highly organized, cognitive, affective, and defensive patterns are replaced by more primitive action processes. I do not presume to have even touched on all of the clinical issues related to inconsolability; even on the clinical level, there are many questions that remain to be answered. For instance (and this is true of moods and other complex affective configurations in general), it is not always crystal clear what factors or group of factors are capable of precipitating such reactions, and even more enigmatic is the process whereby the inconsolability gradually diminishes and then disappears. From the clinical perspective, I have tried to demonstrate that the analytic work can best be maintained by dealing with the inconsolability as a resistance and dealing analytically with those factors that at least appear to contribute to the interference with the process of consolation. I have been impressed with the frequency and the clarity of the role that both pregenital and oedipal components play in the evaluation and maintenance of the inconsolability. A further understanding of these interrelationships may provide us with a better knowledge of a number of "atypical" clinical pictures that often frustrate our attempts at diagnosis and classification. In that vein, it is not easy to define precisely *what* inconsolability is. At times, it appears to have the structure and genesis of a symptom; at other times that of a mood or the mourning process. In some cases, the defensive elements are most conspicuous; in others, the inconsolability seems to be the nodal point of a complex character structure. In most of my cases, the clinical picture suggests a mixture of a number of the above.

Similarly, we are still relatively ignorant of why some individuals are much more prone to becoming disconsolate than others. Studies of the neonate and very young infants demonstrate differences at birth in terms of their enjoyment of being cuddled, proficiency at self-consolations, approachability, and relative ease of satiability, but, to the best of my knowledge, no systematic follow-up studies are available that might demonstrate how, and if, these variations play a part in later vulnerability to inconsolability. There is considerable clinical evidence to suggest that these individuals who have not received "good enough mothering" or who have otherwise in the course of early development suffered early trauma may not have sufficient inner resources to utilize efforts at consolation and may also in adult life suffer more frequently from problems of inconsolability.

REVIEW OF SELECTED LITERATURE

I do not intend to offer a comprehensive review of all of the analytic literature that may contribute to our knowledge of these phenomena. There are only a few systematic contributions that focus, primarily, on inconsolability, although fragmentary allusions to it are scattered through the literature. Quite arbitrarily, I have chosen to limit myself to brief comments on those contributions which stimulated my own thinking on the subject.

1. The 1955 paper, "Say You're Sorry," by Kubie and Israel, contains a poignant report of the case of a five-year-old girl whose withdrawal, remoteness, and sadness can be viewed as manifestations of inconsolability. Although the clinical data are limited, the patient's intense feelings of guilt, her preoccupation with whose "fault" it was, and her inability to accept (or to make use of) solace, all seem similar to what is observed in adult patients with inconsolability. Particularly interesting was the patient's refusal to respond to the author's approaches until the precisely correct words were utilized. I believe that this almost magical reaction is tantamount to a game where one individual expects another individual to "guess" what he is thinking.

2. David Milrod's (1972) paper, "Self-Pity, Self-Comforting, and the Superego," is a pioneering effort to delineate some special problems relating to consolation and its vicissitudes. Milrod's focus is on patients whose self-pity as a major vehicle of consolation "may constitute a persistent major characteristic of a person who uses a grievance, even if imagined or provoked, as the stimulus to withdraw for a long spell of feeling sorry for himself" (p. 505). He stresses the narcissistic withdrawal in these patients and suggests that they may suffer from significant defects in ego boundaries and the tendency to use projection as an important defensive operation. Milrod also emphasizes what he calls a "unique bittersweet gratification" which these patients derive from "a narcissistic orgy, tinged with masochism" (p. 507), and he attributes much of the comforting obtained in the self-pitying to the "rewarding" function of the superego.

3. Herbert Schlessinger's two papers, the 1978 article on "Developmental and Regressive Aspects of Making and Breaking of Promises" and the unpublished essay on "The Nature and Regressive Determinants of the Keeping of Promises" constitute a comprehensive source of information and observations on the phenomenon of the promise. He points out that the earliest precursors of the promise are related to "the primitive experiences of regularity in wish fulfillment" (1978, p. 30) and gratification; and he stresses that for younger children, the promise has a different meaning and significance than it does for adults. This is especially pertinent in regard to the solipsistic manner in which

children may hear and experience parental assent, half-promises, and offhand promises as serious and sacred vows. He also discusses the way in which the child "rather than renouncing the [forbidden] wish . . . renounces certain possibilities of realistic gratification in the hope of thus assuring ultimate gratification of the infantile wish sometime in the indefinite future" (unpublished). Schlessinger also notes the importance of promises in the analysis; he points out that although analysts carefully avoid making promises, nevertheless, it is inevitable that the patient will feel that promises have been offered.

4. Roy Schafer's well-known contribution on "The Loving and Beloved Superego in Freud's Structural Theory" (1960) is a thorough, insightful exegesis on Freud's ideas regarding the loving and protective aspects of the superego, ideas which he never developed as comprehensively as its critical and punitive aspects. Freud always stressed that the superego had access to libidinal as well as aggressive energies. Thus, the ego could be loved as well as hated by the superego. This "loving" encompasses a guiding, protecting, taking care of, soothing of the self—functions that are crucial in the processes of consolation and inconsolability. Freud (and Schafer) point to the special need for such "loving" in situations of "overwhelming danger" of a real order where feelings of helplessness may ensue. Schafer reminds us that these same feelings of helplessness and the dread of "traumatic helplessness" are involved in all levels of Freud's genetic series of "danger" situations. At these times, there may be a need and a longing for the loving, protective parents, but there is also a dependence on the loving aspects of the superego. All of these considerations are of great importance in coping with frustration and disappointment, with obtaining consolation, and the process of inconsolability. I need hardly add that one of the major factors that deter the superego from acting in a benevolent fashion in these situations is the aggression the individual may direct toward the love objects or the superego itself. This aggression, whether it is overt or whether it operates internally, is invariably involved in the blocking of consolation efforts and the emergence of inconsolability.

5. The contributions of Winnicott to this topic warrant far more

space than is available. He has devoted a good deal of his writings to the issues of consolation, inconsolability, soothing, holding, aloneness, and the capacity to be alone. Most of his principal conceptual contributions are well known, so a summary of his work is not necessary. I would, however, remind the reader that many of those concepts—the transitional object, the "good enough" mother, the idea of the facilitating environment, and the concept of "holding"—were developed around the issues of the need for consolation, the ways in which consolation occurs, and the state of what I am calling inconsolability. I will focus on one point only: what Winnicott (1953) refers to as the

> intermediate area of experience, between the thumb and the teddy bear, between the oral erotism and the true object-relationship, between primary creative activity and projection of what has already been introjected, between primary unawareness of indebtedness and the acknowledgement of indebtedness . . . an intermediate area of *experiencing*, to which inner reality and external life both contribute . . . the perpetual human task of keeping inner and outer reality separate yet inter-related . . . therefore studying the substance of illusion, that which is allowed to the infant, and which in adult life is inherent in art and religion [pp. 89–90].

Winnicott sees illusion as a creative, productive, adaptive process that brings together inner and outer reality and that the child can use—he would say *needs* to use—to deal with anxiety and states of the depressive type. It is a process that "may reappear" and be utilized at later ages.

Winnicott argues that the mother has the responsibility gradually to disillusion the infant, but this is impossible unless she first has been able to provide sufficient opportunity for illusion. I think that you will recognize a parallel with the work of Mahler, Pine, and Bergman (1975) on the rapprochement phase and the danger of the precipitous deflation of the child's sense of omnipotence.

What Winnicott is saying is that, after all, life is hard and that the "intuitive" parent recognizes that making the child face and conform to every bit of "objective" reality is too much of a strain. Part of that recognition entails illusion, fantasy, religion, creativity, and play; all of these modalities are crucial to the process of consolation. Where these modalities have not been "allowed" to the child, that child has been deprived of powerful weapons against all of those "one damned things after the other" with which I began this presentation. It may well be that blessed is he who can appropriately make use of illusion in just the way that Mrs. K. hoped that her brother could "go along with the 'make-believe' " without *really* making his niece believe that she could marry him.

REFERENCES

Kubie, L. S., & Israel, H. (1955), Say you're sorry. *The Psychoanalytic Study of the Child*, 10:289–299. New York: International Universities Press.

Mahler, M. S., Pine, F., & Bergman, A. (1975), *The Psychological Birth of the Human Infant*. New York: Basic Books.

Milrod, D. (1972), Self-pity, self-comforting, and the superego. *The Psychoanalytic Study of the Child*, 27:505–528. New York: Quadrangle.

Schafer, R. (1960), The loving and beloved superego in Freud's structural theory. *The Psychoanalytic Study of the Child*, 15:163–188. New York: International Universities Press.

Schlessinger, H. (1978), Developmental and regressive aspects of making and breaking of promises. In: *The Human Mind Revisited: Essays in Honor of Karl A. Menninger*, ed. S. Smith. New York: International Universities Press, pp. 21–50.

——— (n.d.), The nature and regressive determinants of the keeping of promises. Unpublished manuscript.

Winnicott, D. W. (1953), Transitional objects and transitional phenomena. *Internat. J. Psycho-Anal.*, 34:89–97.

5

SOME REMARKS ON THE ANALYSIS OF DREAMS AND OF NEUROTIC SYMPTOMS

CHARLES BRENNER, M.D.

The importance of dream analysis as part of psychoanalytic technique is too well known to require documentation. During many years psychoanalysis was descriptively defined as the psychotherapy that utilized dream analysis. Though this is no longer the case, a glance at the curriculum of any psychoanalytic institute will illlustrate the importance still placed on dream analysis and interpretation by analysts today. No institute has fewer than two courses on dream interpretation and analysis. Many have three. In contrast, few, if any, have a course on the analysis of symptoms. Courses on symptom formation, yes. Courses on the analysis of symptoms, no (Arlow and Brenner, 1988). It is interesting to speculate about why this is so. The simplest answer to the question why dream interpretation is so emphasized is that Freud himself took that position very early in his analytic development and retreated from it only slightly as the years went on. He gave to dreams a special place in activities of the mind. They were, for him, the *via regia,* the superhighway to the hidden recesses of the mind. It is less clear whether there is a similarly easy answer to the question having to do with the neglect of symptom analysis. I know of no evidence that Freud recommended or practiced it, yet the opinion is widespread that there is no special point in analyzing a symptom. The idea is that if one conducts an analysis properly, the symptoms will disappear of themselves. Years ago a beginning analyst was explicitly warned against symptom analysis. One was told that if a patient's conflicts were correctly analyzed, his or her symptoms would disappear. One was told that one should analyze conflicts, not symptoms. The correctness of the premise is unquestionable. Symptoms arise from conflicts. It is a patient's conflicts that an analyst tries, by every means available, to understand, but to draw from this the conclusion that one need not or, indeed, should not pay attention to symptom analysis seems perverse in the extreme. Dreams, too, arise from conflict, yet they should be analyzed. Why not symptoms? Yet the taboo was (Lewin, 1952) and still is widespread.

Since dream interpretation as part of analytic technique is so much the more familiar subject, I shall start with it. My remarks are not intended to be a thorough discussion of the topic. I shall, as far as possible, omit from consideration what is well known and has been often said and shall rather confine my remarks to what I hope is less well known and less often mentioned.

I wish to draw attention first of all to both the theoretical inconsistency and the practical disadvantages of thinking in terms of the topographic theory rather than in terms of the structural theory when dealing with dreams; to paraphrase—the inadvisability of applying to dreams Freud's theories of 1900 rather than those of 1923–1926. I first suggested that the theory of dreams as we know it from *The Interpretation of Dreams* (Freud, 1900) needed revision and I am as convinced of it now as I was then.

In addition to suggesting the need for a revision of dream theory I outlined at that time what the revisions should be (Brenner, 1955) and expanded the outline some years later in collaboration with Arlow (Arlow and Brenner, 1964). The essence of the revised theory I proposed is that a dream is a compromise formation like any other compromise among id, ego, and superego (see also Brenner, 1982). Its special psychological features are not best explained by postulating that dream formation begins in a system Ucs. according to the primary process and that it is only subsequently that a dream is subjected to the secondary process by a system Pcs., which both acts as a censor and imposes on the dream elements a kind of logical, editorial revision (Freud, 1900). The special psychological features that characterize dreams are readily explained by assuming a degree of regression and suspension of ego functions during sleep. In particular, the sense of reality that is so characteristic of most dreams results from the suspension of reality testing during sleep. In contrast with adult waking life, fancy is accepted as fact by adults during sleep, just as it so often is by children during waking life as well.

What are the advantages of revising in this way the psychoanalytic theory of the psychology of dreaming? For one thing, what were exceptions to the old theory are consonant with the revised one. This is true of punishment dreams, for example, as well as for dreams in which a feeling of reality is *not* maintained throughout the dream, as when a dreamer thinks to himself, "It's only a dream." For another thing, it makes explicit a feature of dreams in general that might otherwise escape attention. The feature I refer to is this: unintelligibility in dreams is always a consequence of defense. It does not result from the fact that dream thoughts have been "translated into the primary process," as though that were analogous to translation into an unfamiliar, foreign language. Dreams may well be unintelligible to anyone other than the dreamer for a variety of reasons, but when the dreamer himself does not know what the wishes are that are experienced as fulfilled in a dream it is invariably because of a need to avoid or minimize the unpleasure due to anxiety, guilt, or depressive affect that those wishes would arouse were they not disguised, distorted, and otherwise defended against. Finally, it seems to me that perhaps the chief value of the suggested revision is that it places dreams in a proper perspective among the great variety of mental phenomena. They are no longer to be thought of as a sort of exception, as phenomena of a special kind but rather as subject to the same general laws as are other mental phenomena and understandable in the same conceptual framework. In this respect the proposed revision conforms to Freud's original aim, that of relating dream psychology to the psychology of neurotic symptom formation, the psychology of such everyday phenomena as slips and errors, and eventually to normal psychology as well.

If one turns now from such broad and general considerations to something much more limited, there is one feature of dream analysis that is worth spending some time on. What is usually referred to as the text of a dream, or its manifest content, is never the dream itself. It is only what the dreamer—in this context, the patient—tells us. If one is willing to be precise about it, one will admit that in fact one person can never know the manifest content of another person's dream. One can only try to reconstruct it from the dreamer's account of it. One's first reaction to this admission may be some sense of disappointment or even of disillusionment, but a moment's reflection will suffice to dispel it. After all, what is important in analysis is not "a dream," it is what the dream means—what it can tell us about the dreamer. The report of any dream is actually a statement of the dreamer's first, spontaneous associations to it. The words he uses (insofar as they are not repetitions of words that appeared in the dream itself), his tone of voice, his affect as he tells of his dream, in a word, the whole of what we usually call the "manifest content" is doubly valuable precisely because it is not just his memory of a conscious experience during sleep. It is the dreamer's associations to that experience, i.e., to his dream. Keeping this fact in mind is important because otherwise one may be tempted to pay too little attention to the patient's report of his dream and to try to get as clear and full a description of it as possible from him, as though that's what one should do before asking him to associate to it. "Tell me that again" and "How was that, exactly?" are not usually useful questions to ask about a dream. It has no "text" to be elicited and examined via associations. One has something better to work with than a "text," one has the patient's first associations to it, and they are just as often valuable in dream analysis as his later associations will be. Sometimes they are more so. In any case they are not to be disregarded in an effort to clarify "the dream." They must be included among the associations that one hopes will lead to some understanding of the wishes and conflicts expressed in the dream.

To give an example: a young woman in analysis said, "I had a dream last night, but I don't feel like telling it to you. It's kind of vague anyway. I think it was that my mother married my brother, sort of. It was something weird and stupid like that." She went on to say, "You'd think a dream like that would upset me, but I wasn't upset at all that I can remember. It just seemed like, you know, ordinary."

The patient had nothing more to say about her dream, but if one views her account of it as her associations to her nocturnal experience, and if one has some knowledge of the analytic context of the dream, one can go a fair distance toward analyzing it. The context was this. The patient was angry with me because of a recent interruption to her treatment, an interruption to which she reacted as she had done in childhood when her father left on one of his frequent short business trips: it was another proof that he did not love her as much as she wished, that she could not have him all for herself, and that he probably loved her mother and brother better than he loved her. Her way of dealing with her feelings of jealousy and resentment was to be very agreeable, very docile, very good, and, in particular, to convince herself and her father that she thought him the best, the wisest, and the most brilliant father who had ever lived. In her mind, to tell me a dream was to do me a great favor, to give me a chance to shine in her eyes. Just as she used to flatter her father by getting him to teach her something, she tried to overcome her anger at me by telling me a dream, even though she "didn't feel like it," so that I could show off by explaining to her what it meant. And what better gift could she offer than a dream of incest? What analyst would not like a patient who brought him *such* a nice dream? After all, analysts think every patient wants to marry her father. It's everyday stuff to them or, as she put it, "ordinary." They don't even know how "weird and stupid" everyone thinks they are. But how could she dare talk to me that way? It would be too upsetting.

One can surmise, therefore, that during her sleep the patient had been angry and jealous. She wished she had me all to herself, that I had no other patients and no family but her. At the same time, she was angry at me and wanted to attack me and humiliate me as she felt humiliated by my not loving her as she wished me to. All of this was a repetition of, a transference from, her childhood feelings for her father. Neither her wish to have me for herself nor her wish to avenge herself on me could reach consciousness directly during her sleep. Both would have aroused too much anxiety. The former was repressed altogether. It must be guessed at from what she recalled of her dream. One must know that if a lonely, jealous little girl says, "Mama and Johnny should get married," what she really means is that they should go away together and never come back and she and daddy will get married and he will stay with her forever. The wish for revenge fared little better during her sleep, as far as one can judge from her account of the dream itself, but it came more into the open in her first associations, i.e., as she told her dream. It was given expression in "I don't feel like telling it to you, . . . something weird and stupid . . . ordinary. . . ." The very act of telling me her dream expressed her ambivalence. It was a reaction formation against her anger and at the same time a much watered-down expression of love.

It is probably because too little explicit attention has been paid to the fact that a patient's report of a dream can be so useful in analyzing it that published reports of dreams in the analytic literature so rarely read like what one hears from patients in one's practice. So often it seems as though the meat of the dream is missing, that only its bare bones are on the page. Thus, for example, the dream in the illustration given above would, I think, usually be reported in one of two ways. Either "The patient dreamed that her mother and her brother were married" or "The patient reported the following dream, 'My mother and my brother were married.' " These are both accurate statements of the manifest content of the patient's dream, but notice how much they omit of her account of the dream, much of which was so valuable in interpreting it, i.e., in getting to its unconscious meaning.

To focus on what a dreamer's conscious experience must have been while one listens to the account of a dream is to run the risk of neglecting what may be even more important clinically, i.e., the clues as to the meaning of the dream that are contained in the account itself. It is this account that is the stuff of dream analysis, not the analyst's reconstruction of the dream as the analyst thinks the dreamer dreamed it.

I turn now to my second topic, the analysis of neurotic symptoms as part of psychoanalytic technique. As I noted earlier, this topic is a neglected one, for reasons that are not entirely clear. As I also noted, I believe the neglect to have disadvantageous consequences, as I shall attempt to illustrate in what follows.

One obvious fact about a neurotic symptom is that it is a persistent or recurrent phenomenon. It is not a single incident. Symptoms present themselves as objects of study again and again and often over a long period of time. One can observe repeatedly the psychic context in which they reappear as well as the context that is associated with their recession or disappearance. This information is often helpful in forming a conjecture about the nature and origins of the conflicts underlying a symptom, as the following vignette illustrates.

A woman in her early 50s had had many conversion symptoms throughout her adolescence and adult life. Moreover, she mistrusted and disliked doctors. None of them was any good, none could cure her, their medicines only made her worse. But on the few occasions when she had been seriously ill physically—a broken limb, an acute cholecystitis, profuse vaginal bleeding—she had been a changed woman. She became a sensible, cooperative, appreciative patient. Her conversion symptoms and her distrust of doctors disappeared. It may be added that her father had died when she was only two years old and that her childhood was dominated by jealousy of her paternal cousins, whose fathers had lived, as well as by jealousy of boys and men in general.

From all of this one can conjecture that her hysterical symptoms were, at least in part, compromises between her wish to force the world to substitute for her lost father by treating her with special love and care and her need to punish herself for having such wishes. When she was physically ill, however, her conscience was clear. She need fear no more. She felt punished by her illness and could freely demand and enjoy the special care she was so guilty about wanting at other times.

There are forms of psychotherapy that focus on symptoms exclusively. By whatever different names they are called—conditioning, behavior modification, sex therapy—they have in common an intentional neglect of the dynamics and history of the psychic conflicts of which symptoms are but one of the consequences. They focus only on the symptoms and they seek to cure the symptoms, not to remove their cause, unlike analysis, which, by contrast, seeks to remove the causes of symptom formation by enabling a patient to deal better with the conflicts that caused his symptoms in the first place, with the result that his symptoms disappear along with the other improvements in his mental life. For an analyst, what is of principal interest is the nature and origin of a patient's conflicts, not this or that symptom, i.e., this or that compromise formation.

There is no question of the correctness of this view, as was said earlier. It is the whole of a patient's conflicts that must be focused on in analysis, not just one or another symptom. At the same time, one must remember that a symptom, like any other compromise formation, can lead to a better knowledge of the conflict of which it is a consequence if it can be analyzed. In this respect it is no different from a dream. Like dreams, symptoms are valuable in analysis as roads that can lead to a better understanding of a patient's conflicts.

Does an analyst, then, ask a patient to associate to symptoms as the patient may be asked to associate to a dream? Certainly. There is no reason for not doing so. No reason in principle, that is. Just as in the case of a dream, there may be a good reason for not doing so now and then, but in general one should ask a patient to associate to a symptom, i.e., to talk about it as freely as possible. There is no better way to get to the meaning of a symptom, to reach some understanding of the conflicting forces in a patient's mind that have produced the symptom in question as a compromise among themselves.

Understandably one does not expect to achieve a thorough knowledge of the dynamics and genesis of a long-standing symptom or of the conflict of which it is a consequence either quickly or easily. Still, it is surprising how much one sometimes can surmise about a symptom rather soon. This is true in all likelihood for more than one reason. At least one important one is that many symptoms express childhood conflictual wishes in a rather direct and childish way. They are like naïve or childhood dreams and fantasies in this respect. We all know how transparent and informative such fantasies are at times. For example, if a young boy says that he wishes his father would die so that he can have his gold watch, it is not difficult to guess at the incestuous, parricidal, and castrative wishes that gave rise to the child's fantasy. Note, by the way, that we are not considering whether the child can tolerate conscious knowledge of those wishes—whether, if he is in analysis, any of them can be interpreted to him at the moment. All we are concerned with is our own conjecture or understanding of them. To continue with our analogy, some of the underlying wishes are equally evident if an adult patient reveals that he has never been able to keep a watch; that his father gave him a nice one when he graduated from high school, which he promptly broke; that he got another, even nicer, from his father when he finished college and that he lost it after a few weeks; and that a third watch came some years later as a Christmas present, also from his father, that he lost as well, so that now he buys only very cheap wristwatches for himself, keeps them for a year or so till they are worn out, and then buys a new one. Are not this patient's incestuous, parricidal, and castrative wishes as obviously involved in his symptomatic behavior as were those of the child in his fantasy? Indeed, the adult patient's symptomatic behavior in this example tells us even more than does the child's fantasy, namely, that he is guilty and self-punitive about his oedipal wishes. And, we may add, no dream, early in analysis, would be likely to be more informative about a patient's conflicts than was this account of symptomatic behavior with watches.

To return to an earlier point, it is useful to keep in mind the point of view that one does not approach the analysis of a symptom expecting to "analyze" it fully in a single hour. One learns as much as one can from each attempt to analyze a patient's symptoms, knowing that one will never learn all that one would like to know at any one time.

As another example of this, early in her analysis a young woman mentioned that she had been quite uncomfortable a couple of weeks before on the occasion of a trip to a bank. She had been invited to have lunch in the bank by a friend who worked there. When she arrived, her friend took her to the lunch room. It was a windowless room below street level with only a single door. The patient felt anxious and had to excuse herself. I called to her attention that she had thought of this event just after telling me of her dead sister, who had died as a youngster, before the patient was born. Her sister's picture, the patient had told me, was kept on the patient's dresser throughout her childhood. The patient had always felt that her parents compared her unfavorably with her sister, that she was often bad while her sister, she was told, had always been so good.

"I hated her when I was growing up," the patient had said. "I guess I was glad she was dead. Of course, if she hadn't died, I'd never have been born." There was a pause, then, "Sometimes when I was little, I wished I'd been the one who'd died instead of her."

The patient's response to my intervention was that she did not see how an underground room could have reminded her of her dead sister, since her sister was not buried under the ground, but interred in a vault in a mausoleum above ground level. "Of course," she added, "as we went into the dining room in the bank I saw that it was right next to the vault." She went on to say that she often became anxious in tunnels or in elevators, especially if traffic stopped in a tunnel so that one could not get out or if the elevator doors failed to open promptly.

It is apparent from this bit of symptom analysis that the patient's claustrophobia was at least in part a consequence of conflict over jealous and murderous wishes involving her sister and her parents. One can guess that a combination of "I hated her"; "I wish I were her"; "They'll hate me for hating her"; "Why do they go away, why don't they come back and stay with me?" were all involved in the anxious fantasy of being entombed like her sister, mourned and beloved by parents who longed for her return, instead of the patient being lonely and longing for her parents to return, as had so often been the case during her childhood. It is equally apparent that this is far from a complete analysis of the symptom. It sheds no light, for example, on the patient's childhood fantasies about why her sister died, nor on her own oedipal wishes—her sister was five when she died—penis envy, and fantasies of anal birth. But it is a useful step, even though it is only a step, in the direction of a better understanding of the nature of the patient's conflicts and of their childhood origins.

Another point I would like to make about symptom analysis is this: a symptom often disappears in the course of analysis. Whenever it does so, one may be sure that its disappearance is the result of a shift in the balance among the derivatives of id, ego, and superego that make up the conflict of which the symptom is a compromise. The balance among these psychic elements may shift for many different reasons (Brenner, 1969)—a "transference cure," a "flight to health," a change in a patient's life situation—but the one I wish to consider here is that which comes about as a result of progress in analyzing the conflict. Substantial analytic progress necessarily brings about changes in the various compromise formations that are part of every patient's conflicts—in his neurotic symptoms, in his inhibitions, in his capacity for instinctual gratification, and in many of his character traits. When a symptom disappears as a result of analytic progress, its very disappearance is further evidence concerning the wishes and conflicts that were responsible for it in the first place.

For example, a woman in her 30s was anxious while flying in an airplane. She complained particularly of the fact that, should something go wrong, she was just a passenger. There was no way she could get to the controls and try to save the situation. Not that she could fly a plane herself. She had no experience whatever as a pilot. But the feeling of being unable even to get to the controls was somehow associated with great anxiety whenever she let herself dwell on it. Her further associations included the fact that on one occasion when she flew in a small, private plane she experienced no anxiety. She attributed this to the fact that there was at least a possibility for her "to do something" if necessary in a small plane, where she sat in the cockpit.

This patient's major conflicts centered about the fact that her younger sibling, her junior by four years, was a boy, while she was "just a girl." She was partly furiously jealous, partly hopelessly dejected, and constantly guilty in consequence of what she unconsciously considered to be her castrated, inferior state. If one knows what the controls of an aircraft look like, it is easy to guess that for this patient to sit at the controls of a plane with the steering wheel in front of her body unconsciously gratified her wish to have a penis herself. Incidentally, the colloquial term among pilots for a control stick is *joy stick,* i.e., penis. So the patient's conscious thought about being unable to get to the controls is understandable as a derivative or representative of two closely related unconscious ideas. The one, that if she were a man, if she had a penis, everything would be fine. She would not have to be upset, because there would be no danger of anything terrible happening. The other unconscious idea was a wish to kill and castrate her brother and, for that matter, her father as well, a wish that frightened her very much. To put things more connectedly, her symptom could be understood as follows. To fly a plane symbolized for the patient being a man with a penis. Being "just a passenger" symbolized being "just a girl," inferior and castrated. The anxiety she felt corresponded to the dangers — punishment and retributive genital injury—associated with her jealous, murderous, and castrative wishes, wishes that were stimulated whenever she had to be a passenger, while some man with that big control lever in front of him flew the plane.

At the time she first told of her fear of flying, the patient was hardly conscious of jealousy of her brother, much less of being angry at him and wanting to have his penis for herself. She was conscious of some related ideas, for instance, bitterness over the fact that this is a man's world, in which women are but second-class citizens, but not of personal bitterness toward her brother. If anything, she was rather more protective toward him than he seemed to enjoy. As analysis progressed, she became more aware of the various elements of her penis envy: depressive affects, jealousy of brother and father, rage at them and at her mother, guilt and fear of abandonment, of genital injury, and of loss of love. Nothing more was heard of her fear of flying and when she next flew, some months later, there was no mention of anxiety. The symptom disappeared as the conflict changed. The fact that it did so was additional confirmation that the symptom had really been part of the conflict it was attributed to.

Incidentally, this brief report also illustrates something about neurotic symptoms that is self-evident, in a way, and yet cannot be said too often. For an analyst to think of a patient as "a case of phobia," in this instance, "of flight anxiety" does both himself and his patient a disservice. It is an incomplete and, hence, an inaccurate statement. Because it fails to do justice to the patient's symptom it may also impede the analytic work. Take the case of the patient just mentioned. A complete, accurate statement of her symptom would be that whenever she had to fly with nothing in front of her body, while a young man with whom she had no personal contact sat with a big control lever in front of his body and was the boss of the whole venture, she became anxious. When, however, she sat next to the man in charge, with something in front of her body as well, she was not a bit frightened.

When her symptom is described like this, in a way that really does it justice, one might react to the description by saying that she suffered from "flight anxiety" all right, but add that it was flight anxiety of a very special kind. True. But it is equally true that every patient's every symptom is "of a very special kind," just as every patient's every dream is unique. Generalizations are necessary and valuable in their proper place, but they have their limitations. When it comes to analyzing a patient's symptoms, what one wants to know are their individual, their unique, features. Generalizations about symptoms are useful in calling attention to similarities among symptoms found in different patients. Being aware of such similarities may give one a useful hint about some of the elements of a patient's conflicts. At the same time one must remember that similar compromise formations are not always indicative of similar wishes and fears, just as one must remember that similar wishes and fears can give rise to very different compromise formations. In other words, such a hint must be used with caution. It should not be uncritically accepted as true for the case in hand simply because it is reported to have been true for others that seem on the surface to be similar.

The reminder that dissimilar symptoms can result from similar wishes and fears brings us to still another point that must always be kept in mind during one's clinical work. It, too, is familiar, but, like the last point, it bears repetition. When either infantile instinctual wishes or self-punitive and self-destructive tendencies or a combination of the two give rise to psychic conflicts of major proportions, the resulting compromise formations are never limited to one or several neurotic symptoms. There are always characterological consequences as well, some of them clearly pathological, the so-called neurotic character disturbances, some well within normal limits, and others that are hard to label with certainty as normal or pathological. In other words, a patient's symptoms are never isolated phenomena. Their dynamic bases and their origins are always closely related to those of other important compromise formations of the same individual. They are part of an organic whole, part of the totality of his mental life. Whatever may be the compromise formations that result from an individual's psychic conflicts, the ones that we call symptoms are as much a part of the person as are all the others. In fact, they differ from normal compromise formations rather in degree than in kind (Brenner, 1973, chaps. 8 and 9). One should always remember that a symptom or, for that matter, a neurotic character disturbance, is part of how a patient thinks, feels, and behaves when he is rejected, when he is loved, when he is lonely, when he is part of a crowd, when he is inhibited or frightened or angry, when he feels frustrated or gratified, as the case may be. Like any other psychic phenomenon, a symptom fits into a patient's life. However long-standing and repetitive it may be, its appearance or intrusion into a patient's consciousness is each time a result of what the patient was thinking and experiencing at the moment, just as every dream, whatever its infantile latent content, has some reference to and is in some degree the result of events of the moment in the dreamer's life. It is not quite correct to think, as we so often do, of a neurotic symptom as something distinct from the organized, integrated, and normal part of a patient's ego. Saying that one patient has an intact ego and that another does not is really only a shorthand way of trying to differentiate between patients with many severe symptoms and patients with few mild ones. It is a useful shorthand, perhaps, for the purpose, but it is disadvantageous rather than helpful when one carries it over into one's clinical work with patients and applies it in the analytic situation.

For instance, a patient complains of recurrent backache, or headache, or stomachache. "Analyzing his symptom" means much more than asking what comes to his mind about backaches or headaches or stomachaches in general. Such associations "to his symptoms" are not to be ignored or neglected. Whatever a patient may say deserves attention. But they are only part of the story. It is equally important to learn about a particular episode of pain, the one that occurred yesterday, today, or over the weekend, perhaps. What a patient was doing, thinking, or feeling when he noticed the pain, what he thought of when he felt it, and so on, are likely to furnish the best clues to the unconscious conflicts of which the symptom, in this case, of pain, is a part.

Not that patients should be quizzed about their symptoms any more than about their dreams or anything else. Spontaneous expression is obviously the ideal, but when a patient consistently omits details of the sort just mentioned and talks of his symptoms only in generalities like "I always feel faint in a crowded bus" or "It's the takeoff that makes me nervous every time" one can be sure that he is avoiding the details for a reason, usually an unconscious one, and this should be brought to the patient's attention and, one hopes, analyzed like any other important resistance.

It is when a patient's resistance is not too strong, when he is able to talk freely about a symptomatic episode, that one can see most clearly the relationship between his symptom and the other aspects of his life that are dynamically related compromise formations. For instance, the patient who was anxious when flying, as described above, had a recurrence of the symptom on one occasion after she had been free of it for many months. The obvious question was, "What was it that had precipitated her relapse?" As she talked about the episode, she remembered that when she was anxious, she had, as she expressed it, "An empty feeling in my stomach. A real sick feeling." She could not remember the last time she had been sick to her stomach. She paused for several seconds, then proceeded with obvious reluctance. The last time she could remember was when she had performed fellatio on her boyfriend at his request. She had not enjoyed it at all. She had felt humiliated and used. It had made her sick to her stomach. On the plane, she said, she did not eat a thing. She had just passed up the meal altogether. Luckily she had had a good lunch earlier in the day. She had gone to a special place with a fellow worker and had had two large boiled sausages, which was sort of a treat for her. She used to love them when she was a girl, but has eaten them infrequently as an adult.

It must be added that the flight in question was part of a business trip. She had just been promoted to a position of greater responsibility and was flying to a conference as a result. It should also be added that to be promoted meant to her that her chief, an older man, preferred her to her colleagues, many of whom were men, something she equated, though at first only unconsciously, with having her father prefer her to her brother, who had been a principal rival in her childhood and a chief object of her jealousy.

I hope that this brief account will serve to persuade the reader of what was abundantly substantiated by the analytic material; namely, that being in a plane en route to the conference after her recent promotion symbolized unconsciously the gratification of frightening, guilt-laden wishes. It meant to her that she had triumphed over her brother by biting off his penis, that she had it now, and that she was the favored sibling, the boy in the family. For this crime she had to pay, and pay she did with anxiety, nausea, hunger, and disgust with herself for being such a "sissy" as to be frightened by flying. But what is of particular interest in the context of this discussion is to note that the same childhood wishes—to be a boy and her father's favorite—that resulted in her symptom had equal relevance to other aspects of her adult life. For example, they influenced her choice of vocation, and they accounted for much of the pleasure she got from her work, as well as for inhibitions and unhappiness in connection with it. In a very real sense, then, this patient's symptom, on the occasion just described, was part of her reaction to her promotion. It is equally true that one cannot understand the symptom without reference to the patient's unconscious conflicts and to their origins in the instinctual wishes and fears of her childhood. It is this fact, indeed, that has been most emphasized by analysts, beginning with Freud himself, in their elucidation of the psychology of neurotic symptoms. But what I am trying to add to this and to emphasize is that each time a symptom reappears, it is because something in the present has activated the childhood instinctual conflict of which the symptom is a result. The "something" may be, as in this case, a change in the patient's life situation. It may be a sexual experience. It may be what is happening in analysis, in particular, something in the transference, and so on. Whatever the reason, the past has become active in the present as a neurotic symptom, just as the past is continually and repeatedly active in the present in so many different ways. One must bear in mind that a symptom is one of the many. It is different from the others in certain respects, but never entirely divorced from them, and what is of practical importance, its connection with the other aspects of a patient's life can furnish important clues to the understanding of the conflicts that underlie them all.

I suggest, then, that there has been a tendency to value symptoms at less than their true worth analytically. Symptom analysis, carried out in the way I have attempted to describe and illustrate, contributes significantly to an understanding of the nature and origins of a patient's psychic conflicts. It is not a superhighway to "the unconscious" any more than dream analysis is. It is often, however, like dream analysis, a valuable path for the analyst to follow. Both can lead to most useful results.

REFERENCES

Arlow, J. A., & Brenner, C. (1964), *Psychoanalytic Concepts and the Structural Theory*. New York: International Universities Press, chap. 9.

——— ——— (1988), The future of psychoanalysis. *Psychoanal. Quart.*, 57:1–14.

Brenner, C. (1955), *An Elementary Textbook of Psychoanalysis*. New York: International Universities Press, chap. 7.

——— (1969), Some technical precepts in psychoanalysis. *J. Amer. Psychoanal. Assn.*, 17:333–352.

——— (1973), *An Elementary Textbook of Psychoanalysis*, 2nd ed. New York: International Universities Press, chaps. 7–9.

——— (1982), *The Mind in Conflict*. New York: International Universities Press.

Freud, S. (1900), The Interpretation of Dreams. *Standard Edition*, 4 & 5. London: Hogarth Press, 1953.

——— (1923), The ego and the id. *Standard Edition*, 19:1–59. London: Hogarth Press, 1961.

——— (1926), Inhibitions, symptoms and anxiety. *Standard Edition*, 20:75–174. London: Hogarth Press, 1962.

Lewin, B. D. (1952), Phobic symptoms and dream interpretation. *Psychoanal. Quart.*, 21:295–322.

6

SOME PATHOGENIC ASPECTS OF THE PRIMAL SCENE: A DEVELOPMENTAL VIEWPOINT

MARJORIE HARLEY, PH.D.

This paper is based on two assumptions: the first is that reconstruction of the preverbal period need not be incompatible with the principles upon which the analytic method rests. Rather, reconstructions dealing with some of the basic data of preoedipal experiences may contribute substantially to the patient's understanding of the essential connections between his past and present and bring him in closer touch with himself. As Blum (1977) pointed out, the notion of preverbal reconstruction is not nearly so novel as some are prone to believe. Examining the issues from a historical vantage, he reminded us that Freud's reconstruction in his self-analysis of what the meaning of the birth and death of his younger brother, Julius, was to the second year of life and encompassed both the anal phase and the rapprochement subphase of separation-individuation.

The second assumption is that knowledge of the preoedipal period derived from observational studies has not only enlarged the mainstream of psychoanalytic developmental theory but has pertinence for clinical psychoanalysis. I am well aware that there are some analysts who believe that knowledge gained through direct observations, rather than from strictly analytic data, has little clinical relevance, and that it will in some way replace or contaminate our heritage of psychoanalytic theory. In this respect, I would underscore my hearty agreement with Blum (1977) who has clarified how data from these observational studies have broadened our frame of reference and enriched rather than detracted from the value of what already has been learned from analytic reconstruction.

There has been the further belief expressed by some that the application of knowledge arrived at from direct observations carries the threat of a substitution of such data for strictly analytic data. In this connection I must own that I believe a comparison of the pitfalls of confusing observational data with analytic data on the one hand, and, on the other, of confusing the analyst's intellectual store of analytic data with the data that emerge from the analytic process is a legitimate analogy.

Finally, it has not always been easy for me to understand, when analyzing patients with minor ego deviations, how one can isolate such deviations, rooted in the first years of life, from the later structural conflicts (Harley, 1986). On the contrary, it has been much easier for me to attempt to perceive some of the ways in which the earlier problems have not only contributed to, but also have influenced, the texture and patterning of the ensuing neurotic constellations.

Against this background I shall proceed.

It is in general useful to reexamine and hence also to reassess certain time-honored psychoanalytic concepts within the context of our ever-increasing awareness of the complexity of genetic-dynamic factors, and especially of our rapidly expanding knowledge of the intricacies and variability of ego development.

In more recent years, an interest was expressed in the reassessment of the primal scene as a determinant in pathological outcomes (Esman, 1973; Blum, 1977; Panel, 1978). In these discussions, the primal scene was viewed within the framework of our accretions of knowledge gained since Freud's initial conceptualizations of the infantile neurosis: for example, our greater understanding of how antecedent and subsequent experiences may alter one another's meanings; of how the mind may snatch these multiple memories, meanings, and fantasies and compact them into a few or even a single, often seemingly traumatic, memory (that is, the telescopic nature of memories); or our increased awareness of the subtle and almost infinite ways in which defensive screening maneuvers may be utilized so that less adverse experiences may obscure more adverse ones.

In his incisive discussion of the Wolf-Man's pathology, Blum (1977) reminded us that the reconstruction of the primal scene experience at 18 months and its retroactively traumatic effect in the phallic-oedipal period were yet another manifestation of Freud's genius. At the same time, he pointed to the fact that this single experience and the later, associated experiences that tended to organize themselves around the original event, in and of themselves, could hardly have accounted for the Wolf-Man's severe pathology. In this context, Blum also called attention to Freud's omission of the possibly more traumatic effect of the Wolf-Man's malaria with its attendant high fever.

As Esman (1973) noted in his overview of the literature, scarcely anyone would doubt the universality of primal scene fantasies, whether these be based on actual occurrences or merely on the uncanny ways children have of knowing something "mysterious" is going on in the parental room: that is, their ingenuity in combining their phase-specific bodily sensations, concomitant fantasies, and associatively linked observations for the concoction of their notions of what is taking place behind the closed door, even though they remain on the other side of that door. The theory of libidinal phase development, the child's proneness for quick regressions, the fluidity between zonal outlets, the still-limited extent of cognitive development would all tend to account for the conglomeration that makes up the content of these infantile sexual theories. I am inclined, however, to attribute a more disturbing influence than does Esman to the ubiquitous primal scene fantasies, which are, after all, an essential ingredient of the infantile neurosis with which the child must cope. Nonetheless, I agree that they need not inevitably lead to a pathological outcome, even though they be based on actual exposure to adult intercourse.

The aim of this paper, however, is not to deemphasize the pathogenic importance of the primal scene. As Esman (1973) and Blum (1977) each in his own way indicated, the ultimate effect of actual primal scene exposures and/or fantasies must be assessed within the framework both of developmental factors and the ways in which these experiences may have combined and interacted with other genetic-dynamic forces in the child's total experience. It is from this vantage that I shall discuss fragments from an analysis in which the primal scene in fact was discernible as a major etiological determinant, albeit as but one of a number of major determinants in the total mosaic of the patient's experience.

The patient, a highly intelligent, married man in his late 20s, the father of an infant daughter, and already well-established in his profession, came to analysis because of recurring episodes of impotence and anxiety lest he not maintain a superior level of work. He regarded his fear of flying as only a peripheral symptom unless he was confronted with the necessity to take a plane trip. He was also uncomfortably aware that he depended too much on his wife's success, albeit she was in a different field, to sustain his own sense of status. He additionally questioned his capacity for meaningful relationships: specifically, he felt he was far too preoccupied with his desire to be special. He had had enduring friendships, some of them dating back to his high school years, but he feared these relationships were too much motivated by the need to be respected and admired. They did, in fact, contain this narcissistic, exploitative element, but he was prone to castigate himself and to discount his genuine liking for his friends and his interest in their welfare. He would often question his capacity to love, a question which stemmed from his narcissistic concerns, but also from his enormous fund of destructive aggression which he did not overtly express and rarely allowed himself to be aware of. He was prone to uncomfortable and diffuse states of excessive inner excitations, not only in conjunction with anxiety-provoking situations but also with positive situations: for example, in planning a vacation trip, the purchase of a new car, an important gift for his wife, and so forth. More than once he expressed the feeling that as his analysis progressed, something both wonderful and disastrous would happen. Since adolescence, he had had a recurring fear that he was potentially psychotic.

Developmentally, the patient had achieved a certain, although not optimal, degree of object constancy. He did manifest some structural deviations, but these did not reflect excessively severe pathology, and the weight was on the side of intrapsychic conflicts. In brief, I considered him to be a patient for whom the analytic method could be appropriately and usefully applied.

It soon became evident, through the elucidation of certain transference manifestations, that in repeated periods of his late adolescent and adult life, the patient had derived the ability to function successfully through what appeared to be a magical, primitive identification with some older man who had achieved status and whom he simultaneously idealized. He would find himself on occasion adopting certain mannerisms of this other person, sometimes only a verbal expression or an insignificant gesture, and then of having fleeting moments in which he even felt himself to be this other person. In short, this apparent fluidity of self-boundaries showed itself only in relation to specific individuals (and, of course, in the transference), and then only in a transitory way, although no doubt it was reflective of some weakness in his ego structure. By the same token, it was extremely important for him to be the special one in the eyes of the individual he chose to emulate, if not become. Otherwise, he would feel lost and ineffectual.

During the early months of the patient's analysis, we could piece together the following fragments of his life story. He had been the youngest of four children, three boys and a girl, and throughout childhood had often bathed and slept with his sister, a year older than himself. When he was in early prepuberty, a brother had been born and then another brother and sister in quick succession. His mother apparently had been depressed for the first few years of his life, and her orphaned cousin, a young woman in her early 20s, had contributed much time to his care until the middle of his second year. At that time she had left abruptly to care for an ailing aunt in a neighboring town and later had married. The patient, however, had had sporadic contacts with her throughout his childhood and had remained steadfastly fond of her, retaining the notion, which seems to have been a factual one, that she had been equally devoted to him and had provided good mothering. A frequent anxiety was that if he allowed himself to become attached to me, he would have to sustain the pain of my loss.

His depressed mother was ill-prepared to withstand the child's excessive attempts to cling to her after the cousin's departure. Around the beginning of his third year, a neighbor, recently divorced and childless, moved to a nearby house. Especially noteworthy in the patient's early history was the role of this neighbor who became attached to the child in a possessive, engulfing way. He was much with her, accompanying her to various places, including her own home where he spent many hours each day. He recalled how she told him horror stories, including tales of murder and mutilation, and of big, black, poisonous spiders, and how she exposed her breasts to him when he asked to see them. Later we could ascertain that this memory of seeing her breasts additionally served to screen the sight of her genitals. When he was in his fifth year, that is, in the oedipal period, his parents took a trip, and he lived with this neighbor and shared her bed.

This woman fed the child's omnipotence strivings by indulging his every whim when he was still quite young, and, as his verbal and cognitive development proceeded, by repeatedly assuring him he would do great, wonderful things when he grew up. She projected an image of herself as an omnipotent, omniscient being who, in the child's eyes, had a kind of Midas touch in that everything she came in contact with seemed to turn to gold, including himself.

This intense relationship with the neighbor continued throughout most of the patient's childhood. The fact that it petered out seemed to have been due to several factors: perhaps it was inevitable as the child's increasing maturity rendered him a less gratifying object for this woman's extremely pathological needs; it was also no doubt facilitated by the child himself, who turned to his mother for protection against the neighbor's seductiveness.

The character of the patient's positive oedipal configuration, as it revealed itself for some time, is noteworthy and, as might be expected, was further complicated by the neighbor who served as an alternate oedipal object. Up to the time of his analysis, the patient felt he had always adored his mother and he could think of her only in terms of her innate goodness: for him she was endowed with somewhat of a spiritual quality, and it was as though she had been untouched by earthly sin. Yet he acknowledged that his image of her was unexplainably vague, almost as though she were unreal. Throughout later childhood and prepuberty, he had spent much of his free time in her company, believing that in this way he was making up to her for his father's seeming lack of consideration, and that he had the capacity to be a more satisfactory mate for her. However, this positive oedipal relationship was marred, not only by the child's preoedipal longings but by his too fluid self-boundaries: therefore, to love his mother was, in part, to be like her, and ultimately to be her. He sewed as she sewed, helped in diapering and in other ways in caring for the younger siblings, and accompanied her on shopping expeditions where he showed much interest in her choice of clothing. I would here add the fact that his one-year-older sibling, a girl with whom he had bathed and slept, doubtless augmented this feminine identification, as did the mother herself.

The patient had been more deeply involved with his father than he could realize until the treatment was well under way. He saw his father as a harsh, sadistic dictator whom he could never please, who had been especially disparaging of him, and who had treated the mother with little consideration, upbraiding her for allowing him to remain overly attached to her instead of sending him out to engage in peer activities.

The distorted, positive oedipal situation and a basic fear of women enhanced, if not in some measure induced by, his persisting image of the neighbor, on one level as a powerful, phallic mother, strengthened the child's negative oedipal strivings which he expressed through his masochistic provocations of his sadistic father. At the same time, this sadomasochistic relationship protected him from too much closeness with the father. This would have meant becoming too much like him, an identification against which he had struggled as far back as he could remember. On the other hand, he sought out older, idealized men who would magically impart their power to him and who were substitutes for the father and patently homosexually tinged. In a deeper sense, however, they were substitutes for the magical neighbor who had so reinforced his narcissism.

The patient's proclivity for splitting, as it revealed itself in the transference, was evident in respect to the neighbor and his mother. In brief, he seemed for a long time unable to consider ever having harbored any negative feelings for his mother, although there were veiled hints and glimpses that initially the neighbor had been the "good" one, and his mother the "bad" one. Later in childhood, however, he had come to view the neighbor as the epitome of earthiness and evil. He felt she had fooled him by the assumption of both her omnipotent role and her false predictions in respect to his own omnipotence. He further recalled instances wherein this feeling of omnipotence which she had fostered in him had been abruptly deflated by her, albeit she would again restore it.

A paramount feature displayed by the patient, and one very much related to the theme of this chapter, was a repeated doubting of the reality of his perceptions and the validity of his judgments, a characteristic that appeared to pervade many facets of his life. He frequently complained that he really did not know what was what, what was fact and what was fancy. Hence he was never sure of his assessment of financial ventures, of the actual value of material things he might buy, of his professional decisions, and so it went. Always he would have the feeling: Am I seeing things as they really are; how can I trust the accuracy of my perceptions? It was as though the major issue was not so much the specific conscious content of his concerns as it was the all-pervasive feeling of his inability to perceive and evaluate things as they really were.

As for the reconstruction of the early primal scene exposures: already in the first year of his analysis, the patient would periodically begin to experience excitement as he was approaching my office. These feelings would increase in intensity during the hour, and he would move his legs and arms restlessly, complaining of the sexual arousal and diffuse tension he experienced throughout his body, as well as a concomitant, diffuse anxiety, none of which he could relate to any specific ideational content. He would implicitly implore me to alleviate these feelings and experienced what he verbalized as an "impotent" rage, which was in part directed against me. This rage was also, however, as he himself sensed it, less object-directed and more generalized. In addition, he acknowledged the validity of my suggestion that my seeming impassivity further intensified his rage, since he could not draw me into the arena of his excitement in which he felt so alone. Occasionally, in the midst of this extreme discomfort he reported he had had an attack of diarrhea preceding the hour. When I verbalized for him that it was as though he experienced these exciting, yet uncomfortable feelings to be more than he could contain, he responded almost with surprise that I seemed, indeed, to understand how he felt. At this point, I suggested the possibility that he was reexperiencing old feelings that were related to his having been in some way overexcited as a very young child. In short, my initial attempts at reconstruction were somewhat global.

Then came the time when, as the patient experienced these bodily states, he would also be hypersensitive to any sound I might make: my slightest movement, of which I myself was usually unaware, would distract him and he would complain of a ringing in his ears. On these occasions, primal scene innuendos frequently were present, either in dream material or other communications. My thought that he might well have sustained early and repeated overstimulation (Greenacre, 1952) led to my reconstructing that possibly he had spent time very early in life in his parents' bedroom. I suggested that at an age so young his parents' excitement would have aroused a corresponding bodily excitement in himself; that he would have felt overwhelmed by these strong sensations, abandoned to deal with his own excitement, and with no one to relieve him. His response was to recall a movie he had seen some years previously.[1] In this movie, a little boy stares in fascination through a store window at a still, mechanical man. Suddenly, the mechanical man moves and the child is terror-stricken. As the story goes, for the first time the child knows what fear is and flees from the scene. Aside from this association, the patient responded only blandly to my suggestion.

Several months later, when it seemed timely again to suggest the possibility that he had been exposed to these early primal scenes, I was met with the same bland response. At that moment, however, the patient recalled a dream of the previous night, in which a very young child was holding himself up by the bars of a cage, and pressing his nose against the side of the cage as though staring at something. He spoke of this cage as being the kind in which wild animals were kept, and then associated once more to

[1] This was Saroyan's *The Human Comedy*.

the little boy who had pressed his nose against the store window and had been so startled by the movement of the mechanical man. It was at this juncture that the patient recalled the family custom of having the crib of each of the youngest of the children in the parents' bedroom during his or her first year or more. This had been a matter of expediency. The patient, in reporting this to me, said that of course he had known this all the time, and yet had not known he had known it, and he was genuinely surprised by his denials and repression.

More than a year after he had confirmed the fact of his early primal scene exposures, and without any instigation on my part, the patient began to speak, as he had many times before, of how he allowed himself no curiosity whatsoever about me. He was sophisticated enough to know that other patients were curious about their analysts' personal lives; yet he preferred never to think of mine. Later he could concede he would be too frightened to know anything personal about me, and he himself was puzzled by what this fear could be. He volunteered how he knew where my home was because he had seen the address listed in the phone book when he had originally looked up my office number. Whenever he was in my neighborhood, however, he had refrained from driving along the street where I lived, even though this might mean having to take a more indirect route to his destination. Again, as he put it, he was afraid to look. The fear of what he might see was obviously more in the foreground than was the forbidden aspect of looking. We dealt with this material in a number of ways: for example, in the context of what he might discover about my sex life; of his fear lest he learn I was a dangerous, seductive woman like the neighbor, a fear he had voiced frequently in his analysis; and also of his desire to maintain in the transference relationship the excitement deriving from both his forbidden, oedipal, primal scene fantasies and other fantasies linked to his experiences with the neighbor. Nonetheless, he persisted in his massive repression and denial of all curiosity in respect to my personal and professional life.

Many months later, when he was dealing with his masturbation conflicts, the patient again became highly sensitive to the sounds I made, this time while I was engaged in needlepoint, thereby making a kind of rhythmic noise. He said he had the absurd fantasy that I had a problem and was masturbating. At that time, I interpreted this fantasy as a projection of his own masturbatory activities about which he was so anxious and guilty. He appeared to accept and even confirm this interpretation by proceeding with additional material having to do with his masturbation and acute castration conflicts.

Ultimately our understanding of the fantasy of my masturbation deepened when the patient opened an hour by recalling in only slightly modified form a dream he had reported much earlier in his analysis: "A woman was sitting next to a wall and I was staring at this woman's face, feeling horror that had to do with something about this woman, I don't know what." Among his associations was the thought that the wall was like a night deposit bank box, and that "night deposit" made him think of sex and his nocturnal emissions in adolescence. At this point he said another image from the dream came to mind; namely, he was observing someone, he thought himself, with his nose pressed against the bars of a cage, and again came the memory of the little boy and the mechanical man. He thought I was the woman in the dream because my chair was placed near the wall, and he referred again to his fantasy that I masturbated in my chair. Now he said he was feeling very disturbed and again beset with the frightening thought that he simply did not know what the true state of affairs was. Would he ever be able to trust his own judgments and perceptions? He was, he said, again getting "lost in this feeling"; he could not control this, and now he expressed the urge to flee from my office because his anxiety and excitations were reaching such an unbearable pitch. He was also experiencing what he knew was an old feeling, namely, that no one would believe him. In my own dilemma of the moment, and also in my effort to reach him empathically, I said I could sense he felt real desperation. His response was a spontaneous and excited, "That's it exactly," and, to my surprise, he began to sob, saying he was sobbing with relief. He became calmer and said again that the noise of my sewing made him think I was masturbating.

At this juncture, I dared to make what I characterized as a "tentative" suggestion: that possibly his neighbor had masturbated when his parents had been away and he had shared her bed. To this, his response was almost immediate and decidedly spontaneous: "Yes, yes, you're right; you're on target." He went on to say this must be true, he just felt the ring of truth in it. He paused for a few moments as though reflecting, and then said this was the reason he had feared as a child that people would not believe what he said; he now could see that it was he himself who did not wish to believe the reality. He also recalled that not infrequently as a child he had the sensation that his own bed was shaking; and yet when he steadied himself with his hand on the night table, he realized that, in fact, the bed was not shaking at all.

Although the patient left this hour, which was on a Friday, in a state of seeming hope and exhilaration, by the time he arrived for his Monday hour he made no further mention of the reconstruction. In fact, he did not allude to it for many weeks until, at what I thought was an appropriate moment, I suggested that the whole incident had been so terrifying and disturbing to him that he again had to drive it from his mind. He acknowledged this was so: that whenever he thought of the reconstruction, his mouth became excessively dry, and his anxiety well-nigh unbearable. At times, it was as though he half-remembered the event, and then it would slip away, as does a dream sometimes. Yet he knew it was not a dream. He could feel at those times he did not want to remember. And now again he had the urge to flee the hour.

The following weekend the patient took a professional trip involving plane travel, which, as may be recalled, he feared. He was most afraid, not at the take-off or the landing, which he realized would be more realistic, but while the plane was in midair. Upon his return, he reported the following: on this plane trip he had felt abandoned to his own terror which had seemed to find expression in the excitations that again had suffused his entire body, and he had felt as though he were trapped. Also on this trip, for the first time, his fear had assumed more specificity, and he had realized that he was especially overwhelmed by these frightening excitations when the going was rough and the plane vibrated. It was as though, he said, he feared a bodily dissolution, as though he and the plane were one and that the excitations would cause them both to explode. At that moment he had had what he thought was an actual memory of the movement of the bed he had shared with the neighbor, and he had been startled and relieved by the connection his mind had so suddenly and spontaneously made.

Some time later, the patient spoke of two apartments he had rented which the landlord was to convert into one larger apartment. He planned to utilize a wide hallway, which would connect the two apartments, for a room containing many books of information and which one might use for any activity. I was struck by his expression of "any activity," though it was clear that consciously he meant this would be like a family room in which one could read or play games, and so on. He then told even more specifically of his plans for this room which would involve extravagant expenditures. He had a number of associations regarding his reluctance to reveal his plans to me. For example, he felt that dealing with so much money would be something he should not do, as though he were a "kid" spending money in ways in which only the "grownups" should spend it. He also thought of this room, which was a hall through which people would pass, as a place where one could see all he had done to enhance it, and it was a place where one could both see and be seen. In short, it represented a condensation of forbidden primal scene activities, his exhibitionistic and scoptophilic drive components, his oedipal replacement of his father who had spent money easily, and last, but by no means least, a place in which forbidden masturbatory activities could take place.

I turn now to the main aim of this chapter; namely, to attempt to assess the effect of the patient's early primal scene exposures and fantasies as these combined and interacted with other untoward aspects of his ego and drive development.

I should first inject, however, that I am inclined to believe that the patient received adequate mothering from the cousin in the first year of life and that this (aside from his constitutional anlage) may well have accounted for some of his basic ego strengths, and particularly for the basic trust and capacity for a therapeutic alliance which he manifested in the analytic situation.

To start from the beginning, I would first consider the relationship between the primal scene events in the first year or so of life, and the developmental conflicts of the second year, and some of the ways in which the ensuing ego problems contributed to the patient's oedipal anomalies and his later structural conflicts.

Those of us who do not impute elaborate ideational content to the oral phase would doubtless agree that such early and massive auditory, kinesthetic, and visual stimulation attendant on primal scene exposure would lead predominantly to states of excessive bodily excitations, allowing of course for the fact that some individual infants would be more vulnerable to external stimuli than others. These bodily states, which my patient appeared to have sustained, were compounded by the incomplete separation of the infant from the other, so that the parents' excitement was fused, as it were, with his own. Further, these excessive excitations contained both libidinal and infantile rage components, without specific aim (Greenacre, 1952), and augmented an abiding and heightened sensitivity to both internal and external stimuli. Moreover, the rage component served to increase the patient's aggressive potential and his later sadomasochistic tendencies, and to contribute to his ego-drive imbalance. The extreme anxiety stirred by the disparity between the states of persisting, excessive, inner excitations and the immature organism's inability to contain them contributed to the delay of the formation of self-boundaries. Thus this factor of overstimulation was conducive to a prolongation of primitive identifications, intensifying the patient's later bisexual strivings and castration complex.

In addition to the stress trauma incurred by the early primal scenes, it appears that another kind of stress trauma occurred at the peak of his rapprochement crisis, compounding the tensions accumulated in the first year and further affecting ego and drive development. Here I have in mind the loss of the caretaker cousin which entailed, in effect, his abandonment to his depressed mother, who, at that time, was ill-equipped for the task of mothering. It seems probable that the bland unresponsiveness of a depressed mother would have muted the mother-child interaction and thus hindered the child's development toward a firmer sense of separateness of self. The result was a previously traumatized, helpless child and a helpless mother, so that the rapprochement problems fell far short of optimal solution, as was apparent in later transference enactments. Further, the child's intensified proneness for tension, originating in the early primal scenes, was taxed anew, not only by the expectable anxieties of the developmental crisis of the second year but by the cousin's abandonment. In this instance, the issue was not the fear of object loss; rather, it was an actual object loss which the child sustained. And it seems reasonable to infer that the patient's massive repression of his aggression, apparent in his later reaction formations, and particularly in his transference manifestation, harked back to this happening. All of the aforementioned anxieties and stresses of these untoward happenings in the first two years of life impeded his individuation.

The consequent persistence of his infantile omnipotence strivings was unfortunately extended and exaggerated by the neighbor's entry into the child's life with her emphasis on her own and his grandiosity. This narcissistic interplay between child and neighbor provided still another increment to his severe castration complex: for example, on the one hand, he would feel fantastically omnipotent and then suddenly, in the midst of this feeling, he would, like all small boys, be confronted with the frightening thought of castration. But for him this thought would have been all the more frightening because of its marked contrast to his sense of grandiosity, and also because, as may be recalled, the neighbor had exposed her genitals to him.

On a conscious level, the patient had worshiped this neighbor, primarily because of her seeming omnipotence and the other gratifications he derived from her. On a deeper level, as I said earlier, he had perceived her as a frightening, devouring, phallic woman as well as a frightening castrated woman. She therefore, in no small measure, played a role in his intense, unconscious fear of, and hostility for, women, a hostility that may well have been enhanced by the fact that additionally she was an object for displacement of his anger related to the emotional loss of his depressed mother and his retrospective anger against the cousin who had forsaken him.

The child thus entered the oedipal period with a heightened readiness for excitations and an attendant ego-drive imbalance, with insufficiently firm ego boundaries, associated with greater than average bisexual strivings, with the groundwork laid for an extremely severe castration complex, and with the ingredients for pronounced sadomasochistic oedipal primal scene fantasies.

I shall now discuss briefly the significance of the child's exposure to the neighbor's masturbation in the phallic-oedipal phase in terms both of the early primal scenes and of the future course of his oedipal development.

In respect to the relationship between the early primal scenes and the oedipal primal scene equivalent, that the two were connected in the patient's mind is evident in the way he linked the terror of looking in the dream cage-crib scene and the horror of looking at the woman against the wall with the fright engendered by looking at the mechanical man who so suddenly moved. I might add parenthetically that the mechanical man, in addition to activating the memory traces of the sudden movement of the parents (the *strangeness* of which was so frightening to the infant), also represented the child's uncontrollable erections. But the basic link between the early primal scene trauma and the oedipal trauma was that of the bodily excitations, and the main effect of the earlier experiences on the later one showed itself in the context of his heightened excitation and anxiety level, and hence of his enhanced total organismic stress.

As for the influence of the oedipal event on the child's subsequent oedipal development, it is especially important to bear in mind his insufficiently developed self-boundaries, that is, his incomplete individuation. We have seen, for example, in his airplane fantasy, how his proclivity for massive identification with the other would have lent him the illusion that the neighbor's seemingly strange and uncontrollable excitement was in a sense his own, and this massive identification would also have triggered his greater than average castration fears, particularly since he had already doubtless been exposed to the sight of her genitals. In fact, one is led to wonder if the face in the dream at which he stared with such horror was not a screen for her genitals, whether he actually glimpsed them during the masturbatory act, or whether, as is far more likely, this was a later elaboration of memory. In any event, this experience would have assumed for him, at some point, the meaning of his actual participation in a forbidden oedipal, sadomasochistic primal scene, with a converging of dangers from both the positive oedipal object as well as the oedipal rival. In connection with the sadomasochistic character of the child's fantasies, I would again refer to the neighbor's tales of horror and violence which acted as a seduction to his already pronounced proclivity for sadomasochism.

Last but not least, the patient's distorted oedipal relationship with his mother in his latency years, when object love merged into identification, and when he created the image of her as a kind of ethereal, spiritual person, above earthly sin, also served a defensive purpose against the danger of reexperiencing with her the traumatic oedipal situation with the neighbor. In like manner, the negative oedipal strivings toward the father served this same defensive purpose. To be more explicit, the phallic-oedipal primal scene equivalent reinforced the oedipal distortions.

The shaking of the bed to which the patient repeatedly referred not only activated the memory traces of the kinesthetic sensations of the early primal scenes but was associated with mutual masturbation in prepuberty and with his adolescent masturbation. Actually, material dealing with this prepubertal sex play appeared early in the analysis and was utilized repeatedly to screen the oedipal trauma. On the other hand, the oedipal event was an exquisite example of the compression process of time, as could be perceived in the patient's associations to the room he was designing for his new apartment. In short, and as I have already indicated, within this oedipal event were condensed the libidinal and aggressive bodily excitations of the early primal scenes, the patient's later primal scene curiosity, and its exhibitionistic counterparts, his childhood masturbation and other sexual activities. Further, as we later learned, it provided in the light of the neighbor's pathology, and via a backward displacement in time, an added increment to his adolescent fear of going crazy which sprang from his sexual and aggressive masturbatory excitement.

In my initial, fragmentary description of this patient, I mentioned his problem in relation to reality, namely, his repeated uncertainty in respect to the accuracy of his perceptions and judgment. Greenacre (1973) has elaborated on the relationship of early primal scene exposures to denial and hence to a disturbance in the sense of reality. In my patient, I see these early (preverbal) primal scene experiences as having been a contributing factor, but not, in and of themselves, sufficient to explain the extensiveness of this ego problem. As I have shown, my patient had indeed resorted excessively to denial of these disturbing primal scene experiences, and had resorted again to these same denials as the primal scene material emerged in the analytic process. However, the high level of excitation on which he functioned, and which was rooted in the early primal scenes, also interfered with the development of his reality testing. In addition, it is likely that his uncertain perceptions were also traceable to the cousin's sudden departure in his second year and his ensuing feelings of being lost and confused. Finally, the contrast between his neighbor's endowing him with omnipotence and humiliating him was confounding as well and another impediment to the sound development of his reality sense.

In this chapter I have tried to illustrate:

1. how the excessive libidinal and aggressive excitations evoked by early (preverbal) and repeated primal scenes comprised a contributing factor to a patient's disturbed ego and drive development in his preoedipal years;
2. how echoes of these early stress traumas enhanced the traumatic aspects of a primal scene equivalent in the phallic-oedipal period;
3. how both his high excitation level, originating in these early primal scene experiences, and his phallic-oedipal trauma were among the determinants of his severe oedipal problems, including the distortion of his oedipal configuration; and
4. how his perceptual uncertainties were in part attributable to his proclivity for denial arising from the primal scene trauma, but were also attributable to other forces of experience.

My chief aim has been to assess the effects of the primal scene within the context of the patient's ongoing development and in interaction with other developmental vicissitudes.

REFERENCES

Blum, H. (1977), The prototype of preoedipal reconstruction. *J. Amer. Psychoanal. Assn.*, 25:757–785.

Esman, A. (1973), The primal scene: A review and a reconsideration. *The Psychoanalytic Study of the Child,* 28:49–81. New York: Quadrangle.

Freud, S. (1908), On the sexual theories of children. *Standard Edition,* 9:205–226. London: Hogarth Press, 1959.

Greenacre, P. (1952), *Trauma, Growth and Personality.* New York: Norton.

——— (1973), The primal scene and the sense of reality. *Psychoanal. Quart.,* 52:10–41.

——— (1981), Reconstruction: Its nature and therapeutic value. *J. Amer. Psychoanal. Assn.,* 29:27–46.

Harley, M. (1961), Some observations on the relationship between genitality and structural development at adolescence. *J. Amer. Psychoanal. Assn.,* 9:434–459.

——— (1986), Child analysis, 1947–1984: A retrospective. *The Psychoanalytic Study of the Child,* 41:129–153. New Haven, CT: Yale University Press.

Mahler, M. S. (1971), A study of the separation-individuation process. *The Psychoanalytic Study of the Child,* 26:403–424. New York: Quadrangle.

——— (1972), On the first three sub-phases of the separation-individuation process. *Internat. J. Psycho-Anal.,* 53:333–338.

Panel (1965), Memory and repression. W. G. Niederland, reporter. *J. Amer. Psychoanal. Assn.,* 13:619–633.

——— (1978), The pathogenicity of the primal scene. R. A. Isay, reporter. *J. Amer. Psychoanal. Assn.,* 26:131–142.

Rangell, L. (1967), The metapsychology of psychic trauma. In: *Psychic Trauma,* ed. S. S. Furst. New York: Basic Books, pp. 51–84.

7

PSYCHOANALYSIS AND PSYCHOTHERAPY: AN HISTORICAL PERSPECTIVE

ROBERT S. WALLERSTEIN, M.D.

The study of psychoanalytically derived and informed psychotherapy as a vigorous scientific offshoot of psychoanalysis that lives in a complex dialectical interaction with its psychoanalytic forebear is one among Leo Rangell's lifetime preoccupations in psychoanalysis that he and I have passionately shared and discussed together on numerous occasions. I propose in this contribution to a Festschrift honoring Leo Rangell's contributions to our discipline to survey the past, the present, and the possible future of this constantly imbricated and always problematic relationship, reviewing it against the perspectives of my own psychoanalytic lifetime—from the end of the '40s to the present.

I begin with one caveat. I will make no effort at a comprehensive review of the vast and continually burgeoning literature on psychotherapy informed by, or derived from, psychoanalysis, as theory and as therapy. I want rather to present my own particular perspective on the major developmental unfoldings in the history of modern dynamic psychotherapy vis-à-vis psychoanalysis as it has shaped my own involvements in the theoretical discourse and the empirical research activities in which I have been involved. I therefore do not mention many significant contributors to these issues whose thinking helped swell the *Zeitgeist* in which I have appreciatively participated.

I begin with Freud and the birth of psychoanalysis. In a book essay on "The Current State of Psychotherapy" in 1966, I also began with Freud: "Though their roots can be traced back far into history, to soothsayers and ancient prophets, and to priests and primitive medicine men, modern dynamic psychology and psychotherapy derive firmly from the scientific psychology innovated by Freud. The psychoanalysis developed by Freud as a purified product out of the congeries of therapeutic approaches in vogue in his time or experimentally introduced by him and his first co-worker, Breuer—electrical stimulations, rest cures, hypnotic suggestion, forced associations on command, etc.—soon became *the* scientific psychology and *the* scientific therapy" (pp. 183–184). Yet, though he devoted a monumental lifetime to the (almost single-handed) creation of *psychoanalysis* as a theory of mental life and a systematic therapy of the disorders of mental life, Freud himself never moved in the direction of any other psychotherapy than psychoanalysis proper.

By as early as 1905, Freud had already set down in his paper "On Psychotherapy" his criteria for analyzability, i.e., amenability to this rationally understood and powerful new tool for mental therapy. The criteria there stated are those that have always marked our conception of the "good analytic patient"—one who suffers from a chronic neurosis of the kind classically designated as a "transference neurosis," who has "a reasonable degree of education . . . [and] a fairly reliable character," who is well motivated ("driven to seek treatment by their own sufferings"), who is beyond adolescence but still in the prime of adulthood, is not in any situation of emergency, and who possesses a "normal mental condition" (pp. 263–264), that is, is not suffering, in Freud's language, from psychosis, states of confusion, or deeply rooted depression. By implication—and in contrast—psychoanalysts had nothing to offer to patients not suited to the classical analytic method, beyond the same varieties of suggestive and hypnotic techniques that their nonanalytically informed confreres employed.

It is this view—that proper psychoanalysis was the only truly curative and scientific psychotherapy available—that pervaded the period extending over most of Freud's lifetime; it marked the period of the prehistory of psychotherapy—now more narrowly considered as psychotherapy other than psychoanalysis proper[1]—within psychoanalysis. Freud made his own distinction between psychoanalysis as an etiologic therapy and all other psychotherapeutic effort as but a species of outmoded suggestion, hopefully outgrown by psychoanalysis, most sharply in the famous quotation from his 1918 address in Budapest: "It is very probable, too, that the large-scale application of our therapy will compel us to alloy the pure gold of analysis freely with the copper of direct suggestion. . . . But whatever form this psychotherapy for the people may take, whatever the elements out of which it is compounded, its most effective and most important ingredients will assuredly remain those borrowed from strict and untendentious psycho-analysis" (1919, pp. 167–168).

This view of all psychotherapy other than psychoanalysis as nothing but suggestion was carried to its furthest extreme by Glover as late as the 1950s. I summarized Glover's viewpoint in my earlier overview as follows (1966):

> His thesis was that all therapies other than thorough psychoanalysis are merely varieties of suggestion since they rest on elements (which can even include interpretations of unconscious conflicts) that are not fully analyzed back to their genetic-dynamic roots and hence must ultimately be based on the strong transference (suggestive) authority of the therapist. Even inexact interpretations conveyed in the course of an effort at analysis become, in this view, only displacement substitutes, not so inappropriate as the neurotic symptoms and yet sufficiently remote from the real sources of anxiety so that the patient is all too willing, unconsciously, to live up to them [p. 184].

Glover (1931) posed the specific underlying problem as follows: "What is the effect of inexact as compared with apparently exact

[1] It should be already clear that the word *psychotherapy* is often used in two distinct ways. One is as the most broadly encompassing rubric to designate all psychological therapies devoted to the amelioration of mental disturbance. In this sense there is a large array of psychotherapies, both nonpsychoanalytic and psychoanalytic in theoretical conception and execution, and, among the latter, psychoanalysis proper is but one, the one, as it happens, with the clearest specification of its rationale, its methods, and its conditions. In the other narrower usage, the word *psychotherapy* is used to characterize therapy *other than* psychoanalysis and in this chapter will mean, within that usage, *psychoanalytic* psychotherapy unless otherwise specified. I think that the context will make clear at all points whether the word *psychotherapy* is being used in the broader sense or in the narrower sense.

interpretation? If we agree that accuracy of interpretation amongst other factors contributes towards a cure, and if we agree that fresh phantasy systems are discovered from time to time, what are we to make of the cures that were effected before these systems were discovered?" (p. 398). His, not surprising, response was then: "if in former times analysts did not completely uncover unconscious content, then surely the analytic successes of earlier days must have been due in part to an element of suggestion" (p. 406)—since whatever is not fully analyzed rests ultimately on the "strong transference authority" of the analyst. In 1954, almost a quarter of a century *later*—and after the intervening major development of psychoanalytic psychotherapy (in America) as a complex, multifaceted therapeutic enterprise—Glover, nonetheless, carried this viewpoint even further. He said then, "A further case exists: should the analyst's interpretations be consistently inaccurate then quite clearly he is practicing a form of suggestion, whatever else he himself may call it. It follows then that when analysts differ radically as to the etiology or structure of a case—as they nowadays do with increasing frequency—one side or the other must be practicing suggestion" (p. 394). But at times Glover softened the blow: "bad analysis may conceivably be good suggestion" (1931, p. 407).

We can see readily enough the kind of narrowed reasoning—that there must be only a single "correct" interpretive line in every analytic situation and that any deviation from it, based on inexactness, ignorance, countertransference, or whatever, must therefore be only suggestion—that led Glover, building on Freud, to this sharp dichotomization of psychotherapy into only psychoanalysis on the one hand or simply variations of suggestion on the other. Nonetheless, in this way both he and Freud before him did an unwitting disservice to the future development of dynamic psychotherapy with a sound theoretical base in psychoanalytic psychology, in obscuring the complexities involved in the concepts and practice of psychoanalytically informed psychotherapy under the excessively encompassing rubric of suggestion employed to cover (and thereby to blur) a *diversity* of distinct principles and practices.

Thus, the first era in the development of psychoanalytic psychotherapy within psychoanalysis, which I call its prehistory, marked by the delineation of psychoanalysis as a clearly articulated therapy with a defined array of consensually agreed upon principles and practices, with its specific indications spelled out as early as Freud's 1905 paper, and all else—for all categories of patients deemed not amenable to psychoanalysis—swept into the ill-defined, encompassing category of suggestion. Though a counterstream has existed (from at least the period prior to World War II), out of which there has developed the psychodynamic psychotherapy which today leads so vigorous and widespread an existence, both inside and outside the ranks of analysis proper, and which, though grounded in the theory of psychoanalysis, is distinct and distinguished as therapy from both psychoanalysis *and* suggestion, the position of Freud and Glover on this issue has, nonetheless, also continued as a persisting psychoanalytic voice, continuingly critical of psycho*therapeutic* efforts that are not "strict and untendentious psycho*analysis*."

For a variety of reasons particular to the historical development of psychoanalysis in relation to psychiatry in America—the self-conscious effort of psychoanalysis to ally itself with organized psychiatry and medicine and to "capture" psychiatry for the psychoanalytic idea; the wide acceptance of the psychobiological doctrine of Adolf Meyer with its emphasis on detailed case histories to show the causal relationships of experiential events; the growth of the mental hygiene movement in America with its melioristic call for professionally guided mental health interventions; the impact of American progressive education and other pragmatically optimistic ideas; and so on—the original development of a psychodynamic psychotherapy was a distinctively American phenomenon.[2] From the beginning in fact, psychoanalysts in America did not give over the still inchoate field of psychotherapy to the

[2] Dynamic psychotherapy is indeed the one distinctively American contribution to modern-day psychiatry, albeit a glorious one. Psychoanalysis was created by Freud in Austria; the descriptive nosology of the major mental disorders was the work of Kraepelin and his school in Germany; electroconvulsive therapy was inaugurated by Cerletti and Bini in Italy, insulin coma by Sakel in Hungary, and the ill-starred lobotomy operation by Egas Moniz in Portugal; the concept of the therapeutic community was developed by Maxwell Jones in England; the modern psychoactive drug era was inaugurated in Switzerland with Largactil, later brought to America as Thorazine; and lithium was first successfully employed by Cade in Australia.

nonanalysts, nor dismiss it as nothing more than the benevolent application of suggestion not warranting, therefore, special study or training. Rather, dynamic psychiatry and psychotherapy developed over the very period (the late '30s and through the '40s) when American psychoanalysis was so enormously swelled in numbers and enriched in prestige by the Hitler refugees, and under psychoanalytic influence propelled itself into the dominant voice within the country's medical schools and psychiatric clinical centers—though that development of dynamic psychotherapy has always been intensely disputatious in addition to being so substantial and vigorous.

In the recounting of this unfolding of psychoanalytic psychotherapy in relation to psychoanalysis, I will focus on the role of the main protagonists in the several panel debates of the early 1950s, brought together into one issue of the *Journal of the American Psychoanalytic Association* in 1954, with, however, first a consideration of the just prior pioneering role of Robert Knight in framing the fundamental conceptions that have marked the nature of psychoanalytic psychotherapy as *psychoanalytic* therapy, which is, nonetheless, distinct from psychoanalysis proper.

Knight's principal concerns as a leader in American psychoanalysis were with its relations to psychiatry. He stated that until the advent of psychoanalysis, "psychiatry still lacked a psychology" (1945, p. 777), and he devoted himself to the articulation of what he called "a basic science of dynamic psychology" (1949, p. 101)—"a basic science on which all competent psycho-therapy must rest . . . [a basic science] the chief contributions to which have been made by psychoanalysis" (p. 102). And here Knight first formulated the proposed fundamental distinction, within a psychoanalytically informed framework, between supportive and expressive psychotherapeutic approaches. "Of the various possible ways of classifying psychotherapeutic attempts . . . two large groups could be identified—those which aim primarily at *support* of the patient, with suppression of the symptoms and his erupting psychological material, and those which aim primarily at *expression*" (1949, p. 107; my italics). The explicit bias in favor of the more expressive approach as more definitive, and therefore more desirable, was at the same time made clear: "Suppressive or supportive psychotherapy . . . may be indicated . . . where the clinical evaluation of the patient leads to the conclusion that he is too fragile psychologically to be tampered with, or too inflexible to be capable of real personality alteration, or too defensive to be able to achieve insight. . . . The decision to use suppressive measures is made actually because of contraindications to using exploratory devices" (pp. 107–108).

In a subsequent paper (1952), Knight further distinguished the goals of supportive and expressive approaches, and within the latter the goals (and indications) of psychoanalysis proper: "By the term 'primarily supportive' I mean to imply the *intention* to support and reconstruct the defense mechanisms and adaptive methods customarily used by this patient before his decompensation and the *implementation* of this intention by the use of explicit supportive techniques" (p. 118)—and he went on to indicate an entire array of "supportive techniques," actually the first such detailed listing in a psychoanalytic article. Among expressive modes, psychoanalysis proper is clearly the most far-reaching: "Psychoanalysis offers the best method available to achieve the more ambitious goals of fundamental alteration of character structure, with eradication or reduction to a minimum of neurotic mechanisms. . . . Psychoanalysis attempts the ultimate in exploration, with a goal of the maximum in self-knowledge and structural alteration of the personality" (p. 120). And (other) expressive psychotherapy is given a distinctively different place: "The greatest field . . . for exploratory psychotherapy, which does not involve the more ambitious goals of psychoanalysis, lies in those clinical conditions which are expressed as relatively recent decompensations arising out of upsetting life experiences" (p. 120). Thus, the first clear emergence of the declared distinctions among psychoanalytic therapies from the most supportive to the most expressive: a spectrum from supportive psychotherapy to expressive psychotherapy to psychoanalysis proper.

It is these developments presented by Knight in this series of papers that framed the panels within American psychoanalysis over the early 1950s all brought together in a dozen articles in the *Journal of the American Psychoanalytic Association* in 1954. Collectively they staked out the dominant conceptions about the nature of psychoanalytic psychotherapy—and the controversies about them—that have marked what I call the second era in the relationship of psychotherapy to psychoanalysis, that of established diversity of goal and of technique (the spectrum of psychoanalytically based psychotherapies ranging from the most supportive to the most expressive) within a unity of theory (psychoanalysis), an era that lasted for approximately another 20 years after its full delineation in these manifestos of 1954.

What then are the central positions about the nature of psychoanalytic psychotherapy—derived from the theory of psychoanalysis but applied to a broad spectrum of patients not deemed amenable to classical analysis—and its relationship to psychoanalysis proper that were delineated at that time, and what were the controversies generated around those positions? The central confrontation was between two major viewpoints on the most appropriate way to conceptualize this relationship between dynamic psychotherapy and psychoanalysis. Basically, the issue lay between the viewpoint advanced by analysts like Alexander and French (1946) and Fromm-Reichmann (1950; Bullard, 1959) (but altogether a distinct minority) who saw the historical trend as blurring, if not ultimately altogether obliterating, the technical distinction between dynamic psychotherapy and psychoanalysis, and the viewpoint espoused by analysts (actually the great majority) of whom E. Bibring (1954), Gill (1951, 1954), Rangell (1954), and Stone (1951, 1954) served as major spokesmen who conceived the scientific problem to be the more adequate clarification and preservation of the conceptual and operational distinctions between the two. It was these diametrically opposed viewpoints that were contrapuntally propounded so sharply at the panels published in 1954.

Those who "blurred" the distinction between dynamic psychotherapy and psychoanalysis took two somewhat discrepant positions. The one, the more popular and widespread, and seen by its opponents as the more dangerous in its push toward the dissolution of the distinctness of psychoanalysis was that of Alexander. His call was for the total integration of psychoanalysis into psychiatry and medicine: "That psychoanalytic concepts . . . are necessary for every psychiatrist is by now rather generally accepted . . . psychoanalytic theory [has become] the common property of whole psychiatry and through psychosomatic channels of the whole of medicine" (1954, p. 724). With this "unification" of psychoanalysis with psychiatry, "a sharp distinction between psychoanalytic treatment and other methods of psychotherapy which are based on psychoanalytic observations and theory is becoming more and more difficult. . . . In their actual pratice . . . all psychiatrists become more and more similar, even though one may practice pure psychoanalysis and the other psychoanalytically oriented psychotherapy" (p. 725). Indeed, any distinction between psychoanalysis proper and other uncovering or expressive procedures was declared only "quantitative" (p. 729), and in fact, "the *only logical solution* is to identify as 'psychoanalytic' *all* these related procedures which are essentially based on the same scientific concepts, observations and technical principles" (p. 731; my italics).

In the fullest extension of the Alexander position, "the *only* realistic distinction is . . . that between primarily supportive and primarily uncovering methods" (p. 730; my italics), i.e., collapsing *all* expressive treatment modes, expressive psychotherapy and psychoanalysis proper, into the one category of psychoanalytic psychotherapy, and Alexander (like Knight) adumbrated a list of supportive therapeutic techniques, comprising in this listing gratification of dependent needs, emotional abreaction with reduction of emotional stresses, intellectual guidance assisting the patient's judgments through objective review of stressful pressures, aiding the ego's neurotic defenses when the patient is unable to deal with the unconscious material, and manipulating the life situation when the patient is unable to cope with life circumstance. On the other side of the dichotomy are all expressive approaches, psychoanalysis included, which were stated by Alexander to vary only in quantitative and not in critical parameters.

Fromm-Reichmann (1954), somewhat differently than Alexander, took the position that the effort to treat psychoanalytically the borderline, and, even more, the overtly psychotic individual, required not just major modifications of technique (with which, of course, all would agree) but also systematic revision of the theory of "classical psychoanalysis" into the more modern "dynamically oriented psychiatric theory" (p. 713) based on the interpersonal conceptions of Harry Stack Sullivan. This she defended as being a more up-to-date version of psychoanalysis, and she tried to buttress this assertion by calling on Freud's famous definitional dictum on psychoanalysis—that every therapy that is based on the concepts of transference and resistance can call itself psychoanalysis.[3] Set this way, Fromm-Reichmann's dynamic psychotherapy could simply be redefined as psychoanalysis, with again, as with Alexander, psychoanalysis and psychoanalytically based psychotherapy becoming indistinguishably close on a merely quantitative continuum, only in her case with psychoanalysis assimilated to the new interpersonal theory of dynamic psychiatry rather than Alexander's statement of the opposite direction of flow, psychoanalytic psychotherapy blended almost indistinguishably into psychoanalysis. In both directions the distinctions have been blurred, if not yet entirely obliterated.

Both sets of views, those of Alexander and of Fromm-Reichmann, did at the time have some wide popular appeal, though they were also the distinct minority perspective within the then reigning context of the ego psychology metapsychological paradigm in American psychoanalysis. Since then the Alexandrian conceptions have essentially dropped out of psychoanalytic discourse, though his notion of the corrective emotional experience has had some checkered survival in varieties of more active psychotherapeutic approaches and can also be discerned, albeit in highly transmuted form, in varieties of psychoanalytic emphases on the role of the psychoanalytic *relationship* as a major component factor—alongside working through and insight—in effecting analytic change. Fromm-Reichmann's views (rather, her *techniques*) have survived more directly but essentially within a small group of colleagues working in the arena in which these notions originally took root, the (modified) psychoanalytic psychotherapy of the severely psychotic, frequently in institutional settings.

[3] Freud's definition was stated in the context of his history of the psychoanalytic movement (in 1914) as follows: "the facts of transference and of resistance. Any line of investigation which recognizes these two facts and takes them as the starting point of its work has a right to call itself psychoanalysis, even though it arrives at results other than my own. But anyone who takes up other sides of the problem while avoiding these two hypotheses will hardly escape a charge of misappropriation of property by attempted impersonation, if he persists in calling himself a psychoanalyst" (p. 16).

By contrast to these positions, those who strove to "sharpen" the distinctions among the range of psychoanalytically based psychotherapies, including psychoanalysis, aimed in their treatment planning to select the therapeutic modality from this differentiated spectrum that was best fitted to the psychological structure of the individual patient. This, of course, was the opposite of the position taken by those who would "blur" these distinctions between psychoanalytic treatment modalities, in effect collapsing them all to the position that good psychotherapy is all analytic or is all analysis, and then logically pushing the limits of this "analysis" to its utmost extension. On one level, this can be conceptualized as a concern with the limits to which the applicability of a particular treatment method can be pushed, as against the choice of the most appropriate treatment method for each individual patient (to be sure, staying within the range of psychoanalytically grounded therapeutic modes).

The initial problem for those who sought to "sharpen" the distinctions between the various psychoanalytically grounded therapies was, of course, a definitional one. This was put at the beginning of Rangell's contribution in 1954 as follows: "That this investigation is not focusing on an already settled problem is attested to by the experiences of the Committee on Evaluation of Psychoanalytic Therapy, set up within the American Psychoanalytic Association in 1947. In the years of its work since then, the Committee was never able to pass the initial and vexatious point of trying to arrive at some modicum of agreement as to exactly what constitutes psychoanalysis, psychoanalytic psychotherapy, and possibly transitional forms" (1954, p. 734). Actually, Gill (1954), Rangell (1954), and Stone (1951, 1954) all sought to begin with a definitional statement for psychoanalysis, the parent therapy and the one whose dimensions were most clearly conceptualized and articulated. It was Gill's statement that came to enjoy the widest currency—"Psychoanalysis is that technique which, employed by a neutral analyst, results in the development of a regressive transference neurosis and the ultimate resolution of this neurosis by techniques of interpretation alone" (p. 775)—and he went on for several pages to explicate each phrase of the sentence in extended detail.

Clearly, this definition circumscribes psychoanalysis far more precisely than did Freud's 1914 definition which stated that *any* therapy that *recognizes* the two facts of transference and resistance and takes them as the *starting point* of its work can call itself psychoanalysis. In fact, in contradistinction to Freud's definition, Gill had even earlier (1951) stated that "the designation 'psychoanalysis' is reserved for the technique which analyzes transference and resistance. Psychoanalytic therapy is any procedure which *recognizes* transference and resistance and rationally utilizes this recognition in the therapy, though this may be done in many different ways, and part or all of the transference may not be analyzed" (1951, p. 62).

It is these "many *different* ways" in which "part or all of the transference may not be analyzed" which, of course, represent then the various distinctions made in the psychoanalytic therapies (other than psychoanalysis) between the expressive and the supportive modes. In that same earlier (1951) paper, Gill put the major demarcation between these expressive and supportive modes as follows: "The gross major decision is whether the defenses of the ego are to be *strengthened* or *broken through* as a preliminary toward a reintegration of the ego. . . . The decision to strengthen the defenses is made in cases in which this is all that is necessary, or in those in which this is all that is safely possible" (p. 63). And he then added to the sophistication of conceptualization of supportive techniques through his elaboration of ways of strengthening defenses, (1) encouragement of ego activities in which defense is combined with adaptive gratifications and the discouragement of maladaptive gratifications; (2) avoidance of unwitting attacks on defenses vital to the patient's psychic equilibrium; and (3) following from Glover's conception of "The Therapeutic Effect of Inexact Interpretation" (1931), the fostering of neurotic compromises which allow partial discharge of drive derivatives thereby rendering the work of defense against the remainder easier.

Stone (1951) also essayed to list the principles differentially operative in psychotherapy as distinct from psychoanalysis, but he conflated supportive *and* expressive approaches (just distinguishing these together from psychoanalysis proper). Stone also laid out his listing (the most elaborated to that point) of the indications for psychotherapy over psychoanalysis as follows: (1) limitations of time or money that precluded psychoanalysis; (2) patients too ill or with life situations too unpropitious to be amenable to psychoanalysis; (3) oppositely, patients with illnesses too slight to warrant psychoanalysis; (4) acute reactive disorders; (5) transitional states, psychic readjustments, shifts in developmental phase; (6) requirements of preparatory, preanalytic work, or on occasion follow-up or afterwork; (7) some "more specific indications" in certain character and illness patterns; and (8) arguably, patients with too much secondary gain. Again, this listing of Stone's did not try to separate out those most appropriately steered to expressive from those most appropriately steered to supportive approaches. It did, however, make clear the basis for Gill's (1951) statement concerning the indications for psychoanalysis: "Analysis then is clearly the procedure for a middle range in which the ego is sufficiently damaged that extensive repair is necessary, but sufficiently strong to withstand pressure" (pp. 63–64).

From the above, the rest naturally follows. A primarily supportive psychotherapy becomes the preferred mode for those patients whose failed psychic equilibrium is to be restored via "strengthening the defenses" through the variety of techniques adumbrated now by Knight, Alexander, Stone, Gill, etc. We could consider these patients "too sick" to be amenable to psychoanalysis. Gill (1954) discussed this category of patients this way: "A major contraindication [to psychoanalysis] is the presence of severe regressive factors or the dangers that such may develop. The instances of rather sudden onset of psychosis shortly after beginning psychoanalysis are to be attributed to the regressive pressure of the technique per se on a precariously balanced personality" (p. 780). A primarily expressive psychotherapy becomes the preferred mode for those patients with acute reactive disorders, or in transitional states (Stone), whose ego is not unduly damaged (Gill), who can tolerate the effort at "analyzing the defenses" to the extent necessary via the established methods of interpretation and working through leading to the requisite insights and resolutions. These on the other side we could consider the patients "too well" for psychoanalysis in the sense of not requiring or warranting a treatment so ambitious and far-reaching.

This way of conceptualizing the nature of the different therapeutic modes and of their differential indications puts expressive psychotherapy into an "intermediate" position—certainly in techniques—between supportive therapy on the one hand and psychoanalysis on the other. This was a conception most explicitly developed by Gill (1954): "I have one major point to make. I believe we have failed to carry over into our psychotherapy enough of the nondirective spirit of our analyses" (p. 786). "My stress on this point arises from my feeling that discussion of therapeutic results in psychoanalysis and psychotherapy too often views them as polar opposites, with psychoanalysis regarded as producing structural changes, and psychotherapy as unable to produce any significant intrapsychic change, but only altering techniques of adjustment through transference effects or shifts in defensive techniques" (p. 787). "I would raise the question . . . as to whether there is not more to be said on results and mechanisms in prolonged psychotherapy with more ambitious goals by a relatively inactive therapist and in intensive [he means expressive] psychotherapy" (p. 789).

This is called by Gill an "intermediate type of psychotherapy" (p. 789). "This is the psychotherapy . . . whose goals are intermediate between rapid symptom resolution [i.e., supportive psychotherapy] and character change [i.e., psychoanalysis], where techniques are in a sense intermediate—for example, relative neutrality and inactivity; transference dealt with, though not a full regressive transference neurosis; interpretation the principal vehicle of therapist behavior—and, I suggest, where results are likewise intermediate" (p. 789). And "I wish not to be misunderstood. I am not suggesting that psychotherapy can do what psychoanalysis can do; but I am suggesting that a description of the results of intensive [again, he means expressive] psychotherapy may be not merely in terms of shifts of defense but also in terms of other intra-ego alterations" (p. 793).

All of this, of course, adds up to the statement that in contrast with the maximalist goals of psychoanalysis in terms of fundamental conflict resolution and character reorganization, the goals in all other psychotherapies range from the most minimal to the increasingly more ambitious, with no agreement as to how asymptotically close to those of psychoanalysis they can reach in the different kinds of patients treated psychotherapeutically. Gill (1951) put it thus: "In psychotherapy the goal may be anything from as quick relief of a symptom as possible, with the restoration of the previous integrative capacity of the ego, through a whole range of more ambitious goals *up to* analysis, the most ambitious of all. The choice of therapy may be divided into that which determines the minimum necessary to restore the ego to functioning, and that which strives for the maximum change that is possible" (p. 63; my italics).

This relates closely to another issue that was also not really *resolved* in these debates of the '50s; this is the degree of real distinctness among this array of psychoanalytic therapeutic approaches from supportive psychotherapy to the "intermediate form," expressive psychotherapy, to psychoanalysis. Are these really qualitatively distinct, or are they crystallized nodal points along a continuum, or are they less distinguishably just a (quantitatively varying) continuum—another statement of the "blurring" vs. "sharpening" argument at the heart of those debates. Gill, as is clear from my quotations from him, made the sharpest conceptual distinctions. Stone, characteristically, tempered his commitment to this distinction: "One may think of a continuum from the free play of human relationships in which there is no conscious psychotherapeutic intention—but which obviously play an enormously important psychotherapeutic role in the lives of relatively normal people—to the objective and precise relation between the surgeon and his patient, which Freud idealized. The well-defined psychoanalytic technique [psychoanalysis proper] and brief psychotherapy [Stone's phrase then for his own amalgam of supportive-expressive psychotherapy] are both far from either pole, and yet definitely removed from one another in these opposite directions" (1951, pp. 221–222). Rangell perhaps best expressed the degree of consensus achieved within the majority position that I have labeled as that of those who sought to "sharpen" these distinctions in his statement: "In this view, the two disciplines [psychoanalysis proper and psychoanalytic psychotherapy], at far ends of a spectrum, are qualitatively different from each other, though there is a borderland of cases between them. An analogous comparison can be made to the fact that conscious is different from unconscious even though there exists a preconscious and different degrees of consciousness. Day is different from night, though there is dusk; and black from white, though there is gray" (1954, p. 737).

Rangell's own principal contribution to the debates published in 1954 was his effort to state the major similarities and differences between what he called psychoanalysis and dynamic psychotherapy. He stated each under two headings. In regard to the similarities he stated the evident, that both are psychological treatments influencing other human beings through verbal discourse, and that both are rational therapies built on an "identical body of metapsychology" (p. 737). In regard to the differences, he stated these to be in technique and in goals, and these he developed more fully.

In regard to technique, Rangell singled out that "the crucial differentiating point relates to the role and position of the therapist" (p. 741). He illustrated with an analogy:

> Let us consider that the mental apparatus exerts around it a field of magnetic energy. In psychoanalysis, the therapist takes up his position at the periphery of this magnetic field of his patient, not too far away, so that he is useless and might just as well not be there, nor too close, so that he is within the field interacting with it with his own magnetic field. . . . Immune from repulsion or attraction . . . he sits at the margin, like a referee in a tennis match so that he can say to the patient . . . [p. 740].

> In psychotherapy, in contrast, the therapist does not sit consistently in that seat, though he may sit there momentarily. He is, rather, generally on the court with his patient, interacting with him, the two magnetic fields interlocked, with the therapist's own values, opinions, desires, and needs more or less actively operative [p. 742].

In regard to differences in goal, Rangell again used an analogy, this one borrowed from Gitelson who

> compares the therapeutic process to a complicated chemical reac-

> tion, which, once set under way, will continue to a state of final dynamic equilibrium. During the state of transition of this chemical reaction, many intermediate reactions will have occurred. . . . At any given point, external interfering agents may be introduced which . . . can change the end point at which equilibrium is attained. The therapeutic process can be looked at from this point of view. Psychoanalysis aims at the establishment of the reaction (transference neurosis) and the maintenance of optimum conditions for its final complete resolution. It is not only oriented toward such a final end point, but, in contrast to psychotherapy, is potentially capable of attaining it. Psychotherapy, on the other hand, either from necessity or from choice, introduces the external agent and brings the reaction to an end at any intermediate point of stability [pp. 742–743].

Two other major contributions from the debates published in 1954 have not yet been presented—Bibring's delineation of basic therapeutic principles which are intended, through differential selection and combination, to be capable of characterizing all psychoanalytic therapies, from psychoanalysis to supportive psychotherapy, and the Leo Stone–Anna Freud discussion of the problem of the "widening scope" of psychoanalysis. Bibring's (1954) widely influential article delineated five distinct "basic therapeutic principles," each aimed to its particular goal: (1) suggestion, the induction of mental processes in the patient independent of his rational or critical thinking; (2) abreaction, emotional discharge, which with the abandonment of the traumatic theory of the neurosis has become progressively less salient; (3) manipulation, a mobilization (or redirection) of emotional systems existing in the patient in the service of the therapy and/or the exposure of the patient to novel experiences, "learning by experience"; (4) insight through clarification, i.e., enhanced self-awareness and differentiation of self-observation in the absence of resistance; and (5) insight through interpretation, i.e., the processing of unconscious material with resistance, intense ego involvement, and working through. All psychotherapies, not only psychoanalytically based psychotherapies, but even psychotherapies conceptualized within other psychological reference frames, could be classified, according to Bibring, by the different selections and combinations of these five central therapeutic principles, in the conduct of the therapy. Bibring's classification has continued in active use until the present day.

The other equally influential contribution from those same debates was the discussion by Stone (1954) of what he called "The Widening Scope of Indications for Psychoanalysis": "One might say that in the last decade or two, at least in the United States, any illness or problem which has a significant emotional component in its etiology has become at least a possible indication for psychoanalysis . . . this generally expanding scope of psychoanalysis. . . . Hopeless or grave reality situations, lack of talent or ability (usually regarded as 'inhibition'), lack of an adequate philosophy of life, or almost any chronic physical illness may be brought to psychoanalysis for cure" (p. 568). Stone was warily receptive of this trend, albeit also skeptical—it is, of course, the argument again over extending the applicability of the true (or best) therapy to the margins of its possible indications as against fitting differentiated therapeutic approaches to the nature and needs of the patient.

Stone's final assessment on this issue was: "I should like to return . . . to the basic question posed by our 'widening scope,' i.e., what *are* the true indications for analysis?" (p. 591). The "scope of psychoanalytic therapy has widened from the transference psychoneurosis, to include practically all psychogenic nosologic categories. The transference neuroses and character disorders of equivalent degree of psychopathology remain the optimum general indications for the classical method. While the difficulties increase and the expectations of success diminish in a general way as the nosological periphery is approached, there is no absolute barrier" (p. 593).

Anna Freud (1954) in her discussion of Stone's paper singled out this issue to indicate that her own biases and predilections ran directly counter to such sentiments. She said,

> For years now, our most experienced and finest analysts have concentrated their efforts on opening up new fields for the application of analysis by making the psychotic disorders, the severe depressions, the borderline cases, addictions, perversions, delinquency, etc., amenable to treatment. I have no wish to underes-

> timate the resulting benefits to patients, nor the resulting considerable gains to analysis as a therapy and science. But I regret sometimes that so much interest and effort has been withdrawn from the hysteric, phobic and compulsive disorders, leaving their treatment to the beginners or the less knowledgeable and adventurous analytic practitioners. If all the skill, knowledge and pioneering effort which was spent on widening the scope of application of psychoanalysis had been employed instead on intensifying and improving our technique in the original field, I cannot help but feel that, by now, we would find the treatment of the common neuroses child's play, instead of struggling with their technical problems as we have continued to do [p. 610].

Truly a call for narrowing the scope of indications for psychoanalysis, a position to which Anna Freud steadfastly adhered all her life, and against all the popular and current trends.

It is in the context of this crystallization in the early '50s of these conceptualizations of the nature of psychoanalysis and of psychoanalytically based psychotherapies that a group of us at The Menninger Foundation (Wallerstein, Robbins, Sargent, and Luborsky, 1956) undertook a major empirical study of psychoanalysis and psychotherapy, of what changes occur with these treatments (the outcome question), and of how those changes come about or are brought about (the process question). The project's original (1956) statement of differential treatment indications for the range of psychoanalytic therapies (including psychoanalysis) being studied was embedded in the context of the prevailing definitions and clarifications set forth in the panel publications of 1954 as follows:

1. "Psychotherapeutic counseling is indicated when an individual with a basically healthy personality reacts in an unhealthy way to a life problem largely because of not perceiving or knowing the facts needed for solution of a particular dilemma. . . . Counseling is appropriate in cases of situational maladjustment; occupational misplacement . . . some marital problems" (p. 252).

2. "Supportive psychotherapy is indicated for:

> a. Basically healthy individuals overwhelmed by a severe problem or anxiety so that their optimal effective functioning is temporarily paralyzed, . . . Acute combat fatigue . . . Acute reactive states

> . . . states of object loss (some depressive reactions) . . . some traumatic neuroses (panic states). . . .
> b. Chronic, severe personality disorders with major ego-defects of several varieties . . . those (principally "character disorders") with disruptive, alloplastic symptoms. . . . Treatment is aimed to help them discharge their impulses in a more socially acceptable way which will reduce their overt symptoms and ameliorate the disruptive consequences of the symptoms. . . . The borderline states—those with "fragile egos" are another group in this category. . . . Treatment is often sought at a point of accelerating collapse and represents an effort to stop the regression and stabilize the individual on whatever possible level of functioning. . . ." (pp. 252–253).
>
> "Appropriate to this treatment modality are the borderline psychotic, some overtly psychotic, plus a large group of patients who suffer from "impulse neuroses." Many cases of addiction and perversion likewise fall here. . . ." (p. 254).

3. "Expressive psychotherapy is the treatment of choice for persons with the requisite ego-strength, intelligence, and tolerance for anxiety who have a serious, but *relatively circumscribed* neurotic conflict . . . significant help and change can be effected without having to uncover the infantile genetic roots. . . ." (p. 254; my italics). Appropriate . . . are patients who fall into the categories "symptoms neuroses" and "character neuroses" . . . (p. 255).

4. "Psychoanalysis is the therapy of choice where ego strength, anxiety tolerance, intelligence and capacity for developing insight are of requisite degree and where *the neurotic conflict is sufficiently intense and pervasive* that satisfactory resolution can only come . . . through the development of the transference neurosis and the re-creation, in consciousness, of its prototype—the repressed infantile neurosis. As distinct from patients treated by expressive psychotherapy, the neurotic conflict is more pervasive and less circumscribed; and the psychotherapeutic effort, likewise, less specifically goal-directed. . . ." (p. 256; my italics).

Here, elaborated in the design of an empirical program of psychoanalytic psychotherapy research devised in the early 1950s is the full application of the conception of dynamic psychotherapy and of its relationship to the psychoanalysis from which it derived that came to dominate the (American) psychoanalytic scene in the decades of the 40s and 50s as one major aspect of the fruition and hegemony in America of the ego psychological metapsychology paradigm.

I have emphasized at several points how particularly American was this burgeoning of dynamic psychotherapy, distinct from but inextricably linked to psychoanalysis, and the principal vehicle of the capture of American psychiatry during that era by the psychoanalytic idea—which is not to say that these conceptions remained limited to the American scene. Comparable ideas soon took root elsewhere, mostly in England, and in northern and central Europe. And in 1969 (a decade and a half after the 1954 publications in America), the International Psycho-Analytical Association for the first time devoted a major panel, at its Rome Congress, to "The Relationship of Psychoanalysis to Psychotherapy." In my opening presentation as chairman of that panel (Wallerstein, 1969), I began by stating that this marked "the growing concern within the world-wide family of psychoanalytic endeavour with what has seemed for so long primarily a peculiarly American creation, the body of theory and practice of psychoanalytically based or psychodynamic psychotherapy, in all of its complex relationships with its psychoanalytic parentage" (p. 117).

I undertook to set the framework for the 1969 panel "by setting down what I feel to be the major scientific issues within this area of the relationship of psychoanalysis and psychotherapy as a sequence of *questions*, with a relatively brief statement after each, of the major, often dichotomized, positions that have been taken in relation to each of them by typical outstanding proponents of the various viewpoints" (p. 117). And at the end of my presentation I restated these major questions around which I had tried to organize the issues for discussion by the international panel in the following words:

> (1) Is there a scientific psychotherapy apart from psychoanalysis? (2) What are the similarities and the differences between psychoanalysis and dynamic psychotherapy? (3) How important are the differences (or the similarities)? Should the differences be blurred or should they be sharpened? (4) What are the proper boundaries of each therapeutic modality? *or* when does "modified" psychoanalysis or psychoanalysis with parameters become psychotherapy?

(5) How are differential treatment indications determined? Is the patient fitted to the treatment or the treatment fitted to the patient? (6) What are the proper dividing lines across the range of psychotherapies conceptualized within the framework of psychoanalytic theory? Is the major dividing line between the expressive-uncovering therapeutic modalities (of which psychoanalysis is one) and the suppressive-supportive therapeutic modalities? Which divisions are meaningful, in theory and in practice? (7) What is the relation to non-psychoanalytic therapy? Can a theory of psychoanalytic therapy extend to a psychoanalytic theory of therapy? (8) Can derivative conflicts, can any conflicts, be substantially resolved by means short of psychoanalysis? (9) What are our problems as psychoanalysts in doing psychotherapy? [pp. 125–126].

What is clear from this listing is that the issues and controversies that characterized the panel reports a decade and a half earlier were still very much with us, not appreciably altered, let alone resolved, in the crucible of the accumulated clinical experience and the expanded theoretical knowledge accrued during the intervening time. Nor can it be said that this assessment was at all modified by the considerations of the international panel from the wider vantage point of the varying experiences of psychoanalysts in the diverse national and regional centers of psychoanalytic activity with all their differing historical developments as well as differing ecological settings.

What then is our psychoanalytic understanding of psychoanalytic psychotherapy today, in the late '80s, almost three and a half decades later than the landmark publications of 1954. In the intervening years, new diagnostic and therapeutic conceptualizations have been advanced in regard to the categories of the borderline patients (Kernberg, 1975) and the narcissistic character (Kohut, 1971, 1977). These newer considerations have certainly added both urgency and cogency to the persisting efforts in psychoanalytic ranks to maintain a firm handle on the distinctiveness of psychoanalysis and of psychoanalytically based psychotherapy with their differentiated spheres of application to the array of psychopathological formations, with all the shifting perceptions of this differential applicability as our clinical experience with these new paradigmatic patients of our time has cumulated. This has, of course, been the more striking as the more classical symptom pictures around which our original conceptualizations were elaborated, have correspondingly dwindled in our consulting rooms.

Clearly, the landscape of psychotherapies required reassessment in the light of these developments in theory and these shifts in our patient population. Toward this end the Southern Regional Psychoanalytic Societies sponsored a symposium in Atlanta in 1979 at which three of the central protagonists in the discussions published in 1954, Gill, Rangell, and Stone, were invited to update their views on "Psychoanalysis and Psychotherapy, Similarities and Differences, a 25-Year Perspective." The three chosen were three who were in essential agreement during the debates of the early '50s, representatives of the then majority "classical" position, that maintained a connectedness along a spectrum of psychotherapies, with, however, an articulated distinctive crystallization of differentiated psychotherapeutic modalities along that spectrum—from psychoanalysis to supportive psychotherapy—each with its specific applicability to a particular, nosologically reasonably coherent, segment of patients specifically amenable to it.

It is this selection for the panel in 1979 of three contributors who a quarter century before had spoken with so united a voice that renders all the more impressive the major divergence of views—on precisely the same questions and issues—that marked their discourse in 1979, and that reflects at this point, currently, substantial shifts in the climate of thinking about psychotherapy and psychoanalysis and their relationship that I had indicated in 1969 (just a decade earlier) had to that point persisted essentially unchanged. It is this that I call the contemporary, or the third, era in the development of psychoanalytic psychotherapy within psychoanalysis that I will now review and assess: it is an era in which the broad *consensus* (despite the significant deviations of Alexander and Fromm-Reichmann) that had characterized mainstream psychoanalytic thinking in this area, as represented by Gill *and* Rangell *and* Stone and that reflected the rise of psychodynamic psychotherapy as a distinctive offshoot of psychoanalysis—that I have called the second era—has given way, since the decade of the '70s, to this current third era of fragmented consensus and enforced new thinking about the nature of the psychoanalytic psychotherapy enterprise and its relationship to its psychoanalytic heritage. In the context of this review of the 1979 panel, I will also present the highlighted findings from The Psychotherapy Research Project of The Menninger Foundation (Wallerstein, 1986) as the results of that study of psychoanalytic and psychotherapeutic courses and outcomes and follow-ups over a 30-year span resonate impressively with one of the three major positions of the 1979 Atlanta debate, that of Rangell (though articulated quite independently).

Actually, Leo Stone's views, which were the most subtly nuanced in 1954, have also been those that have survived most unaltered in the retrospective a quarter century later. Basically, Stone adhered to the distinctions he had earlier advanced of the (quantitatively) greater reality orientation of the psychoanalytic psychotherapist. For example, "The therapist's activity, instead of taking a reductive direction, slanted toward the genetic-infantile environment, or its currently unconscious representations, tends to preserve the patient's cathexis of his real and immediate environment—his cathexis of persons, of problems as such, and conflicts as such—and (very importantly) his cathexis of the essential realities of the patient-doctor relationship" (1982, pp. 86–87).

Stone then added a characteristically subtle new distinction he was drawing between the nature of interpretation in psychotherapy as compared with psychoanalysis. "But instead of orienting itself to facilitating the spontaneously evolving transference neurosis of the basic psychoanalytic situation, it is usually based on the therapist's conception of what constitutes the major and currently active conflict or conflicts in the patient's presenting illness or disturbed adaptation, and the relationship of such conflict or conflicts to his actual objects. . . . Interpretations, moreover, tend to be holistic, integrative . . . minimizing the distinctions between defense and impulse, infantile and current, emphasizing large, accessible, and readily intelligible personality dynamisms" (p. 87).

This stance was, of course, quite consistent with the fact that neither in the 1950s nor again in 1979 did Stone clearly try, within the range of psychoanalytic psychotherapies, to demarcate the more interpretive (expressive) from the less interpretive or non-interpretive (supportive)—as had Knight and Gill and our own Psychotherapy Research Project. Stone's long-time consistency in this regard was expressed in a skeptical discussion in this 1982 paper of Knight's original proposal of the expressive-supportive distinction. "The essential idea [of supportive psychotherapy] is that the therapist aligns himself with the patient's defenses, fostering them rather than seeking to weaken them. While this is conceptually and schematically reasonable, it does not lend itself readily to technical specification; and I would feel some doubt that it can often be achieved in a direct and purposive sense" (p. 92). All in all, Stone has exhibited a remarkable consistency of viewpoint on the basic elements of psychoanalytic psychotherapy and of psychoanalysis (and of their relationship) over the three-decade span from his first writing on this specific topic in 1951 until this most recent in 1982. It is a steadiness of perspective that contrasts sharply with the significantly altering views of the other principal protagonists in the 1979 panel discussion.

The individual whose views have shifted most radically over this intervening time span (though he would not necessarily agree with this assessment) is Merton Gill, who, following upon Knight, was clearest in the early '50s in his distinct delineations of psychoanalysis, expressive psychotherapy, and supportive psychotherapy, each with distinctive characteristics, different techniques and goals, and each indicated for a different segment of the psychopathological spectrum. The very radical shift that I see in Gill's views follows as a direct consequence of his evolving preoccupation with the overriding primacy of the interpretation of the transference as *the* criterion of psychoanalysis and of what is psychoanalytic: the earliest possible interpretation of the transference, including the searching out of all possible implicit transference allusions (i.e., making the implicit transferences explicit from the very start of the treatment), the focus on the here-and-now as against the genetic thrust ("there-and-then") in the transference interpretation, and the elaboration of all the implications of what Gill calls the "two-person" as against the "one-person" view of the two participants' contributions to the transference. It is Gill's position (1979, 1982, 1984) that all of this was both implicit and explicit throughout the corpus of Freud's work, but that in practice it has often been accorded only lip service, both by Freud and by all of us who have come after. Here I want only to pursue the implications of Gill's current views about the transference for his (now significantly changed) views on the nature of psychoanalysis and psychotherapy and their relationship. These implications he made explicit in his contribution to the 1979 Atlanta symposium published in a revised version in 1984.

Gill (1984) has developed these new views on psychoanalysis and psychotherapy with his customary logical precision. He summarized his 1954 paper in one sentence as follows: "The thrust of my 1954 paper was to *insist on the difference* [between psychoanalysis and psychotherapy] and at the same time to *recognize* that the two are on a *continuum*" (p. 162; my italics). He then reviewed the "intrinsic criteria" by which analysis is usually defined ("the centrality of the analysis of transference, a neutral analyst, the induction of a regressive transference neurosis and the resolution of that neurosis by techniques of interpretation alone, or at least mainly by interpretation" [p. 161]) as well as the often commonly indicated "extrinsic criteria" ("frequent sessions, the couch, a relatively well integrated patient, that is, one who is considered analyzable, and a fully trained psychoanalyst" [p. 161]). From there he comes to his taking-off point: "The question of the relationship between psychoanalysis and psychotherapy is even more important in practice today than it was in 1954 because of the practical difficulties in maintaining the ordinarily accepted extrinsic criteria of analysis. . . . The question becomes: How widely can the range of extrinsic criteria be expanded before the analyst must decide for psychotherapy rather than psychoanalysis?" (p. 162).

After reviewing the difficulties that analysts have in today's world in maintaining the usual external criteria of psychoanalysis (requisite frequency, the use of the couch, the appropriate psychopathology, proper training of the therapist, and so on), Gill then goes on to say: "The changes I will propose are more radical than a simple extension of the recommendation I made in 1954 that we carry more of the nondirective spirit of psychoanalysis into our psychotherapies." Rather, "I will argue that with the definition of analytic technique at which I will finally arrive, it should be taught to *all psychotherapists* and that how well it will be employed will depend on their training and natural talent for the work." And, "I mean that analytic technique as I will define it should be employed as much as possible even if the patient comes less frequently than is usual in psychoanalysis, uses the chair rather than the couch, is not necessarily committed to a treatment of relatively long duration, is sicker than the usually considered analyzable patient and even if the therapist is relatively inexperienced. In other words, I will recommend that we sharply *narrow* the indications for psychoanalytic *psychotherapy* and *primarily practice psychoanalysis as I shall define* it instead" (p. 163; my italics). What we see here is a proposal now to assimilate to psychoanalysis what Gill in 1954 had taken such pains to demarcate separately as the related but distinct arena of expressive psychotherapy or, in other words, to blur, perhaps to obliterate altogether, the differences that he once felt it so vital to maintain. In effect, this is a revival of the position of Alexander that Gill once led the effort to reject.

Gill clearly acknowledges the basis for these radically altered views: "The reconsideration I am proposing is an outgrowth of my changed views on transference and its analysis which I shall soon summarize" (p. 164)—and he ends his summarizing with the statement: "My reconceptualizations of these intrinsic criteria of analysis, namely transference and its analysis, the neutral analyst, the regressive transference neurosis, free association, and the role of experience in addition to interpretation lead me to the conclusion that the centrality of the analysis of transference . . . is [alone] the distinguishing feature of psychoanalysis. It is what distinguishes it from psychotherapy. It remains for me to try to show that it can be maintained *even in an expanded range of external criteria*" (p. 172; my italics).

Gill then develops his ideas that even a necessary frequency or the use of the couch *may* be dispensable in proper psychoanalytic work:

> while the couch is ordinarily considered to be conducive to regression, it may enable an isolation from the relationship which has

> a contrary effect. No universal meaning of any aspect of the analytic setting may be taken for granted. It follows that no universal prescription can be given for this or that type of case. One may generalize that analytic work goes better with healthier patients lying down and sicker patients sitting up and with frequent sessions for both kinds of patients but a particular patient may not conform to the rule. The meaning of the setting must be analyzed in each instance. Nor is degree of pathology the only variable which determines a patient's response to the analysis of transference. Apart from pathology, some take to it like a duck to water and can work despite infrequent sessions, while others never seem to find it congenial [p. 174].

Gill then, once again, deals specifically with the impact of each of the usual external parameters of the psychoanalytic situation. About frequency, he states: "It would seem obvious that one can accomplish more with greater frequency simply because there is more time to work. But if greater frequency is frightening to a particular patient, frequent sessions may impede the work despite interpretation. One cannot simply assume that more is better. The optimal frequency may differ from patient to patient. We must not confuse optimal frequency with obligatory ritualized frequency" (p. 174). About the couch, he similarly states: "The argument that psychoanalytic technique cannot be used in the face-to-face position because of the reality cues afforded the patient is a variant of the mistaken idea that it is the external stimulus rather than the patient's interpretation of that stimulus that matters. Discussions of the issue seem to gravitate to quantitative terms as though there are fewer stimuli if the patient cannot see the analyst. It may be that the patient facing the analyst is exposed to a wider range of stimuli but the patient's response is to the quality not the quantity of stimuli" (p. 175). And about the experience of the therapist, he states: "Therapists use the technique to whatever degree their skill and comfort in exposing the transferential experience of the relationship permits" (p. 175). And lastly, of the relatively long duration and open-endedness of analytic work, he states: "I do not know the lower limit in duration for the use of the technique I advocate, but I have used it successfully in once-a-week therapy preset to last no longer than nine months" (p. 175). And so on.

Gill declares that central to all the views about the dimensions of the psychoanalytic experience that he is questioning is an "implicit assumption about the psychoanalytic process which I would like to question. It is that analysis is a kind of all-or-none proposition, yielding its positive results only if carried through to the end . . . this belief is often a vain illusion. Freud compared interrupting an analysis to the interruption of a surgical operation. I suggest, on the contrary, that in the changed way of conducting it which I am proposing, analysis may be a process with progressively cumulative benefits, interruptable at various points without necessary loss of what has been gained" (p. 176). Surely, setting up the prevailing view of psychoanalysis as a conception of an all-or-none endeavor is something of a straw man since analysis can assuredly stop in all stages of incompleteness, quite aside from the understanding that, of course, in theory, analysis is *never* complete. That is not, however, to amalgamate every expressive psychotherapy to psychoanalysis as Gill wants to do, just as long as the interpretive thrust is to the interpretation of the transferences in the here-and-now.

Where then would all this leave the field of psychotherapy vis-à-vis psychoanalysis? Gill asks this question in this way: "Should the use of the technique I describe in less than the optimal setting for an analysis still be called psychoanalysis?" (p. 176). Gill obviously feels that the answer to this query is yes. The other name he proposes at this point is "psychoanalytic psychotherapy" which he now says "should be reserved for a technique which *does not* deal with the transference in the way I have suggested is the essential criterion of analytic technique" (p. 176; my italics)—in other words, "psychoanalytic psychotherapy" should be the designation for that therapeutic approach which is *not* psychoanalysis (i.e., does not systematically interpret transference), i.e., what Knight originally, and Gill after him, called in the '40s and '50s, psychoanalytically oriented supportive psychotherapy.

There is yet, however, a third position to be distilled out of the 1979 Symposium, that enunciated there by Rangell and one to which I feel the data of our Psychotherapy Research Project of The Menninger Foundation (Wallerstein, 1986, 1988) provide compelling support. It is neither the unchanged position propounded by Stone nor is it the radical return to the once rejected views of Alexander that Gill has felt driven to as a logical consequence of his own shifts in conception of the essence of the psychoanalytic enterprise. It is, if it needs to be characterized, a position that can be seen as between the two, albeit far closer to Stone's than to Gill's new position.

Rangell's main argument in the 1979 Symposium consisted of staking out his own modified position in regard to his evolving perception of the relationship between psychotherapy and psychoanalysis, a position I have dubbed in my own writing on this subject (1986, 1988) as the "infiltration" of psychoanalysis by psycho*therapeutic* techniques, while, nonetheless, maintaining conceptual clarity around their array of differences. Rangell states this conception as follows: "But just as analysts apply analytic principles freely and copiously to their practice of dynamic psychotherapy . . . with ever-increasing complexity and length of psychoanalysis, the opposite also holds. There is no analysis without its share of each of the technical maneuvers noted by Bibring (1954), which he also described as occurring in both techniques but which typically one considered to characterize mainly psychotherapy. There is no analysis without some of these mechanisms, which are not inadvertent but built-in and by design. Nor are they of themselves necessarily parameters but accessory and preparatory modes intrinsic to the treatment. There is no analytic case treated by interpretation alone, in spite of Gill's definition of 1954. If this were a prerequisite, no treatment would qualify as analytic" (1981, pp. 670–671).

This is the crux of Rangell's argument throughout his 1979 Symposium presentation, based, he stated, on his full-time and diverse clinical practice of some four decades. The rest is but amplification. For example, in returning to the theme of the similarities and differences between psychoanalysis and dynamic psychotherapy that he had discussed in 1954, he states, "Since the comparisons of 1954, increasing experience and precision of technique have led to a lessening of the differences between the two. Structural change of time-enduring quality, also thought previously to characterize mainly psychoanalysis, can be achieved in analytic therapy carefully chosen and performed. . . . I have been able to reach convincing elements of patients' infantile neuroses in consistent analytic psychotherapy, with results comparable to what I have come to expect in psychoanalysis" (pp. 679–680). And in further amplification, he goes on to state, "Empirically, it is not uncommon in practice for there to be a gap between the trains of free associations and the infantile experiences to which we believe they lead. While it might be assumed to be a distinguishing mark between psychotherapy and psychoanalysis that such a gap between data and interpretation exists only in psychotherapy, I would like to point out that this also occurs regularly in psychoanalysis and that this point is not sufficiently appreciated" (p. 680).

But the essence of this position, this acknowledged "infiltration" or intermingling between analytic and therapeutic techniques in all therapies, psychoanalysis and psychotherapy alike, is that, nonetheless, the two are still both distinct, psychoanalysis from psychotherapy, and that separately categorizable techiques predominantly characterize each. Rangell put this thus: "While I have been largely discussing overlapping areas, there are also lines of demarcation between the two fields today as there were in 1954. I said then that there is day and night, although there is dusk (Rangell, 1954). There are still differences in quality and quantity, in consistency and goals, in the uniformity and relentlessness of the method of approach. The distances between the observational data and the genetic mysteries to which they open doors are generally less in psychoanalysis than in dynamic psychotherapy. Again a disclaimer: it is possible in an individual case to bridge this synapse effectively in psychotherapy while this distance may remain wide and the links over it sterile and theoretical even in a well-conducted analysis" (p. 682). And in conclusion, "As a long-range observation over the years, empirically there is in numbers a large borderland in which therapeutic procedures are practiced in a gray area between 'psychoanalysis with parameters' and steady intensive psychotherapy which is not quite psychoanalysis. My belief today is that it is still possible to draw a line between the two, although it is also true that in many cases this line is difficult to define" (pp. 682–683).

This is the panorama then of the current third era debate, with its crystallized, quite discrepant positions on the nature of the relationships between psychoanalysis and the psychoanalytically based psychotherapies, as epitomized by the three protagonists in the 1979 Symposium, Gill, Rangell, and Stone, who were so together in their viewpoints during the critical panels of the early '50s that had staked out the then emergent second era consensus. Though that second era consensus had its major dissenters, Alexander and Fromm-Reichmann, it, nonetheless, was a consensus to which the overall psychoanalytic community cohered, while the sphere of dissent either dwindled away (the Alexander position) or retreated to a particular niche in the intensive therapy of the flagrantly ill, the institutionalized overt psychotic (the Fromm-Reichmann position). It is clear that there is no comparable consensus emergent today among the varying current perspectives on these issues.

Our own Psychotherapy Research Project of The Menninger Foundation was conceived and designed in the early '50s within the crucible of the crystallizing second era consensus on the delineation of the spectrum of psychoanalytic therapies from the most purely expressive at the one end to the most purely supportive at the other with major nodal points along this spectrum for psychoanalysis, expressive psychoanalytic psychotherapy, and supportive psychoanalytic psychotherapy. The definitions we used, the indications we prescribed, and the procedures and techniques that we said differentially characterized these different therapeutic modes have already been stated. The final clinical accounting of these "Forty-Two Lives in Treatment," the chronicle of their treatment courses and outcomes, and their subsequent life courses and outcomes over a 30-year time span has been recently published (Wallerstein, 1986, 1988).

The writing up of these results took place in the context of the new ferment and fragmented consensus that I have said characterizes this third, latest, era in the history of dynamic psychotherapy in America. Our systematic empirical findings bear directly on these very issues and in a manner most congruent with the conclusions of Rangell based in his instance on his own clinical observations in a solo practice. To summarize drastically from the 1988 paper, itself a summary of a very large book (almost 800 pages):

The project cohort consisted of 42 patients, half in psychoanalysis and half in varying admixtures of expressive and supportive psychoanalytic psychotherapy. During the course of these treatments some were deliberately and some de facto shifted from psychoanalysis to psychotherapy; within the segment in psychotherapy there were also some planned, as well as some unplanned, shifts along the expressive-supportive dimension. In studying the individual case write-ups of each of these 42 patients from their pretreatment Initial Studies through to the posttreatment Termination Studies and then the planned Follow-Up Studies (with follow-up data on 100 percent of the cohort), with an effort in each instance to account for the changes achieved and the bases on which these had come about or been brought about, I elaborated our own new and enlarged array of supportive therapeutic mechanisms, some 12 in all—our own data-based reorganization and amplification of the various listings presented earlier by Alexander, Knight, Gill, and others. Using our project data as the base, I spelled out the operation of each of these discerned mechanisms in various of the patient case histories (and subsequent life histories).

What did I then overall assert on the basis of these findings that could throw empirical light on the conceptual issues concerning the relationships between psychoanalysis and the psychoanalytically derived psychotherapies in their similarities and differences? In my paper, I brought our overall Project conclusions together as a series of sequential propositions regarding the appropriateness, the efficacy, the reach, and the limitations of psychoanalysis and of psychoanalytic psychotherapies (varyingly expressive and supportive). I can recapitulate those propositions here as follows:

1. In regard to the distinctions so regularly made in the psychodynamic literature between so-called "structural charge" presumably based on the interpretive resolution of unconscious intrapsychic conflicts, and "behavioral changes" that are presumably all that can come out of all other nonexpressive, noninterpretive, change mechanisms, I question strongly the continued usefulness of this effort to so tightly link the kind of change achieved to the intervention mode, expressive or supportive, by

which it is brought about. The changes reached in our more supportive therapies, and via intrinsically supportive modes, seemed often enough just as much structural change as the changes reached in our most expressive-analytic cases.

2. Therapeutically induced change will be at least proportional to the degree of achieved conflict resolution—though it is clear that there can be significantly more change than there is true intrapsychic conflict resolution, change brought about on all the varying supportive bases adduced (therapeutic change, therefore, on bases other than interpretation, working through, and achievement of insight).

3. Effective conflict resolution turned out not to be necessary to therapeutic change. An almost overriding finding was the repeated demonstration that a substantial range of changes were brought about via the more supportive psychotherapeutic modes and techniques, cutting across the gamut of declared supportive *and* expressive (even analytic) therapies, and these changes were (in many instances) quite indistinguishable from the changes brought about by typically expressive-analytic means.

4. Counterpart to the proposition based on the tendency to overestimate the necessity of the expressive (analytic) treatment mode and of its operation via conflict resolution in order to effect therapeutically desired change has been the other proposition based on the happy finding that the supportive psychotherapeutic approaches so often achieved far more than initially expected of them and did so in ways that often represented indistinguishably "structural changes" in terms of the usual indicators of that state. Most of the treatments (psychotherapeutic and psychoanalytic alike) had been substantially altered during their course in varyingly supportive directions, and more of the patients (again, psychotherapeutic and psychoanalytic alike) had changed on the basis of designedly supportive interventions than had been expected or predicted beforehand.

5. Just as more was accomplished than expected with psychotherapy, especially in its more supportive modes, so psychoanalysis, as the quintessentially expressive therapeutic mode, was more limited than had been anticipated or predicted. This, of course, significantly reflected the nature of the patient population at The

Menninger Foundation who were considerably "sicker" than those in the usual outpatient private practice setting, so often brought or sent to The Menninger Foundation for intensive psychoanalytic treatment (within a protected sanatorium setting) on the basis of so-called "heroic indications." Certainly, these disappointing outcomes of analytic treatments with these sicker patients invites a repositioning of the pendulum in its swings over time around this issue, more in the direction of "narrowing indications" for psychoanalysis along the lines marked out by Anna Freud (1954).

6. Put all together, the psychoanalyses as a whole as well as the expressive psychotherapies as a whole were systematically modified in the direction of introducing more supportive components in widely varying ways, they by and large reached more limited outcomes than promised (hoped) and, as indicated, with a varying but often substantial amount of that accomplished by noninterpretive, i.e., supportive, means. The psychotherapies, on the other hand, often accomplished a good deal more than initially expected and promised, and again with these cases, however, the admixture of intervention techniques was originally projected, with much of the change on the basis of more supportive modes than originally specified.

In summary of all this I say in my 1988 article:

> In the light of the conceptual and predictive framework within which the Psychotherapy Research Project of The Menninger Foundation was planned and implemented three decades earlier, there is, of course, considerable and real surprise to the overall Project findings; that these distinctive therapeutic modalities of psychoanalysis, expressive psychotherapy, supportive psychotherapy, etc., hardly exist in anywhere near ideal or pure form in the real world of actual practice; that real treatments in actual practice are inextricably intermingled blends of more or less expressive-interpretive and more or less supportive-stabilizing elements; that almost all treatments (including even presumably pure psychoanalyses) carry many more supportive components than are usually credited to them; that the overall outcomes achieved by those treatments that are more "analytic" as against those that are more "supportive" are less apart than our usual expectations for those differing modalities would portend; and that the kinds of changes

> achieved in treatments from the two ends of this spectrum are less different in nature and in permanence than again is usually expected, and indeed can often not be easily distinguished [pp. 149–150].

Overall, these conclusions from an intensive empirical study of the processes and outcomes of psychoanalysis and psychoanalytically based psychotherapies as conceptualized within the formulations of the mainstream consensus of the early '50s, conclusions emerging now in the 30-year clinical accounting and overview of the latter '80s, in the midst of this third era of what I have called a "fragmented consensus" among colleagues of once like-minded perspective, place our findings and our views, like Rangell's, between those of Gill and of Stone today. These findings and conclusions do not support Gill's effort to so totally redraw the distinctions within the spectrum of psychoanalytic psychotherapies, in effect collapsing all expressive and exploratory approaches into more or less psychoanalysis, while pushing all supportive approaches back toward an undifferentiated suggestion.

Nor, however, do these findings and conclusions simply support reiterations of the consensus staked out in the '50s on clear-cut differences among a range of psychoanalytic psychotherapeutic modalities which could be distinctively employed on the basis of reasonably clear-cut indications for different categories on the psychopathological spectrum. Though the differences between psychoanalysis and expressive psychotherapy and supportive psychotherapy are there and are real, the boundaries and the seemingly specific deployments are also all much less clear-cut, with inevitable infiltrations, advertent or inadvertent, of admixtures of more supportive techniques and modes into even the efforts at the purest of expressive-analytic approaches. As I say of this in my 1988 paper: "None of this was where, three decades ago, we expected to be today. From another perspective, in terms of the corridor comments made by practitioners in informal interchanges about the conditions and nature of professional practice, what they regularly find that they do in actual practice as against how it is conceptualized for formal presentation in professional meetings, our PRP research conclusions are far less surprising" (p. 150). On this overview, I feel Leo Rangell to be one of those colleagues in full accord. And implicit in all this is, of course, my own agenda for the continuing study of the mechanisms of psychoanalysis and psychotherapy during this present third era of their interrelated history.

REFERENCES

Alexander, F. (1954), Psychoanalysis and psychotherapy. *J. Amer. Psychoanal. Assn.*, 2:722–733.

——— French, T. M. (1946), *Psychoanalytic Therapy: Principles and Application*. New York: Ronald Press.

Bibring, E. (1954), Psychoanalysis and the dynamic psychotherapies. *J. Amer. Psychoanal. Assn.*, 2:745–770.

Bullard, D. M., ed. (1959), *Psychoanalysis and Psychotherapy: Selected Papers of Frieda Fromm-Reichmann*. Chicago: University of Chicago Press.

Freud, A. (1954), The widening scope of indications for psychoanalysis. *J. Amer. Psychoanal. Assn.*, 2:607–620.

Freud, S. (1905), On psychotherapy. *Standard Edition*, 7:255–268. London: Hogarth Press, 1953.

——— (1914), On the history of the psycho-analytic movement. *Standard Edition*, 14:1–66. London: Hogarth Press, 1957.

——— (1919), Lines of advance in psycho-analytic therapy. *Standard Edition*, 17:157–168. London: Hogarth Press, 1955.

Fromm-Reichmann, F. (1950), *Principles of Intensive Psychotherapy*. Chicago: University of Chicago Press.

——— (1954), Psychoanalytic and general dynamic conceptions of theory and therapy: Differences and similarities. *J. Amer. Psychoanal. Assn.*, 2:711–721.

Gill, M. M. (1951), Ego psychology and psychotherapy. *Psychoanal. Quart.*, 20:62–71.

——— (1954), Psychoanalysis and exploratory psychotherapy. *J. Amer. Psychoanal. Assn.*, 2:771–797.

——— (1979), The analysis of the transference. *J. Amer. Psychoanal. Assn.*, 27(Suppl.):263–288.

——— (1982), *Analysis of Transference. Psychol. Issues*, Monogr. 53. New York: International Universities Press.

——— (1984), Psychoanalysis and psychotherapy: A revision. *Internat. Rev. Psycho-Anal.*, 11:161–179.

Glover, E. (1931), The therapeutic effect of inexact interpretation: A contribution to the theory of suggestion. *Internat. J. Psycho-Anal.*, 12:397–411.

——— (1954), The indications for psycho-analysis. *J. Ment. Sci.*, 100:393–401.

Kernberg, O. F. (1975), *Borderline Conditions and Pathological Narcissism.* New York: Aronson.

Knight, R. P. (1945), The relationship of psychoanalysis to psychiatry. *Amer. J. Psychiat.*, 101:777–782.

——— (1949), A critique of the present status of the psychotherapies. *Bull. N.Y. Acad. Med.*, 25:100–114.

——— (1952), An evaluation of psychotherapeutic techniques. *Bull. Menn. Clin.*, 16:113–124.

Kohut, H. (1971), *The Analysis of the Self.* New York: International Universities Press.

——— (1977), *The Restoration of the Self.* New York: International Universities Press.

Rangell, L. (1954), Similarities and differences between psychoanalysis and dynamic psychotherapy. *J. Amer. Psychoanal. Assn.*, 2:734–744.

——— (1981), Psychoanalysis and dynamic psychotherapy: Similarities and differences twenty-five years later. *Psychoanal. Quart.*, 50:665–693.

Stone, L. (1951), Psychoanalysis and brief psychotherapy. *Psychoanal. Quart.*, 20:215–236.

——— (1954), The widening scope of indications for psychoanalysis. *J. Amer. Psychoanal. Assn.*, 2:567–594.

——— (1982), The influence of the practice and theory of psychotherapy on education in psychoanalysis. In: *Psychotherapy: Impact on Psychoanalytic Training,* ed. E. D. Joseph & R. S. Wallerstein. New York: International Universities Press.

Wallerstein, R. S. (1966), The current state of psychotherapy: Theory, practice, research. *J. Amer. Psychoanal. Assn.*, 14:183–225.

——— (1969), Introduction to panel on psychoanalysis and psychotherapy: The relationship of psychoanalysis to psychotherapy—Current issues. *Internat. J. Psycho-Anal.*, 50:117–126.

——— (1986), *Forty-Two Lives in Treatment: A Study of Psychoanalysis and Psychotherapy.* New York: Guilford Press.

——— (1988), Psychoanalysis and psychotherapy: Relative roles reconsidered. *Annual Psychoanal.*, 16:129–151. New York: International Universities Press.

——— Robbins, L. L., Sargent, H. D., & Luborsky, L. (1956), The Psychotherapy Research Project of The Menninger Foundation. *Bull. Menn. Clin.*, 20:221–278.

8

PSYCHOANALYSIS AND THE QUEST FOR MORALITY

JACOB A. ARLOW, M.D.

In this volume dedicated to the psychoanalytic contributions of Leo Rangell, it seems most appropriate to consider certain issues concerning morality. Such issues have been prominent in his writings. While a good deal, if not most, of the psychoanalytic literature concerning the superego and conscience deals with the harsh, primitive nature of moral judgment in psychopathology, Rangell considers the other end of the spectrum, the compromise of integrity, the ease with which moral imperatives and strictures are abandoned, disregarded, and compromised. In a series of contributions (1974, 1976, 1980), he discussed the manifold motivations and mechanisms by which the individual circumvents his obligations and responsibilities. In the light of the realistic, narcissistic, and instinctual gratifications attainable by disregarding conscience, we well may ask, "What is it that makes the individual a moral being? What motivates him to renounce personal pleasure and advantage in response to some inner imperative or prohibition?"

This communication is intended to serve at least three purposes: first, to examine the ontogenesis of the moral imperative from a perspective that differs somewhat from the one that emphasizes the centrality of the vicissitudes of the Oedipus complex in superego formation; second, to consider some striking clinical variations of superego functioning as forms of regression to a more primitive expression of morality, actually a type of protomorality;

and third, to consider some of the technical implications that result from conflicts within the superego, in other words, the consequences of a clash of moral values.

As we are well aware, there is no naturally inherent morality. A moral code is a social acquisition, the product of centuries of experience in communal living. It represents the accumulated wisdom of what the society can and should expect of the behavior of its individual members. Much has already appeared in psychoanalytic literature on how the moral imperative is fostered in the psychology of each individual by the specific child-rearing practices, by the influence of the family, and by the nature of the educational and religious institutions of the society. In its broadest sense, the purpose of pedagogy is to mold the character structure of members of the emerging generation so that their character traits will be consonant with the cultural ideals and values of the society (A. Freud, 1935).

As will be discussed later, it is a mistake to assume that the moral values that dominate the superego functioning of any particular individual are in all respects identical with the traditional moral code of the community. Beyond the bounds of what is prescribed and proscribed by statute and law, there is a vast area of possible choices, where individual conflict between moral values and self-seeking, lustful, aggressive, vengeful, materialistic, and narcissistic tendencies abound. In addition, there are the special situations, where a moral code particular to a family or a subgroup in the society articulates values at odds with those of the surrounding culture.

During treatment, derivatives of antisocial tendencies are commonly the subject of concealment or repression. Accordingly, the demonstration of their manifold influence has long been emphasized in the literature of psychotherapy. Clinical experience emphasizes and reemphasizes how deep-seated and powerful are the immoral forces of the mind, but, as Freud (1923) reminded us, man is at the same time powerfully moralistic. Why should that be? What is it that makes possible and fortifies man's quest for morality? This is the first question I propose to address.

Certain biological characteristics peculiar to man predispose him to seek morality as a necessary condition of his existence.

Two of these are of primary importance. I refer to the extended period during which the human infant is dependent upon caretakers for its survival and to the inherent biological role of pain and pleasure. Unlike most other animals, the human infant for a comparatively long time is unable to sustain itself independently. Without the loving care of a mothering object over an extended period of time, it would soon perish. The psychological consequences of this well-known fact are enormous. It raises to the highest degree of significance the role of the "other" in the mental life of the individual. In time, other persons beyond the immediate caretaker come to play roles of significance to the individual. As a result of his very biological nature, man is not solitary. He is inherently a communal animal. It is this interdependence, this connectedness with others, that places the stamp of humanity on man.

What serves to strengthen this inherent bond to the caretaker is the fact that her life-sustaining activities are subjectively experienced by the infant as suffused with pleasure. Physiological need tension is experienced as painful, gratification as pleasurable. This pleasure-unpleasure principle, which dominates mental life, clearly must have been of survival value in the course of evolution. Noxious elements, for the most part, are painful, ultimately life-threatening, and therefore to be avoided. Contrariwise, life-sustaining activities tended to be experienced as pleasurable, to be sought after repetitively, to be reexperienced and enjoyed. This combination of pleasure with nurturance and protection, emanating from the interaction with the mother, is what Freud (1905, 1921) referred to as the anaclitic object choice.

In recent years, studies in developmental psychology and in psychoanalytic observation of infants have contributed much to our understanding of how this pleasure-unpleasure continuum is modulated and endowed with increasing meaning through the mother-infant interaction.[1] This process is effected primarily through sensory modalities—vision, touch, hearing, smell—and, after a year or so, is augmented by the contribution of cognitive development by way of symbolic representation through speech.

[1] The literature on developmental psychology has grown so vast that it would be impossible to cite in one place one's indebtedness to the many contributors. A number of comprehensive summaries of the literature have appeared in recent years.

The young infant fixes his gaze on the mother's face. By nature he is predisposed to respond to certain perceptual configurations and to draw from them specific affective signals, to which he responds, usually in a similar and/or complementary fashion. The expression on the mother's face may enhance or inhibit the child's natural smiling response. In general, in the early months of life, the child's emotional experience is in a large measure determined by the affective stimulation and responsiveness furnished by the mother. Infants deprived of this interaction will not thrive and may eventually die (Spitz, 1945, 1946).

But while visual experiences, mediated primarily through the infant's fixation on the mother's face, seem to dominate the early experience, other sensory modalities are represented as well. Many observers have commented upon how affective communication and sharing of emotions are mediated through the process of "moulding" the infant to the body of the mother, either during nursing or when being held or carried. On the other hand, muscular tension in the mother and muscular rigidity in the child seem to indicate an affective dissonance between the two.

Another factor that enters into the shaping of the child's affective experiences is the mother's voice, particularly its quality. While we need not necessarily agree with those who have suggested that the fetus *in utero* is responsive to the mother's voice, we must acknowledge recent findings that indicate that the infant recognizes and distinguishes the mother's voice from other voices and responds in specific ways to variations in its quality. The tone of her voice and the rate of her speech reflect the nature of the mother's affective mood. The child experiences these in the total configuration of the caretaking experience and feels what we would characterize as good or bad, that is, pleasurable or unpleasant.

While the sense of smell plays a lesser role in the perceptual experience of human adults, it is a very significant part of the experience of the human infant. Child observation and other studies all indicate that the caretaker's smell is an important part of the total sensory and perceptual gestalt that comes to be associated with the concept of the person fulfilling the mothering role. As a consequence of the totality of this affective intercommunication, whether she intended it or not, the mother becomes the arbiter of what is pleasurable and what is *good,* that is, to be sought after and repeated, as opposed to what is unpleasurable and therefore *bad* and to be shunned and avoided.

The mother's pleasure is enhanced by the child's favorable response to her ministrations. She expresses her pleasure in many ways, which the child is quick to perceive. This is the primordial experience of approval, of feeling good, which soon becomes transformed in a sense of doing the right thing. In the nursery, one may observe how an infant, at the state when he is beginning to crawl, may bump into an object or find himself thwarted in some way. He will then turn and look at his mother and, depending on what he perceives in her response, especially her facial expression, he seems to make the decision whether or not to cry. In the same way, when he overcomes some obstacle or begins to learn to raise himself from the crawling to the standing position on his own, he will smile broadly and look to his mother for a complementary, confirmatory response. The child at this stage is experiencing judgment all the time, although as yet no moral issues are involved. Nonetheless, for him the judgment is most important as far as his internal emotional state is concerned. We may consider this stage of experiencing judgment as the precursor of morality—not true morality, but what we may call the stage of protomorality.

The gradual and progressive understanding of the meaning of the spoken word serves to consolidate this developing protomorality. The child now begins to connect his pleasurable perception of the mother's positive reactions to the spoken words she customarily exclaims under those circumstances; "good boy," "good girl," as the case may be. Every act, no matter how neutral morally from the adult's point of view, becomes for the child fraught with a sense of judgment, approval, or disapproval.

A major turning point in the development of morality takes place when the child begins to grasp the meaning of the spoken word and to place the spoken word in its appropriate context in object relations, especially involving the mother. The vicissitudes of the most ordinary, most commonplace steps in development become the subject of expressions of approval and/or disapproval.

For a meal easily taken, the child perceives a smiling face and a soft, probably grateful voice, saying "good baby." If he extricates himself from some difficulty, he learns that he has done "the right thing." If he persists in his attempts to put a square peg into a round hole in the playbench, he hears an exasperated voice saying, "No, that's wrong." If he is clumsy or hurts himself or falls ill, he perceives on his mother's face expressions that to him represent unpleasure, disapproval, or condemnation. He has been judged "bad." Little wonder that many children, somewhat later on, experience guilt when they hurt themselves or fall ill or feel shame and humiliation when they discover, in attempting to solve some problem, that they have done the "wrong" thing. Thus, concepts of right and wrong, good and bad, have their origin in an affectively laden set of very early object relations that have only the most distant connection to morality, if they have any connection at all. What is right and good, brings pleasure, and should be pursued is what mother approves. What is wrong and bad, brings pain, and should be avoided is what she disapproves of.[2]

It should be clear from what has been said that the pursuit of drive gratification and the nature of object relations cannot be separated one from the other. They are part and parcel of the same process. As I have indicated elsewhere (Arlow, 1980), based on psychoanalytic experience, one may conclude that the mind assimilates new experiences and perceptions in terms of the fundamental criteria of familiar or unfamiliar, pleasant or unpleasant. Memories and perceptions consonant in nature are grouped together and more or less abstracted into organized systems that expand and are transformed in the course of the individual's life. Thus, the early cycle—physiological experience of what is pleasant, good, right, and acceptable, in contrast to what is unpleasant, bad, wrong, and unacceptable—becomes the dynamic background against which later, more highly developed concepts of good and evil are examined and processed.

The culmination of the process of separation-individuation (Mahler, 1971) in the emergence of a sense of self and an appre-

[2] Somewhat later the role of the mother as comforter is appreciated—a new experience for the child, a combination of a painful expression on the mother's face together with loving, pain-easing ministrations (Furer, 1967).

ciation for the "other" constitutes the next major turning point on the path toward developing a sense of morality. This is a gradual process and, before the crystallization of the concept of the self is relatively complete, it is really not possible to speak of the internalization of the caretaker's norms of behavior. Take, for example, the experience of a 15-to-18-month-old child, who stands in front of the bookshelves, vigorously and joyfully emptying their contents onto the floor, all the time saying, "No, no, mustn't." He is repeating the memory of a prohibition, but he has not yet made the prohibition his own, and in his behavior he plays out, without distinction, the roles of both mother and child. Contrasting with this is the situation some months later, when the child stands in front of the bookcase and looks around to see if the mother is watching before he embarks upon his foray of defiance. Now he has a specific mental representation of the mother which, *in this particular context,* is associated with a prohibition she had promulgated in the past. He has a decision to make. Is he willing to take the chance of being caught in the act and thereby run the risk of mother's disapproval and the loss of her love? At this primitive, concretistic understanding of causality, the child feels that the danger resides in being caught in the act, but a new element has been added. The child is aware of the mother's potential affective response to his behavior.[3] He thinks of it, however, only insofar as it concerns how she may behave toward him. It is the possibility of pain from the threatened loss of mother's love and the fear of punishment by her that is of concern to him. This is not yet a feeling of guilt.

With the strengthening of the quality of object constancy, the actual or potential presence of the mother or caretaker ceases to be a necessary condition for how the child resolves conflicts over the do's and don't's that have been put before him. It is sufficient for a *mental representation* of the adult authority–love object to appear at the appropriate time of conflict. It is at this level of functioning that one can speak with accuracy about the internal-

[3] To have this kind of conflict signals that the child has achieved some degree of a coherent object concept relating to the mother. The mother who may punish and the mother whose love he wants are now being represented by a specific person. This implies that two types of object representations, pleasant and unpleasant, good and bad, have been fused into one object concept.

ization of parental demands. The transition to this stage of mental organization is by no means an insignificant step. The manner in which so-called superego figures are represented in dreams and the ease with which individuals commit wrongdoing, when they feel that they will not be seen or caught, are only two examples of how easy it is to regress from a true internalization of norms of behavior to the level of the need for external control.

There is, however, a special step in the development of morality which is frequently overlooked and which I would like to emphasize. I refer to that stage in the child's development after the consolidation of object constancy, in which the child takes into consideration the pain, both physical and psychological, that his behavior (and wishes) may occasion in others. It is a process that has both conscious and unconscious components, that is, it is related to a transient identification in conscious and/or unconscious fantasy with the "other." It is a combination of both empathy and sympathy, which unite into a state of mind I call compassionate identification. Back to the little boy at the bookcase. He takes a giant step toward true morality when he introduces a further thought into the intrapsychic debate, namely, "I love her and therefore I do not want to cause her pain. It would cause me pain to do so." This step represents a major advance in object relations, one that is fundamental for the development of morality. This is the capacity to feel sorry, to feel remorse, an element previously noted by Furer (1967).

Studies of the relationship to the ego ideal have given due account of how the approval of others for doing right and good is ultimately transformed into self-satisfaction and approbation, and the vicissitudes of the erotic ties to the original object or objects represented in the ego ideal have been spelled out in detail. What I am trying to emphasize here is how the erotic tie, expressed through an identification with the object of potential aggression, serves to strengthen the individual's morality. The golden rule, in its positive and negative forms, is an exercise in compassionate identification. It is only when such compassionate identification plays some part in the child's thinking that he can really respond to the admonition, "Don't do that to so-and-so. How would you like it if someone did that to you?"[4]

[4] Abrogating this compassionate identification is a necessary condition for criminality, for training people to kill in war, and for genocide. It was a campaign of propaganda that

By the time the young child arrives at the oedipal phase, his protomorality is dominated by the fundamental potential catastrophes of childhood, namely, fear of the loss of the object's love and fear of punishment. The triadic nature of the oedipal constellation is an effective introduction to the process of socialization. Love and idealization, hostility and fear of retaliation, overwhelm the dominant object ties of the individual, generating conflicts that have to be resolved one way or another as the broader process of socialization begins. Since most neurotic psychopathology results from a regressive reactivation or persistence of conflicts from this stage, what we observe in our patients' behavior, dreams, and symptoms are reactivated or persistent forms of the primitive wishes, but also of the protomorality of this early period of the individual's life. In the subsequent years of development, on many occasions, the voice of conscience may repeatedly express itself in terms of this childhood protomorality, even as the individual acquires higher standards and moral concepts that are more appropriate socially. Moral integrity in the sense of independence from external control, whether the threat of punishment or social disapproval, is perhaps at once the highest and most difficult psychological attribute to attain.

With the depersonalization of conscience, i.e., with the disappearance of the need for a conscious awareness of the mental representation of the moral imperative, true morality becomes possible. What had formerly been an interpersonal relationship now becomes an intrapsychic function. What had been experienced as a conflict with other persons has been transformed into an intrapsychic conflict. What was formerly a wish to maintain or reestablish harmonious relations with the important objects now appears as a pursuit of inner harmony, of a freedom from tension experienced as guilt, fear of punishment, and loss of love. In the main, it is this quest for inner harmony that brings patients to treatment.

Moral imperatives constitute a significant dimension of all intrapsychic conflicts. Successful resolution of such conflicts through

---

rendered Jews, gypsies, and others less than human that made it possible for the Nazis to engage many otherwise civilized Germans in perpetrating their horrendous atrocities. It is a well-known fact that certain psychopathic criminals lack the ability to feel compassion, not just for their victims, but for people in general. Some fundamental quality of empathy seems to be missing in their psychological constitution. Loving and winning the love of others do not seem to be all that important to them.

adaptive compromise formation leads to mental health and progressive development. Unsuccessful resolutions, i.e., failed compromise formations, eventuate in inhibition, symptoms, and character deformation. The goal of psychoanalytic therapy is to further the process of conflict resolution, to bring about a more harmonious integration of the elements in conflict in the form of appropriate, adaptive compromise formations. In this context, appropriate and adaptive mean realistic and mature, that is, the kind of objective judgment the individual would make as a grown person. In treatment, the individual confronts not only his primitive childhood wishes but also the primitive, irrational, uncompromising way he judges himself and others in keeping with the infantile protomorality and the primitive judgment characteristic of the period when his conflicts began.

Let me cite two examples to illustrate this point.

The first concerns a young woman who knew by the age of four that she had been adopted. She did not know what the circumstances of her having been given up for adoption were. She elaborated many different fantasies concerning the event and the nature of her parents. Prominent among these were ideas of having been abandoned by both her mother and her father, and she felt very angry with them. Like so many adopted children, when she grew up, she decided to search out her biological parents. She had many different and conflicting ideas of what she hoped would happen. Among these were ideas of confronting her mother concerning the "crime" she committed in giving the patient up and achieving revenge by humiliating her through her sudden reappearance in the mother's life.

I will not dwell on this part of the patient's experience, significant as it is in the patient's problem. What was interesting beyond the events of the meeting was the information the patient gleaned about her biological father. The fact was he never knew that he had this child. What had happened was that the father had returned to his hometown after many years of absence, looked up his old girlfriend, and had relations with her on this one occasion. He then left the town and never returned. The biological mother never informed him of her predicament. This knowledge hardly affected the derivatives of the fantasy system the patient had built up around the biological father, an imaginary figure with whom she had been involved in her fantasies for many years. At her urging, the mother informed the father that he might expect a communication from the daughter of whose existence he had never known. The patient wrote to him and received in turn a warm, but cautious, response. When he failed to reply to her second letter, she became furious and began to think of her lifelong fantasies of revenge, including the idea of murder.

These fantasies had unconsciously served as the motive force behind a repetitive pattern the patient had pursued. She would choose lovers who were bound to disappoint her and, after suffering for a period of time at their hands, she would drop them in great anger. This patient's quest for justice, rooted in her childhood fantasies, was really a primitive form of morality, a seeking of revenge against a fantasied, not a real, person. As a child, her rage is understandable. As a grownup, aware of the facts of what really happened, her rage is unreasonable. One of the goals of treatment would be to enlist the capacity for compassionate identification with the plight of the mother and father to enable the patient to make a more realistic judgment concerning her biological parents, her vision of her past, and the role of her violent, guilt-laden fantasies of revenge. A large portion of this patient's moral life, caught up in childhood conflicts, has lagged behind the development of the rest of the patient's morality. Just learning the facts concerning her adoption was not sufficient. Only when the patient could effect a compassionate identification with the plight of her mother and father could she begin to resolve her inner turmoil and restore her inner moral equilibrium. In passing, one might note that this type of thinking applies to most judgments that patients make of their parents, to the end that many therapeutic experiences constitute a search for the "villain." During therapy, the analyst has to avoid permitting his sympathy for the patient to interfere with the development of compassionate identification (Arlow, 1981).

The second illustration comes from the case of a man whose whole life was devoted to issues of social justice. He regarded himself as a victim of injustice. When he was but a few months old, his father died of an infection. He and his mother moved in with the maternal aunt's family, where there were several other children. For several years, the patient lived under the illusion that his uncle was his father and that he had two mothers, one who worked and one who stayed home, although he knew quite clearly that the tie to his mother was the fundamental one. Inevitably, in a quarrel with his cousins, they told him that he was not the son of their father. When his mother confirmed the fact at the end of the day, the patient was both crushed and enraged. He wanted to know where his father was. When he was shown a photograph, he became even more angry. "That is not a papa; that's a picture." The mother tried her best to explain the meaning of death to this two-and-a-half year old. Thus, in one day he was deprived not of one but of two fathers. He yearned for the love of the uncle whom he knew and he hated the father whom he had never known.

In later life, this ambivalent attitude toward father figures was lived out in two contrasting sets of behavior. To some authority figures he attached himself with the utmost of filial devotion; toward others he demonstrated unremitting antagonism. What was striking was the fact that, while the patient had great compassion for his mother, having been left a widow with a child at an early age, there was hardly any feeling expressed for the tragic end of a man so early in his life. As we can imagine, part of this patient's problem concerned guilt over his aggressive wishes as well as fear of retaliation from the object of his aggression.

I have chosen both these cases because they demonstrate a fundamental issue, namely, how the vicissitudes of unfortunate object relationships predispose to unconscious immorality. What these two cases have in common is that both patients were angry with someone who never really intended them any harm. In the face of the pain and humiliation they suffered as children, rational judgment in that relationship and compassion were impossible. Since such primitive drive-laden fantasies are repressed and their derivative expressions appear in consciousness, it becomes necessary to explore the psychological depths in which the problem is rooted and thus aid the patient to advance to a resolution of his conflicts that will represent psychic harmony and moral reintegration.

Patients like these, who have sustained cruel blows of fate in childhood, for which they were not to blame in any way, often develop into a character type Freud (1916) called "the exceptions." Having been unfairly deprived of many of the joys and satisfactions of childhood, to which they were entitled, they feel no compelling need to limit their desires or to deny themselves in general in order to conform to the rules of social interaction. They feel they have already been denied more than enough. Since the rules of fair play have not been applied to them, they see no reason to comply with rules. They are, in their view, entitled to be exceptions to the rule. Some patients dramatize the dynamics of this character trait in courtroom fantasies, in which they confront a reproachful legal authority with their own angry claims against the order of things.

In fact, there is much in the psychoanalytic view of mental functioning and in the psychoanalytic approach to therapy that may be analogized to a court of law. The specific manifestations of individual psychology derive from intrapsychic conflict, conscious and unconscious. Many contradictory claims of the personality compete in an effort to establish dominance over the rest of the mind. The forces in conflict within the mind align and realign themselves in different combinations under varying circumstances. In structural language, it is up to the ego to judge what kind of compromise will prove most advantageous under the given circumstances. In fact, certain clinical entities lend themselves readily to explicit portrayal, whether in dreams or in fantasies or in actual life, in terms of a courtroom trial. This is particularly true of the phobias and of anxiety states, as encountered in work inhibitions, social anxiety, examination phobia, exhibitionistic conflicts, e.g., stage fright, erythrophobia, and, of course, in the wide spectrum of obsessive-compulsive disorders, in which the contribution of the prosecuting attorney is particularly severe. In these cases, which form the bulk of psychoanalytic practice, the patient seeks treatment because he wants to be freed from that harsh judge who is himself. The patient suffers from the ravages of the protomorality psychologically translated into the fear of being abandoned, the fear of loss of love, and the fear of punishment. Beyond the primitive fear of being punished in a retaliatory way for his own hostile and forbidden impulses lies the individual's wish to regain, in his mind, the lost or disrupted harmonious relationship to those internalized object representations whose good will and love at one time represented the difference between life and death.

Freud's (1913, 1923) basic conceptualization of the origin of conscience related to the vicissitudes of the Oedipus complex. In characteristic fashion, he coined a striking aphorism, namely, the superego is the heir to the Oedipus complex. He found this formulation particularly felicitous in his attempts to understand the origin of religion and morality in primitive peoples and subsequently in more advanced cultures. Subsequent psychoanalytic studies, however, have indicated that this view has to be modified and that notions concerning the origin of morality in general and conscience in the individual have to be expanded. Without negating the role of the events following upon the conflicts of the oedipal phase, we have to take into consideration the most significant role of events prior and subsequent to the so-called resolution of the Oedipus complex. As indicated earlier, morality has its roots in fundamental biological and experiential relations from earliest childhood. More than that, the moral identity of the individual continues to develop for the rest of his life. Each phase of development and every new role the individual is called upon to play present new moral challenges and expand and test the strength of conscience and of character. In this respect, the transformations during the period of adolescence are perhaps the most important, for it is then that the individual makes the most intense effort to establish his own identity in terms of his sexual, professional, and moral identity. The attempt to resolve in a definitive way the lingering conscious and unconscious conflicts from childhood endows that period of development with the greatest significance for the specific nature of the individual's moral character. It is during this period that the individual's quest for specific ego ideals may lead to identifications with ideal objects. Sometimes these adolescent identifications prove to be transitory. Sometimes their influence persists for the rest of the individual's life. The morality of the individual changes and develops during adult life as a result of critical experiences (Blum, 1985). Such critical experiences are characteristic for particular phases of the adult life cycle (Erikson, 1968).

There are, furthermore, certain problems to the psychoanalytic concept of the superego, to which I would like to call attention. It is obviously incorrect to assume that, in any given society, its members will all subscribe to the established moral code in its entirety. While the code represents an inexorable dimension of social reality, its translation into moral imperatives in psychic structure obviously differs from individual to individual. Although they may be cognizant of the realistic exigencies pertaining to the moral code, as it is expressed in legal prescriptions, individuals nevertheless differ from each other as to the extent they are willing to honor the code fully. There are subgroups within any community who take exception to the authority of the received morality and who, consciously or unconsciously, function to shape the character structure and the superego functioning of their children accordingly. Beyond these considerations, one must take into account individuals for whom the special events of their lives have resulted in a unique combination of inwardly maintained moral directives. These factors have to be taken into account in the course of psychoanalytic therapy.

In the symptom neuroses and in the character neuroses, for the most part, the offender is the self who cannot renounce or control guilt-laden instinctual wishes, so that the resultant difficulty represents a compromise between impulse and punishment. Moral judgment is directed against the self, which now has to suffer pain or experience inhibition. But what happens if someone else, in a real or imagined sense, is the guilty one? In some forms of depression, as Freud (1916) pointed out, by a process of identification with the transgressor, the individual turns the accusations against himself. Serving as a proxy for the culprit, the depressed patient, through his illness, achieves a dubious victory of revenge.

But there are those cases in which the individual has been subjected to real suffering by someone who unequivocally violated the generally accepted moral code and, what is more, the perpetrator, if we may call him that, has gone unpunished. The moral order of the child's world was broken down. The criminal has gotten away with it and now seems to be beyond the reach of retaliation and punishment. This is the combination of factors that one encounters in a clinical syndrome that has not been accorded the attention it deserves in psychoanalytic studies. I am referring to the clinical picture of criminality out of a *borrowed* sense of guilt.

Freud describes certain characters who pursue a pattern of criminality in order to assuage a sense of guilt. Either they justify the persistent feelings of guilt, genetically related to some imagined childhood oedipal crime, and/or they enlist the forces of the law in actualizing a scenario in which they will be punished. In the case of the syndrome of criminality from a borrowed sense of guilt, the individual was not himself the culprit. It was someone else, usually a parent, who was culpable, and most often the patient was the victim. The patient identifies with the wrongdoer and experiences the guilt that he thinks the wrongdoer should have felt. There is a sense of moral outrage that the wicked have gone unpunished. What is more, in most cases, the criminal is out of the reach of the patient. He cannot confront him or in any way wreak vengeance for the pain that the criminal occasioned. What is most disillusioning is the fact that the wrongdoer not only gets away with it, not only goes unpunished, but he may even be enjoying the fruits of his immoral behavior. What happens in these cases is that the patient acts out a fantasy of punishing the wrongdoer. By a process of identification with the culpable object, the individual assumes the object's crime and the attendant guilt and, by perpetrating criminal and self-destructive acts, arranges for the culpable object to be punished in the person of his own self. It is as if the only way to catch up with the wrongdoer and to bring him to a court of justice, where he would get the punishment he deserved, is for the individual to stand in his place, to commit crimes for which the culpable person could be punished. It is a self-induced, self-destructive, pyrrhic victory.

The following obviously limited clinical presentation may illustrate how these dynamics operate. The patient, a young woman of unusual intellectual endowment, came to treatment complaining of depression, insomnia, fear of going insane, and inability to work. She could not follow through with her assignments and lived in constant fear that she would be fired. She indulged excessively in marijuana and was afraid that she would be arrested, which would be ruinous to her professional career.

Her parents were divorced when she was five years old. The father had a nervous breakdown. He never supported the patient in any way and, after a few visits shortly after the divorce, he disappeared from the patient's life. As a gifted student, the patient was able to obtain a first-rate education, achieving an advanced degree, enabling her to embark upon a career that was full of promise. Her relations with men were stormy and unhappy. In her treatment, it was not difficult to demonstrate her suppressed rage at the abandoning father, her fantasies of killing him, and her guilt over such wishes. Going crazy meant losing control of her impulses. During treatment, the patient sought out and found her father, who had by now established another family and was engaged in a successful and, as the patient felt, a glamorous profession. During this time, the patient became very active in organizations protecting the rights and welfare of abandoned children.

In the transference, the patient experienced separation as an abandonment. On several such occasions, she would begin excoriating herself, tearing furiously at her own body with her nails. From her associations, her dreams, and her fantasies, it became clear that she was venting her rage against her father, but had directed the physical assault against her own body. On the one hand, the patient identified with her father, saying, "I am a crook, a criminal, like him." At the same time, she imagined bringing him to court and having him jailed for failing to provide child support. During this time, as a result of her punitive identification with her father, she tried to get punished, setting herself up to be fired, sabotaging her efforts to get another job, and exposing herself to the possibility of arrest.

She had a fantasy of bringing her father to a session for a definitive confrontation in the presence of the analyst, who would act as the judge. In her mind, the record of her analytic productions was the bill of indictment against her father. It was reassuring to have the confrontation in the analyst's office, where she felt she would not lose control and become murderous. When she saw how proud her father was of his son by his second wife, she felt that she had been cast off because she was defective. Her murderous wishes made her feel guilty, and she wanted the analyst to punish her for these hostile wishes against her father. In that context, she said, "I feel beaten, tortured, arrested, and jailed," things that she had wished her father to experience.

After a period of several years, in which the father and the patient did not communicate with each other, the father broke the silence and reestablished relations with the patient. The patient, by this time, had had an opportunity to appreciate her own conflictual wishes of vengeance and self-punishment. She could accept his justifications for his behavior, limited though she considered them to be. Most of all, however, she appreciated that he had been a sick man with serious problems of his own. Who knows what difficulties and injustices he had experienced in his early life? She could now remember how, before she was four years of age, he had been a devoted and loving father. Some memories of pleasant activities and play together came to her mind. She could feel for him. She could not completely forgive him, but she was ready to let her painful memories fade in significance.

For this patient, the treatment expressed not only a wish for justice to be done, but also a quest on her part for inner moral harmony. Not only did she want to fulfill her lifelong wish for her father to be brought to justice and be punished, she also felt guilty because of her violence and vengefulness. Its primitive nature and intensity clashed with her more adult, rational apprehension of morality. Somewhere deep in her mind she had retained the memory of a happy, loving attachment to the father of her early years, of a time of mutual trust and love. The ability, after years of treatment, to effect a compassionate identification with him was crucial for her recovery.

Clearly, it is impossible in the course of one presentation to encompass the many different forms the problem of moral integration assumes during psychoanalytic therapy. Because the psychoanalytic compact requires unequivocal confrontation with the truth, painful as it may turn out to be, entering upon this form of treatment implies a basic moral commitment on the part of patients. Only when the individual reaches the point where he decides that he can no longer tolerate what he has been experiencing and that he is prepared to make a fundamental change in himself, can we anticipate a successful outcome of the arduous, joint pursuit of inner truth that analysis signifies. What the patient is really seeking is a higher, more effective integration of himself as a moral being.

One of the major goals of treatment is to modify and diminish the influence of infantile protomorality and childish, primitive morality and to institute instead the more rational, compassionate mode of adult moral judgment. In psychoanalysis one learns not only to have compassion for oneself, but also for others. It has been said that ethical behavior consists of how the individual relates his behavior to his moral standards. If this is so, then ethics becomes the measure of one's ability to care and to be concerned, that is, to love. As I have tried to demonstrate in this presentation, in the development of human morality, the deepest roots go back to the wish to love and be loved. One could paraphrase Freud's famous dictum about the goal of psychoanalytic treatment to read: "Where superego was, there shall ego be."

REFERENCES

Arlow, J. A. (1980), Object concept and object choice. *Psychoanal. Quart.*, 49:109–133.

——— (1981), Theories of pathogenesis. *Psychoanal. Quart.*, 50:488–514.

Blum, H. P. (1985), Superego formation, adolescent transformation, and the adult neurosis. *J. Amer. Psychoanal. Assn.*, 33:887–909.

Erikson, E. H. (1968), The human life cycle. *International Encyclopedia of the Social Sciences*. New York: Crowell-Collier.

Freud, A. (1935), Psychoanalysis and the training of the young child. *Psychoanal. Quart.*, 4:15–24.

Freud, S. (1905), Three Essays on the Theory of Sexuality. *Standard Edition*, 7:125–245. London: Hogarth Press, 1953.

——— (1913), Totem and Taboo. *Standard Edition*, 13:1–165. London: Hogarth Press, 1955.

——— (1916), Some character-types met with in psycho-analytic work. *Standard Edition*, 14:309–333. London: Hogarth Press, 1957.

——— (1921), Group psychology and the analysis of the ego. *Standard Edition*, 18:67–143. London: Hogarth Press, 1955.

——— (1923), The ego and the id. *Standard Edition*, 19:3–66. London: Hogarth Press, 1961.

Furer, M. (1967), Some developmental aspects of the superego. *Internat. J. Psycho-Anal.*, 48:277–280.

Mahler, M. S. (1971), The study of the separation-individuation process and its possible application to borderline phenomena in the psychoanalytic situation. *The Psychoanalytic Study of the Child*, 26:403–424. New York: Quadrangle.

Rangell, L. (1974), A psychoanalytic perspective leading currently to the syndrome of the compromise of integrity. *Internat. J. Psycho-Anal.*, 55:3–12.

——— (1976), Lessons from Watergate: A derivative for psychoanalysis. *Psychoanal. Quart.*, 45:37–61.

——— (1980), *The Mind of Watergate: An Exploration of the Compromise of Integrity*. New York: Norton.

Spitz, R. A. (1945), Hospitalism—An inquiry into the genesis of psychiatric conditions in early childhood. *The Psychoanalytic Study of the Child*, 1:53–74. New York: International Universities Press.

——— (1946), Anaclitic depression. *The Psychoanalytic Study of the Child*, 2:313–342. New York: International Universities Press.

9

PUNITIVE PARENTHOOD AND CHILDHOOD TRAUMA

HAROLD P. BLUM, M.D.

Punitive child abuse is a widespread, multidimensional phenomenon that cuts across social, educational, economic, and cultural boundaries. It is not associated with any single form of psychopathology or psychiatric diagnosis, in the caretaker or the child. Far more frequently than we have wanted to acknowledge, it occurs in the most protean forms ranging from psychological maltreatment or physical punishment, to starvation and abandonment. The far-reaching variable consequences of punitive abuse encompass destructive and self-destructive syndromes, including, at the extremes, suicide and murder.

Different forms of maltreatment coexist and are dynamically interrelated. It should be emphasized that sexual abuse is also an aggressive assault, usually with its own inherent punitive motives and determinants. Punishment is a manifest or latent component and both a cause and consequence of child abuse; it may be combined with sadomasochism and narcissistic rage, and may appear in disguised, dissociated derivatives. This chapter will deal with abusive punishment and the relationship between childhood trauma and punitive parenthood. Childhood trauma may decisively contribute to a sadistic, punitive superego. The trauma may be experienced as an assault and punishment, and may intensify unconscious guilt, leading to later enactment of punitive and self-

Dedicated to Leo Rangell. The R. L. Scharf Lecture, Psychoanalytic Institute of New York University, April 23, 1988.

punitive behavior. Superego pathology is an important consideration in child abuse, but no one determinant can be artificially isolated from other pathogenic factors. Parental ego impairments can be anticipated. The cases to be referred to here were in the milder categories and are not representative of different and more malignant psychopathology.

Inappropriate punishment of children can be noted throughout recorded history. While cultural custom and social sanction (e.g., in punitive initiation rites) should not be confused with anomalous punitive parenthood, aberration has a cultural context, and psychoanalysis recognizes differences and underlying interrelationships. The discipline of caretakers, teachers, and employers often took the form of deprivations and humiliations, beatings, and sexual exploitation. The pathogenesis and consequences of different forms of mistreatment cannot always be differentiated; but there is a difference between sexual overstimulation and the trauma of extreme pain and panic, torture and terror. Sexual overstimulation per se (e.g., parental nudity) is not likely to be as deeply traumatic as punitive aggression and violence.

Before this century of the child, virtually all the child-rearing and pedagogical texts and tracts advocated, like Schreber's father, corporal and coercive punishment. "A child is being beaten" was considered normal and healthy, necessary for the child's moral and psychosocial development. There was a fine line between harsh discipline and child abuse. Abuse could be disguised as appropriate punishment, "for the child's good," even more painful to the disciplinarian. Beatings continued through childhood, and could be so severe at adolescence that flight from home prevented maiming and murder. An ordinary house could actually be a chamber of horrors. These traumatized children grew up into punitive, abusive parents, repeating cycles of psychologically crippled caretakers and children, as in the Bible: "The iniquities of the fathers are inflicted on the children to the third and fourth generation." Neither the rod nor the child was spared. Long before the radiological recognition of infantile fractures, there were obvious black and blue marks and scars from parental punishment. Parents had virtually absolute authority, and in past centuries there were no legal strictures protecting the child.

Masturbation was rampantly suppressed cross-culturally, and the little "sex offender" could be severely punished. Not only were children castrated, ostensibly to sing in choirs, but infants could be castrated in the cradle with parental impunity. Some sexually abused children were genitally mutilated, castrated for their parents' and their own incestuous behavior. Atrocities were condoned and rationalized.

The discovery of the importance of unconscious fantasy led Freud to abandon the seduction theory, but not to neglect trauma. Two interrelated, complementary theories actually evolved—the theory of unconscious conflict and fantasy, and the theory of psychic trauma. Fantasy and reality were both important, and not necessarily readily differentiated. Psychoanalysis illuminated the child's inner impulses and motives, his own seductiveness and provocation, the child's hidden pleasures, but also the anxiety, rage, shame, guilt, and confusion associated with child abuse. Oedipal guilt and punitive trends are greatly magnified when oedipal fantasy becomes reality. Trauma is co-determined by the activation and validation of unconscious fantasy, and by the intensity, duration, and potential mastery of the traumatic situation.

One particular child might be chosen as sexual object and/or sacrificial or punitive scapegoat. The abuse might be direct or vicarious, through spouse, servants, or other surrogates. Punitive abuse might have occurred only briefly and sporadically, such as after parental illness, injury, or intoxication, or might be an ongoing part of a pathological, sadomasochistic caretaker-child relationship.

The uncovering of punitive and perverse parenthood contravened the usual silence on the subject. Freud's (1896) description of the preanalytic treatment of 12 women and six men, all 18 of whom had been sexually abused in childhood, was revolutionary. The traumatic scenes were partly recalled, and then reconstructed and reconnected with later symptoms and inhibitions. The seduction theory was never simply seduction, and Freud's (1896) attention to parental authority, power, and punishment is still noteworthy:

> All the singular conditions under which the ill-matched pair conduct their love-relations—on the one hand the adult, who cannot

> escape his share in the mutual dependence necessarily entailed by a sexual relationship, and who is yet armed with complete authority and the right to punish, and can exchange the one role for the other to the uninhibited satisfaction of his moods, and on the other hand the child, who in his helplessness is at the mercy of this arbitrary will, who is prematurely aroused to every kind of sensibility and exposed to every sort of disappointment, and whose performance of the sexual activities assigned to him is often interrupted by his imperfect control of his natural needs—all these grotesque and yet tragic incongruities reveal themselves as stamped upon the later development of the individual and of his neurosis, in countless permanent effects which deserve to be traced in the greatest detail . . . every such relationship between children postulates a previous seduction of one of them by an adult [p. 215].

The pathogenesis and consequences of these relationships, outlined in the Oedipus myth, clearly involve much more than seduction. Blinding denial of incest, oedipal guilt, and punishment are ubiquitous, as depicted in the Oedipus drama. Seduction as an overextended (abused) concept is not implied in the terminology of "seduction theory or seduction trauma."

The fragility of parental ego regulation and superego ideals and strictures is readily discerned in fairy tales, fokelore, and world literature. Consider the well-known nursery rhyme, "Rock-a-bye baby in the tree tops / When the wind blows the cradle will rock / When the bough breaks the cradle will fall / Down will come baby, cradle and all."

The baby will not always be held, and the holding environment may fail. When passions become too great, the gentle rocking may give way to withdrawal or punitive reactions. The parental "breaking point" may come and/or the baby's psychic organization may collapse under the internal and external pressures. One is also reminded of the "Old lady who lived in a shoe / Who had so many children she didn't know what to do, / She whipped them all soundly and sent them to bed." Here, too, is a description of the overwhelmed caretaker (overwhelmed by many rather than one particular child) where aggressive and punitive reactions take the place of nurturance and reciprocal comfort.

The particular mix and match of parent and child are very important, and there are factors in both (parties) partners that may excessively strain and distort the relationship. Sensitivities, temperament, age, phase, sex, and sibling position, the child's capacity to elicit mothering, and that child's meaning to each parent and to the parental relationship are important considerations (Mahler, Pine, and Bergman, 1975). The exceptionally difficult or handicapped child, the child who easily cries and is not easily consoled, the parent or child with very low frustration tolerance and regressive vulnerabilities—all such factors may be major contributors to ensuing problems. Some children seem to be remarkably resilient, as if they were relatively "invulnerable" to abuse. The parent may not be able to bond and may have limited empathy for a particular child, and the child may not be able to read and adapt to parental cues. Predisposed parents are far more likely to regard the child with punitive disappointment (Helfer, 1976). Some parents may primarily respond to the child when he is hurt, or prefer that the child exploit, hurt, and punish the parent. Other parents play sadomasochistic games or are inappropriately preoccupied with the child's punishable transgressions. Punishment is rationalized as induced by the child's seductions, infractions, and provocations. When responsibility is assigned to the child, collusion is invited or demanded since the child cannot give informed consent. Delinquent parents may punish to enforce collusive silence and submission and to conceal abuse while continuing abuse. Reporting abuse may then increase guilt and invite punishment of and by the caretaker, as well as offering a sense of power and revenge.

The "sadistic superego," so often associated with imperious and imperative commands, inconsistent controls, with punitive and self-punitive attitudes, may be poorly internalized and subject to internal splits, inconsistencies, and regression. Rigid prohibition and overpermissiveness may alternate or coexist as if there were several superegos. Blame and guilt are readily projected and denied, with superego vulnerability to compromise of standards and integrity (Rangell, 1974). The archaic, punitive superego is usually associated with a pathological ego ideal, impossibly perfectionistic demands, and untamed, omnipotent, infantile ideals. Irrational expectations of the infant and child and the child's failure to meet the parent's infantile ideals and expectations may result in punishment of the child. The child is then seen as disappointing and frustrating, conveying and evoking a sense of failure in the parents (Blum, 1981, 1987). Identifying with the aggressor, his own punitively experienced parent, the child may be punished as the parent was or wished to be punished. Punitive attitudes are associated with a lack of empathy and appreciation of the child's real needs and interests (Steele, 1970).

The seduced child may not repeat sexual abuse but aggressive abuse of children, pets, or other surrogate victims. A majority of prostitutes, muggers, and rapists have been abused children. Aggression, retaliation, and punishment coincide and sometimes defy differentiation. The youthful delinquent may reactively develop into the harsh, disciplinary martinet. One such case was that of an adult father who worked within the legal profession. Analytic rules were regarded as unnecessarily stringent and occasionally disregarded; the onset of analysis was compared to joining the military. The feelings of harshness were by no means confined to the analytic situation and pervaded the parent-child relationship. He enforced severely strict discipline at home and associated to the house as a "courthouse." He was especially strict with his daughter who was subject to disciplinary measures for anything from interruptions, staining clothes, to not doing homework. Any sign of disrespect could be punished. Disobedience was a major threat, and "talking back" could not be tolerated. Coercion could be rationalized and justified, while compliance and conformity were rewarded.

In the transference relationship, the patient constantly searched for the analyst's condonement or condemnation, approval or disapproval. He was also attuned to any alteration or infraction of the rules by the analyst and was ready to hear clarifications as castigations, and interpretations as insults. The analyst's nonverbal behavior, his movements in the chair, breathing, his silence or tone of voice were regularly screened for criticism and reproach. There was also no paucity of reprimand for the analyst's technical errors and imputed mistreatment of the patient. The analyst, at various times, was accused of beating a dead horse and having an ax to grind about the whole issue of abusive and punitive attitudes. As the analysis proceeded, he became increasingly aware of the exaggerated, irrational, and inappropriate nature of his accusatory and punitive attitudes. With analytic work, he very gradually became more benign and tolerant of human frailty and less inclined to attempt to seduce or provoke fierce battles over trivial points.

What was the background of his need to punish and to be punished, to want to hurt, humiliate, and coercively mistreat others? This patient was raised in an atmosphere of overstimulation, seduction, and intimidation with inconsistent and insufficient regulation and restraint. From earliest years he was allowed to bathe and toilet with his mother. There was no direct evidence of primal scene exposure, but there was definite parental nudity and display in scant underclothes. The patient shared a room with his only sister, with parental denial and silent condonement of sibling sexual exposure and exploration. Actually, sibling sexual exploration continued through latency and into preadolescence with incestuous play accompanied by conscious sexual arousal and excitement. The sibling sex play was a shared secret amalgamated with family secrets. The patient had grown up with intense, unconscious oedipal guilt, which was also based upon the guilt of his parents, embedded in fantasies of punishment.

But important, positive values had also been transmitted, which were reinforced in adolescence. An alteration of standards occurred with contradictory ego ideals and with successful repression of forbidden impulses. There was extraordinary internal disharmony, but the compromise on a conscious level resulted in strict, righteous, and self-righteous attitudes. The sexual delinquent had become the prohibiting puritan. From another viewpoint, what was repeated was not the sexual seductions of childhood but reactive behaviors which were dominated by disapproval and rigidity. Prohibitions extended to almost any infractions. They were paradoxically not directed against his child's sexual curiosity and masturbation. Too readily subject to superego regression, the patient could be more or less mature in his inconsistent standards and values, only to become harsh and punitive. He was in many subtle forms readily subject to corruptive "sops to his conscience" and compromise of integrity. The benevolent, protective parent and the good self were isolated from the punitive parent and denigrated self almost to the point of a split in the ego and superego systems (Shengold, 1979). The patient, identified with the aggressor, could severely castigate his child without self-criticism. The patient's daughter also repesented his sister, an object of sexual temptation and guilt, as well as his "bad self." He was unconsciously fearful that his child might repeat the forbidden activity of his own childhood.

The harshly mistreated child may represent not only alien aspects of the self or sibling, but also of the parent. In this role reversal, which also occurs in the treatment transference, the child will represent the parent's parent, and the parent will represent the child. The infantile parent then demands parenting from the child. The role reversal may represent a kernel of historic truth of simultaneous parent-child regression. The parent's own parent-child conflicts and traumas will be revived by the experience of parenthood (Rangell, 1970; Mahler, Pine, and Bergman, 1975). The patient's guilt was alleviated by projection and externalization, but also by inviting counterattack and self-punitive atonement. His own childhood seduction was now replaced by punitive provocation and circuitous self-punishment through his own child's distress. Punishment for incest was postponed and inflicted on the next generation. This patient was stimulated in analysis to explore, reintegrate, and master his childhood incest play. The "doctor game" of the transference and childhood was modulated, with attenuation of the neurotic repetition (Levin, 1985). He was able to understand the revival of unconscious conflict coincident with parenthood. In projecting guilt and punishing the child "culprit," he was also identified with the victim for whom he paradoxically lacked sympathy. The victim often represents a dissociated, disowned, despised self or object.

I shall now turn to the case of an affectionate, yet abusive, punitive parent who was not herself abused in childhood or as an adult. There was no history of violence, nor of her being deliberately neglected, molested, or cruelly punished. Stating that she was abusing her child, she insistently pleaded for immediate treatment. However, unlike abusive parents who seem unconcerned or even self-righteous, this patient was filled with conscious shame, guilt, and remorse. She was confused and mystified by her punitive responses and attitudes toward her child, whom she also loved. It was rare to find a patient interested in psychoanalysis with child abuse as the chief and initial complaint, not associated with addiction, perversion, or psychosis. (In common contrast, punitive parenting was uncovered in the analysis of the prior patient.) Intelligent, earnest, with capacities for observation, reflection, and verbalization, she was motivated toward understanding. Though she was afraid to explore her inappropriate, irrational behavior, she identified with the analyst's attitude, aims, and commitment (Kanzer, 1985). The analytic pact and prognosis were favored by her personality resources and resolve. But it was threatened by the patient's concern about psychological and social implications, and by her feelings of shame and humiliation. She was at times uncertain of the boundaries between strict discipline and excessive punishment. Tested for trust, tolerance, and benevolent neutrality, the analyst was used for confession and control, as an external superego, with the patient alternately seeking forgiveness and punishment, condemnation, and absolution.

This mother was the product of an affluent, liberal Christian, rural background with permissive rather than authoritarian attitudes toward children. Neither the patient nor her siblings remembered her parents as tyrannical, irresponsible, or impersonal. At first she had tried to conceal the difficulty from her family, hoping that the problem would be surmounted with more maternal experience. The episodic, impulsive abuse intensified during her child's second year of life, and she seemed less inhibited about disparaging her child and motherhood in the presence of her husband and siblings. It was apparent that the anxiety and dismay of the family and their unified concern influenced her decision to seek psychiatric consultation. She had unconsciously provoked and entreated her relatives to provide rescue, regulation, and support in responding to her cry for help. She consciously aspired to be a good mother, and the abuse was a secret stigma, with concomitant feelings of inadequacy and failure. She was "failing in life's most important task."

Her relationship with her child had not been easy from the

beginning. Ambivalent about becoming pregnant, she was eager to please her husband and to fulfill herself as a woman. Pregnancy was uneventful and a rather gratifying experience. She consciously anticipated a pleasurable and benign motherhood and did not foresee that the supposed "little heaven" could become "a living hell." Her baby was born after heavy labor, obstetrical intervention, and disillusionment with natural childbirth. Her initial response to her newborn was cautiously pleasurable, and she had an affectionate investment in his care, e.g., holding, feeding, changing. Would direct analytic observation of their dyadic affective exchanges and relationship have foreshadowed the disorder to follow? (It was not possible to determine if there was a subtle disturbance in attachment, eye contact, or empathy.) However, her son became colicky and then hyperactive, irritable, and very difficult to soothe or to calm. Neither member of the dyad really seemed to enjoy the other; the mother felt that she did not satisfy the child and that the child was not satisfied with her caregiving and nurturance. Moreover, the mother's self-confidence and self-esteem were injured, reviving earlier feelings of inadequacy and self-reproach.

She gave chilling descriptions of some of the struggles with her child. These struggles largely occurred after the child had become a willful, temperamental toddler. When the child had been excessively demanding and when she felt depleted and imposed upon, free play could be transformed into a tense standoff with the danger of escalation into open warfare. With regression, hostile behavior and verbal abuse were immediate. She would scream, curse, express hatred, and call him scatological names. Sometimes she resented the child's crying, which might only provoke more anger. Frustration, anxiety, rage, and blame could escalate when the mother was particularly vulnerable. At highest tension she "went for the throat," and slapped the child in the face and head.[1] By the time the child was three, he verbalized self-blame, but he also asked his mother if she wanted to kill him (possibly repeating her exclamations), and asked for a new

[1]Head injury is common in child abuse and may be self-inflicted as well. This is related to the real and symbolic meaning of the head. The softer cranium of the child provides less shielding against brain injury so that neurological and psychological trauma may coincide. There were no medical injuries in this case.

mother. It is significant that in this treatable case, the punitive abuse was circumscribed and relatively controlled and mild. The child's physical condition never required medical care.

She recognized that she resented the child's being a child. She could sometimes try, without conviction, to justify spankings on the grounds that the child had driven her "to the end of her rope" and deserved it. She would complain that he was the type of child that if "you give an inch, he takes a mile." After these brief "devastating" battles, she was filled with remorse and regret. She wanted to undo the damage, compensate the child for his grief and misery, and win an affectionate reconciliation. She would verbally apologize, explain that she had lost her temper, did not mean what she said or did, in effect asking the child's forgiveness and forbearance. Her own grief, remorse, and self-condemnation could be extreme. Disclaiming her awareness, and "knowing" again, she could transcend her projection and denial, asserting reality. She wanted more shared parenting from her husband. She envied his being away at work, and not protecting their son while she was confined to the house. Before her treatment she was prone to argue with her husband. But she could signal and elicit his holding action and external restraint. She could affectionately teach, read, or play with her child only to sometimes grapple with explosive feelings if he resisted. Her insensitivity was circumscribed and changeable, and she could enjoy understanding and feeling understood by her son.

Her child, though resourceful and resilient, was at risk and had many complaints about minor problems. There were, for example, nightmares and tendencies toward head-banging. Prior to treatment, the mother did not interfere with her child's head-banging, observing it with a mixture of anxiety and anger, and almost a "perverse satisfaction." He could reconcile with his remorseful mother, and they could restore affectionate communication. He was able to turn to alternate objects such as his father for surrogate parenting, and increasingly to find alternate paths for befriending and playfully engaging his mother. Peer relations became age-appropriate, and he responded to adult strangers without excessive anxiety, vigilance, or overinvolvement.

Analytic work with the mother revealed infantile qualities (beneath the surface of composure and maturity) with unresolved oedipal and preoedipal conflicts and fixations to trauma. Regressive and acting-out proclivities coexisted with intact ego capacities. (Some derivative sublimations cannot be discussed here.) Though narcissism, aggression, masochistic character, and unconscious beating fantasy were all very important, I shall concentrate mainly upon the patient's problems with unconscious rage, guilt, and the need to punish and be punished. Hostile transference was sustained and associated with denigration of the analyst and analysis, and external improvement. Some features of the mother-child abusive interaction appeared quite differently in the analytic work than in the historical account. For example, the child's reputedly excessive demands were often reciprocal to the mother's own impulses and fears of transgression; the blame of the child was often an externalization of the mother's own guilt, shame, and feelings of self-accusation and self-reproach. Traumatic experiences from the mother's past were reenacted with role reversal associated with identification with the aggressor. Closely identified with her child, the mother found it very easy to reverse aggressor and victim, guilt and innocence.

The patient associated her child's masturbatory interests with her own fears that the child would grow up to be perverted and oversexed. As her own unconscious fantasies came into focus, it became clear that her fantasies were determinants of her child's punishment. He was more likely to be punished not just when he was demanding or provocative, but when his mother experienced the activation of unacceptable fantasies in the transference and in her external life. Until early adolescence, she was a "nightwalker." She would visit her parents' room and their bed before returning to her own bed. Her complaints of her child's hyperactive imposition and intrusiveness turned out to be a derivative (on one level) of her own primal scene intrusions with unconscious oedipal guilt.

The patient was dismayed at the erotic nature of many of her daydreams and her dreams. There were many dreams of voyeuristic-exhibitionistic nudity, related to the transference and to her farm experience. In one dream, a tidal wave threatened the patient, the revival of trauma. The patient associated to having been overcome by a wave of fury at her child, but she regained her mental balance before attacking the child, or feeling that she should be "knocked out" by a tranquillizer. (Wondering if she needed drugs involved fantasied punishment and soothing.) However, she also recalled experiences where a wave had left her topless and publicly exposed on the beach, and her earliest embarrassment at scenes of public exposure. The child's intrusions and transgressions represented and activated her own conflicts. The tidal wave was repeated in the tides of transference and her enactments with her child. The child had to be controlled and condemned for the mother's "misbehavior." Further, this mother's guilt after punishing the child clearly resulted from the attack, but "unconscious guilt" had also been present prior to the attack. Projection of her unconscious guilt led to blame and punishment of her child. The punishment did not fit the crime or alleviate guilt, but only perpetuated guilt in conscious awareness. Unconscious crime led to punishment, but then to the crime of punishment (Menninger, 1970) and recurrent guilt. She was a guilty criminal, a criminal from a sense of guilt (Freud, 1916), and a criminal bribed by remorse in a "vicious cycle."

Shortly after the birth of a sibling, when the patient was approximately three years of age, she was accidentally injured and became extremely ill. Multiple systems were involved, requiring hospitalization. This was a protracted illness, associated with familial stress. Torn between her desperately sick daughter and her new infant, the patient's mother doubtless regressed, in degree, with her daughter. A long period of anxiety and parental vigilance followed in the months of gradual recuperation. The convergent double trauma of the birth of a sibling and the patient's own, nearly lethal, illness had repressed pathological sequelae. Development was disrupted just as self and object constancy was established. Residues of separation and dependency issues remained unresolved. The traumatic experience and ensuing preoedipal regression impeded oedipal-phase and superego development, as well as ego integration. Her fantasies of violence and punishment had been validated, and derivatives would be repeated in parenthood. There was a partial arrest at the level of the archaic, punitive superego, identification with the aggressor, and infantile narcissistic ideals.

As the trauma was repeated in the transference, issues of trust, abandonment, and rescue came to the fore. Though she had been "rescued," and had fantasies of analytic rescue of herself and her child, she initially could not trust herself or the analyst. She had unconsciously felt abused and betrayed. At the time of the traumatic illness, she thought she must have been an ugly, sickly child, displaced by a sibling rival—a child who felt that she was bad, unloved, and unlovable—and was being punished. What had she done to deserve such punishment? And what had her parents done so that the whole family experienced punishment? Her parents probably had similar questions and reactive responses. Unconsciously, she was her parents' punishment, and her child was her punishment.

Infantile trauma and guilt were anlage of her adult fear that she and her child would be victims and losers. She vigorously denied reaction to loss, e.g., to canceled sessions or vacations, but her anger was evident. She had nightmares of being lost and of her child being lost and found. To her, the analyst's cancellation was a "get lost" message which could be transmitted to her child. She ambivalently turned toward and away from her child and motherhood.

She had been a habitual nail-biter and still bit her cuticles. She thought of a dog who turned vicious and bit kids and who had to be destroyed; a cat who was killed after running away. The loss and death of animals as well as her love and wish for pets were reported just after an analytic vacation. On her own birthday she associated to a feast with suckling pig. Her child reproduced her experience of nurturance, but also her own greedy, devouring self, and envy of her nutured sibling. All three were "suckling pigs." She responded to her child's whining or crying as to a rival's demands and as if she were being deprived or reproached, as a loss of love and a cry for love. There were many associations to parasites and exploiters, and she thought of her fears of being drained and depleted by the analysis and by her own infant. A dream image of a fungus under her breast led to associations of object loss and breast-penis castration, along with fears of inability to give nurturance. Her son was also identified with her younger sibling, and on this sibling's birthday she dreamed that her son had died. Her own feeling of being abused and degraded were derivatives of her unconsciously feeling castrated, deprived, and punished. She had unconsciously wanted to eliminate her sibling and now her child. Her sibling's birth coincided with her near death; her murderous wishes and fantasied punishment had been complete repressed with elements of kill or be killed.

Her ambivalently loved child was unconsciously her own and her mother's excrement—everything that was sick and that she despised in herself and her family. She was extremely upset by a novel where the mother could not protect and seemed to sacrifice her own child. She had presumbly felt abandoned and sacrificed during her illness. Following recovery, she was excessively clinging to an overanxious mother—a factor in her intolerance of separation—her need for a nightlight, her sleeping with her parents, and her later adult sleep disturbance. Needy of my presence, approval, and nurturance in a maternal transference, she longed for warmth and tenderness and wondered if she should not have had a female therapist. She wanted so much to be soothed and comforted as well as nurtured. In her mothering, she also identified with the rescuer and comforter.

Both in the transference and in her relationship with her child she was likely to erupt with anger when she herself was not soothed. Hostile feelings toward the analyst were protracted and sometimes seemed intractable. She identified with a psychiatrist's daughter who was raped and murdered on a roof. She was both aggressor and victim in unconscious incest and its punishment, and in reactivated infantile trauma. Her trauma also had residua of rage reactions and intensified sadomasochism (Glenn, 1984). By latency there was sufficient benign development so that she had caring relationships, and usually affectionate play with her friends and dolls. The adult disorder was dramatically foreshadowed in a singular violent attack on a doll concomitant with sleep disturbance.

The maturation and taming of the archaic punitive superego were a most significant dimension of the patient's analysis. This patient differed from those abusive parents who were themselves abused and repeated their own childhood punishments. She could recognize her own regressive loss of control, and she valued self-control, sensitivity, and kindness. She felt quite insecure and lacked confidence as a mother, alternating self-blame and blame of the child. (The search for historic truth in past trauma should not be derailed into accusation and infantile blame.) Because of projection and fear of retaliation, her child could be regarded as accusatory and reproachful. With regression, she was not able to empathize with the child and could not deal with her own dependent needs and demands for nurturance. She unconsciously competed with her child to be mothered. Her high expectations for herself, so clearly related to her infantile ideals, were associated with impossible expectations for her child. The child should not have limitations or shortcomings and could be punished for the mother's own unacceptable demands and disappointments. Frightened of her own infantile longings projected onto the child, she fantasied that the child should be capable of independence, and even of providing comforting and nurturance for the mother. Traumatic elements contributed to the acting-out diathesis, identification with the aggressor, and the victim, as well as the rescuer and comforter (Blum, 1987).

The traumas of her infantile illness and childhood seductive overstimulation left her unable to sustain nurturant, protective attitudes. She could transiently, but globally regress to a female fury, a Lady Macbeth who could withdraw her affection, with affectionate holding transformed into assault. Parenthood reactivated a return of the infantile repressed. Her transformation from a social, articulate, and knowledgeable woman into an infantile, punitive parent was characterized by activation of archaic superego substructures. Superego arrest and regression were associated with her episodic dyscontrol, the projection of blame and guilt, punishment of the child for the mother's own transgressions and shortcomings, and self-punishment of the mother through identification with and the effect upon her of the child's hurt and humiliation.

It is important to note here that there was ego plasticity and resilience, with positive accomplishment inside and outside analysis. Recovery from childhood trauma is complex, with many unpredictable developmental vicissitudes. Why was the trauma transmitted intergenerationally? Repressed hostility centered upon her own child rather than being more diffusely expressed toward such targets as herself, other individuals, groups, or "natural" threats. Several factors may have predisposed to the still unpredictable outcome. Her extended infantile traumas had structural as well as dynamic consequences (Rangell, 1967). The traumatic situation, including sibling birth, was concretely repeated, with the victim role reversed by obligatory identification with the aggressor when she became the attacker. Her sibling and her illness represented parental punishment and rejection. Another point concerns the paradoxical demand to be an ideal mother, probably of an idealized child representing a narcissistic object. Such failure also was unconsciously punishable, and punishment was omnipotent and omnipresent. The punishment may have or acquire its own hidden rewards and masochistic gratification, its own adaptive value and secondary gain.

In concluding, I will remark about the tormenting burdens upon the analyst in the analytic treatment of abusive parents. Distrust, traumatic anxiety, and fear of recurrence or retaliation fuel massive resistance. Child abuse may raise serious questions about the appropriateness and effectiveness of psychoanalysis. The analyst may be conflicted about responsibility for the welfare of the patient and his or her child and possibly complicity in abuse. Analytic regression and acting out may endanger the child. Issues of responsibility, blame, and exposure complicate and confuse analytic issues. The analyst may lose objectivity, becoming judgmental and critical or compassionate and conciliatory; or he may have rescue fantasies concerning the parent, child, and analyst being rescued from rage, revenge, and violence. Indignation, shock, horror, outrage may pervade the transference-countertransference field. Paradoxically, an opposite form of difficulty may supervene. The analyst may defend against his own violent fantasies with disbelief or underestimation of the disorder, and such patients may be mistakenly appraised as unlikely to maltreat their child again. The time required for analytic change is an important consideration. Countertransference pressures may be intense, complicated by familial, social, legal, and ethical issues. Parameters may be necessary with these patients, but should not be based upon countertransference. Analysis, or modified analysis, if indicated, would permit in depth treatment and research. Such patients test the limits of analysis and the analyst.

SUMMARY

Punishment is an important determinant of child abuse. Punitive parenthood does not necessarily follow from an abused childhood but may be related to other forms of childhood trauma. The punitive superego does not necessarily derive from punitive parents. Trauma may be unconsciously experienced as punishment by the child, and often by the child's parents. Such trauma in early childhood may disrupt superego development, leading to partial arrest, regressive vulnerability, reinforcement of the archaic, punitive superego, and variable superego splitting, inconsistency, and dysharmony. The trauma tends to be transmitted intergenerationally, and repeated in behavior, as well as in transference, dreams, and daydreams.

The repetition of trauma and the influence of the sadistic, punitive superego converge in punitive parenthood. Such parents are guilty because of their punitive abuse but are also "criminals from a sense of guilt." Internal demands to punish and be punished both contribute to and follow from the abuse. Reporting abuse can paradoxically intensify guilt and invite punishment of and by the caretaker. A vicious cycle of conscious and unconscious guilt may ensue, despite remorse and efforts to mitigate and master trauma.

In these cases complicated by ethical, legal, social, and familial issues, the countertransference may be of special importance and intensity. The punitive parents described here, with circumscribed, relatively controlled disturbances, were treatable by psychoanalysis with minor modifications.

REFERENCES

Blum, H. (1981), The maternal ego ideal and the regulation of maternal qualities. In: *The Course of Life*, Vol. 3: Washington, DC: National Institute of Mental Health, pp. 91–114.

——— (1987), The role of identification in the resolution of trauma. *Psychoanal. Quart.*, 56:609–627.

Freud, S. (1896), The aetiology of hysteria. *Standard Edition*, 3:189–221. London: Hogarth Press, 1962.

——— (1916), Some character-types met with in psychoanalytic work. *Standard Edition*, 14:309–333. London: Hogarth Press, 1957.

Glenn, J. (1984), Psychic trauma and masochism. *J. Amer. Psychoanal. Assn.*, 32:357–385.

Helfer, R. (1976), *Child Abuse and Neglect*. Cambridge, MA: Ballinger.

Kanzer, M. (1985), Identification and its vicissitudes. *Internat. J. Psycho-Anal.*, 66:19–30.

Levin, E. (1985), The doctor game revisited: Doctor's treatment of their own children. *Internat. J. Psychoanal. Psychother.*, 10:505–524.

Mahler, M. S., Pine, F., & Bergman, A. (1975), *The Psychological Birth of the Human Infant*. New York: Basic Books.

Menninger, K. A. (1970), The crime of punishment. *Internat. J. Psychiat.*, 9:541–564.

Rangell, L. (1967), The metapsychology of trauma. In: *Psychic Trauma*, ed. S. S. Furst. New York: Basic Books, pp. 51–84.

——— (1970), The return of the repressed "Oedipus." In: *Parenthood*, ed. E. J. Anthony & T. Benedek. Boston: Little, Brown, pp. 325–336.

——— (1974), A psychoanalytic perspective leading currently to the syndrome of the compromise of integrity. *Internat. J. Psycho-Anal.*, 55:3–12.

Shengold, L. (1979), Child abuse and deprivation: Soul murder. *J. Amer. Psychoanal. Assn.*, 27:533–560.

Steele, B. (1970), Parental abuse of infants and small children. In: *Parenthood*, ed. E. J. Anthony & T. Benedek. Boston: Little, Brown, pp. 449–478.

10

AUTOHYPNOSIS AND SOUL MURDER: HYPNOTIC EVASION, AUTOHYPNOTIC VIGILANCE, AND HYPNOTIC FACILITATION

LEONARD SHENGOLD, M.D.

Leo Rangell in his recent work has been integrating and adding perspective and content to his earlier papers. One favorite theme that he has repeatedly emphasized is the importance of decision making (1969, 1971, 1987)—of choice operating at all levels of consciousness. One of the achievements of a successful analysis in his view would be that "Decision making, at an unconscious and derivatively derived preconscious-conscious levels, becomes less encumbered or even freed from neurotic inhibitory influences by the changes which have taken place within the intrapsychic process" (Rangell, 1987, p. 244). The freeing up of the power to decide is part of "an increased executive functioning of the ego over the entire scope of the patient's trial intrapsychic actions" (p. 245).

This chapter is about autohypnosis—an important and sometimes unacknowledged kind of "neurotic inhibiting influence" which adversely influences the freedom of operation of what Rangell (1987) calls the "core" of the intrapsychic processes. Autohypnosis specifically affects the power to make choices and decisions. It also is intricately involved with the functioning of another of Rangell's main recent concerns: the operation of the superego in conflicts centering around what he calls "the syndrome of the compromise of integrity" (Rangell, 1974, 1976, 1980). Autohypnosis inhibits the alertness of the ego, and thereby can evade the ego's and the superego's responsibility for what has happened, what is happening, and what can happen. No one can hold to a truth that has not been reliably registered. No one can resist properly or make an appropriate defensive choice about an impulse which is pretended away from, rationalized, and disowned. No one can make a decision on the basis of what has been experienced under the deceptive conditions of autohypnosis.

Psychoanalysis has dealt with alterations in consciousness and hypnosis from the beginning of its history as a cathartic technique that first featured the therapeutic use of hypnosis and developed from a theoretical basis that stressed "hypnoid states" (Breuer and Freud, 1893–1895). The occurrence of these specific kinds of altered states of consciousness[1] has never been in doubt, but psychoanalysts have not worked out an aesthetically and scientifically satisfactory integrated understanding of their nature.

Hypnosis can be defined as an artificially induced state resembling sleep and characterized by greatly increased suggestibility toward the hypnotizer. It can proceed to various depths, from superficial to deep. These "degrees" of hypnosis also characterize autohypnosis.

The analyst quickly becomes familiar with the phenomenon of hypnosis through hearing frequent requests from his patients to be hypnotized—a passive turning toward the parent figure-analyst that ranges from a longing for symbiotic merger to a desire for sexual submission in intercourse.

I am convinced from my work with patients that conditions of autohypnosis are part of ordinary mental functioning—part of the everyday range of states of consciousness between deep sleep and full, wide-awake alertness (Lewin, 1950, 1955). However, it seems sensible to view as pathological the overuse, prolonged intensity, or excessive duration of autohypnosis. It has been my observation that such pathological use of autohypnosis occurs regularly in those who have been subjected to what I have called *soul murder* (see Shengold, 1975, 1979).

Soul murder is a dramatic term for the deliberate attempt to

[1]I am not in this presentation going to attempt a much-needed classification and differentiation of different alterations of consciousness.

interfere with another person's separate identity and his capacity to experience joy and love. It is what happens where emotional deprivation, sexual abuse, physical and/or mental torture and brainwashing flourish—in actual or psychological concentration camps. Soul murder usually takes place in childhood, where the child's initial, almost complete dependence on the adult makes for the easy possibility of tyranny—a tyranny that can involve a regimen of seduction and torment, frequently alternating with indifference and neglect. Soul murder is a crime most often committed by a psychotic or psychopathic parent; almost always the soul murderer has also been abused and deprived in childhood and is operating under a compulsion to repeat his or her own traumatic past. The child-victim desperately needs to be rescued, yet usually can turn only to the very parent who does the seducing and tormenting for deliverance. This makes for an overwhelming need to experience the bad (and sometimes horribly bad) aspects of the parent as good; to achieve this necessary delusion, brainwashing and denial are required. This has been powerfully depicted in fiction by George Orwell in *1984*, which ends with the soul-murdered Winston Smith "loving" the "Big Brother" who has destroyed his humanity. The denial and the brainwashing are partly accomplished by the use of hypnosis and autohypnosis. Autohypnosis is specifically described as part of the denial-fostering mode of thought and language that Orwell calls "doublethink" (1949, p. 17).

Freud expanded Bernheim's theory that hypnotic phenomena are based on the universal susceptibility to suggestion. For Freud (1921) suggestibility is fundamentally the transference of an infantile sexual tie to the parent onto the hypnotist. Ferenczi had been the first to hypothecate this; in 1909 he stressed the transference of very early erotic, *masochistic* drives and feelings directed toward the parent. Transference is obvious in an act of hypnosis performed by a hypnotist on a subject. It is present but hidden in what appears to be "spontaneous" *auto*hypnosis.

Freud believed in a phylogenetic origin for the tendency to be hypnotized. The hypnotist's technique evokes in the subject a predisposition toward compliance to the parent which has survived in the unconscious from the early history of the human family. This archaic subservience toward the primal father is revived in the course of the individual's development. What is reawakened is "the idea of a paramount and dangerous personality, towards whom only a passive-masochistic attitude is possible, to whom one's will has to be surrendered" (Freud, 1921, p. 127).

Fliess (1953) observed that the hypnotist by his technique of manual "passes" and verbal suggestions arouses the subject's erogeneity to effect the use of this sexual excitement for the establishment of a particular kind of transference—a transference that precipitates an identification. This is enhanced by the repeated suggestion to "go to sleep" delivered by the hypnotist in an authoritative but somnolent tone; he himself sounds as if he were going to sleep. Freud formulates that the hypnotized person identifies by incorporating the hypnotist and depositing him as part of his superego. With the exception of the tie with the hypnotist, all contact with the outside world is cut off, and the hypnotist who has taken over some of the functions of the superego can now abolish reality testing. In autohypnosis, of course, the continuing presence of the mental representation of the hypnotist as part of the superego can give rise to the same effect (denial) from within.

DEFENSIVENESS OR MENDACITY

Freud observed that there was something pretended and gamelike about hypnosis because its power is really based on the phylogenetic subjection to the primal father. Fliess (1953) added that the hypnotist's command to sleep is pretended—neither the hypnotist who sounds sleepy nor the subject really goes to sleep. This reflects for Fliess the dangerous deceptivity of the primal parent. Freud (1921) felt that "Some knowledge that in spite of everything hypnosis is only a game, a deceptive renewal of these old [primal horde] impressions, may, however, remain behind and take care that there is a resistance against any too serious consequences of the suspension of the will in hypnosis" (p. 127). It has been frequently noticed that these resistances to morally offensive, hypnotic suggestions occur despite complete suggestive compliance in other respects; here, then, the "game" has a benevolent effect on the self-protective power of the conscience.

In contrast, for those who have experienced effective soul murder, the encounter with the primal parent/Sphinx (Shengold, 1963) has resulted in an identification of such *continuing* power that the moral resistance of the conscience has been severely compromised. For them, the gamelike or pretense quality of hypnosis has acquired a preponderantly malignant and destructive (i.e., *dangerously* deceptive) rather than a saving effect; all the more dangerous because for many of the formerly abused victims the universal transient tendency to autohypnosis has become compulsive: a chronic defensive necessity.

Lewin (1955) depicts psychoanalysis as inherently linked to suggestion and hypnosis: "*Genetically*, the analytic situation is an altered hypnotic situation, as the analytic hour is an altered hypnotic session" (p. 169; my italics). He enjoins us to be aware of "the ratio between sleep and waking in the analytic patient" (p. 198). He portrays the analyst as the waker or arouser, who sometimes also soothes (i.e., puts the analysand to sleep a little). Fliess (1953) describes the subtlety of the *autohypnotic* phenomena that occur in analysis. The analysand, instead of associating freely, can escape into a first degree of hypnosis that can go unnoticed by both patient and analyst. This makes for a kind of contact that precludes responsibility for what is said and felt; it amounts, says Fliess, to "hypnotic evasion."

Kris (1952) has made us familiar with the concept of regression in the service of the ego. A regressive shift away from full, clear consciousness can principally serve either the ego's need to defend against or its need to further the discharge of drive tensions. (An example of the latter would be the approach to a loss of consciousness at the moment of orgasm.) In performing either a primarily defensive or a primarily releasing function, shifts in states of consciousness are carrying out the basic psychic tasks we assign to the ego—the mediation between the drive representations of the id and the external world, the screening out and the letting through of instinctual drive representations. Fliess (1953) and Dickes (1965) stress the defensive use of autohypnosis against libidinal and aggressive impulse (Fliess's *hypnotic evasion*).

In a 1967 paper I noted autohypnotic phenomena that transcended the defensive function and used the term *hypnotic facilitation*. Gill and Brenman (1959) mention "the appearance of vivid and intense outbursts of feeling" (p. 48) occurring during hypnosis and describe it as a frequently noted phenomenon. I will not try to bring up to date Dickes's excellent review (1965) of the literature on shifts of consciousness.

My clinical material is from victims of soul murder, those who have been seduced and abused as children.

AUTOHYPNOTIC VIGILANCE[2]

A young woman, L., who had been seduced by an adult man as a child of five, was subject to repetitive, contradictory, symptomatic states that involved alterations of consciousness. During these periods of perceptible autohypnosis, there was a simultaneous shutting off of emotion and perception and a hypersensitive searching for and awareness of certain signals that meant to her the possible reliving of a trauma from childhood. She could be at the same moment both blocking out and hyperaware of inner and/or outer reality. Sometimes this manifested itself in her insisting on the figure while ignoring the ground; sometimes by being overconcerned with the surroundings but neglecting the central meaningful event. There were a number of confusing and contradictory combinations of impulse and defense against impulse that involved simultaneous awareness and denial of the significance of the same events. She was therefore both an expert witness, even a sensitive detective preternaturally alert to clues, and a completely unreliable observer. Her predominantly good character included transient paranoid suspiciousness, and masochistic, guilt-ridden self-doubt. Sometimes simultaneously and sometimes alternatively she played the roles of Cassandra and of that unfortunate lady's disbelieving audience.

L. reported one day that she had left the previous analytic

[2]This section is a longer version of a brief communication that appeared under this title in 1978.

session feeling "sleepy and out of things." She had been in a characteristic hypnoid state:

> I didn't even know how to open the door or whether to leave it open; it was as if I weren't quite there, and I had no awareness of you or of leaving your office. And yet when I went out into the waiting room, I heard the sound of a man urinating from the bathroom. I am sure it was a man—from the sound. And before that, as I was closing the door, you had a phone call and I heard the change in your voice. You weren't talking to a patient, but to someone you didn't want to hear from.

The patient was, as usual, right. I was by this time familiar with her not knowing what was going on and a concurrent uncanny accuracy about perceptual details. The patient who had succeeded her on the previous day had been a man; he reported that he had urinated before coming into his session. Just as L. was closing the door to my office, I had received a telephone call from an insurance salesman, and although the young woman could only have heard me say "hello" and "no," I had *not* welcomed the call. Despite the patient's alteration of consciousness, her perceptions had been accurate and had registered almost instantaneously.

As a child of five, she had been seduced to perform fellatio after she had opened a bathroom door on a man who was urinating. His anger at the intruder ("someone you didn't want to hear from") turned to sexual excitement, and he started to masturbate. The girl especially remembered the sound of his excited breathing. She was "fascinated—as if hypnotized" by this exhibition and was easily induced to suck on his penis. When she first reported this incident, she had not yet remembered the terrifying overstimulation and shock that ended this initially tolerable and even pleasurable contact. Despite the terror, the sexual encounter was repeated several times. The man was a relative, a father-substitute who lived for a time in the large family house; part of his duty was looking after the children.

In later life L.'s autohypnosis blocked the sexual excitement that could have resulted from perceptions unconsciously linked to the memory of the earlier seductions. At the same time the hypnosis was compatible with, and perhaps even enhanced, a concentrated hypercathexis of perceptory signals—i.e., there was a *hypnotic vigilance*. She often listened intently for sounds of the analyst's breathing and was aware of nuances of change. These would evoke a "sleepy feeling," or an increase of it if it were already present, and she would often say something like, "I am aware of the breathing, but now it's almost as if you aren't even there."

I believe this is an instance of a not uncommon symptomatic state—simultaneous hypnotic evasion and what I call hypnotic facilitation. The alteration of consciousness as she left the session served both to ward off and to repeat the past (Fliess, 1953; Dickes, 1965; Shengold, 1967). The hypercathected listening and watchfulness also functioned both for defense against and for discharge of derivatives of instinctual drive (e.g., voyeuristic excitement). To be seduced while she was hypnotized meant that she was passive and therefore not responsible for what had happened and what was happening. (Like all soul murder victims, she had to spare the aggressor and take on the guilt for the seductions; this had in time become the mainstay of her masochistic character.) The excited beginning of the seduction was easier to repeat than was the subsequent terror, overstimulation, and rage. Ultimately, it was the overwhelming fear associated with her rage—a rage that could reach the pitch of wanting to bite and kill—that was evaded by the hypnosis. The analysis clearly brought out the evolution of the wish to suck the penis into the wish to bite it off—castration by biting followed by the expectation of terrible retaliation. (There was an even deeper fear of the sheer annihilative intensity of her rage, a more primal reaction to overstimulation.) The alteration in consciousness also served to keep the incestuous object of her feelings (the fantasied parent in the guise of the actual seducer) out of conscious awareness. There was a compulsion to repeat the past traumatic events, and the expectation of repetition made for a characteristic alertness to signals (for L., especially auditory signals) as part of a generalized watchfulness that was compatible with autohypnosis.

I have frequently found *hypnotic facilitation* part of the significance of autohypnotic phenomena. Hypnosis allows for the attainment of a forbidden satisfaction without responsibility for it.

The latter is at least the conscious intention. This is marvelously illustrated in a short story by Balzac, one of the *Contes Drolatiques, The Venial Sin,* in which a boy is seduced by a woman who pretends she is asleep. I will return to this story.

HYPNOTIC FACILITATION: PATIENT M.

The Balzac story was mentioned to me by my patient, M., who in the course of his analysis recognized something of himself in it. M., although in his 30s, still lived with his seductive and psychotic mother, who did everything she could to keep her son from moving out. During the analysis he remembered that as a child he had been seduced by his mother in a variety of bizarre ways, which included her playing with and sucking on his penis but usually centered around her manual invasion of his anus, frequently in connection with extended enema rituals. He simultaneously identified with his mother and was tied to her as a sexual object—in disguised fantasy. His sexual experiences, casual and joyless, were exclusively with women. His masturbatory fantasies were sometimes homosexual and sometimes heterosexual. (This involved being and having his mother; of course he was not initially conscious of this.) But his masturbation usually could culminate in orgasm only if he lapsed into an altered state of awareness that strongly resembled the first stage of hypnosis. (The alteration was clearly pathological since it reduced the pleasure of his climax.) It was many (seemingly unproductive) years into the analysis by the time he acknowledged the autohypnotic states. The patient (unlike most of the soul murder victims I have seen) had been quite aware of them and accused himself of "deceptiveness" for not telling his analyst about them before. Indeed, he went on to describe the masturbation performed under autohypnosis as also full of:

> . . . fraudulence. It involves pretending that it is happening to me rather than that I am doing it to myself. [He was *actively* reproducing predominantly *passive* past traumatic experiences.] And when I do it I feel *half asleep* [these are the same words used by

> Shakespeare's Desdemona, see below], so in effect I have no responsibility for it, I feel in a fog about the whole thing.
>
> [The pleasure of his orgasm when "half asleep" was compromised:] It's not satisfactory because it is done under a ruse—it's too sudden and too short and I feel immediately discontented with it. It's different from the fuller feeling I get when I'm fully awake and know that I am masturbating.

Here hypnotic envasion and facilitation coexisted, and the sexual discharge that related to forbidden impulses was allowed to occur but in a compromised way.

In the middle phase of his analysis, M. had become involved with intense sexual feelings about his analyst, feelings that were transferred mainly from the psychotic "phallic" mother of his childhood whose contacts he was remembering. These feelings were being worked out as he was also acknowledging first the existence and then the extent of his autohypnosis. He discovered that the full feeling of erogeneity could abolish the hypnosis:

> Last night I was standing near a kiosk. Why did I use that foreign term—I think it's *French*—for a newsstand? I became aware I was in hypnosis and I was staring at a TV magazine with a picture of a good-looking doctor from a soap opera on the cover. The headline said, "Everybody's *Son* the Doctor." I realized the sexual excitement about him. I got an erection and that snapped me out of the hypnosis [my italics].

His fantasy was of fellatio (in slang, "French" sex—actually both the French word "kiosque" and the English "kiosk" are derived from a Turkish word, and Turkey was associated with his mother's family) directed at his own doctor-parent, but he was simultaneously in fantasy being the parent fellating the "Son."

During this period M. had a dream. He started the session:

> I feel sleepy. As I was coming in I thought, if I'm sleepy, I can't get sexually excited. I had an orgasm last night, but I guess I'm still in heat because all week I have tried not to masturbate. When I went to bed last night, I felt hypnotic [M. had by now adopted the analyst's term]. I had the thought, "If I'm half asleep, I'm not responsible." So I started to masturbate, but didn't finish. I remember hoping that a wet dream would finish it off for me. Then,

> after the dream, which wasn't a wet one, I did masturbate when I was still half asleep. I woke from the dream with an erection. Here's the dream:
>
> I was to be analyzed with a different analyst. There was a couch or a stretcher. [He had on the previous day visited a relative who had been hospitalized after suffering some rectal bleeding; he had found him in a hallway lying on a stretcher.] The analysis was to take place in the open air. I had the thought, "This is like being analyzed by a friend." I then woke with an erection.
>
> [He associated:] I don't really want another analyst, but I don't want to have these sexual feelings about you. "The open air"—it reminds me of what I told you about masturbating "against the air."

M. had an unusual masturbatory practice involving trying to have an ejaculation without using his hands, lying on his back, moving his penis up and down, as he put it, "against the air." (A variation was moving his pelvis and penis up against a sheet or blanket ["material" symbolizing mother].) These experiences, which never did culminate in ejaculation without his resorting finally to manipulation, involved movements of his hips and buttocks, which induced anal feelings and excitement. There was frequently also the conscious fantasy of visualizing a woman's body, especially her behind. The seductive "air" represented the active partner who was to bring the passive patient (identified with the woman and with her cloacal parts) to climax. He associated to the "open air" as being connected with "being blown" (the mother had performed fellatio on him in childhood). The phantomlike invisible "airy" presence was also a kind of denial of this past reality. These masturbatory experiences reproduced a teasing, overstimulating sexual contact evoking phallic but especially anal excitement—a repetition of the incestuous contact from childhood when he could not ejaculate and satisfactorily discharge the anal and genital overexcitement. As an adult, the increasing unpleasure of the overstimulation would finally make manual stimulation mandatory and the resultant orgasm would "break" the fantasy; he could then "wake up." The orgasm was a relief, but always a disappointment.

At the beginning of the session, it was chiefly M's passive anal excitement—his wish to be the person with the bloody anus on a stretcher—that he was evading. Perhaps even more distant was the murderous rage at the enforced passivity; this rage was associated with the wish to get rid of the analyst. In the course of his associations he talked of having pictured before the dream "a kind of prostitute I once picked up. I had intercourse with her, but it was unsatisfactory. I was left with the vivid image of her lifting up her knees onto her chest. I was revolted and disgusted by the sight of her anus and the dirtiness around it, a brown discolored area. I never wanted to see her again."

He then told me that for the past few months he had worn pajamas to bed instead of his dirty and usually slightly fecal-stained underwear. The slight staining was due to "continuous sweating" around his anus, which he attributed in part to the (unconsciously defensive) habitual, periodic "steeling" of his perineal muscles and their relaxation in between. This unconscious anal play (which resembled the perianal movements in his masturbating "against the air") made for a rather constant need to evade the concomitant anal erogenous involvement, and this defensive requirement seemed to go along with the almost continuous intensity of his autohypnosis. For M. the hypnotic evasion also seemed to be a chief mechanism for his impressive characteristic and *anal* (Shengold, 1988) defensive ability to isolate his emotions, including rage and vague paranoid feelings as well as his responsibility for his actions.

Several days before the dream his apartment had been robbed (his "room" entered, an anal invasion). When going out to his analysis, he had left his keys in his mailbox, thereby denoting the apartment to which the keys belonged. Also, he had left behind his wallet, full of recently counted bills, on the table in his room "in open view" (symbolically his anus and rectum "in the open air"). M. realized that he had invited the theft. During the session in which he recounted his dream of "open-air" analysis, he suddenly interjected, "Now I realize that I was in hypnosis when I left my keys in my mailbox." The analyst was the one he had unconsciously invited to penetrate his "room," and M. was unwittingly acting out the role of the dirty "anal" prostitute. (The roles were reversible, it was he who paid the analyst.) His "hypnoid state" had facilitated the theft but defended him against the body feelings and emotions associated with what he was reenacting.

It was also during this period of the analysis that he told me about the Balzac story which he found particularly exciting and had often read while masturbating. Although the story is about what is described as a simulation of sleep ("deceptiveness") and not necessarily about a true hypnotic state, it illustrates the symptomatic nature of alterations of consciousness which range from mild hypnosis to deep sleep. (My patient had not been responsibly aware that this story of the seduction of a boy by an older woman represented a repetition of his own past.)

"THE VENIAL SIN"

In Balzac's tale, a young woman, Blanche, virginal and knowing nothing about sex, is married to an impotent old man. When she realizes that he cannot father a child, she consults her confessor; he tells her the story of Ste. Lidoire, who

> . . . went to sleep terribly soundly one very hot day with one leg here and the other there and very little on and a young man full of evil came up and very slyly filled her with child and as the saint was utterly ignorant that this wicked thing had been done to her she was very surprised indeed after some time to have to take to childbed. She had thought the swelling of her pouch must be some serious ailment. Now, Ste. Lidoire did penance as for a mere venial sin, since she had had no pleasure from the wicked act, as the evil man himself bore out, for at the gallows when the noose was round his neck, he declared that the saint never even budged.
>
> "Oh, Father," said Blanche, "you may be sure I shall not budge any more than Ste. Lidoire did" [pp. 53–54].

Blanche decides to seduce a young page of fourteen. She does this by pretending to be asleep as he reads to her, sitting at her feet and looking up at her lap. After much hesitation—she finds it necessary to say to him with her eyes closed, "Go on René . . . I am asleep, you know" (p. 59)—the page realizes her intention, and

> . . . that very same evening . . . [René the page] went seeking and, finding Blanche asleep, forthwith made her dreams very lovely ones. So thoroughly indeed did he ravish that which agonized her, and with such good husbandry did he sow his baby seed that there was really enough left over to have made a couple more, when suddenly the dear woman squeezed her page by the head, crushed him to her, and cried: "Oh, René, you woke me up!"
>
> True enough, no sleep could have survived that onslaught, and Blanche and René together concluded that the saints must sleep very soundly indeed [1832, p. 59].

(Blanche experienced a kind of healthy erotic hyperawareness that is in contrast to the defensive and punitive dimming of pleasure of M. and qualitatively different from the defensive vigilance of my patient L.) The mendaciousness inherent to the hypnotic state—mendaciousness is a characteristic of the primal parent (Fliess, 1956)—is present in the Balzac story. The young woman, an adult, blames the "sin" on the fourteen-year-old page (child); *she* was "asleep": "Come now, René! Do you realize that while I have only committed venial sins, because I was asleep, you have got mortal sins on your conscience?" (p. 60).

Despite the sunny Rabelaisian comic tone, the soul murderer's shifting of guilt onto the child is clearly evoked here. In the story, the defensive *hypnotic evasion* is the predominant motivation; but the alleged shift in consciousness is used to facilitate the "discharge of libido." When Blanche's old husband refuses to believe that "the page could get in [your hole] without waking you," she replies: "Of course I felt it, and nicely too, but, you see, as you never taught me what it was, I thought I was only dreaming" (p. 63).

A CONTRASTING EXAMPLE

Freud wrote to Fliess about a story told to him which seems to involve a true hypnotic state:

> An important and wealthy man (a bank director), aged about sixty, came to see me and entertained me with the peculiarities of a girl with whom he has a *liaison*. I threw out the guess that she was probably quite anaesthetic. On the contrary, she has from four to six orgasms during a single coitus. *But—at the very first approach she is seized with a tremor and immediately afterwards falls into a pathological sleep; while she is in this she talks as though she was in hypnosis, carries out post-hypnotic suggestions and has complete amnesia for the whole condition*. He is going to marry her off, and she will certainly be anaesthetic with her husband. The old gentleman, through the possibility of being identified with the immensely powerful father of her childhood, evidently has the effect of being able to set free the libido attached to her phantasies. Instructive! [1950, pp. 277–278; my italics].

The libido was "set free" and the multiple orgasms achieved only with use of the simultaneously defensive and facilitating state of "hypnosis."

PATIENT L. CONTINUED: A CLINICAL EXAMPLE OF DEFENSIVE AND FACILITATING AUTOHYPNOSIS

Once L. (the vigilant hypnotic) had, unusually for her, failed to pay her bill at the end of the month. Then the analyst had to cancel several sessions without prior notice because of illness, a most unusual occurrence in the analysis. When the analysis was resumed, L. came into the office and, instead of, as usual, tentatively and rather passively putting, almost dropping, the check into his hand, she thrust it out at him aggressively. On the couch, she began:

> I felt like shoving the money at you, and yet I was so glad to see you. I was worried when your phone service called [another unexpected and unwelcome telephone call] to say you were not going to be here. I thought either you were sick or *someone had died* [my emphasis]. But you looked so nice at the door; you looked like you had just had a haircut, like a little child all dressed up for his birthday. It made me feel good to see you.
>
> [Analyst:] You felt good *and bad* to see me.

Why did you say that? I only had good feelings toward you [long silence]. Where did you get the bad feelings from?

[Analyst:] What about your "shoving the money at me"?

Oh, as I was listening to you just now I felt as if I were falling asleep [my emphasis]. And at first I didn't know what you were talking about. I forgot that I had said that to you. How strange!

[Analyst:] It does seem strange that you have to go to sleep to keep from hearing me repeat what you were able to say to me seemingly with full awareness.

Well, what *I* say isn't so meaningful; when you say it, it counts.

This patient was characteristically most threatened by her (oral and anal) destructive impulses and their resultant "bad" feelings. In thrusting the money at the analyst, she was reversing her passivity in relation to the man from her childhood who had thrust his erect penis out for her to suck. The incident from the past was connected with a destructive fury that terrified her; such fury could castrate and kill, and this proved to be what most demanded hypnotic defense—feeling "as if I were falling asleep."[3] The anger was suppressed, the positive side of her ambivalence is stressed, the analyst looks "so nice." This idealization is the reactive disguise for a devaluation—the analyst is reduced to a birthday child with a haircut (presumably the younger brother whose birth displaced her as the family's center of attention; she had wanted more than his hair cut off). When the analyst underlines her "bad" aggressive feelings, she greets this with an isolating silence. When he reminds her of her aggressive "thrusting" action, she resorts to hypnosis to cancel out both the responsibility

[3]Dickes (1965) pointed out a similar instance of hypnosis-called-sleep in Shakespeare's *Othello*. Desdemona is reacting to the devastating verbal (oral) attack of the half-crazed, jealous Othello which culminates with his ironic:

I cry you mercy then:
I took you for that cunning whore of Venice
That married with Othello [V, ii, 88–89].

When Othello leaves, and Emilia asks Desdemona, "How do you, my good lady?" she replies, "*Faith, half asleep*" (my italics; see Patient M.). (The "Faith" shows the denial of the betrayal involved.) Here the "half-asleep" screens out the oral rage of the black man (the father in the dark), primarily in an attempt to deny what had just happened; secondarily, it dilutes Desdemona's own *reactive* rage. For my patient, getting away from her own potentially murderous anger ("someone had died") seemed to be the main motive for the autohypnosis she attributed to the analyst—who had previously handed her the bill, invaded her by the telephone call (an oral-aural penetration), and betrayed her by disappearing.

for the impulse and (especially) the potential for experiencing in feeling the terrible intensities involved. Finally, she gives a wise explanation for the analyst's repetition of her words affecting her more than her initial confession of the "shoving" impulse. (She is not aware that the repeating is an erotic "rubbing.") She has made the analyst responsible for what she feels and what she says; his verbal repetition is an oral invasive thrust (like the phone call and the interpretations); these invasions evoke the past trauma, and must be evaded by autohypnosis. And simultaneously, the hypnosis furnishes an *absence* (a blank space also supplied by her protracted silence), which could facilitate a repetition of the sexual assault of the past. After the session she realized, and subsequently reported, that she had wanted to suck the analyst's penis when she first saw him at the door. That she also wanted to bite and swallow it took much more analysis to become responsibly conscious, to be "owned" by her.

Autohypnosis in both its defensive and facilitating effects works in the service of denial: what is allowed to happen, or what has happened, does not count. (The relevance of this to what Rangell calls the compromise of integrity is obvious.[4]) Autohypnosis is regularly employed by the soul murder victim to spare the soul murderer and to repeat the childhood trauma, directly and in attenuation. Since autohypnosis is often there without the patient's awareness, it must be anticipated and looked for by the therapist. The inherent concomitant evasion of responsibility for what is being said, thought, and felt makes autohypnosis a formidable, even—if not recognized—a potentially insurmountable, resistance to analysis in any patient. Autohypnosis affects the reality testing of both the ego and the superego (Weinshel, 1986). Where hypnotic alterations of consciousness exist to an extensive degree, this should alert the observer to the possibility that they are the result of the actual occurrence of brainwashing—or, in Orwell's terms, of enforced *doublethink*.[5] Often the original trau-

[4]Rangell (1974) views "syndromes resulting from the compromise of integrity [as] *endogenous to human life* . . . as diffuse in behaviour and their ingredients, as *ubiquitous* in unconscious mentation as are the ingredients which will result in neurosis" (p. 7; my italics). I believe one of the endogenous, ubiquitous ingredients that supplies part of the mechanism for the "syndrome" is autohypnosis.

[5]Also compare Rangell's (1974) description of the compromise of identity: "a combined mechanism of distortion, denial, rationalization, *deception* of the self and others [which] bridges across [the] unconscious/preconscious and conscious" (p. 9; my italics).

mata took place under conditions involving autohypnosis; then the altered state returns with the compulsion to repeat. Autohypnosis can operate as part of the mechanism for the isolating, mind-splitting defenses involved in what we psychoanalysts call *denial*—the nonregistration or blanking out of what is happening and what has happened. Where *doublethink* and autohypnosis flourish, soul murder should be thought of. When one comes across the compromise of integrity in private or public life (Rangell, 1980), autohypnosis should be thought of.

REFERENCES

Balzac, H. (1832), *Droll Stories*, Vol. 1. London: Elek Books, 1958.

Breuer, J., & Freud, S. (1893–1895), Studies on Hysteria. *Standard Edition*, 2. London: Hogarth Press, 1962.

Dickes, R. (1965), The defensive function of an altered state of consciousness. A hypnoid state. *J. Amer. Psychoanal. Assn.*, 13:365–403.

Ferenczi, S. (1909), Introjection and transference. In: *Contributions to Psychoanalysis*. New York: Basic Books, 1950, pp. 35–93.

Fliess, R. (1953), The hypnotic evasion: A clinical observation. *Psychoanal. Quart.*, 22:497–511.

——— (1956), *Erogeneity and Libido*. New York: International Universities Press.

Freud, S. (1921), Group psychology and the analysis of the ego. *Standard Edition*, 18:67–143. London: Hogarth Press, 1962.

——— (1950), Extracts from the Fliess papers. *Standard Edition*, 1:175–343. London: Hogarth Press, 1966.

Gill, M. M., & Brenman, M. (1959), *On Hypnosis*. New York: International Universities Press.

Kris, E. (1952), *Psychoanalytic Explorations in Art*. New York: International Universities Press.

Lewin, B. D. (1950), *The Psychoanalysis of Elation*. New York: Norton.

——— (1955), Dream psychology and the analytic situation. *Psychoanal. Quart.*, 24:169–199.

Orwell, G. (1949), *1984*, ed. I. Howe. New York: Harcourt, Brace & World, 1963.

Rangell, L. (1969), The intrapsychic process and its analysis. *Internat. J. Psycho-Anal.*, 50:65–77.

——— (1971), The decision-making process. *The Psychoanalytic Study of the Child*, 26:425–452. New York: Quadrangle.

——— (1974), A psychoanalytic perspective leading currently to the syndrome of the compromise of integrity. *Internat. J. Psycho-Anal.*, 55:3–12.

——— (1976), Lessons from Watergate: A derivation for psychoanalysis. *Psychoanal. Quart.*, 45:37–61.

——— (1980), *The Mind of Watergate: An Exploration of the Compromise of Integrity*. New York: Norton.

——— (1987), A core process in psychoanalytic treatment. *Psychoanal. Quart.*, 56:222–249.

Shengold, L. (1963), The parent as sphinx. *J. Amer. Psychoanal. Assn.*, 11:725–751.

——— (1967), The effects of overstimulation: Rat people. *Internat. J. Psycho-Anal.*, 48:403–415.

——— (1975), An attempt at soul murder. *The Psychoanalytic Study of the Child*, 30:683–724. New Haven, CT: Yale University Press.

——— (1976), Autohypnotic watchfulness. *Psychoanal. Quart.*, 47:113–115.

——— (1979), Child abuse and deprivation. *J. Amer. Psychoanal. Assn.*, 27:533–559.

——— (1988), *The Halo in the Sky*. New York: Guilford Press.

Weinshel, E. (1986), Perceptual distortions during analysis. In: *Psychoanalysis: The Science of Mental Conflict*, ed. A. Richards & M. Willick. Hillsdale, NJ: Analytic Press, pp. 353–374.

11

THINKING AND THE SUPEREGO: SOME INTERRELATIONS

JANINE CHASSEGUET-SMIRGEL, Ph.D.

Many of my American colleagues give preference to ego psychology with which I am not very familiar. Yet I believe that Leo Rangell, who is so attentive both in his writings and his personal attitude to everything that has a bearing on human ethics, could well be interested in my little essay on the superego. I am particularly thinking of his writings on Watergate (1974, 1976, 1980). I hope that the interest we both share in what Freud (1933) has called "the higher side of human life" will reduce the distance separating the eastern shore of the Atlantic from the Pacific West Coast, and that the feelings of friendship and admiration I bear him will do the rest.

It seems to me that where the superego is concerned, there is much misunderstanding among the general public and even among psychoanalysts. Its existence in the mind is quite commonly regarded as an impediment and nothing more, as proof (when the subject has been analyzed) of an unsuccessful analysis. It is considered as a *conservative* element in comparison to the progressivism of a personality where this supererogatory agency, the effect of which is to inhibit the mind, no longer holds sway. Without the superego, without this useless anchor, the mind would navigate the seas—or better, float into infinite space like a balloon freed of its ballast.

Yet the ability to feel guilt is part of "normality." The problem lies in the inability to feel guilt, the need to project guilt, to be persecuted by it; the need to deny, to split, and to erotize it. The fact that this is not in line with the *Zeitgeist* should prompt us to question current ideology, put us on the alert, not cause us to give in to the current trend.

Freud never considered the superego as destined to disappear. Rather we need to amend its excessive severity, the result of "infantilisms" (1937, p. 237) originating in fixation or regression, and also excessive damming up of aggression that is turned back upon the ego (1930). But surely the aggression turned inward against the ego is itself linked to the "infantilisms" that prevent the ego from discharging what it considers are guilty drives, since:

> . . . repressions take place in early childhood; they are primitive defensive measures taken by the immature, feeble ego. . . . Analysis, however, enables the ego, which has attained greater maturity and strength, to undertake a revision of these old repressions; a few are demolished, while others are recognized but constructed afresh out of more solid material. These new dams are of quite a different degree of firmness from the earlier ones; we may be confident that they will not give way so easily before a rising flood of instinctual strength [Freud, 1937, p. 227].

It is difficult to imagine how the revision of these repressions, the distinction between those that are to be kept, even consolidated, and those that are to be discarded, could take place without the activity of the superego, freed in turn of its anachronisms. Even when Rangell (1986) considers that most attributes of the superego are to become ego functions, he by no means abolishes these, but simply infers an extension of ego control. What grounds are there for ever imagining that the aim of a psychoanalysis should be to abolish the moral agency—it is in fact a question of revising it—when Freud (1933) humorously and somewhat bitterly remarks:

> Following a well-known pronouncement of Kant's which couples the conscience within us with the starry Heavens, a pious man might well be tempted to honour these two things as the masterpieces of creation. The stars are indeed magnificent, but as regards conscience God has done an uneven and careless piece of work,

> for a large majority of men have brought along with them only a modest amount of it or scarcely enough to be worth mentioning [p. 61].

Freud goes on to say that the "super-ego is the representative for us of every moral restriction, the advocate of a striving towards perfection—it is, in short, as much as we have been able to grasp psychologically of what is described as the higher side of human life" (p. 66). The idea that Freud and the psychoanalysts coming after him could set out simply to abolish "the higher side of human life" seems inconceivable.

It is important to remember that although Freud speaks in this and in other texts of the severity, the "harshness," of the superego, he has already referred to the possible insufficiency of the superego, for instance, in *Civilization and Its Discontents* (1930). The impression one gets is that the general public, and certain analysts and others on the periphery of psychoanalysis who have joined with the crowd, wish only to see the superego as a sadistic agency that ill-treats the subject and also the world at large, a sort of warder in boots, wielding a whip and yelling, "Schnell, raus" at innocent victims. Sadism and destructivity directed at others can go under the disguise of the superego, it is true, and this presents us with an enormous problem. But in such cases, are we really dealing with the moral agency? Is it not something quite different? The Devil in monk's clothes remains the Devil all the same. It is a fact that patients suffer from feelings of guilt, inhibition, and anxiety related to anachronistic taboos. Such patients generally fall into the category of neurosis. (I am excluding melancholia. Although Freud's study of the subject leads him to discover an agency that opposes the ego, it is far from certain today that this agency is the superego. Is it not primarily of a narcissistic nature? In addition, a solid superego is of precious help where an ego ideal strives to attain an impossible perfection. Francis Pasche [1961] points out that certain superego manifestations of the depressed patient are conducive to its regaining self-esteem. "Culpable, therefore capable," as he puts it.)

On the other hand, we find in contemporary clinical practice that our most serious cases, those of certain borderline patients in particular, concern disorders of moral conscience, accompanied by thought disorders. The temptation is to connect the two. This is what I shall try to do, essentially on the basis of clinical examples, though I am afraid that for reasons of space I shall have to limit my remarks to the study of a particular mechanism that aims at disqualification of the superego.

THE DISQUALIFIED SUPEREGO

I should like to describe more fully the case of a patient about whom I have already written (1988b). For a long time I considered Libya, about 45 years old, a case of phobic hysteria, despite the many dramatic events in her life, both before and during analysis, that should have alerted me to the structure of her superego and her psychic organization in general. In addition, her relationship with me took on a very special coloring. Before long, she had decided she had to take care of her teeth, choosing to go to the School of Dentistry where students learning their trade at her expense made her life miserable. At the same time she was in the habit of whispering in a way that made it impossible for me to hear what she was saying. One day I remarked on the painful dental treatment she was inflicting on herself and linked this to her inhibition when it came to using tongue and teeth in our sessions. She replied that it had been the same in her previous analysis and told me that her analyst had once said, "For six months now I've not understood a word of what you've been saying." This intervention on the part of a colleague whom I respect for his kindness and patience struck me as most unusual. But even then my own smouldering irritation did not put me on the track. I understood her dental martyrdom (under the pretext that she could not afford high dentist fees) as self-punishment for the aggressive and erotic wishes of an oral nature or expressed as oral presentations that are characteristically found in hysteria, this being more plausible since her hysteria, which was in fact a "cover," justified such an understanding of her behavior.

Soon her whole life was transformed into a series of misfortunes. Her husband was unfaithful, the father of her daughter's newborn baby was a drug addict, her son had taken to the bottle.

She was insulted at work and had even come to physical blows with a colleague. Some time prior to this she had been involved in a most unpleasant court case. She had helped an injured cyclist and had been accused of having been the one to cause the accident. In a restaurant she fell, hitting her head badly on the tiled floor. She had a car accident. Her past and present were filled with catastrophes, which, paradoxically, left me quite unmoved, tending instead to exasperate me. I frequently toyed with the fantasy of discontinuing the treatment, or of getting up in the middle of a session. I was sorry I was not a Lacanian. Five-minute sessions would have been ideal for my psychic comfort. But in the meantime I had understood. My patient was suffering from *moral masochism*, a syndrome which I, like my colleague Rosenberg (1982), cannot classify with the neuroses.

In discussing moral masochism, Freud (1924), we remember, said,

> . . . morality becomes resexualized once more, the Oedipus comples is revived and the way is opened for a regression from morality to the Oedipus complex. This is to the advantage neither of morality nor of the person concerned. An individual may, it is true, have preserved the whole or some measure of ethical sense alongside of his masochism; but, alternatively, a large part of his conscience may have vanished into his masochism. Again, masochism creates a temptation to perform 'sinful' actions, which must then be expiated by the reproaches of the sadistic conscience (as is exemplified in so many Russian character-types) or by chastisement from the great parental power of Destiny [p. 169].

It is clear that masochistic satisfaction is obtained at the expense of morality. The ego places itself in a position where it invites punishment at the hands of the superego, such punishment being administered by the various authorities in the social environment or by the analyst, who embodies the superego. At the same time the subject's constant provocative attacks lead to a sadistic discharge which puts great strain on the analyst's countertransference. *I would even propose that this sadistic discharge is part of the undertaking. The aim is not just to be punished by the reembodied and reexternalized superego, but to depreciate it, to deprive it of its abstract, independent, and sovereign character in order to disqualify it.*

The year before writing "The Economic Problem of Masochism" (1924) in which the negative therapeutic reaction is given as the first example of moral masochism, Freud (1923) stated that when faced with the negative therapeutic reaction, "One begins by regarding this as defiance and as an attempt to prove . . . superiority to the physician" (p. 49). Rather than interpret this desire to triumph over the physician as envy, I am more inclined to think that it is a matter of deriding the superego, of ridiculing it. In 1924, Freud shows that moral masochism implies resexualization between the superego and the ego, and regression in relation to the fully developed Oedipus complex that has engendered the independent and impersonal moral agency, this latter now being undermined by the ego's active pursuit of satisfaction. I, for my part, advance the hypothesis that the ultimate goal is to eliminate the superego, to expel it from the Heavens where Kant places it, to seduce it, to entice it into playing sexual games in the nursery—in a word, to debase and pervert it.

Rosenberg (1982) classes moral masochism in the category of the perversions, and rightly I believe (this is, of course, when it dominates a personality—no one is without some measure of moral masochism), opposing it to the *guilt* of the neurotic, though he does not speak of the seduction, the debasement of the superego with which I am concerned.

In my opinion, the subject does not regress to a sexual masochistic position in relation to the oedipal father, as Freud (1924) states, and as is also Rosenberg's view. I believe that he abolishes the father by turning him into a companion, making him an accomplice in his sexual fantasies (and this is true for both sexes). The father's unbearable claim *never to collude with the child,* to act as a barrier against incest, must be invalidated. In the case of men, the very manifest homosexual nature of these provocations aimed at the superego-father he is in the process of dethroning have the effect of depriving the father of his power to forbid where the mother is concerned. A father who allows himself to become involved in such an erotized relationship loses his paternal function. The intent is to transform both the superego and the father into an anodine and/or ludicrous object. This was obvious with two of my patients, as I shall show with a few extracts from their material.

Petljura, who already had two analyses, declared war on me from the start. I do not put the cushions back into place. I have kept him three, no, two minutes less than the day before. I turn the light off because I am miserly. I am a Jew. The Jews were the ones to start racism, etc. Sessions were filled with anti-Semitic remarks of the kind, "Jews should learn to keep quiet. Listening to them, you'd think they're the only ones to have suffered. As if the rest of the world didn't exist. They dehumanize non-Jews. They make a terrible fuss about the gas chambers, as if killing in one way rather than another mattered at all. On and on they go, taking themselves for the chosen people. One day they'll have to climb down a peg or two, etc." At quite an early stage he dreamed that he was crucified, head down. The implication was that he had been crucified by me, by a Jew. This crucifixion head down meant that he endured greater suffering than Jesus. (Identification with Christ is very often prominent in such patients.) Although I was assigned the role of tormentor, I also was the Jew who was denigrated and attacked. I had to "come down a peg or two." For me this switching around was depreciation of the superego, of the father who had to be turned into the provider of sexual pleasure, this being the way to eradicate the father's paternal function, and who must be denigrated: it was the father-Jewish analyst who was the immoral one.

Then came material in which the patient unconsciously identified with the corpses on which his father, a forensic surgeon, performed autopsies, while the father himself, as in this patient's first dream, was humiliated, denigrated, penetrated, and castrated. This was a dream in which his car crashed into the back of his father's car, smashing it, and the patient then associated to the long illness that had left his father a sick man. At this first session he quoted an Arabic proverb that, he said, ran as follows: "A pilgrimage is never complete until the pilgrim has sodomized his camel."

After quite a few of these positions had been interpreted, Petljura later had another dream in which it was obvious that the transference had been intensely erotized and the analyst-superego-father depreciated. He was reading a large erotic book containing some "shockingly revealing" engravings. A little man walked past from behind. He tried to hide the book but only managed to cover up four small pornographic brochures. The patient associated this dream to the self-imposed suffering that his four weekly sessions represented. After I had interpreted the dream, showing how our relationship had been erotized (his masochistic complaints were designed to reduce me to the state of the "little man"), his provocations attenuated. He had another dream. He was reading an account in *The Observer*, an English newspaper, of a trial at which Margaret Thatcher had testified, producing overwhelming evidence for the man's conviction. Then the patient found himself on the quai Branly (a Paris street on the Seine riverbank). He associated to a short, nineteenth-century play, a satirical parody of justice he had just finished reading, in which the author pokes fun at magistrates. When I had interpreted the transference (Margaret Thatcher is me; I am frequently associated with England), he commented that she was ridiculous in his dream. Then I showed him that the aim of his masochistic provocations was to ridicule the moral agency (*The Observer*) and the judge (Mrs. Thatcher, the analyst) who personified the moral agency, venturing that this fantasy was present when he masturbated (quai Branly suggests the word *se branler*, to masturbate). This produced another association. He had relatives living on the quai Branly. Their son had joined a London sect where hanging rites to produce an ejaculation were performed. He was dead. He had hung himself. (It should be noted that in England execution of the death sentence was by hanging.)

I now turn to the clinical material of my patient Romain about whom I have written elsewhere (1984). This provides a good illustration of the way the ego (the patient) depreciates the superego (the external authority). At one point in his analysis Romain went to Switzerland (a haven for French capital whenever the currency loses value). This was at a time when exchange regulations were particularly strict. He was on the night train. The customs men insisted on searching through the case of the other person in Romain's compartment. Romain insulted them, and for calling them "bastards" was led off to the customs office where he was stripped and searched, and held until the morning. The bottle of Wilhelmine alcohol he had bought was confiscated, along with his checkbook. I got the impression, as he related this episode, that the provocation was aimed at me. He had withheld an important fact in his biography from me (he had crossed the border without opening his case), and at the same time in the paternal transference he wanted me to penetrate him homosexually, wanted me to force him to open his case, to strip and search him. And in the process he managed to degrade the categorical imperative to nothing more than a customs man's cap.

As regards Libya, quite a few of her masochistic provocations were intended to *make me feel guilty*, to prove to me that her superego was more upright, more severe, in a word, more perfect than mine. She attacked my apartment, for example, my "bourgeois" social background (she really came from a family higher up on the social scale than mine) and the fact that I took money from my patients. She told me one day that "problems, anxiety, and stupidity" were things I had never had to deal with. After reading an article written by my father's elder brother,[1] to which I had added a short biographical introduction, speaking of how he had been shot in the Warsaw ghetto and mentioning his modest social origins, she told me (with reproach) how lucky I ought to consider myself, since she could never be free of her bourgeois and anti-Semitic family. She held extreme-left political views and, like all the members of the political group to which she belonged, expressed opinions tinged with anti-Semitism.

It seems to me that the subject's constant efforts to make the analyst *feel guilty* are aimed not only at provoking the analyst into a sadomasochistic erotic relationship in keeping with the moral masochism that colors the subject's whole life, but are also aimed at disqualifying the superego projected onto the analyst. The analyst is proved utterly deficient on the moral level and incapable of judging the patient. Far from finding himself in the position of judge, in the countertransference the analyst is painfully experiencing a state of micromania with poignant feelings of unworthiness, when he is not plagued by the fantasy of ridding himself of a patient whose attacks wound him and his values to the core. Conduct of this type can of course be regarded as an

[1] Of all my patients and colleagues, she was the only person to guess the ties of family linking me to the author of this article.

attempt to erotize otherwise unbearable guilt, as Rosenberg (1982) states with good reason. In this connection, I was able to catch a glimpse of Libya's guilt when the defenses I have described became inoperative. She told me one day that the Jews were abominable, because the thought of what they had lived through persecuted her.

I maintain, however, that disqualification of the superego constitutes not only a means of lessening guilt but also of eliminating the paternal function. This in turn affects the thought processes.[2]

THE ARCHAIC MATRIX OF THE OEDIPUS COMPLEX AND THOUGHT

I shall begin by referring to the material concerning my patient Franca, which I presented at the Montreal Congress (1988a):

> I postulated a primary wish to rediscover a universe without obstacles, rough edges or differences, identified with a smooth mother's body rid of its contents—the father, his penis and babies. *These contents represent reality*, because access to the mother's abdomen is closed to the child. In fact, it is a matter of regaining *in thought* a form of mental functioning without shackles, with freely circulating psychic energy, and of recovering the mode of functioning proper to the pleasure principle. In my view, it is the wish to destroy reality which makes the fantasy of emptying the mother's belly so all-important. The following dream came just before the Easter holidays.
>
> *'The whole world has been devastated. Everyone has disappeared but for 34,000 people.* [She was to associate this figure with her bill for analysis in that month: 3400 francs.][3] *The earth has returned to the Ice Age. I am with a few survivors on a sled, on a road that goes all round the world. The feeling is extraordinary, marvellous and rather idyllic. We are thrilled. It is like skiing on soft, smooth snow.'* She had another dream the same night. *She was with her friend, Lewis. They were climbing a staircase. They reached the top of a cliff overhanging the sea.*

[2] Here I am obliged to refer to my previous work on "The Archaic Matrix of the Oedipus Complex" (1984), the principal points of which are dealt with in *Sexuality and Mind* (1986).

[3] See Revelation 7–4: "And I heard the number of them which were sealed" (the People of God, spared by the apocalyptic destruction).

> *He wanted to push her into the sea. She was frightened and fascinated. Then the scene changed. They were in an apartment. She was to introduce him to her mother. Lying in a bath someone was stretched out in the water. She wondered how this person managed to breathe.*
>
> Without going into the detail of the dream, I believe we can discern in it the desire to return to the smooth body of the mother-analyst by destroying all obstacles (the catastrophe of the end of the world, leaving her alone with 34,000 people who represent the analyst, identified with Mother Earth and now totally accessible. It is possible to go all around it on a sled with a feeling of perfect elation.) The second dream shows that it really is a matter of a return to the intrauterine state: falling into the sea, the person in the bathwater [pp. 157–158].

I should like to remark here on "skiing on soft, smooth snow." In my opinion, this does not involve—or rather does not solely involve—the satisfaction of a sexual desire, but represents the return to the mother's unencumbered body, a plunge back into a mental universe free of all constraints.

In a recent paper (1988b) I remarked that the pleasure found in dreams of flight and the pleasure enjoyed by adepts of the deltaplane and the U.L.M. and all the "sliding" sports should not be understood (or not solely understood) as the equivalent of an erection or an orgasm, but rather as representing a will on the part of the subject to regain the maternal body and to install himself in a universe from which all obstacles (the father, babies, and thought) have been eliminated. This is a world in which the subject *moves* unchecked in space where differences between one point and another no longer exist. I have also described the effect this has on the thought process (1987, 1988a), since this smooth and completely unobstructed world of the dream tends to dominate waking thought. I have attempted to show that this repressive mode of mental activity in which all thoughts are equivalent can be identified on the collective level too. The categories of "cause" and "effect" have disappeared. The father is the *cause* of the baby's existence in the mother's body, this plain fact being the prototype of cause and effect (Grunberger, 1983, personal communication). In the fantasy, once the father has been ousted, the subject is able to take possession of the mother's body and the very idea of *cause* disappears. Thus all thoughts float, indeterminate, interchangeable, in an intemporal world without past or future. This produces a psyche in which everything is one and the same. Laws and principles no longer exist.

The original meaning of the word *nomos* ("law" in Greek) is "division," "separation." A fatherless universe where fusion with the mother is possible is a world without law and without separation. The word *law* in every language, I believe, at least since the seventeenth century, is used in two senses, the one being law in the sense of moral and/or legal codes and the other corresponding to the definition given by Montesquieu (1748): "The necessary relationship deriving from the nature of things." When the father has disappeared from the psyche, the different phenomena no longer follow one from the other in an articulated sequence.

Libya had a dream in which a landscape of hills, trees, paths, and cultivated fields was suddenly transformed into a desertlike plain she described as irresistibly beautiful. She went through a period during which she was set on convincing me that the assassination of Aldo Moro was no more reprehensible an act than capitalist exploitation (a popular New Left theme in France at the time). She then proceeded to pay me a considerably smaller sum in cash than the money she owed me. She had a dream in which she cheated on the amount she paid a salesman for the purchase of a car, an Aldo-Moro. The patient was ashamed of this dream, as if it betrayed her. Through association it was established that the Aldo-Moro car represented the parents united in the primal scene and put to death (Aldo Moro's body was found in an Italian car; Aldo-Moro refers equally to Alfa-Romeo and Romeo to love and a couple). Her knowledge of the reality of the primal scene and the murderous hatred directed at her parents, united in the act of coitus, had to be denied at all costs by "cheating"—in this case by regressing to a mode of thinking in which facts are equivalent, interchangeable, in which the act of murder is not different from capitalist exploitation. (In this respect, I believe that it is the fully developed Oedipus complex that places murder above all other crimes.) The dream of "cheating" in order to purchase the Aldo-Moro is a demonstration of the use to which the patient put analysis: a means to help her cheat about the reality of the primal scene. At the same time the Aldo-Moro represented me, united with my husband (the hyphenated name of the car, an Aldo-Moro, was associated with mine). On top of this, the patient later denied the whole episode, and then came up with another version: her husband had taken money from the pile of notes. At any rate, she refused to believe she could be wrong. In short, she was rewriting history in the way history is rewritten in Orwell's *1984*:

> The whole literature of the past will have been destroyed. Chaucer, Shakespeare, Milton, Byron—they'll exist only in Newspeak versions, not merely changed into something different, but actually changed into something contradictory of what they used to be. . . . The whole climate of thought will be different. In fact there will *be* no thought, as we understand it now [p. 46].

I want to emphasize the fact that man strives to free his mind of chaos, even though I have concentrated on the opposite wish to return to a state of chaos. In the Wolf-Man case, Freud (1918) refers to schemas, supposing that these are transmitted phylogenetically:

> . . . which, like the categories of philosophy, are concerned with the business of "placing" the impressions derived from actual experience. I am inclined to take the view that they are precipitates from the human history of human civilization. The Oedipus complex, which comprises a child's relation to his parents, is one of them—is, in fact, the best known member of the class. Wherever experiences fail to fit in with the hereditary schema, they become remodelled in the imagination—a process which might be followed out in detail. It is precisely such cases that are calculated to convince us of the independent existence of the schema [p. 119].

Freud chooses the example of the Oedipus complex to illustrate this hereditary schema. As I have said (1984), all systems of classification are composed of at least three terms: the subject on the one hand, and two categories (in this case the father and the mother). The Oedipus complex is more than just an example of a schema. It is the prototype of all schemas of classification: without a father to separate subject and mother, the subject is in a world of chaos and confusion. It is the fully developed Oedipus complex that will enable the subject to establish categories and to classify impressions (in ways that are no longer purely defensive, i.e., obsessional neurosis), and thus bring order into the primeval chaos, the process that leads to humanization. The impersonal scale of independent values (the superego), which the Oedipus complex supposedly bequeathes as its legacy, goes hand in hand with this ability to classify, this being in turn linked to the acknowledgment of differences. In 1985, I emphasized that genitality is characterized by an ability to acknowledge differences, particularly differences between the child and his father, between the small boy's prepubertal penis and the adult's potent penis, and between the sexes, and that this leads to acknowledging the existence of the genital primal scene. I have also underlined the fact that acknowledgment of differences is equivalent to acknowledging reality. In point of fact, the scale of values that is an inseparable part of the superego we qualify as postoedipal reflects integration of the notion of *differentiation*, rooted in integration of the paternal dimension.

Disappearance of the paternal dimension leads to chaos, and this points to a fundamental link between mental functioning and the existence of a mature moral agency. A fully developed moral agency implies the ability to acknowledge the obstacle that separates the mother from the subject, which amounts to an acceptance of reality. The immature or regressed superego may limit the capacity to think clearly, replacing the formulated laws of scientific discoveries by moral rules. But when there is an insufficient or totally absent superego, this will have the effect of blocking the thought processes, resulting in deformation of thought or undifferentiated chaos.

With admirable intuition Orwell (1948) associates the mental universe of nonthought which he so remarkably describes in *1984* with anomie, a world where the notions of good and bad have been abolished: "In the end the whole notion of goodness and badness will be covered by only six words—in reality, only one word. . . . Don't you see that the whole aim of Newspeak is to narrow the range of thought?" (p. 45). And also: "This was not illegal (nothing was illegal, since there were no longer any laws)" (p. 9). And on April 4, 1984, Winston wrote in his diary:

> Last night to the flicks. All war films. One very good one of a ship full of refugees being bombed somewhere in the Mediterranean. Audience much amused by shots of a great huge fat man trying to swim away with a helicopter after him, first you saw him wallowing in the water like a porpoise, then you saw him through the helicopter's gunsights, then he was full of holes and the sea round him turned pink and he sank as suddenly as though the holes had let in the water. audience shouting with laughter when he sank. then you saw a lifeboat full of children with a helicopter hovering over it. there was a middle-aged woman might have been a jewess sitting up in the bow with a little boy about three years old in her arms. little boy screaming with fright and hiding his head between her breasts as if he was trying to burrow right into her and the woman putting her arms round him and comforting him although she was blue with fright herself, all the time covering him up as much as possible as if she thought her arms could keep the bullets off him. then the helicopter planted a 20 kilo bomb in among them terrific flash and the boat went all to matchwood. then there was a wonderful shot of a child's arm going up up up right up into the air a helicopter with a camera in its nose must have followed it up and there was a lot of applause from the party seats [pp. 10–11].

In this example the insufficient superego has produced thoughts without values attached to them. They become dehumanized and do not belong to the category of reason. Reason implies nonequivalence; it supposes the existence of differences and a hierarchy to order the different terms. On the other hand, the return to moral chaos implies the return to mental chaos. A seven-year-old girl whose godfather had taken to caressing her in a sexual way dreamed that her doll was covered with mud. In her dream she could not see properly, her vision had blurred. In other words, the paternal representative who ignores the taboo preventing sexual relations between child and adult (the eradication of differences) as well as the barrier against incest provokes mental confusion.

SUMMARY AND CONCLUSION

My aim has been to study disqualification of the superego, although I have had to restrict this to certain modes, especially moral masochism and the attempt to inspire feelings of guilt in the analyst. In my opinion, this is more than a resexualization of the relation between the superego and the ego, since it leads to degradation of the moral agency and finally to the elimination of the distinction between father and child who become sexual playmates. The disappearance of the impersonal postoedipal superego, which sets the boundaries of good and bad, leads to thought disorders since thought cannot develop without integration of the oedipal father and the ability to acknowledge differences and a hierarchy of values that goes with such integration. This study is nothing more than a step toward a more comprehensive understanding and a redefinition of "moral insanity."

REFERENCES

Chasseguet-Smirgel, J. (1984), The archaic matrix of the Oedipus complex. In: *Sexuality and Mind*. New York: New York University Press, 1986, pp. 74–91.

——— (1985), *Creativity and Perversion*. New York: Norton.

——— (1987), Reflections on some thought disorders in nonpsychotic patients. Unpublished.

——— (1988a), A woman's attempt at a perverse solution. *Internat. J. Psycho-Anal.*, 69:149–161.

——— (1988b), From the archaic matrix of the Oedipus complex to the fully developed Oedipus complex. *Psychoanal. Quart.* (in press).

Freud, S. (1918), From the history of an infantile neurosis. *Standard Edition*, 17:3–123. London: Hogarth Press, 1962.

——— (1923), The ego and the id. *Standard Edition*, 19:3–66. London: Hogarth Press, 1961.

——— (1924), The economic problem of masochism. *Standard Edition*, 19:157–170. London: Hogarth Press, 1961.

——— (1930), Civilization and its discontents. *Standard Edition*, 21:59–145. London: Hogarth Press, 1961.

——— (1933), The dissection of the psychical personality. *Standard Edition*, 22:57–80. London: Hogarth Press, 1964.

——— (1937), Analysis terminable and interminable. *Standard Edition*, 23:209–253. London: Hogarth Press, 1964.

Montesquieu (1748), *L'Esprit des lois*. Paris: Société des Belles Lettres, 1950.

Orwell, G. (1948), *1984*. London: Penguin Modern Classics, 1974.
Pasche, F. (1961), De la Dépression. In: *A partir de Freud*. Paris: Payot, 1969.
Rangell, L. (1974), A psychoanalytic perspective leading currently to the syndrome of the compromise of integrity. *Internat. J. Psycho-Anal.*, 55:3–12.
——— (1976), Lessons from Watergate: A derivative for psychoanalysis. *Psychoanal. Quart.*, 45:37–61.
——— (1980), *The Mind of Watergate: An Exploration of the Compromise of Integrity*. New York: Norton.
——— (1986), The executive functions of the ego: An extension of the concept of ego autonomy. *The Psychoanalytic Study of the Child*, 41:1–37. New Haven, CT: Yale University Press.
Rosenberg, B. (1982), Culpabilité et masochisme moral ou la culpabilité comme "négatif" du masochisme. *Les Cahiers du Centre de Psychanalyse et de Psychothérapie*, 4.

12

SYNTHETIC AND CONFLICTUAL ASPECTS OF THE SUPEREGO: A CASE STUDY

JULES GLENN, M.D.

In discussions analysts often refer to the strength of the superego as if it were a monolithic structure. The case study I will describe in this chapter reveals the limitation of such quantifications. It demonstrates the superego as a complex whole synthesized from various elements, and that there are internal contradictions within it. Obviously in the case study I emphasize clinical data related to superego formation.

CASE REPORT

I treated Richard T. when he was 11 to 16 years old. The three times weekly psychotherapy possessed the structure and process of analysis, but the results, while good, were limited. Richard was at the start a latency child. He did not have any physical signs of prepuberty or psychological indication of preadolescence at that time. When he was 13 pubic and facial hair appeared and he started to masturbate.

During the consultation his parents and he described his being afraid of dying because of a horrible pain throughout his body.

This article is an expansion of a paper read at the Panel entitled "Superego: Too Much, Too Little" at the Fourteenth Annual Conference, Regional Council of the Psychoanalytic Societies of the Greater New York Area and Philadelphia, June 18, 1988.

With medical reassurance he calmed down in a few days, but had trouble going to school and came home weepy and unhappy. In the background of these symptoms were the following: (1) Johnny, a boy in his school, had been "torturing" him for some months. Johnny kicked the patient, threw him downstairs, and ripped his papers. The school tried to keep the boys apart. (2) At about the same time, Richard's mother had been ill. Her sickness consisted of an undiagnosed infection which caused severe abdominal pain. A gynecologist hospitalized Mrs. T. three times for brief periods and also put her on antibiotics and pain killers. At one point Richard stared out of the window of his house for hours, crying and looking and longing for his absent mother. (3) While she was ill, the father threatened to leave and actually went away on a business trip for a period. Mr. and Mrs. T. had argued openly and seriously for years, and when Mr. T. was about to separate, Mrs. T. became anxious and "hysterical." Shortly before the consultation Mr. T. decided to try to make a go of the marriage and remain with the family, to everyone's relief.

The mother was a sculptor, devoted to her work, anxious and in psychotherapy. She was also devoted to the care of her children, Richard and his four-year-younger brother Jim, but had difficulty in managing them. She could not control her younger son provoking Richard and Richard's violent responses. She once told me she felt fused with Richard and could not frustrate him. She told me that her parents were fragile people who needed the protection of the patient's mother and her sister. Mrs. T.'s father was a rather poor delivery man who relied on the word of authorities. Both Mrs. T. and her sister did artistic work.

My patient's father was a clothing manufacturer, prone to boast of his shady deals, some of which Richard knew about and admired. The father was also a joker, ever avoiding serious matters with humor. He had told the children that he had done poorly at school but was a success nevertheless. In addition, Richard knew of his paternal grandfather's difficulties. As a young man he had been a con man who, when fired from a company he had cheated, attempted to blow up some of its property. He was apprehended and jailed. This man divorced his wife and later remarried her.

Richard's masochistic traits, hinted at in the history, became apparent early in the psychotherapy. Richard brought a powdery white substance, bicarbonate of soda, to his early sessions. He was interested in science and planned to do an experiment, he said, as he poured the powder from one container to another, spilling a little of it, threatening by the mischievous look on his face to spill more as he watched my reactions. Thus I was able to tell him about his provocativeness and eventually to tie this to his relationship with Johnny. Although Richard was skeptical that he provoked his torturer as he was trying to provoke me, he diminished and eventually ceased seeking contact with the boy and hence stirring him up. His messiness appeared at home as well as in my office; his mother was forever urging him to brush his teeth, bathe, and be orderly. This suggested an earlier toilet-training conflict with his mother, which was never truly confirmed. His mother said that toilet training had been easy.

Identification with mother and father could be interpreted. Richard's bringing joke books to his sessions and telling jokes and riddles made it clear that he identified with his father who loved humor. Eventually we could see that in his avoiding doing schoolwork, he emulated his father both specifically, as father had been a negligent student, and in a more general way in that he violated rules and lied, saying he had done his homework. A superego defect could thus be traced to his identifying with his father whose morality was shaky. Richard's ego ideal included breaking rules and lying!

Richard developed a number of "illnesses" during the treatment, and it was difficult to determine to what degree they were consciously feigned. He fell, injuring his knee, and could hardly walk at home and in school. However, he miraculously recovered when he wanted to help his father officiate at a local marathon. He had to be able to walk well to do this, and so got completely better in one day. On another occasion he developed fever and vague flulike symptoms. The elevated temperature readings were due to his heating his thermometer surreptitiously, but several physicians thought he might have had infectious mononucleosis or an allergic condition as well. He identified with his mother as a sick person, as a victim, a sign of a punitive superego. But the difficulties he developed resulted at least in part from his dishonesty, apparently a manifestation of a weak conscience.

Richard's superego was an amalgam of strong and weak parts. His provocation and aggressiveness, in part an identification with both parents who fought, also reflected his superego, which demanded punishment for violations. In fact, the identification with the fighting parents added to the punitive aspect of his superego. The provocation and aggression provided drive gratification (both aggressive and libidinal) as he identified with the partners of the primal scene, which required punishment. In addition, he identified with and was close to the sick mother he feared losing when he became ill with symptoms similar to hers.

The father was not all bad in his own eyes or in his son's. His ideal was to make money, and he worked hard at it. He spent long hours at his factory and with customers, took work home, read papers connected with it, and boasted of his accomplishments. The family's wealth and material achievements confirmed his success. The family moved from an apartment to a modest home to a better one and then to a magnificent one they all took pride in planning and supervising. Richard found great pleasure in making suggestions and criticizing the builders and his father's management of them. He spent many session hours drawing pictures of the house and grounds, noting the wonderful structure and being proud of his father while commenting on every deficiency. Through identifying with his hardworking father he set a goal for himself he could not reach. Other aspects of his ego and superego made it hard for him to sustain work. He was spoiled by the material rewards he could obtain without much effort. When the family made one move, the father gave each child a present to make up for his being deprived. The mother said they should have been rewarded for working instead. Richard's Bar Mitzvah and the gifts he received were expensive to the extreme. Just through being his father's son he received presents from wealthy customers of his father. He felt he could and should achieve results without work in certain fields, particularly school.

He thought that learning could occur without effort and that once one learned something it was not forgotten. Because he could not accomplish these feats, Richard felt there was something seriously wrong with him. When he could not grasp something immediately and permanently, he became discouraged and gave up. He spent many sessions discussing learning processes. I, using Richard as the subject, demonstrated learning curves to him. I would offer him a series of nonsense syllables or numerical sequences, which he then learned. At first he could not remember all of them when he tried to learn, but with repeated attempts he got it, only to forget much of it after a week. He then could relearn it more quickly than on the first try.

Through these procedures Richard came to see that learning took effort, and we went about understanding why he did not realize this. We focused on his idealization of his father who could, he thought, accomplish things without hardly trying and his parents' gratifying him so that he did not suffer disappointment and tension.

There was another area in which Richard *could* work, at least after the therapy had proceeded sufficiently. His mother was an artist and he became one too. He created abstract paintings, which he exhibited prominently in the living room of his house. Later he learned to do metal work at camp and was hired as an instructor. These artistic achievements involved identification with his mother, in many ways a safer identification than that with his father who could then cut him down for competing. I am inclined to believe that the ideal involved here should be considered a superego function and structure (ego ideal being part of the superego), but one could argue that this artistic ego ideal is part of the ego as it does not refer to morality. Through his artistic activities, sublimated drive pleasure was achieved. At any rate Richard could attain the ideal with relatively little conflict, spend much time working in this area, going into New York City to take lessons, and loving it.

The power of Richard's superego did not derive solely from identification with external objects, or rather their representations. Unfortunate events intensified castration anxiety and hence the fear of punishment. When Richard was a year old his pediatrician, thinking something was wrong with his penis—perhaps he had dysuria; his parents could not recall and Richard did not remember—passed tubes up his penis one or two times. (We never ascertained what had actually occurred.) Then at three and a quarter, the toilet seat fell on his penis while he was urinating, a freak accident that Richard did not recall. Later in nursery school he complained that his penis hurt. Because of Richard's castration anxiety he had trouble talking about his penis and masturbation during the psychotherapy sessions. It was not until he was a teen-ager that he could discuss it at all, but he would become frightened and avoid details. Nevertheless, he became able to masturbate and enjoy it. He told me that but not his fantasies. As a teen-ager he also dated a girlfriend, but did not engage in sexual activities with her, partly because her parents maintained strict supervision. Probably he selected a girl with strict parents so he could have a relationship without the danger of sexual involvement.

Another factor that determined the intensity of the punitive aspect of Richard's superego was the intensity of his drives, particularly his aggressive drives. (Possibly his sexual urges were unusually strong, but I have no knowledge to that effect.) The patient's anger at his brother was great, as was his fury at his parents. He berated his father and mother for favoring his brother, for not stopping his provocation, and for pressing him, Richard, to work. He hated his brother who would intentionally be noisy when he was trying to concentrate on his homework or listen to music. I believe that the intensity of his drives evoked stepped-up superego activity to combat them.

At the start of the treatment Richard was a frightened, provocative boy who did terribly in school. In addition to the paradoxical superego issues I have discussed, we analyzed his competition with his younger brother who had serious dyslexia and required a special school. Richard envied his brother who he felt could get away with little work and tried to do as little as possible himself in order to be equal with his brother. His conscience also prevented him from surpassing his brother. His goofing off was on the one hand due to a "weak" superego that said, "It's okay, even preferable, not to work—like father," and on the other hand to a "strong" superego that said, "Don't work, don't do better than brother—or father." Two opposite ideals operated in concert.

Richard had a great deal of trouble studying for his Bar Mitzvah. He procrastinated and forgot the prayers and Torah readings required. The Cantor spent extra time helping him to prepare. It became possible for me to interpret his reluctance to compete with his father and become a man. The family emphasis on the non-religious aspects of the ritual did not help him to devote time to preparing for the ceremony. The father spent lots of money on a huge, most lavish party to which he invited more business associates than friends of Richard and himself.

When Richard was 14 he had a dream that revealed the importance of oedipal wishes that his superego opposed.

> I am home in my house upstairs in my mother's bedroom watching TV alone. It's not the house as it is, but the house in one of the plans. My brother and parents are not there. A man got into the house, a genius technician got into the house without the alarm going off. I open the door and see a man with an ax downstairs. I quickly lock the door and go to push the emergency button. I remember to call the police, but the phone wasn't working. I run across the balcony, take apart the alarm, and then cross wires in the alarm so it goes into the 20-30-second delay mode. The terrorist, the man with the ax, runs into the kitchen, slams the alarm box with his ax. Things go into the burglar mode. At this point my father woke me up.

The patient's associations were not thorough, but one can see the role of the superego. Watching television reminded him that he sometimes goofs off, does not study as he should when his parents are away. This, he said, is against the rules. When I said he is punished in the dream for breaking the rules, he noted that the mother's room in the dream is actually his parents' room. He remembered his mother's buying food the previous day, which Richard is neutral about, and purchasing a toy car for his brother, which Richard opposes.

The dream, these associations showed, was about his superego's opposition to his not studying and, related, his forbidden desire for intimacy with his mother, regressively depicted on an oral level, as well as his anger at his mother and brother for her purchasing something for him. One may guess that the dream also depicted homosexual conflicts, but this was never clearly demonstrated. The man with the hatchet, the superego figure, was a representation of Richard's father. At the same time he was

Richard, the furious boy who wished to break into and enter the house sexually and aggressively. The burglar also represented the father as well as the patient, both harboring dishonest desires.

At one point it appeared that Richard had dyslexia, but extensive and detailed educational tests revealed that this was not true. The psychologist who tested Richard suggested tutoring to help him with his schoolwork. His parents backed this educational help and supplied him with tutors. Through Mr. and Mrs. T.'s changed and more demanding attitudes, Richard's affection for and identification with one particular male tutor and with me, and interpretation of superego difficulties, the patient became a rather good student who got mostly A's. As we ended treatment he received A's in chemistry, social studies, art, and a business course in investments, a B in math, a C in English, and a D in French.

I had an opportunity to find out how my former patient was doing a year after the therapy ended. Richard's schoolwork continued to be good, but his SAT scores were low. Two prestigious and a number of perfectly good colleges accepted him. As befits the follow-up of this family with superego pathology, Mr. T. attempted to donate a large amount of money to one of these schools in order to get his son into it. This plan failed, according to Mr. T., who withheld the contribution. However, Richard called the school after being turned down and convinced the admissions officer that he should be accepted. He cited his eagerness and his interest in the metal work in which this university excelled. Also in line with our discussion of spoiling, Richard's father bought him an expensive sports car in his last year of high school. On the plus side, the boy had been working hard and had an exhibit of his metal work locally.

DISCUSSION

This clinical material points to the complexity of the superego. One cannot only talk of weak and strong superegos, quantify their intensity, but can evaluate different aspects and their relationships. The superego consists of a cluster of functions that have to do with the ideals of the individual (the ego ideal), what he should or should not wish, feel, or do, and the punishment for failure to achieve these goals (the punitive part of the superego) (Freud, 1914, 1921, 1923, 1933). Punishment at the superego's request is meted out via the ego. The ideals may be many and contradictory, but they are more or less integrated into a complex gestalt. Despite the integration, intrasystemic conflicts within the superego occur. The ego-ideal aspect of the superego can be demanding in part or lax in part. The punitive aspect of the superego can be weak in part or severe in part.

The superego is a structure in the sense of Rapaport and Gill (1959): "configurations of a slow rate of change" (p. 157). Identification is an essential element in superego formation (Freud, 1921), but we should keep in mind that, while the actual traits of the object are important, the representation one identifies with is not identical with the object. Richard wanted to be like his father—dishonest and industrious. He wanted to be like his mother—artistic and creative. His mother also represented hard work and to a degree (along with father) control over certain drives that were forbidden. Neither parent was able to help Richard control himself sufficiently.

Love for his parents with whom he identified and whom he emulated motivated him to be like them. The identifications also served defensive functions. Identifications with parents lost or potentially lost in actuality or in fantasy can keep the loved person with one. Identification with aggressive objects can guard against fears of their attacks (A. Freud, 1936).

Identification with parents who love the child and whom the child loves results in a "loving and beloved" aspect of the superego (Schafer, 1960). The individual feels proud if he achieves goals of the ego ideal which acts like an object that can love and protect (Freud, 1921).

Identification with punitive aspects of the parents and aggressive urges turned against the self serve to establish and maintain the punitive part of the superego. The intensity of the aggressive urges stems from a number of determinants: (1) the degree of innate and/or unneutralized aggression; (2) environmental experiences that make aggression greater (such as frustration); and

(3) narcissistic rage when one is unable to achieve ideals, the perfection one strives for that one pictures exists or can exist. Richard thought he could achieve goals easily without effort and became furious when he could not.

It is apparent that the superego's structure is overdetermined, but that identifications play a prominent and crucial role in its formation. Brenner (1982) emphasizes the compromise formations that occur in response to the many determinants.

The superego is a *developing* set of functions (Blum, 1985). A description of changes that generally take place as the individual matures will serve as a background for further understanding of Richard's superego. Understanding superego development requires knowledge of the state of the ego and the drives in relation to it, and so I will consider these aspects of the personality as well.

The ego-ideal aspect of the superego grows out of early narcissistic wishes for union and bliss, but becomes more mature as the individual matures. Wishes to be one with the mother of separation-individuation (Mahler, Pine, and Bergman, 1975) and to please the parent of the anal stage fuse to produce sphincter morality. Fears of dissolution, of losing parents' care or their love, of castration anxiety at 18 months (Roiphe and Galenson, 1972) or later during the oedipal period join together with parental identification to form the punitive part of the superego. Richard's early frightening experiences with his penis are relevant here.

The superego of the oedipal child (Glenn, 1978) is in formation and relatively weak. As a result of this and increased drive pressure, many open expressions of drive derivatives appear. These children are thus fun to work with in analysis. Although conflict is present, the child can talk about and enact naughty thoughts, feelings, and activities without fully knowing they are naughty.

With latency (Freud, 1905; Sarnoff, 1976) the child's superego grows and becomes more organized. Sexual thoughts and feelings become more forbidden and hidden. Adaptively the child uses his or her libidinal and aggressive energy, neutralized and transformed, along with other neutral energies, for constructive educational purposes. The defenses evoked give the child's personality a compulsive quality lacking in Richard's case. Interferences with the development of the demanding and punitive aspects of the patient's superego militated against the usual latency development.

In preadolescence (Blos, 1962; Wieder, 1978) drives increase, and the ego and superego often cannot manage them well. Many children of this age become restless, confused, and regress to oral and anal manifestations. There can be ego regression as well. The preadolescent's ego may deteriorate with resultant failures in school achievement. (On the other hand, the increased cognitive capacity of this age group may sustain itself and result in superb academic work.) The deterioration did not occur for a sustained period in Richard's case, probably because the therapeutic work fortified the superego at this time. For a brief period during preadolescence he got hold of firecrackers which he ignited, a displaced expression of anal explosive and aggressive desires. He also wanted to purchase dangerous Chinese stars as a more phallic symbolization of his aggression. He imagined throwing these sharp multipointed weapons at opponents, including his brother, and in karate chopping his enemies. Richard obtained sales catalogues in order to buy Chinese stars and other deadly weapons, but in the end his conscience won out and he refrained from purchasing them.

During adolescence and early adulthood the superego is restructured in order to allow the individual to adapt to new personal, biological, and societal demands (A. Freud, 1958; Blos, 1962). The superego of childhood restricts sexual activity, but the adult whose superego requires that he not engage in intercourse will find himself in difficulty. A marked change of the ego ideal is thus necessary for adaptation. Richard had not progressed far along this road to maturity. His superego did not permit sexual activity to a degree one would expect. On the positive side, his did not deteriorate as many do during restructuring. His attempts, supported by his psychotherapy, to build his superego into an adaptive structure, play a role in these outcomes.

Superego changes during the teen-age years take place under the influence of cognitive changes to formal operations (more abstract thinking), which enables the adolescent to hypothesize and plan better and to develop more abstract ideals (Piaget and

Inhelder, 1969). Although Richard did develop more advanced cognition and was able to plan his future better, he did not build a more abstract idealism.

Teen-agers, as they break away from their parents to become more independent, seek substitute models to serve as a basis for reforming their superegos (A. Freud, 1958; Blos, 1962). They may identify with peer group values or incorporate the ideals of adult mentors or mentors of their own age. The diminished cathexis of parental representations is one of the causes of temporary and maladaptive superego deterioration, while identification with parent substitutes may have adaptive or maladaptive consequences. Richard used his analyst, teachers, and tutors to achieve a stronger and more academically oriented superego; the influence of peers was minimal in his case.

The adaptive superego is flexible, but there is danger that alterability will lead to disadvantageous behavior (Arlow, 1982). The superego requires external support to maintain itself even in adulthood. For Richard, such buttressing came from his parents, teachers, and therapist.

The superego is subject to regression in both structural and temporal senses briefly, for long periods, or permanently. We have seen that teen-agers may engage in activities previously contrary to the standards of their ego ideal. Freud (1921) has demonstrated that group members can identify with a leader who becomes an immoral superego figure, while at the same time the individuals feel glued to each other and their leader by libidinal ties. Hatred often becomes directed toward people outside the group, wreaking havoc. Rangell (1980) has shown that identification with immoral leaders can defend against superego restraint. Arlow (1982), in a telling joke, stated that the superego is like a policeman; when you need it most, it's not around.

There are many, too many, examples. Lynch mobs can commit murder without guilt. In war individuals enact wishes ordinarily forbidden. Gay (1988) has described the Austrians' losing control and slaughtering Jews after Hitler's invasion. The Holocaust is a horrible example of a nation's deteriorating morality under the influence of leaders.

In many instances it is not a matter of simple deterioration of the superego. Rather, new ego ideals replace the old. The usual morality disintegrates and an immoral (to our standards at least) superego replaces it.

The victims as well as the perpetrators may suffer from superego decline. Psychic trauma can cause ego and superego regression. In addition, drugs, including alcohol, may produce loss of control and judgment as ego and superego deteriorate. Extreme economic conditions, such as poverty and starvation, may lead people to commit acts they consider immoral, as stealing. Loyalty to one's family as well as self-preservation may justify such behavior.

The synthetic function applies not only to the ego and id, as described by Nunberg (1955), but to the superego as well. A number of configurations appear, some of which I will discuss. Johnson and Szurek (1952) used the term *superego lacunae* to denote a characteristic of persons whose consciences, while strong and demanding in many ways, have areas of laxity. However, the apparent partial absence of superego may be illusory. Certain people possess superegos that include ideals of antisocial subgroups within our culture. The morality of these people may be consonant with that of our society in certain dimensions (i.e., nuclear family values) while contrary to many usual standards (i.e., murder may be justified to accomplish group goals). Patients with so-called lacunae may be examples of contradictory ideals rather than of superego "holes." Johnson and Szurek describe how these patients enact their parents' wishes. Blum (1988) has suggested that fantasies shared by parents and children may interfere with superego development and even result in "corruption" of the superego. I suggest that in cases with supposed lacunae as well as in antisocial groups the shared fantasies may result in unusual superego configurations. Indeed, socially acceptable superegos also depend on shared fantasies.

It is not easy to ascertain parents' fantasies and thus establish that the child's fantasy is identical or highly congruent with his parents' without the grownups' being in analysis. However, in Richard's case we can be reasonably certain that Mr. T. and my patient shared the fantasy that dishonesty is the best policy and that they were partners in deception. Mother and patient shared an admiration for artistic achievement and felt united through their creativity. These fantasies were components of Richard's ego ideal, and had libidinal implications as well.

Freud (1916) delineated individuals who engage in criminal activity in order to be caught and thus punished for another actual or fantasied wrongdoing. Alexander (1929) recognized that these criminals from a sense of guilt suffer from a corrupt superego that permits certain violations if punishment precedes, accompanies, or follows the "crime." In this way conscious feelings of guilt are averted. He added that a healthier means of avoiding guilt feelings consists of discharging drives through sublimated activity, which entails social achievement. Rangell (1980) has identified a socially and politically malignant form of avoiding guilt feelings, the syndrome of the compromise of integrity. The individual fails to maintain his individuality and to exercise individual ego judgment under pressure of the group. The Watergate scandal exposed this personal defect in relief. Through identification with a corrupt leader, followers and the general population can triumph over the superego without guilt. Rangell's observation leads one to suggest that a child like Richard may use identification with his father defensively to avoid guilt.

Alexander (1929) asserted, agreeing with Freud, that a milder superego, a consequence of changes in society's moral concepts, may ease or alter the content of neuroses. A similar dynamic occurs in psychoanalysis and psychotherapy. A significant source of therapeutic improvement is the change in superego through identification with the analyst as well as through interpretation and insight (Strachey, 1934). The superego becomes more tolerant, thus permitting free association and diminishing self-punitive symptoms and character formation.

The superego's automatic functioning is necessary for optimal adaptation. When it fails, pathological behavior or symptoms may result. When one desires to express or satisfy a forbidden wish, a signal guilt feeling alerts the ego to take steps to stop the expression. The subject often is not aware of this guilt, but he might be perfectly conscious of it.

The superego engages in compromise formation which can be adaptive or maladaptive. The ego ideal can be flexible and realistic and allow the individual to find adaptive solutions, or it can be so rigid and unrealistic that the person develops serious symptoms. Richard's difficulty in school resulted from a compromise formation. The ideal that said, "Be like father and don't work," the ideal that said, "If you don't work, you will achieve anyway," the ideal that said, "Don't surpass father or brother," conflicted but acted in concert and led to minimal effort. The demands of the drives could be partly subdued, while at the same time they could be gratified in masochistic behavior of which poor schoolwork was an instance. The punitive part of the superego took part in this compromise formation.

A more adaptive compromise appeared in Richard's creative work. He achieved an ideal which arose out of identification with mother and which pleased both parents. He sublimated aggressive and libidinal urges and, as Alexander (1929) suggested, evaded conflict with his superego.

I have used quotations to indicate superego demands several times. That requires explanation. The voice of the conscience is called that because individuals often "hear" their superego's admonitions or urgings. Normally this is not a hallucinatory experience. The individual knows it is not a real external voice he hears. Isakower (1939) has noted the importance of the auditory sphere in the production of the superego.

This and other anthropomorphic descriptions of superego functionings in this chapter derive from the prominent role of identification in the formation of the superego. An unconscious fantasy of incorporating the parents into the individual results in a feeling that the parents are actually present, demanding compliance, restraint, and punishment.

SUMMARY

A case study of a boy in treatment from 11 to 16 affords us an opportunity to examine both ego ideal and punitive aspects of superego development. The patient's superego formation entailed identification with a dishonest but hardworking father who had done poorly in school, and an artistic mother. Some preoedipal,

oedipal, latency, and adolescent contributions are discussed. The structure of the superego is overdetermined. The central importance of identification with parents, parent substitutes, and mentors is emphasized, but other defenses and drives are significant too in the synthesis of the superego. The superego also comprises contradictory and conflictual aspects, in part based on opposing ideals and identifications. So-called superego lacunae can result from antisocial ideals, parental encouragement, and shared fantasies. A well-functioning superego results in adaptation rather than disturbed behavior and character and symptom formation. Corruptible superegos, compromises of integrity, and sublimatory modes of evading superego demands are examined. The superego is not fully autonomous, but requires environmental buttressing.

REFERENCES

Alexander, F. (1929), *The Psychoanalysis of the Total Personality*. New York: Coolidge Foundation.

Arlow, J. A. (1982), Problems of the superego concept. *The Psychoanalytic Study of the Child*, 37:229–244. New Haven, CT: Yale University Press.

Blos, P. (1962), *On Adolescence*. New York: Free Press of Glencoe.

Blum, H. P. (1985), Superego formation, adolescent transformation, and the adult neurosis. *J. Amer. Psychoanal. Assn.*, 33:887–910.

——— (1988), Discussion, Panel: Too much, too little. Fourteenth Annual Conference of the Regional Council of the Psychoanalytic Societies of the Greater New York Area and Philadelphia.

Brenner, C. (1982), *The Mind in Conflict*. New York: International Universities Press.

Freud, A. (1936), *The Ego and the Mechanisms of Defense*. New York: International Universities Press.

——— (1958), Adolescence. *The Psychoanalytic Study of the Child*, 13:155–178. New York: International Universities Press.

Freud, S. (1905), Three Essays on the Theory of Sexuality. *Standard Edition*, 7:125–243. London: Hogarth Press, 1953.

——— (1914), On narcissism: An introduction. *Standard Edition*, 14:67–102. London: Hogarth Press, 1957.

——— (1916), Some character-types met with in psycho-analytic work. *Standard Edition*, 14:309–333. London: Hogarth Press, 1957.

——— (1921), Group psychology and the analysis of the ego. *Standard Edition*, 18:67–143. London: Hogarth Press, 1955.

——— (1923), The ego and the id. *Standard Edition*, 19:3–66. London: Hogarth Press, 1961.

——— (1933), New Introductory Lectures on Psycho-Analysis. *Standard Edition*, 22:3–182. London: Hogarth Press, 1964.

Gay, P. (1988), *Freud: A Life for Our Time*. New York & London: Norton.

Glenn, J. (1978), The psychoanalysis of prelatency children. In: *Child Analysis and Therapy*, ed. J. Glenn. New York: Aronson, pp. 163–203.

Isakower, O. (1939), On the exceptional position of the auditory sphere. *Internat. J. Psycho-Anal.*, 20:340–348.

Johnson, A. M., & Szurek, S. A. (1952), The genesis of antisocial behavior in children and adults. *Psychoanal. Quart.*, 21:323–343.

Mahler, M. S., Pine, F., & Bergman, A. (1975), *The Psychological Birth of the Human Infant*. New York: Basic Books.

Nunberg, H. (1955), *Principles of Psychoanalysis*. New York: International Universities Press.

Piaget, J., & Inhelder, B. (1969), *The Psychology of the Child*. New York: Basic Books.

Rangell, L. (1980), *The Mind of Watergate: An Exploration of the Compromise of Integrity*. New York: Norton.

Rapaport, D., & Gill, M. M. (1959), The points of view and assumptions of metapsychology. *Internat. J. Psycho-Anal.*, 40:153–162.

Roiphe, H., & Galenson, E. (1972), Early genital activity and the castration complex. *Psychoanal. Quart.*, 41:334–347.

Sarnoff, C. (1976), *Latency*. New York: Aronson.

Schafer, R. (1960), The loving and beloved superego in Freud's structural theory. *The Psychoanalytic Study of the Child*, 15:163–188. New York: International Universities Press.

Strachey, J. (1934), The nature of the therapeutic action of psycho-analysis. *Internat. J. Psycho-Anal.*, 15:197–223.

Wieder, H. (1978), The psychoanalytic treatment of preadolescents. In: *Child Analysis and Therapy*, ed. J. Glenn. New York: Aronson, pp. 237–259.

13

A THEORETICAL FRAME FOR THE STUDY OF SEXUAL PERVERSIONS

OTTO F. KERNBERG, M.D.

In a schematic outline of the psychoanalytic theories of perversion, one may, I believe, roughly distinguish three groups of theoretical formulations. The first one, basically corresponding to Freud's (1927, 1938a,b) original conclusions about the subject, defines perversion as the fixation at or regression to a psychosexual phase at which a permanent and obligatory deviation from the normal in the sexual aim and/or object is required in order to achieve orgasm. In this theory, an infantile sexual component (or partial) drive (anal, oral, etc.) serves as a defense against an underlying neurotic conflict, namely, against the unresolved Oedipus complex. This concept stresses the centrality of castration anxiety and the Oedipus complex in the etiology of perversion, and views the perversion as a structured defensive organization.

In my view, this traditional concept of perversion continues to be valid for perverse patients who present a neurotic, in contrast to a borderline, personality organization, and normal infantile, in contrast to pathological, narcissism. In fact, in contrast to the tendency of the recent psychoanalytic literature to describe all perversions as if they represented a double layer of conflicts with strong predominance of preoedipal issues, I think one finds patients with typical neurotic personality organization (a firm sense of identity, a capacity for object relations in depth, and predominantly repressive defensive mechanisms) who do present an organized perversion as part of their symptomatology.

A second concept of perversion is represented by the formulations of the British object relations theorists, particularly Fairbairn (1940), Melanie Klein (1945), and Winnicott (1953), whose approach stresses the preoedipal contributions to the psychodynamics of perversion, the psychopathology in the mother-infant relationship, and the central role of preoedipal aggression. What follows is an overall summary of this approach, particularly of Klein's contribution to it.

The child's pathologically intense pregenital and particularly oral aggression—whether its source is a reaction to frustration (Fairbairn, Winnicott), or derived from inborn aggression (Klein)—is projected onto the parental figures, especially mother, thus causing a paranoid distortion of the early parental images. Because the child projects predominantly oral-sadistic but also anal-sadistic impulses, the mother is experienced as potentially dangerous, and the hatred of the mother later expands to hatred of both parents whom the child, in his unconscious fantasy, experiences as a unit. A contamination of the image of the father by aggression primarily projected onto the mother and then displaced onto him and lack of differentiation between the images of the parents under the influence of primitive defensive operations dealing with this aggression produce in both boys and girls a combined and dangerous father-mother image, with the result that all sexual relationships are conceived as dangerous and aggressively infiltrated. Under these circumstances, the primal scene acquires particularly dangerous and frightening characteristics and is perceived by the child with severely sadomasochistic distortions. All of this leads to an excessive aggressivization of oedipal conflicts, so that the image of the oedipal rival typically acquires terrifying, dangerous, and destructive characteristics; castration anxiety and penis envy become grossly exaggerated and overwhelming; and superego prohibitions against all sexual relations (because of their oedipal implications) acquire a savage, primitive quality, reflected in severe masochistic tendencies or paranoid projections of superego precursors.

In addition, the idealization of the heterosexual love object in the positive oedipal relation and of the homosexual love object in the negative oedipal relation are also exaggerated and, as an expression of splitting operations, have marked defensive functions against the threatening condensation of primitive rage and oedipal aggressiveness. The exaggerated, unrealistic idealizations of the love object, matched by the unrealistic, paranoid distortion of the oedipal rival, intensify further oedipal inhibitions and castration anxiety. The genital strivings of these patients with predominantly preoedipal conflicts serve important pregenital functions as well. The penis, for example, may acquire symbolic functions of the feeding, withholding, or punishing mother, and the vagina may acquire the functions of the hungry, feeding, or aggressive mouth; similar developments occur regarding anal and urinary functions. The existence of these features in combination with excessive aggressivization of the pregenital libidinal drive derivatives also contributes to intensifying castration anxiety and the fantasied dangers of sexual relations.

This second approach differs from Freud's thinking in that it stresses preoedipal conflicts, particularly preoedipal aggression, as a crucial contributing factor in the etiology of the perversions, but it continues to emphasize the importance of castration anxiety in blocking the full deployment of genital sexuality. This theory explains the intensity of castration anxiety, the incapacity to identify normally with the oedipal parent of the same sex, and the inhibition of the sexual approach to an object of the opposite sex as derived from the aggressivization of the positive and negative oedipal relationship and the fantastic accentuation of castration fears as genital sexuality becomes the recipient of displaced preoedipal aggression.

A third approach to the psychodynamics of perversion is represented largely by the French psychoanalytic school, particularly by the formulations of Chasseguet-Smirgel (1985b, 1986), Braunschweig and Fain (1971), Grunberger (1976), McDougall (1980), and Lussier (1982), among others. Chasseguet-Smirgel has singularly contributed to this approach, and summarized (1985b) her view pointing to the following central aspects. First, in agreement with Freud, she considers the perversions as a regressive activation or fixation at a partial, pregenital, component drive in replacement of genital sexuality that is interfered with or blocked by castration anxiety. Second, she stresses the universal potential for regression to the anal-sadistic phase, stating that "the anal universe can be considered as a preliminary sketch of the genital universe" (p. 157). This anal regression transforms the symbolic relation to the genital phallus into one of a pseudo-genital fecal phallus that permits the denial of the differences between the two sexes (anal "equality" of the sexes in contrast to genital differentiation), and also implies the abolishment of generational boundaries (the fecal phallus erases the differences between the little boy's and the father's penis, and permits to eliminate the awareness of the vagina as the significant female genital organ). Third, in a secondary defense against the masking of the anal regression, an idealization of anality occurs, with a symbolic accentuation of the aesthetic and formal aspects of art, nature, physical objects, and interpersonal reality. There also develops an idealization of the specific perversion of the individual patient as vastly superior to the "ordinary" genital relations (with their oedipal implications). Fourth, the mechanisms of denial of the differences between sexes and of generations, and of idealization of the pregenital, partial perverse component drive, are accompanied by the mechanism of splitting, which permits at the same time a persistent recognition of reality. At a conscious level, the pervert still recognizes the reality of sexual differences and of generations, and of the need to integrate his perverse strivings somehow, in a nonpsychotic fashion, into his actual sexual behavior. The loss of reality-testing characteristic of perversions in psychotic personality organization signals the failure of this splitting operation, the uncontrollable destruction of the ego by primitive aggression, and the extremely dangerous nature of these patients' perversions.

In short, in this formulation, perverse structures are characterized by regressive analization, denial of the differences of sexes and generations, defensive idealization of anality, persistent recognition of reality, and splitting (both denial and recognition of sexual differences) superimposed on repression.

Chasseguet-Smirgel (1986) stresses that, in both sexes, the early relation to the mother is of fundamental etiological importance in perversions. However, in contrast to the British school, and particularly to Melanie Klein's formulations, she considers the aggression against the mother to reflect archaic aspects of the oedipal situation that derive not from split, part object relations to the breast, but from fantastic distortions of the imagined interior of the mother's body.

Chasseguet-Smirgel considers perversion as ultimately derived from the need to deny the reality of the mother's vagina and the "dark continent" of the interior of the mother's belly, and from the unconscious aggression toward the mother expressed in the archaic fantasy of destruction of the contents of the mother's body, including her father's penis, other babies, and any obstacle opposed to a free-floating, endless expansion in the mother's smooth unobstructed belly.

Chasseguet-Smirgel proposes that aggression against the mother projected onto her as an engulfing primitive genital figure, the need to deny the awareness of the vagina, and the very aggression against the content of the mother's genitals are underlying dynamics that reinforce castration anxiety of the later, advanced oedipal stage in both sexes.

In the French concept of perversion, Freud's stress on the centrality of the Oedipus complex and castration anxiety in determining the defensive regression to a component sexual drive is reaffirmed, with the modification of stressing the archaic Oedipus complex linked to the primary relation to the mother. This view may be considered a modified version of the British view, with a particular emphasis on the defensive mechanisms of denial of the differences of sexes and generations, and the idealization of anality.

Chasseguet-Smirgel (1985b) has applied her understanding to particularly severe forms of perversion, stressing how in such cases the anal quality of the mechanism of devaluation (that is typical in the narcissistic transferences of these patients) leads to the transformation of all object relations into undifferentiated, devalued "segments" unconsciously representing feces. Here, the denial of the differences of the sexes and of generations, the omnipotent equalization of homosexuality and heterosexuality in multiple, polymorphous perverse sexual activities, reflects, in her view, a perverse destruction of object relations by analization of them. In my experience, this generalized destructiveness of all object relations that seem to be regressively "digested" and then "fragmented" into symbolic feces is a dramatic, quite concrete finding in the analytic exploration of most severe cases of perversions. I have explored the relation between these dynamics and the syndrome of malignant narcissism (Kernberg, 1984) in earlier work. In this regard, Fairbairn (1940) had already described the defensive withdrawal from object relations in some patients with severe psychopathology, and the replacement of object relations by a regressive accentuation of perverse sexual strivings.

Chasseguet-Smirgel's emphasis on the pathological consequences of severe early aggression on the process of separation-individuation from the mother, and particularly on the vicissitudes of the normal girl's identification with female functions, and on the little boy's tolerance for the oedipal rivalry with father, dovetail with the work of American psychoanalysts who have stressed the importance of separation-individuation in the genesis of perversion. Thus, Stoller (1968) described the fear of femininity in men, an expression of men's anxiety about losing their sexual identity, as derived from the primary symbiosis with the mother that must be undone in order for a masculine identity to be developed by separating off from maternal identity. Person and Ovesey (1974a,b,c, 1978, 1984) also stress the importance of severe conflicts of separation-individuation and related disturbances in identity formation as common dynamic features of male transsexualism, transvestism, and homosexual cross-dressing in men. Blum (1988) has pointed to the importance of the mechanism of shared unconscious fantasy in the mother-infant dyad as a key etiological factor in preoedipally determined gender identity disorders.

In earlier work (Kernberg, 1984, 1985, 1986, 1988) I have pointed to the striking similarity of the psychodynamics of perversions described by the British and French schools and the psychodynamics of borderline personality organization I have observed over the years. Lussier (1982) in his comprehensive study on fetishism, in which fetishism is used as a paradigm for the general study of perversion, stresses the combination of preoedipal and oedipal conflicts in these patients, the dominance of ego splitting in relation to preoedipal conflicts, and the condensation of such preoedipal conflicts with oedipal ones leading to an extremely sadistic and masochistic conception of the primal scene. He emphasizes the multiple functions of the fetish as a symbol of sadistic control over a woman, a protection against separation anxiety, a reassurance against the destructive affects of aggression derived from preoedipal and oedipal conflicts, and a defense against homosexual urges linked to the submission to a sadistic father and to a castrating phallic mother in the primal scene.

I concluded in earlier work that, in clinical practice, we do not find a single set of underlying dynamics for all cases of perversion. On the contrary, a careful analysis of a broad spectrum of perverse psychopathology points to radical differences in the dynamic and structural preconditions of perverse behavior. More specifically, the study of male perversion (Kernberg, 1986) and of the clinical syndromes of masochism (Kernberg, 1988) led me to conclude that polymorphous perverse fantasies, activities, and capabilities emerge as an essential part of human sexuality at all levels of pathology and normality. The consolidation of a specific perversion as an obligatory precondition for sexual gratification, to the detriment of ordinary freedom and flexibility of sexual gratification in a stable relation with a loved heterosexual object may indicate a severe or moderate or merely a mild degree of pathology according to the patient's predominant level of ego organization and object relations.

Specific sexual perversions in the context of borderline personality organization have a more guarded prognosis and are more difficult to treat than sexual perversions in the context of neurotic personality organization. The severity of the illness and the prognosis are even more guarded for patients with borderline personality organization and the consolidation of a narcissistic personality structure, particularly for cases of malignant narcissism. Thus, the type and severity of the patient's character pathology are fundamental codeterminants of the structure, dynamics, and prognosis of perversion.

Another crucial dimension that, in my experience, codetermines the structure and prognosis of perversion is the developmental level and integration of superego functions. Aggression in the form of criminal activity of the psychopath, and aggression in the form of sadistic violence in malignant narcissism (pathological narcissism in combination with ego-syntonic aggression, paranoid traits, and antisocial features) are characterized by the absence of an integrated superego; indeed, these severe pathologies may also be expressed in a violent sadistic perversion, illustrating the most dramatic type of sexual perversion that can be encountered. In contrast, the relation between perversion and superego pathology in neurotic personality organization has the paradoxical effect of consolidating the perversion (because of the unconscious prohibitions against genital sexuality that represents incest and evokes castration anxiety), but also protecting the patient against uncontrolled expression of aggression and the related deterioration of object relations. An integrated, although excessively severe superego guarantees the "boundaries of playfulness" of the perverse scenario, which has positive therapeutic and prognostic implications. The importance of the type and degree of superego pathology in determining the prognosis and treatment indications of perversions also reflects the general centrality of superego distortions in contemporary psychopathology highlighted by Rangell (1974).

Finally, in my view, the vicissitudes of aggression in the perversions emerge as an essential component of all sexuality, and the relationship between aggression and eroticism appears as a basic psychodynamic factor throughout the entire spectrum of perverse psychopathology, from neurosis to psychosis. Under normal circumstances, aggression is recruited at the service of sex and love and enriches the love life; under extremely pathological circumstances, aggression may recruit sex and love for destructive purposes, reflected in the transformation of perversion into perversity, characteristic of the syndrome of malignant narcissism (Kernberg, 1984, 1985).

In what follows, I expand on the clinical observations made in earlier work. I shall stress the following points of view. (1) In contrast to the traditional relegation of polymorphous perverse features as merely aspects of sexual foreplay, I consider them a crucial aspect of normal sexuality. (2) Organized perversions at a neurotic level of personality organization do present, in both sexes, the psychodynamics originally proposed by Freud, psychodynamics centering on the defensive fixation at a partial, component drive in defense against full genital sexuality with its oedipal implications, the threat of incest, and castration anxiety. For all practical purposes, these cases follow the course of psychoanalytic treatment that is typical for other types of neurotic illness, including neurotic character pathology, and they should no longer be considered as being particularly severe. (3) Cases of stable perversion and borderline personality organization, in contrast, typically present the dynamics described by the British and French schools, with individually varying centrality of different aspects of these dynamic constellations. In general, they present the same condensation of oedipal and preoedipal conflicts under the dominance of preoedipal aggression characteristic of borderline personality organization. I must stress that this condensation includes a regressive primitivization of the oedipal conflicts, an overriding predominance of aggressive over libidinal strivings, and is clinically very different from the more differentiated, defensive regression to preoedipal stages of development to be found in patients with neurotic personality organization. The fundamental question of why some patients with these dynamics develop a perversion and others do not is, in my view, still open. (4) Sexual perversions in the context of a narcissistic personality structure, and particularly in the case of malignant narcissism, do show very fully the psychodynamic constellations outlined by Chasseguet-Smirgel. In fact, the full deployment of a regressive "anal universe" practically overlaps with the syndrome of malignant narcissism plus an organized perversion. Even patients with multiple perverse tendencies and malignant narcissism deploy the same psychodynamic features. (5) Patients with total inhibition of all polymorphous perverse features not derived from repression but from lack of activation of early eroticism (that is, some extremely inhibited borderline but not hysterical patients) have the least favorable prognosis for treatment of their pathological sexuality. They may present most stubborn resistances to psychoanalysis and, in fact, all psychotherapeutic treatments that attempt to resolve their sexual inhibitions. (6) The special position of homosexuality with regard to the realm of the perversions emerges as a major, new development in psychoanalytic thinking.

A consensus seems to be evolving that there exists not one homosexuality, but a spectrum of homosexual psychopathology that parallels that of the other perversions (McDougall, 1986). However, at the healthier polarity of the spectrum, homosexuality presents with the capacity for integration of genital and tender impulses in the same object relation, and does not show the exclusive and rigid characteristics typical for all other perversions. Also, in theory, homosexual impulses should be part of the available pattern of perverse fantasies and behaviors of normal sexuality as well. In fact, the continuity between such homosexual tendencies in neurotic personality organization and in patients who do not present significant character pathology seems to hold true for women but not for men. Many "normal" women are free to experience homosexual impulses and behaviors under socially facilitating circumstances which would trigger homosexual panic in nonhomosexual men. Openly bisexual men usually have more severe character pathology than many openly bisexual women. The explanation for this difference may lie, as Stoller (1975) suggested, in the more stable core gender identity of women derived from their primary identification with the mother, in contrast to the need of the male to disidentify in the course of separation-individuation. In addition, there is some evidence that the stronger social and cultural prohibitions against male as contrasted to female homosexuality may constitute a second reason for these differences (Liebert, 1986).

THE FUNCTIONS OF POLYMORPHOUS PERVERSE INFANTILE SEXUALITY AND ITS IDEALIZATION AS PART OF NORMAL LOVE RELATIONS

I believe that we have not explored sufficiently the theoretical implications of the improvement in sexual functioning that we find in patients who obtain maximal benefit from psychoanalytic treatment. Regularly, in cases where a full resolution of the patient's psychopathology is achieved, we may observe that erotic excitement is intimately linked to derivatives of aggression, so that libidinal and aggressive impulses coalesce in sexual play and intercourse, and in the activation of implicit homosexual excitement and gratification in the mutual identification that takes place as part of intercourse and orgasm. In addition, it is striking how these normal, polymorphous perverse fantasies and activities include a symbolic activation of the earliest object relation of the infant with mother, and of the small child with both parents, condensing preoedipal and oedipal relations with them. A correlation of this finding is that the normal perverse components of sexual play and intercourse, such as fellatio, cunnilingus, anal penetration, and exhibitionistic, voyeuristic, sadistic, and masochistic sexual play, maintain the intensity of their erotic value because they activate such unconscious fantasies regarding the oedipal and preoedipal objects. If, as in narcissistic personalities, such internalized object relations deteriorate, the normal perverse sexual play also may deteriorate into mechanical activities that lose their erotic potential. An essential component that maintains the intensity of a passionate love relation is constituted precisely by normal polymorphous perverse sexuality, which recruits in its function as the receptacle of unconscious fantasy the currently conflictual relations and meanings that evolve between a couple throughout time.

What is also of particular interest is that, insofar as sexual passion includes the freedom of unconsciously integrating love and hatred in polymorphous sexual behavior, an implicit frame of a couple's safe object relation is developed, a frame that tolerates the playful use or "exploitation" of each other as part of sexual play. This frame represents a temporary regressive splitting of the ego at the service of sexual excitement and love which enters into a dialectic contradiction with the opposite tendency also activated in sexual intimacy, namely, the urge for temporary fusion experiences in the sexual relationship.

This sexual "use of the object" reflects a normal function of splitting of the sexual object, or, rather, a duplication of it, in which the reality of the object relation is maintained, while a fantastic, regressive one is playfully enacted as part of sexual desire and excitement. In fact, the inhibition of this function, of this sublimatory use of splitting, is related to the decrease in sexual excitement that is part of milder forms of sexual inhibition.

Another important mechanism operant in normal sexual excitement is the idealization of the sexual partner, his or her genitals and body. In earlier work (Kernberg, 1986) I referred to the normal function of idealization of the sexual partner's anatomy, what I called erotic idealization, as a crucial aspect of the normal integration of tender and erotic strivings in both heterosexual and homosexual love relations. This erotic idealization parallels the normal idealization processes described by Chasseguet-Smirgel (1985a), namely, the projection of the ego ideal onto the loved object which characterizes falling in love, and which increases the narcissistic gratification provided by the real encounter with this materialized version of the ego ideal. The idealization of the loved object, then, also carries with it the idealization of the genital encounter, of one's own and one's partner's bodies and genitals, as they touch and merge with each other. Thus, the defensive use of idealization and splitting that we encounter in perversion reappears as part of the normal constellation of eroticism and mature sexuality.

THE QUESTION OF "NORMAL" AND "TRANSITIONAL" HOMOSEXUALITY

Male homosexual patients with neurotic personality organization and the corresponding structural characteristics of their world of object relations typically show the dominance of an unconscious submission to the oedipal father related to guilt over their oedipal longings for the mother and castration anxiety. In other words, they present a defensive structuralization of the negative Oedipus complex within the context of a consolidated ego identity, a prevalence of total or integrated object relations, a predominance of oedipal strivings, and defensive mechanisms centering upon repression. In their love relations, they are often able to have stable object relations which include both genital excitement and tenderness toward the same man, illustrating that the concept of perversion does not preclude the capacity for integrating genital and tender feelings in the same object. These patients often present polymorphous perverse fantasies and activities, and they may engage in a broad range of sexual behaviors as long as the obligatory homosexual condition is maintained.

The question of the boundaries between homosexuality in a neurotic personality organization and the normal homosexual components of male sexuality has no simple answer. One might assume, theoretically, that in parallel to the existence of polymorphous perverse infantile sexual trends of other types, homosexual impulses would be freely available and show in occasional homosexual excitement and experience. If homosexual tendencies simply behaved like other polymorphous perverse trends, we would expect a spectrum of homosexual responses—from a perversion in the sense of the habitual and obligatory restriction, at one extreme, to occasional homosexual impulses, fantasies, and behaviors, at the other. In clinical practice, however, we see very few cases of homosexual behavior in male patients who otherwise would present no major character pathology.

On the contrary, by far the large majority of male patients we encounter who present casual homosexual behavior or a casual bisexual orientation belong to the borderline spectrum of pathology. Thus, from a clinical viewpoint, there appears to be a discontinuity between neurotic male homosexuality and normality, and male orientation toward one or the other sex does not seem to follow the usual distribution of polymorphous perverse sexuality.

In female homosexual behavior, however, the situation is different. In my experience, occasional homosexual involvements on the part of women who are essentially heterosexual and do not present severe characterological problems are quite frequent. Sociologists have described the ease with which, in the context of group sex experiences, women accept homosexual as well as heterosexual encounters, while men with a heterosexual identity sharply reject any homosexual approaches. The defensive rejection of the normal preoedipal dependency on the father on the part of adolescent boys may contribute to this rejection of longed-for closeness with other men (Blos, 1987). The theoretically expected continuity between nonobligatory homosexual trends within a normal population, on the one hand, and an obligatory homosexual perversion at a neurotic level of personality organization, on the other, probably exist for women but not for men.

If this clinical observation is valid, one might speculate that two important factors may be operative here: first, as mentioned before, the hypothesis formulated by Stoller (1975) indicating that female core gender identity is cemented in the primary identification with mother, and therefore women may be more secure in their gender role identity as well, accepting their homosexual impulses as derivatives of the unconscious psychological bisexuality without excessive anxiety. Men, in contrast, whose core gender identity implies disidentifying from mother, and who therefore experience less certainty in their basic gender role identity, may be more prone to repudiate the feminine aspects of their sexual identity. A failure in the mother's relating to her infant child as a little boy—which would further weaken the little boy's identification with his own masculine gender as part of his identification with the mother—may significantly contribute to this dynamic feature. A second factor may be the existence of strong cultural biases against male homosexuality in our own culture, even against any overt physical manifestation of closeness between men, which may discourage casual homosexual impulses and behavior in men. Less cultural repudiation of female sexuality may facilitate the manifestations of occasional homosexual behavior in women.

PERVERSION AND HOMOSEXUALITY AT A NEUROTIC LEVEL OF PERSONALITY ORGANIZATION

Obligatory homosexuality in a neurotic personality organization is frequent in men and in women. As mentioned before, the oedipal constellation and castration anxiety are dominant features in these types of perversion, and the most typical object relation represented in the homosexual relation is the submission to the oedipal parent of the same sex, that is, the negative Oedipus complex, as a defense against the positive Oedipus complex interfered with by severe castration anxiety.

The men are patients whose homosexual identification is with themselves as the child being loved by the mother, while their longings for the mother have been displaced onto motherly men who protect them from both a forbidden relation with the mother and from the rivalry with the dissociated, cruel, and sadistic father. In other cases, and sometimes in the same patient, the identification may be with the giving mother, while the patient projects his sexually dependent self onto his homosexual object (Freud, 1914).

In the case of women, similar relations obtain, with the patient sexually submitting as a little girl to motherly women, thus avoiding the unconsciously forbidden relation with the father; or the identification is with the motherly and sexually available women, while the submissive, dependent sexual self is projected onto the homosexual partner. Homosexual women who identify with the oedipal father, while projecting their oedipally dependent self onto their homosexual object, usually have a more complex and more pathological structure. Homosexual women who adopt a "male" role in the relationship, and who, in their gender role identity (in their physical appearance, clothing, and behavior) accentuate their identification with men, usually also present significant repudiation of the feminine aspects of their personality, of their identification with the mother in the preoedipal relation, and, by the same token, indicate significant preoedipal conflictual roots condensed with oedipal conflicts. The "wish-fulfillment type" of the female castration complex described by Abraham (1920) thus presents more complex dynamics than those he suggested, and many cases of female homosexuality based upon a narcissistic personality structure and borderline personality organization also present with a surface identification with a male role in relating to other women (thus revealing the preoedipal roots of their envy of men).

As has often been mentioned in the literature, all perversions except homosexuality and masochism are more frequent in men than in women. This seems to be true at the level of neurotic and of borderline personality organization. One also encounters in women very frequent masochistic and sadomasochistic fantasies and behavior that are not organized as a perversion, but quite freely expressed in masturbatory fantasies and in nonobligatory sexual behavior, while organized masochistic perversions in a strict sense seem to be more frequent in men. I have seen some typical cases of masochistic perversion in women with neurotic personality organization. One patient was able to achieve orgasm only if her arms were twisted severely during intercourse, thus producing intense pain. She related that behavior to the struggle with a boyfriend who was forcing her to have sexual intercourse, twisting her arms. She experienced an intense pleasure on that occasion, which then organized her masochistic perversion.

Similarly, exhibitionistic fantasies and behavior are frequent in women without leading to an organized perversion. Fetishism, voyeurism, pedophilia, and sadistic perversion at any level of personality organization are relatively rare in women.

The generally held assumption that castration anxiety is a more powerful force in male than in female psychology, and that this final common characteristic of all perversions is therefore stronger in men, may explain this difference. McDougall's (personal communication) observation, however, about the severity of primitive forms of castration anxiety in women with strong preoedipal conflicts points to an open question in this area. Severe inhibition of all sexual enjoyment derived from preoedipal conflicts and predating the dominance of repressive mechanisms is more frequently seen in women, probably signaling the danger to the full expression of female sexuality under conditions of severe and early repudiation of their primary femininity in the context of conflicts around aggression with the preoedipal mother.

PERVERSION AND HOMOSEXUALITY AT A BORDERLINE LEVEL OF PERSONALITY ORGANIZATION AND IN THE NARCISSISTIC PERSONALITY

At this severe level of psychopathology of perversions, the dynamics described by the British and French schools appear as central in the patients' unconscious life, and coincide with the psychodynamics of borderline personality organization. The interesting question of why some of these patients develop an organized perversion, while most other patients of this group present, instead, the chaotic coexistence of multiple, polymorphous perverse infantile sexual traits has not yet, in my view, been answered satisfactorily. The presence of multiple perverse traits that do not amount to an organized perversion is frequently present in both male and female borderline patients. I have seen sadistic and masochistic, voyeuristic and exhibitionistic behavior in borderline women, and even highly regressive, bizarre masochistic behaviors in both sexes. The most severe types of aggressive perversions, however, have been described almost exclusively in men. It is an open question to what extent biological features of the expression of aggression as well as cultural determinants contribute to both a higher intensity of aggression and its channeling into sadistic sexual behavior in men. There are, however, well-documented cases of severely sadistic perversions in women, and many such cases in the legal system may never reach a psychiatrist. The novel *Die Klavierspielerin (The Pianist)* by Elfriede Jelinek (1983) penetratingly describes the relation between a sadistic, voyeuristic, and masochistic perversion in a woman, and her sadomasochistic and homosexual relation to an extremely envious, sadistic, and invasive mother.

In earlier work (Kernberg, 1986) I described two dominant types of dynamics in male homosexuality at the level of borderline personality organization. First is a consolidated homosexuality in a nonnarcissistic borderline patient in which dominant preoedipal dynamics involve the wish to submit sexually to the father in order to obtain from him the oral gratifications that were denied from a dangerous, frustrating mother. The other type is a narcissistic personality structure consolidated with a dominant homosexual identification. In this latter case, there is usually a much better surface functioning (in terms of object relations and nonspecific aspects of ego strength), but also a much more stable and deeply rooted homosexual organization. I have found similar characteristics in female homosexuality at a borderline level.

When the borderline structure is not complicated by a narcissistic personality, the chaotic object relations overshadow the homosexual dynamics; but when the borderline personality organization exists in the context of a narcissistic personality, the homosexual orientation is much stronger. At the same time, object relations are not as chaotic—at least in ordinary social functioning. In these narcissistic patients one finds a dominant unconscious fantasy of incorporating, as part of the homosexual identity, the characteristics of both sexes, so that the envy of the other sex can be successfully denied. This development provides the background for extraordinarily severe resistances in psychoanalytic treatment.

For practical purposes, I have found that, in both men and women, if the perverse tendencies are multiple and the organization of the personality is clearly borderline, the overall prognosis for treatment depends on the intensity or severity of aggression, the degree to which superego functioning is maintained (so that, at least, ordinary conventional morality is available), and the presence or absence of a narcissistic organization, that is, the integration of a pathological grandiose self.

Borderline personality organization per se plus multiple perverse tendencies, in the absence of severe superego pathology, without primitivization of aggression, and without a narcissistic personality structure, has a relatively good prognosis for fundamental reorganization of the patient's sexual life and resolution of his psychopathology in general. Also, in these cases with better prognosis, the very availability of multiple perverse tendencies may improve their sexual life at a time when the borderline personality organization has been resolved.

PRIMITIVE ELIMINATION OF ALL PERVERSE FEATURES AS PART OF GLOBAL, SEVERE SEXUAL INHIBITION

The study of borderline patients with severe inhibition of sexual desire, including significant limitations of the capacity for obtaining pleasure from masturbation or in any sexual interaction with another person, has revealed the enormous difference between sexual inhibition resulting from repression (typical for neurotic personality organization) and that derived from earlier stages of development, the unavailability or early repudiation of the erotic excitement of bodily stimulation. Severe conflicts in the mother-child relation in the first few years of life, the absence of a sustained, gratifying mother-infant relationship that permits kindling of skin eroticism seem leading etiological elements here.

Men with an incapacity for longing and tenderness and for erotic excitement have profound fears and experience deeply engrained rejection of women, with severe paranoid tendencies that complicate their intense anxiety over their sexual functioning. One might say that, in these cases, castration anxiety is so infiltrated by the fear of annihilation by a fantasied, primitive, sadistic mother image, that all sensuality is suppressed or extinguished.

In women, typically women with borderline personality organization and severe conflicts around preoedipal aggression, these sexual inhibitions are particularly resistant to analytic treatment. They are usually linked to a profound repudiation of feminine identity, a conception of the female body as genitally destroyed and repugnant, and, by projection of aggressive impulses, male genitality is also experienced as dangerous and repugnant. One female patient's exclusive masturbatory fantasy was that of a deeply humiliating scene, in which she was prostrated on a hard bed, surrounded by groups of nuns who were watching her while the mother superior of the convent used a mechanical apparatus to penetrate her exposed genitals. This scenario contained no physical closeness, no contact of male and female genitals, and only the awesome, frightening, humiliating atmosphere of a world dominated by sadistic and voyeuristic women. This patient had a history of severe problems of separation and individuation from what she experienced as an extremely sadistic, oerwhelming, invasive mother. The mother forbade all expression of sexual curiosity in the family, and dominated her passive and distant husband. The patient struggled with enormous difficulties in separating from an archaic, primitive maternal image that interfered both with her identification with a feminine role and with her reaching out toward her father and heterosexuality.

In conclusion, I have attempted to present an overview of the dynamics of perversion in the light of a structural frame of reference that attempts to integrate levels of personality organization with object relations, vicissitudes of aggression, superego development, and narcissism.

REFERENCES

Abraham, K. (1920), Manifestations of the female castration complex. In: *Selected Papers on Psycho-Analysis*. New York: Brunner/Mazel, 1979, pp. 338–369.

Blos, P. (1987), The role of the dyadic father in male personality formation. *Sigmund Freud Haus Bulletin*, 10:7–14.

Blum, H. P. (1988), Shared fantasy and reciprocal identification, and their role in gender disorders. In: *Fantasy, Myth, and Reality*, ed. H. P. Blum, Y. Kramer, A. Richards & A. Richards. New York: International Universities Press.

Braunschweig, D., & Fain, M. (1971), *Eros et Anteros*. Paris: Petite Bibliotheque Payot.

Chasseguet-Smirgel, J. (1985a), *The Ego Ideal: A Psychoanalytic Essay on the Malady of the Ideal*. New York: Norton.

——— (1985b), *Creativity and Perversion*. New York: Norton.

——— (1986), *Sexuality and Mind: The Role of the Father and the Mother in the Psyche*. New York: International Universities Press.

Fairbairn, W. R. D. (1940), Schizoid factors in the personality. In: *An Object-Relations Theory of the Personality*. New York: Basic Books, 1954, pp. 3–27.

Freud, S. (1914), On narcissism. *Standard Edition*, 14:69–102. London: Hogarth Press, 1957.

——— (1927), Fetishism. *Standard Edition*, 21:147–158. London: Hogarth Press, 1961.

——— (1938a), An outline of psycho-analysis. *Standard Edition*, 23:143, 202–204. London: Hogarth Press, 1964.

——— (1938b), Splitting of the ego in the process of defense. *Standard Edition*, 23:273–274. London: Hogarth Press, 1964.

Grunberger, B. (1976), Essai sur le fetichisme. *Rev. Franç. Psychanal.*, 40:235–264.

Jelinek, E. (1983), *Die Klavierspielerin*. Reinbek bei Hamburg: Rowohlt.

Kernberg, O. F. (1984), *Severe Personality Disorders: Psychotherapeutic Strategies*. New Haven, CT: Yale University Press.

——— (1985), The relation of borderline personality organization to the perversions. In: *Psychiatrie et Psychanalyse: Jalons pour une Fecondation Reciproque*. Quebec: Gaetan Morin, pp. 99–116.

——— (1986), A conceptual model for male perversion. In: *The Psychology of Men: New Psychoanalytic Perspectives*, Vol. 7, ed. G. I. Fogel, F. M. Lane, & R. S. Liebert. New York: Basic Books, pp. 152–180.

——— (1988), Clinical dimensions of masochism. *J. Amer. Psychoanal. Assn.*, 36:1005–1029.

Klein, M. (1945), The Oedipus complex in the light of early anxieties.

In: *Contributions to Psycho-Analysis*. London: Hogarth Press, 1948, pp. 339–390.

Liebert, R. S. (1986), The history of male homosexuality from ancient Greece through the Renaissance: Implications for psychoanalytic theory. In: *The Psychology of Men: New Psychoanalytic Perspectives*, Vol. 8, ed. G. I. Fogel, F. M. Lane, & R. S. Liebert. New York: Basic Books, pp. 181–210.

Lussier, A. (1982), *Les Deviations du Désir: Etude sur le Fetichisme*. Montreal: Quarante-Deuxième Congrès Des Psychanalystes De Langue Française.

McDougall, J. (1972), Primal scene and sexual perversion. *Internat. J. Psycho-Anal.*, 53:371–384.

——— (1980), *Plea for a Measure of Abnormality*. New York: International Universities Press.

——— (1986), Identifications, neoneeds and neosexualities. *Internat. J. Psycho-Anal.*, 67:19–31.

Person, E. S., & Ovesey, L. (1974a), The psychodynamics of male transsexualism. In: *Sex Differences in Behavior*, ed. R. C. Friedman, R. M. Richart, & R. L. vande Wiele. New York: Wiley, pp. 315–331.

——— ——— (1974b), The transsexual syndrome in males: I. Primary transsexualism. *Amer. J. Psychother.*, 28:4–20.

——— ——— (1974c), The transsexual syndrome in males: II. Secondary transsexualism. *Amer. J. Psychother.*, 28:174–193.

——— ——— (1978), Transvestism: New perspectives. *J. Amer. Acad. Psychoanal.*, 6:301–323.

——— ——— (1984), Homosexual cross-dressers. *J. Amer. Acad. Psychoanal.*, 12:167–186.

Rangell, L. (1974), A psychoanalytic perspective leading currently to the syndrome of the compromise of integrity. *Internat. J. Psycho-Anal.*, 55:3–12.

Stoller, R. (1968), *Sex and Gender*, Vol. I. New York: Science House.

——— (1975), *Sex and Gender*, Vol. 2. London: Hogarth Press.

Winnicott, D. W. (1953), Transitional objects and transitional phenomena. *Internat. J. Psycho-Anal.*, 34:88–97.

14

CONSENSUAL SADOMASOCHISTIC PERVERSIONS

ROBERT J. STOLLER, M.D.

As time has passed, an attribute of Rangell's I have always admired has become essential for me: his commitment to his daily, concrete, unending clinical experiences as the anchor—the stabilizing force—for his theorizing. But have not all psychoanalysts, from Freud on, claimed to do that? Is not that habit the criterion for distinguishing us from avowed philosophers? Is not that effort—to ground one's understanding of human nature in observation—Freud's great advance in the progress toward the science, the objective study, of subjectivity?

Yes, we all answer. Of course. We *all* start, we say, with observations (granting that no observing is free of preconceptions, that no data are not interpretations). Still, some analysts—Platonic idealists—are, by nature or accident, less constrained by data and others—nominalists—more so. Psychoanalysis needs both, best of all, as with Rangell, in the same person.

This, however, is the chapter of a nominalist, who believes psychoanalysis is always in danger of slipping its gears and trying to run as a theory machine undeterred by the friction of clinical realities. Few analysts are worried that our reports are our unconfirmable, private versions of the clinical situation. That perhaps insoluble problem, to which Rangell has unendingly attended, is the fundament on which I place this chapter.

So I want to do something risky, at least to me: to try to pull an audience of psychoanalytic readers away from its natural expectations—in this case, a proper psychoanalytic presentation—to something more primitive, a return to raw (using that word as double entendre) data. In choosing this style of presentation, I use the style itself—presenting a mass of observations—as a vehicle of information, thereby suggesting that we should learn more about sadomasochistic behaviors and that our theory and the vocabulary that conveys it have run too far ahead of our facts. (Maleson [1984] and Grossman [1986] show how the multiple meanings given to *masochism* and *sadism* over the decades have led to confusing theory, not only on sadomasochism but on our understanding of "normal" and "pathologic" development.)

Though everyone knows how to squeeze pleasure from pain—someone else's or our own—it takes more doing to move such skill to an organized activity that is one's preferred or necessary form of erotic behavior: a perversion. Therein lies a familiar problem for psychoanalytic explanations: what is the connection between a full, day-and-night commitment to a behavior—erotic, for instance—and just a whisper? There is nothing like a well-done piece of analytic treatment for finding answers to such questions, but I have never analyzed an erotically perverse sadomasochist. Nonetheless, in recent years I have acquired information I can share on—let us call it—an ethnography of consensual sadomasochistic practices. I need not belabor the obvious: the observations that follow cannot replace those from analyses. There is no harm, however, in reminding colleagues that nonanalytic data can support and advance analytic theory and practice. (This chapter has been read and discussed with me by all my major informants. They agree that the observations herein are, in their experience, accurate.)

A PSYCHOANALYTIC "ETHNOGRAPHY"

A colleague suggested that, after my years of hiding from reality in my office, I should get out into the world a bit and observe, in their natural habitat, people with marked gender aberrance. Because of his connections with the Sheriff's Department of West Hollywood, he thought I might be given an escorted tour of the natives. But the Station Commander decided—I do not know why—that I should not observe the gender disordered but instead talk with the lieutenant assigned to drawing up rules to regulate B&D (Bondage and Discipline) establishments, those that cater professionally to people—mostly men, infrequently women—who need a safe place to perform, for a fee, sadistic or masochistic acts. So I was invited to visit three such places, two owned by men: *Chaney's* and *The Club Kincaid*, and one by a woman: *Chez Nous* (the different names—my pseudonyms give the feel of the actual ones—perhaps reflect different attitudes in male versus female owners), to talk with the owners, employees, and customers, and to tour the chambers, see the paraphernalia, and learn how they were used.

I soon had other informants—patients and nonpatients—who began teaching me the vocabulary and practice of S&M/B&D. All these informants—owners, employees, a manager, and habitués of B&D establishments; a freelance professional dominant ex-submissive woman; a piercing expert; a homosexual ("kinky") S&M therapist of homosexual S&M men, his lovers, and friends; pornographers, homosexual and heterosexual; and simple practitioners of S&M—have provided a flood of information.

THE SADOMASOCHISTIC PERVERSIONS

I now believe that *there is no sadomasochistic perversion* but, rather, many sadomasochistic perversions. I draw this conclusion not only from my own observations but from reviewing the literature. Yet until recently—before loading up on facts—I had no reason to doubt the psychiatric and psychoanalytic wisdom that there is such a perversion in which someone gets genitally excited by having inflicted or by inflicting pain, and that it is a radical distortion from "normal."[1] Then I began meeting sadomasochists. And so now I would say that there is sadomasochistic behavior in which pain and/or humiliation are linked with pleasure, but those who seek it do not make up a homogeneous enough group to warrant classification as a unity, a diagnosis.

[1] I.e., penis-in-vagina; in adults; monogamous—in purest form by means of marriage; no naughty fantasies; no whips or nails, hardly a slap; no mismanagement ("sexual dysfunction"); in a relationship sturdy with respect, responsibility, and caring.

Let me complicate things more. We all accept that perverse sadomasochism includes not only the inflicting of physical pain but also certain scenarios in which flagrant humiliation—for instance, master/slave—are features in the erotic play, in the absence of physical, on the flesh, pain. If then, enacting humiliation is also accepted as defining the perversion "sadomasochism," we have broken the boundaries of our definitions, for one will find humiliation/revenge fantasies—undoing, repair, reversal, mastery (Blum, 1978)—in *all* perversions. So we cannot avoid definitional problems by simply excluding from "the perversion sadism" or "the perversion masochism" those behaviors in which the inflicted pain is psychic rather than physical. For instance, there are people who, while not directly excited by, say, the lash of the whip, are profoundly turned on by the idea that being whipped puts them into a special, high-intensity contact with another person. They hate pain; they love to play at subjugation.

Other instances: here are names of some perverse behaviors, not classified as sadomasochism, at the center of which—expressed manifestly or invisibly—is the depiction of humiliation, the central depiction of S&M: transvestism, pedophilia, excretion, homosexuality, voyeurism, exhibitionism, rape (Stoller, 1975, 1979, 1985).

Now on to patterns of behavior that, were I even to speak only briefly of them, would take hours to describe. (For each category to be listed shortly, sense the "et ceteras.") I mention this now only to underline the earlier statement that there are many, many sadomasochistic perversions, not "*the* sadomasochistic perversion." In order to impose at least minimal order on this mass of observations, I shall divide behaviors into techniques, modes and roles, settings, and body parts. I suspect that this list is quite incomplete. And keep in mind that behind these rough listings are aesthetic sensibilities, nuances as exquisite as the efforts of painters, composers, and poets to get things exactly right. Shapes, size, colors, smells, textures, sounds, hardness and softness, decorations, materials used, effects produced, and so on, make the difference between exquisite, moderate, or no pleasure. (Even the words used count: a woman patient will only say "SM," not "S&M," to label her practices.)

Let two examples of nuances stand for the rest. (1) People who like to be paddled have available to them dozens of differently shaped and textured paddles, from which they choose, if they can find it, only one that produces *exactly* the right pain. (2) For some—sometimes the sadist, sometimes the masochist—seeing blood or welts or bruises is a high excitement. Just as movies strain for verisimilitude in their sadomasochisms (stories of war, athletics, adventure, torture, and spooks), so do the S&M scenarios of erotic play. (S&M players, by the way, say it is unfair that so many people's main entertainments in films, TV, books, and theater are flagrantly sadomasochistic yet socially encouraged. There are pornographic films for sadomasochists made up entirely of pieces spliced together from legitimate movies.)

Techniques

Whipping: whips (long, short, thick, thin, rope, leather, cloth, braided, unbraided, with or without knots and studs); paddles; canes; hands (open, fisted, palm, dorsum); switches (single, bundles); leather straps; chains, knouts.
Piercing: nails (sharp, blunt); needles; spears; arrows; jewelry; knives.
Tattooing.
Scarification.
Cutting: knives; razors; teeth; surgical instruments; scissors.
Hanging: suspension of body; suspension by neck; by limbs; from wires; from chains; from instruments driven through the flesh.
Electric shocking: different machines for delivering different sensations of shock (e.g., cattle prod, vibrator, medical machines).
Stretching on racks: different machines to stretch different body parts and to represent notable infernal apparatuses.
Mouth gagging: cloth; adhesive tape; ball-in-mouth; dildo.
Imprisonment: in cages; in black darkness (closets, blindfolds, diving bell); masks; boxes; trunks, coffins, refrigerators, barrels, packing crates.
Altered consciousness: by suffocation; by anesthesia; by hanging; by drugs; by prolonged suffering.
Mummification; cocooning: in loose leather bags; form-fitting leather costumes; bandages; plastic; blankets; mesh fabric; head and/or body plaster casts; latex; rubber.
Iron maidened.
Tickling: feathers; cloth; fingers.
Bondage: rope, twine; cotton thread; wire; leather; cloth; in harness (e.g., pony game); chains; nylon stockings; handcuffs; steel shackles; rubber tubing; straitjackets.
Excrement (expelled, retained, ingested, smelled, dirtied by): urine; feces; sweat;

semen; vaginal fluids; anus licking; enemas; catheters; other urinary and rectal foreign bodies.
Hair pulling or shaving: scalp; eyebrows; eyelids; body; genitals.
Burning: branding; dripped hot wax.
Wrestling: females; males and females; males; mud.
Stomping: high heels; bare feet.
Nonsuicidal wrist and ankle slashers.
Amputees.
Breathing control (air deprivation): diving helmets, masks.
Infantilism: diapers; cuddling; feeding with milk bottle; enemas.

Note the common feature, at least for those of us outside the games: suffering, not necessarily pain in the usual sense. A second common feature is the gross, dramatized expression of powerlessness for the participant playing the masochistic role and of power for the designated sadist. Though frequently implied, humiliation need not be a part of the overt scenario.

Modes and Roles

1. Top: bottom. A top is the person who, in a particular episode, chooses to be the manifestly dominant person, while the bottom is the person dominated. There are, however, as many different styles of topping and bottoming as there are players. For instance, there is "the pushy bottom," a person who takes an apparently submissive role but insists on giving the orders. (A dominant tells me that, in his and his colleagues' experience with consensual S&M, bottoms are erotically more lively, demanding, and needy than tops. Because it is the top's responsibility, for safety's sake, to do nothing beyond the accepted rules, the bottom is the pampered one, appearances to the contrary.) Subheadings of top and bottom are master-mistress/slave, mistress/serving maid (male or female), horse/rider, teacher/student, mother or father/child, warrior-amazon/captive, doctor-nurse/patient, madam/customer, priest/penitent, sheik/harem girl, executive/employe(e), director/ingenue, or any other two-poled power relationships imaginable. *Passive* and *active* would seem fine descriptive words for sadomasochistic activities, but when we enter the participants' minds, we find that—just as is the case everywhere—passivity can be a (covert) way of controlling, and activity can be a (covert)

way of indulging in passivity. (By no means are bottoms usually passive.) Likewise with the terms *dominant* and *submissive*.

2. Pain-as-pleasure: pain-as-pain. Some in the S&M scene suffer these various kinds of discomfort-pain-agony without the sensations themselves being pleasurable. (The opposite of "pleasure," we know, is not "pain," for there are pains that are pleasure and pains that are not.) For these people, it is not the direct experience of pain that they seek but rather that, in experiencing pain, they please their master. No sadomasochists like all kinds of pain. The distinctions, though fine, are precise: *this* part of the back smarts marvelously when whipped; half an inch away is agonizing.

3. The sex of the participants. Some people can perform sadomasochistic acts only with people of the opposite sex; some only with people of the same sex; some enjoy the acts with people of either sex, the enjoyment being different depending on the sex of the partner; and for some the sex of the partner is irrelevant: only the S&M counts.

4. Feminine: masculine. In this mode, it is not the sex that counts but whether the person, sometimes regardless of sex, is acting in a manner that the participants agree is a feminine way or a masculine way.

5. Erotic: nonerotic. By no means are all sadomasochistic scenarios aimed at creating erotic pleasure. In many situations, the techniques listed above are used for relaxation, dramatizations, and, for some people, may never be connected with erotic excitement. For others, the sadomasochism is foreplay, and, for some of these, continuing the sadomasochism leads to orgasm, while for others, the sadomasochism gives way to sexual intercourse in the usual styles, heterosexual or homosexual depending on the participants' tastes.

6. Physical: mental. For some people, the scenario does not include any of the physical techniques listed above but simply the playing out of parts, such as mistress and her servant. For others, the physical pain-inflicting activities are necessary. For many, the play acting is crucial but must also include the physical.

7. Autoerotic: interpersonal. Most sadomasochists need partners, but some want to practice alone. I do not include in the

latter group those who are unable to find partners and thus fantasize them but rather those who "play" by themselves (e.g., a man who drives nails into his testes) without an overt scenario.

8. Cross-dressed: not cross-dressed. Though there are no statistics, everyone in this business knows it is not uncommon for men who, during their play, take the submissive part to dress in women's clothes. This is also the case among those who hang themselves and who use other techniques for reducing consciousness. Some dominant women on occasion dress in men's clothes during sex play.

9. Overt: covert. The people I study practice their sadomasochism overtly, in the sense that they understand their scene—its rules, participants, and functions—in serving pleasure. On the other hand are the people who would not classify themselves as aberrant and who redefine the sources and purposes of their pleasure: a practicing sadist tells me of a non-S&M friend, a fighter pilot who flew combat missions with an erection. Other examples are those who use one or another of the techniques and modes listed above as religious practices. (I have treated a woman—not a perverse SM—for whom the crucified Christ is an erotic object; for some He is a *raison d'être* for erotic suffering; we are told of religious ecstacies that culminate self-torture in mystics and of the passions of flagellantes.)

10. Consensual: nonconsenual. As to moral issues, this is the important category. In an endeavor in which the central feature is one's playing with danger, participants who choose unwilling partners or who go beyond the agreed-on rules between partners introduce high risk into what is otherwise theater.

Settings

Consensual sadomasochism is theater—an amusement park—not only in its pornography but in its playgrounds in the real world. When the participants are practicing in private, they nonetheless have complex, ritualized ways of setting the scene and then playing their parts appropriately on that stage. The professional establishments are even more grossly prepared in this way, with their special lighting, instruments of torture and punishment, vocabulary, names of the places and participants, dramatic cosmetics and costumes. Catering to the various tastes are medieval prisons, torture chambers, physical examination rooms, operating tables, creaky chateaus, religious habitats, military posts, harems, and so on. Red and black are favored colors.

Anatomy

I suppose that any part of the body that can be reached can be the source of a masochistic procedure, for instance, genitals, breasts, anus and rectum, urethra, body skin, limbs, torso, face. Human ingenuity can drive to unbelievable extremes. (The reader will appreciate, in this regard, the remarkable report of de M'Uzan, 1973.)

Dynamics

What is going on? What do the players experience as their reasons for these behaviors, these desires, these demands, these aesthetics? What stories are being told in these games? (In other words, what dynamics are at work?) They are, I believe, the same I have described for sexual excitement in general (Stoller, 1979), but with the spotlight even more focused on the business of risk.

Let me run through these elements, underlining qualities familiar to sadomasochists. *Dehumanization* is grossly emphasized in the overt scenarios. We see that in the enactments of master/slave; the groveling, smeared, or bound victims; the Nazified masters. *Illusion of danger*, the appearance of *risk*, *mystery*, and *secrecy* are also essential features. Though I have not described these features in detail, each sadomasochist I talk with describes the ways in which the players negotiate the "contract" (Smirnoff, 1969), so that, within the illusion of danger is the already arranged promise that absolute limits are not exceeded. By far the most important element to be established is trust. And they all appreciate sophisticated partners who know exactly how to play within the rules of the game while seeming—with exquisite nuance—to be exceeding the limits. They fear and despise the mad practitioners, those whose excitement depends on nonconsensual sadomasochism: the rapists, the slashers of strangers, the brutes whose dehumanization practices are no longer consensual games. The art of sadomasochism, then, is its theater: its delicious simulation of harm, of high risk. Mastery. From trauma to triumph (though the triumph is—at least by the standards of outsiders—Pyrrhic).

ARE THE PEOPLE MENTALLY ILL?

Here we must beware the game of name-calling hidden in otherwise decent concepts such as *narcissism, borderline, deneutralized libido, prepsychotic masquerading as normal*. None of these terms has been defined clearly enough that observers agree when evaluating a live person. So I avoid them. I can only say that in the highly selective sample that my informants present is no one who is psychotic, prepsychotic, or latently psychotic by the standards clinicians accept. And these people, were one to try to apply character diagnoses to them, are as varied as I expect are the readers of this chapter. All are stable in employment, almost all are college graduates or beyond, lively in conversation, with good senses of humor, up-to-date on politics and world events, no more or no less depressed than my social acquaintances, and so on.

I know that mine is a selected group, but there may be a generalization useful for our thinking about most perverse people: psychoanalytic theories that start by calling perverse people borderline, prepsychotic, and so on, do not do justice either to the massive areas of successful function present in many perverse people or to the massive areas of pathology present in those we do not label perverse. (Freud [1905]: " . . . we cannot escape from the fact that people whose behavior is in other respects normal can, under the domination of the most unruly of all the instincts [desires], put themselves in the category of sick persons in one single sphere of sexual life" [p. 161].) Or to the finding that every person ever described in our literature, regardless of diagnosis or outcome, has been perverse. At any rate, to argue that all sadomasochists are the same at bottom and that the differences between them are unimportant tramples truth to encourage theory. In regard to character structure, they have little in common. In life style and interests, they share only S&M.

That brings us back to the nominalism versus realism/idealism dilemma: are there common features that unify these innumerable S&M behaviors (with, thereby, common dynamics and etiology)? Is there an essence masochism, an essence sadism, that, like Galen's humors or Freud's libido, suffuses the body, seeping into every cell and synapse, dripping down the axons? Is sadomasochism an "it," a distinct entity? Is the issue not the same as with, say, "depression"? We would not say there is no such thing as bipolar depression, though each such depressed person has uncounted different features from the next. Yet we would be wrong to say that everyone who is depressed, from the gentlest to most severe, has the same condition.

A FEW MORAL ISSUES

I must say more about this nuclear aspect of sadomasochistic practices, for, more than anything else, it marks a change in my beliefs. Presuming that others are as I was, it may interest the reader to note my change in attitude.

The point is this: granting the monstrous deeds that can be committed by those acting nonconsensually, I now think most of the sadomasochistic acts I have listed are not as bad as they seem. (A Brahmin turns green watching us eat hamburger: Whose stomach secretes the truth?) When the actors know the rules and can trust their partners, there is less damage done than in many ordinary human relations, erotic or otherwise. An imitation of humiliation is carefully constructed *never* to produce true humiliation; cutting the flesh need not cut the spirit. The imitation of trauma is not traumatic. Constant, high attention to one's partner's experience is more caring and safer than the blundering, ignorant, noncommunicating obtuseness that governs so many "normal" people's erotic motions. So, though I find my informants' games unappealing, I no longer extrapolate and think these people are unmitigated freaks. (We should distinguish those who harm from those who, in trying to undo the effects of harm inflicted on them early in life, play at harm. I believe it is immoral for psychoanalysts to hide their moralizing in jargon-soaked theory.)

I am not saying that those who use sadomasochistic practices are paragons of enlightened behavior; the ones I have talked to express the kinds of sadness, loneliness, anger, and anguish that enliven most people's relationships. I do believe, however, that my sadomasochistic informants have something to say about the value of open-hearted communication, at least when people are making love. Therein perhaps is another of God's wry jokes: we can learn something about loving in the melodramas of harm (just as the Book of Job—that wondrous sadomasochist text—has always been the great comics' handbook). The sadomasochists I know have been saving their souls by risking their skins. "Life is so much more painful than the wounds of the flesh" (*Piercing Fans International Quarterly*, n.d.).

Well, these lovely sentiments may be too innocent. Perhaps, were I actually to witness a sadomasochistic game, I would be more cautious; the reader should know that my knowledge comes from photographs, videotapes, descriptions by informants, and the brief tours of the B&D clubs mentioned above (when no customers were in action). Still, I think the above facts can somewhat modify the tenor of psychoanalytic discussions of sadomasochism.

A FEW WIDER ISSUES

If the reader is not appalled by my sympathetic position, let me add a few footnotes that touch on larger issues.

The Question of a Universal Sensual-in-the-Flesh Masochism

Informants who have gotten into genital or nipple piercing report that, once the initial pain is over (and, for some, during it), the continuous stimulation of the area by the inserted jewelry is very specifically erotic. And if the jewelry is pulled on, the erotic sensation markedly increases. For those, male or female, whose nipples were previously erotically insensitive, there now is always erotic sensitivity. Whether these manifestations are specific only to sadomasochists or whether these people have discovered something about human tissue in general is beyond my capacity to judge.

How common are the little sadomasochisms of everyday life, covert but observable: the skin pinching, cuticle tearing, gum picking, colonic treatments, deep massage, hairpulling-dreamy-self-and-other stimulations? Are anlagen to low-powered masochism present in infancy and childhood with excretion pains and reliefs, teething, sneezing, unassuageable penile and clitoral erections?

The Influence of Culture in Causing "False Perversion"

Piercing and tattooing have moved out of the S&M community, especially with young adults. As members of other cultures do now and have done for thousands of years, these non-S&M people, male and female, are having a fine time with the new fads. I suspect that for many the behavior is, psychodynamically speaking, not perverse. Yet—a preliminary impression based on what informants say they have heard—nipple and genital piercings create the same erotic sensations in these otherwise nonsadomasochistic faddists' responses as my S&M informants enjoy. (Perhaps the informants know something we do not about the flesh.)

We also need not find cryptoperversion in the adolescents who two years ago were into leather, last year wore metal studs on their clothes and collars, this year dress in latex, and next year advertise pacts with the Devil by tattoos on their rear ends.[2]

[2] Perhaps a more accurate position is to say these fads are evidence of hidden perversion, but only if we concede that the dynamics—though not the full flowering—of perversion are present generally in erotic life (Freud, 1905) and in its expressions in fashion and art.

Sadomasochism, Altered States of Consciousness, and Strong Religions

The people who practice the most extreme forms of physical mortification—in my studies, all men (the B&D club proprietors tell of rare women)—describe an experience they reach toward and can achieve only if they go to the outer limits of physical torture: an altered state of consciousness more valuable to them than any other experiences in their lives. (See Stein [1965] for a discussion of such states in children with severe pain.) We have also heard these reports from philosophers of the drug culture; from those of other societies and religions who use drugs, physical pain, starvation, or other means of altering consciousness, especially practitioners of certain Eastern religions. We learn the same from some people with near-death surgical and other physical illness experiences, people who were drowning, and some who only by chance survive certain types of suicide attempts. Some victims of political torture report that they escaped their torturers by transforming the physical agony into a mind-altering experience. And perhaps we are also looking in on the same mechanisms of dissociation people anesthetized by hypnosis describe, as well as Breuer's hypnoid states that facilitate amnesias, conversion reactions, and multiple personalities.

At any rate, you may agree that the experience of extreme suffering points us to frontiers of human behavior well beyond the exotica of perverse sadomasochism.

GLIMPSES OF ETIOLOGY

This has already been a long discourse, and yet it has not even touched the areas that interest me most: origins of the sadomasochistic scripts. Unfortunately, I have no solid ground, only hints, such as the need we all have to master the traumas and frustrations that emanate from the "sadists" of infancy and childhood: parents.

I have, however, a clue, to be stated as a hypothesis that needs clinical confirmation: the major traumas and frustrations of early life are reproduced in the fantasies and behaviors that make up adult erotic life, but the story now ends happily. This time we win. In other words, the adult erotic behavior *contains* the early trauma. The two fit: the details of the adult script tell what happened to the child (Stoller, 1979). We, then, are detectives trying to retrace the original events.

I had a meeting with eight people—men and women; homosexual, bisexual, and heterosexual—who consider themselves sadomasochists. The four who are the most into physical, pain-in-the-flesh S&M (rather than master-slave scenes in which physical pain is not a big item) had had massive physical disease with terrifying medical interventions in childhood. As a result, they had to be confined, severely and for long periods, without the chance to unload their frustration, despair, and rage openly, and appropriately (Stein, 1965). Hence perversion. Each described the process by which they consciously forced themselves to master what at first, in infancy and childhood, was uncontrollable physical agony and terror by taking the pain and working with it in their heads, eventually via daydreams and altered states of consciousness, till it was converted into pain-that-is-pleasure: voluptuous pain. They consciously, desperately, successfully taught themselves to erotize suffering. Their triumph is their perversion.

One woman had vertebral disease so severe that, because of unremitting pain, for days she could not sit: attending school, for instance, was an agony. She was subjected to physical exams, laboratory tests, and painful orthopedic treatments and prostheses. Her husband has had severe asthma since birth, with frequent, prolonged, severe medical emergencies and hospitalizations. A second woman in childhood had episodes of violent headaches, with vomiting, disturbances in sensorium, and nonauditory hallucinations, diagnosed then as migraine and/or epilepsy. A second man, the one with the fiercest practices, had the worst childhood experiences with pain because he was born with a life-threatening illness. From birth on, he suffered innumerable penetrating medical procedures—needles, cutting, blood-letting—requiring even now, in mid-life, weeks-long hospitalizations. (Details of these informants' agonies will be published elsewhere.)

Each of these informants has told me of S&M friends who had

comparable traumatic pain experiences in early childhood. Before our meeting together, none had realized this dynamic might be etiologic in a significant number of sadomasochists.

The etiologic hunch is that the more severe the suffering, the greater the need for S&M; the more the suffering was physical, the more physical suffering will be manifest in the perversion. But far more clinical evidence is needed. For instance, are there those who had a comparable anguished childhood but no adult perversion, or nonsuffering childhood but adult perversion; why do some undo the past with a preference for receiving and some for inflicting suffering?

The idea that severe, prolonged, traumatic pain can contribute to perverse S&M has four foundations in general theory: Freud's discussions (e.g., 1920) on how we master painful experiences; A. Freud's description (1936) of a mechanism—identification with the aggressor—that especially expedites that transformation; Loewenstein's (1957) mechanism of seduction of the aggressor; and Rangell's (1967) model —explication—that shows how and why psychic traumas *are* trauma. (Rangell gives us the term *traumatophilia*, a defense that exactly fits the outcome of my informants' struggles. It is part of that series of related but not synonymous terms—*counterphobia, reaction formation, neutralization, sublimation, erotization of anxiety*—covered by *mastery*.) Then, more specific, are reports that elaborate the mechanisms of making pain pleasurable: Laforge (1930) and Fenichel (1934) on erotizing anxiety; Stein (1965) on how severe childhood illness and confinement can lead to altered states of consciousness and interfere with "outward expressions of aggression by active play" (p. 71); Valenstein (1973) on how physical illness in early childhood can lead to masochism; Freedman (1978) on a unique, perhaps-not-quite-S&M perversion; Glenn (1984) on three patients who became masochistic following childhood surgical traumas. Blum (1987) underlines the crucial part identification plays in the child's struggle to master trauma: "Identifications occur with anxious parents who are themselves frightened by the child's illness or injuries; and such identifications with the medical staff who all too often contribute to, rather than alleviate, the trauma. Illness, hospitalization, and surgery, perceived as an assault (as in "heart attack''), may also intensify the untamed aggression in the identification with the aggressor'' (p. 615).

The case descriptions in these reports do not, however, match those of my informants in that none of the former are described as full-blown perverse sadomasochists. In addition, the childhood illnesses and ensuing traumatic procedures, though severe, were not as prolonged in their severity as with my informants, nor, in most cases, beyond the range of the experiences (e.g., tonsillectomies, colic, otitis media with or without mastoiditis) of other children. I suspect the answers to questions about the specificity of the adult erotic choices lie in the precise details of the inflicted traumas and the complex mass of forces in the family—preoedipal and oedipal attitudes and behaviors of parents—pressing on the child. These then evoke intrapsychic maneuvers, fantasies that in time solidify into character structures (one type of which is our erotic life), to deal with these forces (plus, it is always worth conjecturing, the deep tides of innate dispositions).

CONCLUSION

I am suggesting that we augment our present psychoanalytic theories and findings on sadomasochism with as many observations gathered from as many sources as possible. By adding such ethnographic, nonpsychoanalytic-treatment-derived data to what psychoanalysts now think on this subject, I believe we can in time come to better explanations and to useful ideas for treatment.

REFERENCES

Blum, H. P. (1978), Psychoanalytic study of an unusual perversion. *J. Amer. Psychoanal. Assn.*, 26:785–792.

——— (1987), The role of identification in the resolution of trauma. *Psychoanal. Quart.*, 56:609–627.

de M'Uzan, M. (1973), A case of masochistic perversion and an outline of a theory. *Internat. J. Psycho-Anal.*, 54:455–467.

Fenichel, O. (1934), Defense against anxiety, particularly by libidinization. *Collected Papers*, Vol 1. New York: Norton, 1953, pp. 303–317.

Freedman, A. (1978), Psychoanalytic study of an unusual perversion. *J. Amer. Psychoanal. Assn.*, 26:749–777.
Freud, A. (1936), *The Ego and the Mechanisms of Defense*. New York: International Universities Press, 1966.
Freud, S. (1905), Three essays on the theory of sexuality. *Standard Edition*, 7:135–243. London: Hogarth Press, 1953.
——— (1920), Beyond the pleasure principle. *Standard Edition*, 18:7–64. London: Hogarth Press, 1955.
Glenn, J. (1984), Psychic trauma and masochism. *J. Amer. Psychoanal. Assn.*, 32:357–386.
Grossman, W. I. (1986), Notes on masochism. *Psychoanal. Quart.*, 55:379–413.
Laforge, R. (1930), On the erotization of anxiety. *Internat. J. Psycho-Anal.*, 11:312–321.
Loewenstein, R. M. (1957), A contribution to the psychoanalytic theory of masochism. *J. Amer. Psychoanal. Assn.*, 5:197–234.
Maleson, F. G. (1984), The multiple meanings of masochism in psychoanalytic discourse. *J. Amer. Psychoanal. Assn.*, 32:325–356.
Rangell, L. (1967), The metapsychology of psychic trauma. In: *Psychic Trauma*, ed. S. S. Furst. New York: Basic Books, pp. 51–84.
Piercing Fans International Quarterly (n.d.), 20:19.
Smirnoff, V. N. (1969), The masochistic contract. *Internat. J. Psycho-Anal.*, 50:665–671.
Stein, M. H. (1965), States of consciousness in the psychoanalytic situation. In: *Drives, Affects, Behavior*, Vol. 2, ed. M. Schur. New York: International Universities Press, pp. 60–86.
Stoller, R. J. (1975), *Perversion*. New York: Pantheon.
——— (1979), *Sexual Excitement*. New York: Pantheon.
——— (1985), *Observing the Erotic Imagination*. New Haven, CT: Yale University Press.
Valenstein, A. F. (1973), On attachment to painful feelings and the negative therapeutic reaction. *The Psychoanalytic Study of the Child*, 28:365–392. New Haven, CT: Yale University Press.

15

A DEVELOPMENTAL APPROACH TO ACTING OUT

HEIMAN VAN DAM, M.D.

When I was asked to write an essay on some of the works of Leo Rangell, I became impressed by his many writings which combined his interests in infant and child analysis, on the one hand, and their integration into his work with adult clinical and theoretical issues on the other (Rangell, 1954, 1961, 1963, 1968; Panel, 1969).

My contribution to this Festschrift is an attempt to follow the path that Rangell has laid out so fruitfully and so successfully over the many years of his creative writings. In this presentation, the origin of the language of action (or motor language) and thought in infants and children will be discussed and contrasted to symbolic verbal language and thought. At times it is necessary to make reconstructions of early childhood in order to integrate in the ego of the adult patient these nonverbal actions with verbal thought processes. A clinical example will be utilized to demonstrate the usefulness of this approach with adult patients, who still use the original language of action in the transference. This is what is understood as acting in the transference. I conclude with a brief discussion of the clinical data and comments on some selected papers from the vast literature on acting in the transference. It is impossible, however, to do justice to all the authors and panels that have dealt with this subject over the years.

THE ORIGINS OF THE LANGUAGE OF ACTION

In his 1954 paper, Rangell shows how certain people ward off social anxiety by anchoring themselves to a familiar object. In the case of poise, it is the circumoral region, the snout, which is stimulated. In Rangell's example, it was a cocktail glass that was held by the patient. What this patient revealed in her analysis was a sensorimotor way of dealing with anxiety that had its antecedents in the earliest experiences of her infancy. The subsequent mode of dealing with excessive stimuli bore the stamp of that period. An infant utilizes his body to deal with unpleasurable situations. For instance, when hungry, the infant cries or kicks. Rangell even used the term "action in the service of the ego."

Action is used by infants and older children as a form of thinking, instead of verbal thought processes, as described by Galenson (1971; Galenson, Miller, and Roiphe, 1976). Although verbal thought processes such as symbol formation and metaphors can be found as early as the second year of life, the child continues to rely when dealing with conflictual anxiety situations much more on motor action than on verbal thought for a period that extends well beyond the preverbal era. Although children acquire speech at an early age, motor action remains a preferred channel for discharge and problem solving for a long period of time. Even in adulthood one can see motor actions accompanying speech.

Infants and children continue to use motor action because of the way they deal with their earliest conflicts. The infant's concept of what is pleasurable ("good") and what is unpleasurable ("bad") is at the heart of the matter. What is pleasurable is swallowed, incorporated, and what is unpleasurable is spit out, gotten rid of, externalized, or projected. Action is the prototype of dealing with conflict. Conflicts during the first year of life are largely between the infant and his environment. Motor action is intended to change the environment to provide or get rid of what is lacking or bothersome. Once Rangell's patient with problems around poise became aware that what was bothering her was not the crowd, i.e., a projection, but an internalized conflict, resorting to action became more ego-alien.

There is much that can be learned from studying motor actions in infants and small children. Some motor activities promote further development, such as the smiling response. It promotes the transition from the autistic phase into the symbiotic phase. Other motor activities, such as rocking and head-banging, are in the service of drive-tension discharge, are maladaptive, and may lead to serious developmental arrests. Crawling, on the other hand, plays an important role in differentiating the infant from the symbiosis with his mother and in establishing a clearer body ego. At a later stage, walking initiates the practicing subphase and learning about the external world (Mahler, 1974). In other words, motor activities are highly important for the development of the psychic apparatus. Mahler, Pine, and Bergman (1975) have described the role that locomotion plays in the development of the body ego and in the differentiation of self and object. Equally important are the contributions of motor activities for the development of memory and the secondary process. For instance, the rooting reflex in the neonate contributes to the laying down of memories of successful nursing episodes.

As early as 1895, Freud (1950) discussed the development of the experience of satisfaction in infants. He speaks of the laying down of a motor image of a specific action that has led to satisfaction. Later on, states Freud, the memory of this motor image may activate hallucinations. As the infant matures, motor actions are not only used for direct discharge of drives but can be used for memory, detour, delay, learning, and anticipation. A good example involving detour, delay of discharge, and learning is an infant searching for his favorite blanket. Let us assume the infant has already learned to remember the satisfaction of being nursed by the mother. He has also discovered that his wish to suck cannot always be satisfied; the mother has disappeared. He has found that discharge of his needs for motor actions in the service of the oral drive are possible by sucking on the blanket. The next time the need to suck arises he has a choice either to scream and to kick or to take purposeful action in the direction of his blanket if he can delay his need for immediate discharge. Motor action can be very much in the service of the ego. It involves thinking without any verbal content. All that is involved are memories of visual, olfactory, tactile, and sucking experiences, which can be turned into a reality experience by the use of the motor apparatus.

Piaget (1937) has made observations on infants independent of psychoanalysis. He was struck by what he calls sensorimotor intelligence, which reaches a stage of "dynamic realism" before verbalization and conceptual thought. For instance, an infant may be able to perform raking in a raisin or finding an object hidden behind an obstacle, i.e., be capable of making inferences without and before the development of speech. Animals, of course, do this all the time. When speech develops, it is at first, as Piaget shows, less capable of adaptation and conceptualization than action already is. Sensorimotor intelligence is only gradually replaced by verbal language and thought. As Piaget puts it, the child uses in the presence of every new problem the same primitive processes of adaptation (i.e., sensory motor action) although diminishing in importance with age. In other words, action in children is the original form of thinking and problem solving. Examples of other forms of thinking not involving verbalization are mathematical and artistic thought processes as well as in the well-known thought processes of dreams. Freud was well aware of the importance of action language when he stated the reverse—that thought is trial action. As will be demonstrated, acting in the transference is a primitive, regressive form of thinking and communicating. Looked upon in this way, it can be dealt with therapeutically.

The proneness to action in man has a long history both ontogenetically and phylogenetically, as studies by ethologists have shown. It may be useful to remember this in order to maintain a tolerant and empathic attitude toward acting out, so that it can be studied and treated in one's patients as a defense and as content material. These formulations of action as primitive thought are also consistent, I believe, with Rapaport's (1967) concepts on the development of thought.

A great deal of action language remains under the influence of the needs of the drives, whereas verbal language and thought soon are governed by reality testing. During the course of childhood the language of action becomes integrated with and subordinated to ordinary logical thinking. The energy saved by thought processes is then used for purposeful action. In individuals where this development is interfered with, both processes, action and thought, may not become integrated, and continue to function independent of each other. Motor action and specifically acting in the transference should be dealt with as a developmental fixation or regression. One can approach it with the same degree of empathy, tolerance, and analytic curiosity as any other fixation or regression.

It is obvious, therefore, that the analyst, whether he works with children or adults, strengthens his patient's ego when he puts into words experiences that have been carried on quite consciously at times on nonverbal somatopsychic levels. Some analysts reject out of hand the idea that preverbal and nonverbal experiences can ever be verbalized. Any time one makes an interpretation referring back to the oral or anal phase of development, one is of necessity dealing with preverbal and nonverbal behavior. Also, much more of oedipal behavior is in the form of motor action than is usually acknowledged. There may be limits to what can be verbalized, just as there are limits to what can be remembered from very early periods. Part of the problem, however, is that one is not always attuned to what patients bring us in nonverbal ways. Many early experiences are remembered very accurately but not in a way that is easily deciphered by patients and analysts. The latter all too often are tuned in to the patient's verbal productions only. Describing the treatment of his adolescent patient Dora, Freud (1905) stated: "He that has eyes to see and ears to hear may convince himself that no mortal can keep a secret. If his lips are silent, he chatters with his fingertips; betrayal oozes out of him at every pore. And thus the task of making conscious the most hidden recesses of the mind is one which it is quite possible to accomplish" (pp. 77–78). Freud, of course, also used infant and child observations wherever he could. His best known observation on infants is the use of a spool by his 18-month-old grandchild who mastered object loss by throwing the spool away and retrieving it with the words *gone* and *here*. He saw this tendency to repeat at work in his adult patients (Freud, 1920), in the transference, and in acting out.

The task of an analyst is to put into words for his patient what the latter may not be conscious of. Even though conscious of his actions, the patient may not have integrated them by seeing the necessary connections.

DEVELOPMENTAL AND GENETIC RECONSTRUCTIONS

Originally when Freud thought that the ego had only one defensive function, namely, repression, to make conscious what was unconscious was the ultimate goal in analysis. As the ego became better understood, the lifting of repressions was only one of many goals. Nowadays the goal is much broader—to provide a patient with insight which then leads to change. Sometimes, this insight is provided by the analyst making a reconstruction of the patient's past, based on data from the patient's analysis as well as data that come from other areas of the analyst's experience. There is no way that it could or should be otherwise. One can only hope that one's reading of the professional literature will be of benefit in one's work. We hope that the right author will come to mind at the right time when working with patients. Included in this reservoir of knowledge are also data from papers and presentations in the area of infant observation. Lampl-de Groot (1976) has raised the question whether the mere intellectual knowledge of these early childhood phenomena will interfere rather than aid with an empathic understanding of the experiences our patients had as infants and children. One should hope for a recall in an affective, empathic way in order to be of maximum benefit to one's patient. In one sense, the analyst's words are a model for the patient. Therefore, it is essential—not just important—that the analyst has an empathic knowledge of early childhood and not just an intellectualized knowledge that defends against an affective experience. However, an interpretation or reconstruction that is made in an intellectualized way can hardly serve as a model for the patient's ego. It should be self-evident that reconstructions are not made just for the sake of digging up the past. They are made as a means to an end. The purpose is the undoing of infantile regressed modes of functioning via the gaining of insight into what brought these patterns of behaving about in the first place. For instance, what Rangell did with his patient with the drinking glass was to reestablish connections with the past, how his patient dealt with potential humiliation as a child, and what made her feel castrated and humiliated in the first place.

Ernst Kris (1956) gives a clear-cut example of how impossible it is to recover what exactly took place in one's childhood. Anyone who has worked with or observed little children knows that very often there is a massive accumulation of traumas that eventually produces symptoms. Often the parents are unaware of the full chain of events, let alone the fantasies that become interwoven with this chain of traumatic occurrences. Kris wondered how much can be recalled in an analysis 20 years later. To reconstruct all the events is obviously impossible. What one can hope for and should strive toward is an understanding of patterns of reacting and patterns of fantasies. Kennedy (1971) makes the distinction between the genetic constructive approach, which reconstructs the patient's past on the basis of what the patient tells us, and the developmental approach, which comes from other sources available to the analyst. One ends up in reconstructing events that are definitely incomplete and probably inaccurate, but the aim is to undo the regressed patterns of behavior via insight into some of the factors that have gone into its formation.

There are additional problems connected with recall of the past, such as the phenomenon of "telescoping of events." Anna Freud (1951) observed this at the Hampstead nurseries and reminds us: "Though we realize as analysts that past experience is telescoped in this manner, we are in danger of underestimating the extent of the phenomenon, when not reminded of it by the result of direct observation." (p. 27). Anna Freud and others have cautioned that direct observations have limited value; one can study surface phenomena quite well, whereas fantasies, for instance, may not be accessible. In other words, the patient determines which event is significant and not what the analyst or parent would anticipate. Again, direct observation confirms this only too well. What may be traumatic for one child is not for another. Reconstructions or interpretations should therefore not be made in a dogmatic way but should be stated as a working hypothesis.

Some analysts object to the use of developmental data because they fear it will move psychoanalysis away from its basic core—the elucidation of the oedipal conflict. There is an element of truth to this in the limited sense that from the developmental point of view, the phallic-oedipal phase is just one maturational milestone among many. However, with it are associated many achievements such as phallic masturbation, triadic object relationships, sexual curiosity, oedipal fantasies, and castration anxiety. Its resolution is associated with marked changes in drive development, superego consolidation, many new ego functions, that it remains the most significant event of early childhood. Loewald (1979) also noted a decrease of interest in the Oedipus complex and an increase of interest in preoedipal issues. He said that "increased understanding of preoedipal issues, far from devaluating oedipal ones, may in the end help to gain deeper insight into them" (p. 754). Therefore the fear that attention to preoedipal issues would detract from the nuclear position of the Oedipus complex seems on the whole unwarranted. Nevertheless, as mentioned before, many analysts have difficulties in integrating what they do know about early childhood in their analytic work with adult patients. Anna Freud, as quoted by Settlage (1976), also spoke of the reluctance of many analysts to use data from infant observations.

Freud (1937) always favored integrating observational and clinical data, as can be seen when he drew the comparison between the archaeologist and the psychoanalyst. Both the analyst and archaeologist "have an undisputed right to reconstruct by means of supplementing and combining the surviving remains . . . if an object makes its appearance in some particular level, it often remains to be decided whether it belongs to that level or whether it was carried down to that level" (p. 259). Freud makes a clear-cut inference that one needs to know the gradual development of a culture in order to do full justice to a correct archaeological reconstruction. The same holds true for an analytic reconstruction. One needs to be familiar with development in order to make the most accurate reconstruction possible.

Knowledge of the earliest development of children is of great help to the analyst in one more respect as well. Instead of feeling bewildered and anxious because he does not understand the so-called acting out of his patient, the analyst recognizes patterns appropriate to the preverbal and nonverbal period of childhood. As a result, there is less of a tendency toward countertransference and especially counteracting out with the patient, or premature prohibition.

CLINICAL EXAMPLE

At this point a clinical illustration from the analysis of an adult patient will be given that demonstrates quite well several of the points and potential pitfalls that have been described so far. The acting out was looked at from as many viewpoints as possible, including the developmental approach. A reconstruction was made that was quite incomplete; yet it was sufficient to bring about substantial change.

An adult patient was seemingly very dissatisfied with her analysis. It was quite obvious that her dissatisfaction was a repetition of her relationship with her mother. In the transference her dissatisfaction took various forms, such as missing appointments, consulting colleagues, bursts of anger, inability to tolerate the positive transference. Every possible interpretation was used with no outward success. Examples of these interpretations were the following: she would turn to other analysts when she felt misunderstood by me, just like her turning away from her mother to other parent figures in her childhood; her inability to talk about sexual feelings was a repetition of conditions in her home where sexual discussions and masturbation were taboo; her anger was a defense against libidinal desires in the transference, similar to her incomplete entry into the oedipal relationship to her father, who was too involved in his business; aggression was more tolerated than sex in her family, including her going in anger to a neighbor woman's house as a small child; her attempts to cause me pain, humiliation, and castration had parallels in her sexual activities and fantasies—these in turn could be understood in terms of her relationship to peers and siblings in her childhood; her need to be so aggressive in the analysis could be related to a defense against passive homosexual wishes and fears related to her powerful mother. Some of these interpretations had a temporary effect on her behavior, especially aggression as a defense against libido, but soon her complaints and acting out returned in full force.

One particular item stood out: in spite of her extreme conscious dissatisfaction and rage, she often arrived very early for her next appointment, even after a missed session or a gripe session with yet another analyst. Inquiries as to this inconsistency would lead to such denials as "I had nothing better to do." Gradually something began to dawn upon me. She had made a number of references to herself as being a dog chained to my couch. She also felt that I thought her bark was louder than her bite, because I did not become anxious when she became aggressive or threatened to leave the analysis. One of this bright woman's favorite remarks was: "You kick a dog and he barks; you kick an analyst and he says 'transference.' " I drew her attention to the recurrent metaphor of the dog. With considerable reluctance she began to talk about the dogs in her life. There had been many because her mother got rid of them rather rapidly. At least one of them was let loose from the family car on a Sunday afternoon ride. However, another dog was more useful for understanding her seemingly inconsistent behavior. This particular dog was an uncontrollable one, whom she had been particularly attached to during her latency years. It reminded me of an infant I had once studied whose mother was frequently ill. I had observed how this seven-month-old infant had cuddled with the dog and even had begun to make some barking noises whenever her dog barked. The infant had apparently substituted a new and rather unusual primary object, the family dog, for the ailing mother. My adult patient's dog supposedly dated from her latency period. I was reminded of Kris's study, Anna Freud's comments on telescoping, and Sigmund Freud's comparison of the archaeologist and the analyst. The patient's "latency" dog had a tendency to escape from the house whenever someone opened the door. The dog might be gone for quite some time, but eventually it would show up at the elementary school waiting faithfully for my patient. As she unfolded this memory I showed her that in a way she was like her dog, uncontrollable and always running away, but also showing me how much she cared by waiting so long and so faithfully for me upon her return. She scoffed at my reconstruction and dismissed it. I think she was too afraid of giving up and losing her defensive acting out. In addition, the ego requires some time to integrate new experiences. However, from that moment on, this form of acting out in the transference ceased. I do not think that one interpretation alone can undo the acting out. Many interpretations are necessary, because, like all other psychic phenomena, acting out in the transference is multiply determined. The defensive aspects as well as the content of acting out must be shown to the patient, as was done in this case. Interpretations are directed at contributions from all layers. After all, it was her ambivalence to her mother, not just in the oral phase but in every phase of development thereafter, that had led to this identification with her new love-and-hate object, the runaway, loyal, nonverbal dog.

Several features make this vignette of interest. First, the conceptualization that acting in the transference is more than avoidance of a memory; that in fact it is the communication of a memory in a sensorimotor form. In addition, acting out is conceptualized as an infantile form of thinking characteristic of an ego in which the synthetic, integrative function is defective. Finally, what makes this vignette of interest is that the reconstruction was incomplete and inaccurate, which is of course not surprising (see also Glover, 1931).

Several months later the patient's mother came to visit. It was a direct result of the recently improved relationship between the patient and her parents. During the visit, the mother began to reminisce what her own life had been like when she was my patient's age. The mother revealed then, presumably for the first time, that during the first two years of my patient's life, she had been very depressed because she had become separated from her husband who had been drafted on account of the war. The patient had always known about her father's military service during her first two years of life but not about the mother's deep depression. The patient forgot about this new bit of information, and it was not mentioned in the analysis. It came back to her several months later during a discussion about separation from the analyst. It aided in the understanding of her reaction to the planned vacation by the analyst. However, it also made clear that the disappearing and reappearing dog had also stood for her father's temporary absences and happy reunions during the war. In other words, it was an identification with the frustrating, aggressive, and libidinal, oedipal and preoedipal objects—father, mother, and dog.

She also told me that she had learned from her mother that the first word she ever used was *bow-wow*. This suggested to me that her identification and object ties with disappearing and reappearing, loud, barking dogs did indeed go back to her infancy when her mother was so depressed. A sensorimotor experience of early infancy was carefully and accurately preserved to which later related experiences and later phases of development had contributed additional meanings. It had been used defensively as a withdrawal mechanism during much of childhood and reappeared as such in the transference.

DISCUSSION

Although much emphasis is placed on the origins in infancy of the acting out of this patient, it cannot be stressed enough that later childhood traumatic events made spontaneous recovery from this early infantile deprivation impossible. One should not gain the impression that this patient had only a traumatic first year of life and suffered on account of it in her adulthood. Infant and child observations show over and over the resilience and recovery of functions of the psychic apparatus if subsequent phases of development take place under more favorable circumstances. Those patients who have not recovered from the traumatic first year of life very likely need analysis of the remainder of the preoedipal phase, the oedipal phase, latency, and adolescent difficulties as well as problems encountered in adulthood.

What would have happened if the analyst had not been aware of the importance of pets for the development of infants and children? Would the patient eventually have led the analyst into this area of her life by remembering herself? Very likely so, at least for the experience with her dog during the latency period. It is unlikely that she would have been able to verbalize the preverbal and nonverbal aspects of her relationship to dogs as an early object. For this she would need the help of her therapist. Contributing to the ability to bring about change via insight was the empathic attitude of her analyst. This empathy was based in part on knowledge of infant development, but also on my experiences dealing with acting out and play action in children and adolescents. Verbal communication throughout childhood including adolescence is limited, as Freud observed with Dora. Acting out should be understood and dealt with in a similar way as play in child analysis. Prohibition may then be necessary only as a very last resort.

Not all acting out in the transference comes to a sudden halt. Sometimes it gradually loses its intensity as its meaning is becoming understood. Perhaps the difference between the sudden and gradual change lies in the relationship of the observing ego to the acting out, and the extent to which the synthetic function of the ego is available. If the acting out becomes ego-alien, the patient is more likely to give it up. If the defensive aspects remain strong until the end, as in the case cited, the patient tends to cling more to it and only reluctantly parts with the acting out. Again, there are similarities to a child's play, even though acting out is a more primitive form of psychic functioning than play. The significance of pets in the life of children, including their play activities, has been documented by Sherick (1981) and others.

An excellent review of the literature on acting out can be found in a book edited by Rexford (1978), most of which is consistent with what has been presented here. Rexford also includes a review of Freud's writings on the subject. Particularly impressive are the contributions by Blos and Greenacre.

Especially pertinent is Blos's way of utilizing his adolescent patient's acting out to reconstruct that patient's past. "The acting out as a special form of remembering was translated into verbalized memories of his past" (p. 153). Much of the acting out of so-called adult patients is actually an arrest of development at the adolescent level where acting out is phase-specific. Yet Blos at times also adheres to a somewhat negative view of acting out. "Acting out by its very nature has forfeited the capacity of mastery and turned it into an act of avoidance" (p. 155). "Adolescence offers an opportune chance for the treatment of acting out propensities, which . . . represent phase-specific measures in an effort to cope with the actualities of growing up" (p. 163). My thesis is that acting out can be part of a developmental process and can be utilized as a communication that should be dealt with analytically. Therefore acting out can at times lead to mastery, especially the adolescent form. Even courts of law have recognized this. A juvenile delinquent's record may be closed if he has proven that he has integrated his acting-out delinquent tendencies. Often this is done without any treatment. Blos, naturally, is fully aware of this and refers to it as "acting out in the service of ego synthesis" (p. 164). The dilemma posed by Blos is an interesting one. He is right on both accounts—acting out can be regressive and not lead to mastery, and it can be part of the developmental process of childhood and adolescence and lead to mastery. Adolescent issues and forms of communication do not suddenly diminish during adulthood. An exclusively negative view of acting out, especially the adolescent type, is unfounded and unwarranted. One is again reminded of Freud's analogy to an archaeological finding whether the (archaeological) object belongs to the level where it is found or whether it comes from another layer.

Greenacre also considers prohibition or direct intervention useless, even though some analysts still advocate it. Her clinical descriptions and search for etiological factors in early childhood are well known. For instance, she attributes a tendency to imitativeness to patients who act out in the transference, which begins in the second year of life and may involve "other children, adults, or even pets." As I have indicated, the origin may go even further back than Greenacre indicated, namely, to the first year of life. Specifically, in my patient, the depression of the mother and the absence of the father during the symbiotic and early separation-individuation period can account for the fixation at the preverbal level.

Since the appearance of the book edited by Rexford a number of important papers on acting out have appeared, especially those that came from the participants of the international congress in Copenhagen on "Acting Out and Its Role in the Psychoanalytic Process." Anna Freud (1968) mentions that in the analysis of young children the distinctions between remembering, repeating, reliving, and acting out become blurred: "not thought or speech, but motor actions are their legitimate media of expression and communication" (p. 169). The distinction between adult and child may not be as clear-cut as Anna Freud describes it, especially in the regressive analytic setting.

Rangell (1968) addresses himself to the confusion about the term *acting out,* especially as distinguished from *neurotic action.* Rangell and Anna Freud both mention that in recent years analysts have become more understanding and permissive of acting out. Nevertheless a critical and at times moralistic view toward acting out still prevails. With Rangell, I concur that prohibitions ignore the facts that the motivations behind acting out are unconscious. The term *acting out* may well be on its way out as we gain more understanding of disturbances in the function of verbal communications.

SUMMARY

Data from infant observation, child analysis, and acting out in the transference by adult patients are presented to demonstrate that there exists a continuum of primitive thought processes that precede and coexist with verbalization, which may find their ultimate expression in acting in the transference. In addition and as a consequence, it was recommended that acting in the transference be treated as a communication that needs to be analyzed, like play is done in child analysis. As in child analysis, the use of prohibition will play a very limited role.

Analysts need to make use of data available from a variety of sources for psychoanalytic theory formation and technique. Rangell's work draws upon all the sources mentioned in this chapter. Finally, observations on infants and children should alert the analyst to the possibility that pets from infancy or childhood on may play an important role in the psychic life of their adult patients.

REFERENCES

Freud, A. (1951), Observations on child development. *The Psychoanalytic Study of the Child,* 6:18–30. New York: International Universities Press.

——— (1968), Acting out. *Internat. J. Psycho-Anal.,* 49:165–170.

Freud, S. (1905), Fragment of an analysis of a case of hysteria. *Standard Edition*, 7:3–122. London: Hogarth Press, 1962.
——— (1920), Beyond the pleasure principle. *Standard Edition*, 18:3–64. London: Hogarth Press, 1955.
——— (1937), Constructions in analysis. *Standard Edition*, 23:255–269. London: Hogarth Press, 1964.
——— (1950), Project for a scientific psychology. *Standard Edition*, 1:283–397. London: Hogarth Press, 1966.
Galenson, E. (1971), A consideration of the nature of thought in childhood play. In: *Separation-Individuation*, ed. J. B. McDevitt & C. F. Settlage. New York: International Universities Press, pp. 41–59.
——— Miller, R., & Roiphe, H. (1976), The choice of symbols. *J. Amer. Acad. Child Psychiat.*, 15:83–96.
Glover, E. (1931), The therapeutic effect of inexact interpretation. *Internat. J. Psycho-Anal.*, 12:397–411.
Kennedy, H. (1971), Reconstruction in child analysis. *The Psychoanalytic Study of the Child*, 26:386–402. New York: Quadrangle.
Kris, E. (1956), The recovery of childhood memories in psychoanalysis. *The Psychoanalytic Study of the Child*, 11:54–88. New York: International Universities Press.
Lampl-de Groot, J. (1976), Personal experience with analytic technique. *The Psychoanalytic Study of the Child*, 31:273–296. New Haven, CT: Yale University Press.
Loewald, H. W. (1979), The waning of the Oedipus complex. *J. Amer. Psychoanal. Assn.*, 27:751–775.
Mahler, M. S. (1974), Symbiosis and individuation. *The Psychoanalytic Study of the Child*, 29:89–106. New Haven, CT: Yale University Press.
——— Pine, F., & Bergman, A. (1975), *The Psychological Birth of the Human Infant*. New York: Basic Books.
Panel (1969), Nonverbal communication in the analysis of adults. A. Suslick, reporter. *J. Amer. Psychoanal. Assn.*, 17:955–967.
Piaget, J. (1937), *The Construction of Reality in the Child*. New York: Basic Books, 1954.
Rangell, L. (1954), The psychology of poise. *Internat. J. Psycho-Anal.*, 35:313–332.
——— (1961), The role of early psychic functioning in psychoanalysis. *J. Amer. Psychoanal. Assn.*, 9:595–609.
——— (1963), Beyond and between the no and the yes. In: *Counterpoint*, ed. H. S. Gaskill. New York: International Universities Press, pp. 29–74.
——— (1968), A point of view on acting out. *Internat. J. Psycho-Anal.*, 49:195–201.

Rapaport, D. (1967), *The Collected Papers of David Rapaport*, ed. M. M. Gill. New York: Basic Books.

Rexford, E. N., ed. (1978), *A Developmental Approach to Problems of Acting Out*. New York: International Universities Press.

Settlage, C. (1976), Commentary on the 6th pre-congress conference on training. *Internat. J. Psycho-Anal.*, 57:205–210.

Sherick, I. (1981), The significance of pets for children. *The Psychoanalytic Study of the Child*, 36:193–215. New Haven, CT: Yale University Press.

16

DEATH OF A YOUNG CHILD'S FATHER: EFFECTS ON SEPARATION-INDIVIDUATION

ELEANOR GALENSON, M.D., and
BARBARA FIELDS, M.S.W.

Much recent research involving infants has aimed at investigating various aspects of the mother-infant and parent-infant relationship. Whether fully acknowledged or not, the basic foundation for this research has been provided by the clinical descriptions and conceptualizations of the separation-individuation process. Mahler, Pine, and Bergman (1975) were able to discern commonalities of this process as it developed in many mother-infant dyads, while also pointing out unique features of the process in a number of normal mother-infant pairs. Having come this far, however, it has been difficult to identify just how each infant's biological endowment is molded by his environment, in the subtle and gradual process that leads in not too long a time to the unique character of each parent-child triad.

Our research has been aimed at learning more about this process of molding. The study of deviance has often provided clues to understanding normal development, and so we chose to study pathological mother-child interactions, but in a sample of subjects seen in private practice where the serious environmental hazards imposed by poverty would not be operative. There were of course other kinds of environmental influences, but the well-known massive effects of poverty did not have to be taken into account.

A study such as this one could not have been undertaken at all were it not for the vast bank of data already available regarding both normal and abnormal development of babies and parents. These data provided the background for our detailed study of each infant-parent triad. Certain theoretical and clinical formulations have been particularly helpful in planning our research. Fraiberg, Shapiro, and Cherniss (1983) and others have shown that every baby has a special meaning for his parents which is based upon the parents' own experiences, serving as the basis for the parents' "fantasied baby" in contrast to the "real baby." Fraiberg thought that the young infant becomes a "transference object" for the parents by virtue of such fantasies, extending Winnicott's conceptualizations epitomized in his statement that there is no baby without a mother and no mother without a baby. Factors contributing to the formation of the "fantasied baby" are many—the nature of the pregnancy, the baby's actual endowment and biological characteristics, for example. But most potent, particularly since they are largely unconscious and often conflictual in nature, are the unresolved preoedipal parental conflicts that are revived in every adult who parents a child.

These unresolved preoedipal conflicts are of a special nature because the infant is a unique type of "transference object"; the helpless infant requires the assistance of another human being for his very survival. By virtue of this fact, disturbances in the early infant-parent relationship are often due to unresolved preoedipal parental conflicts specifically involving dependency and separation. Resolution of infant psychopathology depends in large measure upon our ability to obtain access to such parental conflicts. These conflicts are revealed in parental behavior with the infant during a limited period, the infant's early years, by virtue of the effect of the baby as "transference object." The collateral study of at least two members of the triad, that is, infant and one or the other parent, is necessary in order to gain access to the parent's preoedipally based fantasies and conflicts. Further exploration of preoedipal parental contributions may be continued subsequently in individual psychoanalysis or psychotherapy with the parents.

Analysts involved in direct infant observational research must possess the capacity both to anthropomorphize with infants and their parents and to utilize metaphor in formulating nonverbal material observed in both infant and parents. Some analysts are blocked from utilizing these capacities and must depend on others for this. For it is largely the *behavior* of both the infant and his parents that provides access to the underlying psychological processes during this early developmental phase.

The problem of understanding and interpreting this behavior was one which the senior author (E. G.) constantly encountered in carrying out individual psychotherapy and psychoanalysis with young children over a period of almost 35 years, an experience shared by all who treat this age group. She found that these therapeutic approaches often modified symptoms but failed to prevent the development of some other form of psychopathology at a later time, modified by maturation but still basically similar to the original problem. Furthermore, mother-child relationships were often severely and permanently disturbed as a result of the treatment process itself, because the therapist had assumed primary importance for the child as a rival for the child's affection and the prototype of a more successful parent. For some children, such substitution may be lifesaving and therefore therapeutically justified. For others, however, the intense attachment to the therapist appeared to interfere with the very aim of treatment, namely, improvement in the mother-child relationship.

Our choice of the treatment modality we will describe was in part the result of this earlier experience. It was also determined by the senior author's work with a clinic population of children under four years and their mothers who were treated for a variety of psychological disturbances in the setting of a therapeutic nursery for both children and mothers. Despite the severity of the psychopathology encountered in many of these infants who came from both middle-class and lower middle-class homes, the therapeutic gains often surpassed those of the young patients E. G. treated in individual private practice.

Analysis of these cases, almost 50 nursery-treated children, supported the conclusion that treatment outcome depended, in almost every instance, upon the extent to which the mother-child reciprocal relationship had been supported and improved. Treatment failure, in contrast, was correlated in great part with the degree to which the therapist had *substituted* for the mother in her therapeutic relationship with the child, and the therapist's failure to engage the mother as "cotherapist" and "copatient." Was this due to parental psychopathology or to poor treatment design?

Our new therapeutic model was designed to deal with the issues already described. We made the following assumptions:

1. The young child's psychopathology results in great measure from a discordance between the parents' "fantasied child" and the "real child"; this is best approached in a therapeutic setting that elicits parental fantasy—i.e., in the presence of both infant and parent in a playroom designed to simulate the home situation as closely as possible.

2. In this setting the behavior of infant and parents is more likely to reveal the fantasies and other psychological processes of both child and parent to the therapist trained to anthropomorphize with this behavior and to utilize metaphor to translate nonverbal material into secondary process language.

3. The presence of the parent during all treatment sessions with the infant supports a more favorable type of reciprocal engagement of the dyad, rather than interfering with its development.

4. Additional therapeutic sessions with the parents alone provide further access to their preoedipal conflicts aroused by the child as a special type of "transference object." As this material became conscious, it could be utilized in concurrent therapy with the parents with us or in the parents' individual psychoanalytic or psychotherapeutic treatment with another therapist, since it is no longer "acted out" so intensively with the baby as "transference object."

Treatment is structured as follows. After the parents are interviewed by the senior author for two or three sessions, each of the parents (if both are available) brings the baby to several assessment sessions with both authors. If treatment is indicated, the infant and at least one of the parents attend two or three therapeutic sessions each week. The baby's behavior serves as the focus of the junior author's work with both mother and child and father and child. The parents also have individual treatment sessions with the senior author at varying intervals, depending upon their individual requirements. Here, too, the infant's behavior remains the focus of the work, and the parents' own reactions are used to further our mutual understanding of the underlying psychological processes in both infant and parents. Finally, both authors consult with one another frequently, correlating the treatment of the family.

The changes in the nature of the infant-parent interaction and in the direction of the developmental process in the infant provide the basis for judging the effectiveness of our treatment method. In regard to the infant-parent relationship, we have utilized the criteria outlined by Mahler, Pine, and Bergman indicating normal progression in separation-individuation, and the behavioral criteria described by Call (1978) as indicators of the normal attachment process. Psychosexual development in the infant is judged by the emergence of phase-derivative behavior as described by Galenson and Roiphe (1971) and Galenson, Miller, and Roiphe (1976). Ego development is evaluated by clinical observation and by psychological testing when appropriate.

The emergence of parental, unconscious, preoedipal material is signaled by parental recall of forgotten memories of childhood experiences and affects, often assisted by the parents' direct questioning of their own parents. The extent to which access to preoedipal material then modifies the parents' behavior with their infant is observed within the nursery and through detailed interviews with the parents. Parents who are concurrently undergoing psychoanalytic or psychotherapeutic treatment elsewhere often bring such issues into their own treatment. Only longer term follow-up will allow evaluation of the overall effectiveness of this treatment modality.

We have seen 65 cases for consultation over the past seven years; 16 families have been in treatment over more than a six-month period, and eight of these are still with us.

One case of infantile autism in a nine-month-old child was largely resolved by age 15 months. Other less malignant symptoms and syndromes included anorexias, sleep disturbances, excessive crying, problems in impulse control, developmental lags, excessive fear of strangers and of separation, and other symptoms of an underlying attachment disorder.

Our findings can be summarized as follows:

1. Marked improvement has occurred in those instances of disordered parent-infant attachment where pertinent preoedipal parental conflict material has emerged into parental awareness.

2. While the parent-child relationship has improved in all our cases, those who have not done as well are children whose parents remain in serious conflict with one another. This is particularly true in the children of divorced parents, but also where one or both parents continue to deny the conflict that in fact does exist between them.

3. A split transference has developed in a number of cases; one author becomes the good and the other the bad object. This has proven to be a workable situation by means of continuous communication between the two authors. Also the parents are informed at the beginning of treatment that the senior author has access to all treatment material and is tacitly "in charge."

CASE MATERIAL ILLUSTRATING THE CONJOINT TREATMENT METHOD

It seems unlikely that the psychological effects of being raised in a single-parent family can be generalized to cover the wide range of situations to which this term is currently applied. Such factors as the psychological status of the single parent, the age and sex of the parent and child, the circumstances surrounding the birth and early years of the child's life, the availability of support systems, both familial and extrafamilial, and the constitutional endowment of the child are but a few of the variables that influence children's development. And even beyond these variables are all the difficulties inherent in arriving at long-term prediction, even where unusual features do not have to be taken into account.

With this in mind, although no general conclusions can be drawn from the case we shall present, the material illustrates the complex interaction of a young child and her mother, their reaction to a trauma they experienced jointly, the influence of the mother's reactions, and the range and complexity of defenses which this very young child was able to muster. We will emphasize in particular the influence of the trauma on the child's object relations and defensive structuralization—an effect that was easily identifiable and that suggests to us that certain roots or precursors of character formation can be delineated at an earlier age than is usually expected. Finally, our experience with this case lends strong support to the argument for initiating intensive treatment of the traumatized young child directly, along with the parent, rather than limiting treatment to the parent only.

Annette's father died suddenly when she was 20½ months old. Conjoint treatment of mother and child was begun when Annette was 30 months of age, and came to an abrupt end almost eight months later under circumstances that will be described below. Our model of conjoint treatment consisted, in this instance, of biweekly sessions with the mother and child together, conducted by B. F., and weekly sessions with the mother alone conducted by E. G. This type of therapy (as already stated) requires extensive collaboration between the two therapists, both in regard to sharing material and working with aspects of transference and countertransference problems which inevitably arise. Both parent and child were informed of this collaboration from the outset.

Annette's mother, Rose, then 36 years old, had been married before, as had Annette's father who was 50 years old when he died, and both parents had grown children by their prior marriages. Rose, the youngest by about seven years of four siblings, grew up in a wealthy but isolated home from which her rather elderly parents were frequently absent. Rose was cared for by a long series of nurses, none of whom she remembered with particular fondness. She has been an "eating problem" all her life—first as a young child, later as a borderline anorectic in her adolescence and adult life. She had been "crazy about" her father, was devastated by his sudden death when she was 22 years old, and described that she had continued feeling his presence as a constant benevolent protector who would always be with her.

Her first marriage at age 20 years to a wealthy man of her own age was marked by mutual infidelity, alcoholism, and drug abuse; the children of this marriage were, not unexpectedly, equally disturbed. Hoping to find stability, if not passionate love, Rose was married again at 32 years to a very wealthy man who was her senior by some 14 years. The pregnancy with Annette was unplanned, but was not terminated because of the mother's intense fear of having an abortion. Spotting began early, however, so that Rose was largely confined to bed during the last seven months of the pregnancy. She became deeply depressed and gained over 50 pounds during this time.

After a normal, full-term, spontaneous delivery, Annette's primary caretaker was a nurse who remained for five months, another nurse until she was 18 months, and a series of subsequent nurses who came and went. However, the mother was hardly ever away from home because Annette's father had also become deeply depressed when Rose was about five months pregnant. While Rose's depression gradually lifted after Annette's birth, her father's depression worsened. He spent many days in bed, distracted only by his daughter with whom he played several special games—whirling a top and stacking coins.

Annette, who was bottle-fed from the start, was always a "finicky" eater and very fussy, often requiring hours of being held before falling asleep. However, by eight months she was a lively active bright baby who spoke her first words at nine months. Her development proceeded well, despite the continuing paternal depression; she discovered her vagina at 16 months, began to masturbate at that time, and was well on her way toward toilet training by 20 months.

Although she was a very attractive child who apparently had great "sending power," she did not go to others as easily as they came to her. Separation from either parent, her various stepsiblings, and the two housekeepers who had been with the family even before her birth precipitated acute distress in Annette, and she would resort to thumb-sucking and retreat.

Annette's father died suddenly during the night, when Annette was 20½ months old. She was told of his death the next morning. She did not attend the funeral, but was present during the subsequent week of the family's sitting shiva. In answer to her repeated requests for her father, her mother read the book *The Dead Bird* to Annette many times. But soon Annette began to sulk, was moody, and had tantrums, particularly at bedtime. Mother and child now spent many hours together in bed, hugging and kissing one another; Annette followed her mother everywhere, including her daily showering. When she momentarily lost visual contact with her mother at a birthday party, she was inconsolable.

This intense attachment was undoubtedly fostered by her

mother, who had been relieved by her ailing husband's death, yet felt guilty and angry at the doctor whom she accused of having neglected him. Annette was encouraged to be the cheerful and gay support for Rose as well as the extended family, a role that she dutifully fulfilled despite her continuing intense fear of separation. However, Annette persisted in searching for her father, a symptom that finally brought her mother to us for consultation.

During her first visit to our playroom with her mother, Annette was a beautiful, gay, and cheerful child of 30 months who politely greeted us but then began to flit from toy to toy. To my question as to what had happened to her father, she answered, "He died, he broke and is in the sky." To my statement that she had come to understand more about Daddy, she said, "Marvellous," and then flung herself sobbingly on her mother's body, saying, "I don't want to come here."

To her next two sessions she brought a plastic horse to which she had developed an attachment eight months after her father's death, i.e., at age 28 months. She called it "My Daddy horse" and took it with her fairly constantly. She maintained her gay smiling face, but said almost at the same moment, "My Daddy doesn't love me, he can't love me, he has no feelings inside," and "My Daddy ran away; I told him not to, but he did."

During the following eight months of conjoint treatment of mother and child, two major themes emerged. One involved the extraordinary attempt that this 32-month-old child had made to organize and integrate the death of her father, while the second concerns the meaning of the father's death to a preoedipal girl.

Annette's mother echoed our own impression that Annette was very advanced in language, which was unusually rich, and in play, which was creative and active, and her impulse control, which was extremely well developed. While this spoke to the presence of a solid inner organization and structure, Annette exuded at the same time a sense of false, even brittle, gaiety, setting her mouth in a broad, tense grimace and saying, "I'm not sad; see, I'm smiling." While she cried sometimes, she denied any painful feelings, particularly sadness and anger. This peculiar affective contradiction was exactly similar to her mother's, who blandly denied sadness despite tears barely held back.

During the next two to three months, while Annette repeatedly asked her mother to make birds out of play dough, the mother struggled with the issue of what and how to tell Annette more about her father's death. Annette's therapist, B. F., initiated the explanation after extensive discussion with the mother. Using toy horses, she pointed out that their hooves were buried, and then read *The Dead Bird* book aloud again, pointing out the various features of death that applied to both her father and the bird—the bodily changes, the funeral, the burial, the grave, and the cemetery. Annette's responses indicated the affective split in attempting to ward off painful feelings while acting out in a game the very burial she feared. This critical session was followed by a remarkable calming of Annette's "hyper" moods and flakiness, and she continued to request details that indicated how difficult it was for her to begin to accept the finality of death.

This permission to explore Annette's need to know more about her father's death relased a flood of anger directed primarily at the mother. Now Annette pretended to telephone to her father, said he was hiding and that she could reach him in a variety of ways.

In the midst of this barrage of anger and curiosity, Annette began to ask her mother where her vagina was—a subject that she had dropped sometime after her father's death. A resurgence of masturbation and various games connected with sexual activity between men and women now appeared, and one day Annette said to her therapist, "You know, daddies have a penis, my Daddy had a penis. Girls don't have a penis, I have a vagina, my Mommy and Barbara [her therapist] have vaginas." Along with this upsurge of anger and return to sexuality, Annette's former fear of monsters disappeared. Annette one day made a snake, "but one who had no teeth," and declared she liked being a girl.

DISCUSSION

This highly condensed presentation of the complex material that emerged from this pair describes a mother who seemed to be attempting to make up for her own lonely childhood and her unresolved mourning of her father by establishing a symbiotic attachment to her child. Annette was to be a cheerful aspect of the mother's self, and to counter her ongoing depression, but she also seemed to represent for the mother the oedipal child for which she had never given up hope.

Annette was used by the father in a somewhat similar fashion: she represented life and hope as a counter to his deep depression. This paternal relationship, distorted as it was, nevertheless seemed to have provided Annette with the basis for an unusually sturdy tie to her dead father. Her persistent quest for him and his penis and her fetishistic use of the plastic horse gave evidence of the remarkable stability of her mental representation of him and the eventual development of oedipal longings for him, once the denial of her sadness over his death was lifted. This defensive denial had been imposed upon Annette by the mother's similar defense, an imposition that seriously interfered with Annette's separation and individuation as well as her psychosexual development.

Had treatment not been instituted, it is probable that Annette would have remained her mother's alter ego and her own "false self." The burden of her anger at the father who left her and the even greater anger at her mother who kept her from claiming her developmental rights of becoming a separate and sexual female might have been unsurmountable for many children less well endowed than this valiant little girl.

But here our story must end, for Annette was killed at 38 months in a terrible accident, leaving those who knew her to accomplish *their* mourning as she had so diligently worked out her own.

REFERENCES

Call, J. D. (1978), Psychological and behavioral development of infants and children. In: *Practice of Pediatrics*, ed. V. C. Kelley. Hagerstown, MD: Harper & Row.

Fraiberg, S., Shapiro, V., & Cherniss, D. (1983), Treatment modalities. In: *Frontiers of Infant Psychiatry*, ed. J. D. Call, E. Galenson, & R. L. Tyson. New York: Basic Books.

Galenson, E., Miller, R., & Roiphe, H. (1976), The choice of symbols. *J. Amer. Acad. Child Psychiat.*, 15:83–96.

——— Roiphe, H. (1971), The impact of early sexual discovery on mood, defensive organization and symbolization. *The Psychoanalytic Study of the Child*, 26:195–216. New York: Quadrangle.

Mahler, M. S., Pine, F., & Bergman, A. (1975), *The Psychological Birth of the Human Infant*. New York: Basic Books.

17

FREUD IN A SECOND GENERATION: SOME PERSONAL REFLECTIONS

CLIFFORD YORKE, FRCPsych, DPM

The contributor to a Festschrift in honor of Leo Rangell has no shortage of appropriate subjects on which to draw. Rangell is interested in everything psychoanalytic, and the scope and range of his writings and other contributions are wide indeed. But there is a second characteristic that has always attracted me to his work: a readiness to look afresh at any given topic, to detect a need to extend and modify existing concepts whenever this seemed called for, while at the same time adhering firmly to basic psychoanalytic concepts without which our psychology ceases to be truly psychoanalytic. He has always been quick to distinguish the schismatic from the true scientific advance.

Perhaps it is these characteristics that have fostered Rangell's very deep interest in the work of Anna Freud. In a memorial paper (1984), he pointed out that, through Anna Freud, Freud's own work was deepened and extended for a second generation. This is a view I totally share, and it seemed to me that on this special occasion, it would be appropriate to say something of Anna Freud from a personal point of view, and to try to convey what it was like to work with her and to watch some of her scientific contributions unfold.

I first encountered Anna Freud when, as a young psychiatrist in training, I heard her lecture at the Maudsley Hospital in London. At the time, I knew little about the speaker, a slight figure in a pinafore dress with voluminous ankle-length skirt. Her head was rather large in proportion to her body, with big enquiring eyes and animated expression. I did not know then that the dress was habitual, self-made with considerable skill, and timeless. I knew she was one of Sigmund Freud's daughters, though I could not have said which, and I knew she had written a book called *The Ego and the Mechanisms of Defense*, though I had not read it. But I cannot help wondering whether that initial experience set something in train. Certainly, it was Anna Freud to whom I turned for advice when seeking personal analysis and who steered me in what turned out to be the right direction.

It took a while to learn about her intellectual history, about her contributions to psychoanalysis, and to understand how much the work we came to know in London owed to her work and activity in Vienna before the *Anschluss* had cut her life in two. At an informal gathering to celebrate her seventy-fifth birthday, she recalled her initial application for membership of the Viennese Psychoanalytic Society. She had sought to be admitted on the basis of her acknowledged interest and involvement, including her services as librarian to the Society. Her father was not convinced that these were appropriate grounds for acceptance, but he agreed to refer the matter to Karl Abraham who was at the time President of the International Psycho-Analytical Association. Abraham's reply was uncompromising: she would have to conform to the rules and read a paper like anyone else. Telling the story with a certain relish, she wondered if that compulsory requirement had alone been responsible for the fact that she had gone on writing ever since. What she did not say was that the initial reluctance had more to do with reticence than any wish to profit from a special relationship.

Anna Freud had drawn on her father's work and built on it with original and extensive contributions of her own. But although she knew that her father's work was of inestimable value, she was never an uncritical follower of his views. She took it for granted, both in matters of everyday life and in personal considerations, that no one was perfect, and she was always aware that Freud had not said the last word on anything and that later developments would continue to add and to modify a very great deal. And then there were certain paths along which she refused to follow him. The concept of a death instinct was a notable example. Although she presented arguments for and against it at the Vienna Congress, as Rangell reminds us, it was clear from her remarks elsewhere that she regarded it as a philosophical speculation which was in no way a basic or even necessary concept in psychoanalytic thinking. She never said this quite so plainly in her written work, though her general view of the subject could perhaps be inferred from her neglect of it. But the importance she attached to the aggressive drive and to death *wishes,* as opposed to *instincts,* is abundantly clear in her publications.

Indeed, the impact of Anna Freud's thinking as it articulates itself on the printed page with deceptively simple elegance is considerable, but it cannot convey a unique way of working. That depended, to an extent not easy to imagine, on a singular form of collaboration with others. It was not until, as an outsider, I joined what felt like an extended family in Hampstead that I came to understand how her work in child analysis was not only fostered by, but even depended on, her creation and development, over a period of many years, of the Hampstead Child-Therapy Course and Clinic—now, after her death, the Anna Freud Centre. From the beginning she had drawn on staff selected and trained by herself and a few close colleagues.

What had been created was a unique instrument for psychoanalytic investigation that went beyond the provision of public service. The services themselves gave rise, in the form of meticulous records, to a mine of detailed information drawn from normality and pathology: from a well-baby clinic, a mother-toddler group, and a nursery school for the under-fives; from extensive diagnostic assessments using a standardized psychoanalytic schema; and from clinical treatment and management.

When I joined her as Medical Director, I found my principal assignment was to take overall responsibility for the diagnostic services and to chair the diagnostic meetings. I found this an exciting and challenging task, in view of her own expertise and unique contributions to the field. But she was always helpful and supportive and taught me a great deal in her unobtrusive but effective way. I began to form the opinion that Anna Freud's contributions to psychoanalytic research were intimately connected with her approach to a coherent nosology based on a deepened understanding of human development. And it seemed to me, too, that in this regard, her work could be set in a broad historical context that gave her a permanent place in the development of psychiatry as well as psychoanalysis (Yorke, 1980). I want to say a little about her approach to diagnosis because this inevitably became a personal involvement and concern.

I have sometimes been asked why I put such emphasis on the diagnostic aspects of Anna Freud's work when she contributed so variously to so many important topics. The short answer lies in the nature of psychoanalytic nosography itself, a matter about which she herself was always very clear. What we see, whether in the adult or the child, is either the result of development or its continuing progress. We see what has gone right or is going right, or what has gone wrong or is going wrong in meeting the demands of what Hartmann (1939) called the "average expectable environment." We see what amounts to transient disturbance, the products of "developmental strain" as Nagera (1966) used to call it, or, more seriously, arrests, deviations, or established reversions or regressions (Yorke, 1983a,b). For Anna Freud these were not simply matters of child assessment in the nursery school or at the diagnostic stage of referral: even the process of psychoanalysis itself can be understood as a matter of continuous diagnostic revision. *A sound nosology draws and utilizes advances in almost all fields of psychoanalytic research.* Anna Freud's interest in it was abiding.

Anna Freud's attempts to systematize diagnosis were crystallized in an approach that rested on three contributants. One of these—the detailed developmental history together with the mental examination, whether in the form of observation, consultation, or psychological testing—is common to every serious worker in the field. What Anna Freud had added was the Diagnostic Profile (1962) and the concept of Developmental Lines (1963). For some years these have been familiar concepts to most psychoanalysts, but a brief restatement of the principles involved may be useful for present purposes.

It was Anna Freud's belief and practice that due weight must be given to *all* available data. Genetic or constitutional factors;

physical illnesses or accidents; apparent or potential mental traumata; benign, advantageous, or malign environmental influences—none of these always reveals the extent of their influences on the presenting clinical picture. It is essential to try to see the various distinctive features in relation to the *whole* personality setting. The various agencies within the mind must be seen in terms of their *dynamic* relationships with each other; mental *economics* assessed in terms of their contending strengths; and the quality and resilience of the agencies as mental *structures* taken into account. It may then be possible to make significant inferences about the current status of internal and external adaptation, and to form a rough idea of how important features of this have come about.

Such an initial Profile can be no more than provisional. But, for all the defects, inseparable from any attempt to produce a coherent framework on the basis of information that is incomplete and often far from reliable, the Profile has the advantage of attempting to assess, on the basis of coherent psychoanalytic thinking, the contributions of a large number of variables to the presenting personality.

But an important point must be emphasized. The Profile represents a *cross-section* of the child's personality, including the pathology and its relation to the symptoms, at a particular moment in time—namely, at the time the child is seen—and in relation to that child's own developmental history. It does so against the background of a hypothetical developmental norm. While it remains, in all essentials, a cross-section, it does so within the context of a developmental matrix, sectioned horizontally, as though all the flux and change of development were frozen for an instant for the critical inspection of the diagnostician.

The developmental history should, however, guard against such a frozen and isolated view. But I began to feel, as time went on, that in this respect, the value of the Profile would be enhanced if its use were implemented by more extended consideration of Developmental Lines. Up to this time, the Profile maker would devote a very short section to the Lines; and restrict his discussion of them to very young children. This was perhaps largely because certain lines were useful in deciding whether a child of three or four had taken the necessary developmental steps to be able to make use of analysis.

Let me reemphasize one or two central points. Developmental Lines are not concerned with the history and establishment of any one part of the personality viewed in isolation, such as the id or the ego, but with the basic interactions between them and "their various developmental levels, and also age-related sequences of them, which in importance, frequency, and regularity are comparable to the maturational sequence of libidinal stages and the gradual unfolding of the ego functions" (A. Freud, 1965). In effect, these Lines put together, in functional form, what the Profile takes apart. They *synthesize* rather than *analyze* (in an everyday or chemical sense). Examples will readily spring to mind; they include such closely scrutinized Lines as the one which leads from dependency to emotional self-reliance and adult object relations via various stations on the way; from irresponsibility to responsibility in body management; from wetting and soiling to bladder and bowel control; from egocentricity to companionship; and many more.

Arrests on Developmental Lines, and reversions along and deviations from them, are important contributants not only to childhood pathology (A. Freud, 1965, 1974) but also to adult disturbance. Not every adult has moved from egocentricity to companionship; not every adult is capable of moving from play to work when the need arises; not every adult is capable of consistent conceptual thinking; not every adult has made the moves from pervasive to signal anxiety; and not every adult has traversed the entire line of development of object relations, which leads from dependence to emotional self-reliance (Yorke, 1983b). Yet, in spite of these obvious facts, the notion that Developmental Lines are mainly applicable to the under-fives is comparatively widespread, and many child analysts still do not consider it worthwhile to make an assessment of them in children of latency age or beyond. This is, perhaps, understandable in the case of certain Lines—of the Line that leads from wetting and soiling to bladder and bowel control, where progress is linked with expectable physiological maturation, or the Line that leads from suckling to rational eating, even though it is well known that attainments on these Lines may be lost in a variety of adult disturbances. Many adult psychotic phenomena cannot be fully understood without the notion of reversion along such Lines (Freeman, 1976). But *arrests* on these Lines beyond the confines of childhood are far from unknown; we have all met an occasional instance where enuresis has persisted uninterrupted into adult life without evident organic cause, and I have described a case of an adult who had never made a proper transition from fluids to solids, and had to supplement his diet chemically (Yorke, 1983a). The rarity of an instance such as this does not, in my view, affect the general argument.

It is still sometimes said that Developmental Lines are no more than descriptive devices of a selective and arbitrary kind. This is emphatically not the case. Developmental Lines are functional associations of elements from the various agencies whose dynamic interaction plays an instrumental part in the psychological disturbance of children—and adults.

Consideration of this kind increased my conviction that assessment by Profile and assessment by Developmental Lines are *not* alternative approaches to diagnosis. They are complementary. The one provides us with a cross-section, with a *horizontal* view; the other with an appraisal, in *vertical* terms, of the significant stages reached by the child's personality in its progress, retrogression, or arrests along many and varied pathways which, taken together, help to form the same diagnostic picture. Of course, the Profile has been elaborated in such a way that it provides a readily available and systematized aid for the diagnostician, while the Developmental Lines are less fully elaborated and have not been gathered into a comparably organized schema. But both approaches are needed: each comes into its own when used in conjunction with the other. Together, they place the pathology in terms of horizontal and vertical coordinates.

The argument calls for illustration. Let us take the case of a ten-year-old boy in whom a brief phase, characterized by a phobia of dog dirt, has given way to a repetitive washing compulsion. He has great difficulty in falling asleep. His daily life is dislocated. He occupies the bathroom for hours on end. His need for reassurance about the effectiveness of his cleaning rituals is unceasing, but no attempt at external remedy can bring relief to his internal and torturing distress. A hitherto outstanding school performance is seriously deteriorating.

His parents are caring, loving, but ambitious, and have a high regard for all things intellectual. He shares intellectual activities such as chess with a small circle of friends, but is not otherwise appreciably engaged with them. His ready and rigid moral disapproval makes it difficult for him to tolerate, let alone share, the everyday peccadillos of his peers. The history further reveals a severe physical illness involving prolonged diarrhea during the second year of life, at a time when toilet training was almost completed; a later refusal to accept his mother's supervision of his bodily care which existed side by side with a personal physical fussiness; a mild dislike of games involving some danger of dirtiness; and a fastidiousness in appearance belied only by somewhat untidy hair. But until the onset of his phobic, and later obsessional-type, disturbance, he gave no great cause for concern: he amply satisfied the expectations of his parents and his teachers, and he was in no way teased by his schoolmates, since his attitudes and behavior fell well short of quirkiness.

It is not too hard to imagine the thoughts of the diagnostician when, faced with such a case, he attempts an assessment by Profile. He will note the anal-libidinal organization confronted by structured defenses manifest in the cleansing rituals; he will note the enormous price paid for their upkeep in terms of adaptation; and he will be struck by the rigidity of a superego under whose widespread proscription the ego displays an intolerance of so many instinctual trends. He will give weight to the many areas in which functioning is unimpaired, though he will note that high cognitive abilities and intellectual endowment are helpless in the face of threatening fantasy, and that the ego is unable to restrict and contain anxiety at signal levels. So he would start his assessment with a rough idea of the general contributions of the different mental agencies to the presenting clinical picture.

Next, he would no doubt reflect on the general psychological matrix in which the obvious abnormalities were to be found. He would examine the instinctual organization, including the contributions toward it of aggression as well as the less obvious libidinal trends. He would examine the manifold indications of ego structure and functioning, beyond those betrayed by the symptom, and he would try to make a fuller assessment of the superego, including structural anomalies, unity or duplicity in aims and controls, as well as the provision and maintenance of ideals and realistic goals. His survey of all these will constitute a detailed study that broadens out from the obvious centers of disturbance to provide a cross-section of the child's personality.

This cross-section must now be complemented by a developmental perspective. Without this, he cannot begin, for example, to tackle the question of libidinal fixation versus regression. Has the child remained restricted to an instinctual level which he would normally have outgrown, or have the more advanced instinctual adjustments of latency only given way under the impact of prepuberty, when defects of ego containment and control have proved unequal to strengthened developmental demands? This is an old psychoanalytic question, but its point is central. It is one thing to recognize the articulation of the different parts of the personality; it is another to know the historical steps by which their interrelatedness has come about. *Depth* must be added to *breadth*. How, in the present example, can the scrutiny of Developmental Lines augment this *vertical* dimension?

Take the line which leads from vegetative excitation, through pervasive anxiety, to signal anxiety (Yorke and Wiseberg, 1976). It is clear that, during latency, anxiety was reasonably well contained, but, with the upsurge of prepuberty, phobic formations occurred which, though initially successful, were progressively displaced until the anxiety became increasingly diffuse and derestricted. Only with the onset of obsessive-compulsive symptoms was anxiety contained, and then only as long as the symptoms were kept in being. Again, the Line that leads from the discharge of excitation via bodily pathways to the increasing (though never exclusive) use of mental ones shows some interesting features. It is by no means straightforward. An increasing enjoyment in, and emphasis on, intellective pursuits shows that forward moves along this Line are quite advanced, if not excessively so; while the boy's attitude to bodily expression, as revealed in the full history, borders on the hypochondriacal. Furthermore, in his compulsive symptom, the excitation is discharged (and the *idea* as well as the *expression* of dirtiness and contamination kept at bay) by repetitive bodily activity. These phenomena require deeper investigation, but they most certainly involve a developmental *deviation*.

What about the Line that leads from egocentricity to companionship? The boy has clearly failed to reach the end point. He uses other children largely for the pursuit of specific intellectual pleasures, and in this respect his relationships fall short of true companionship. It follows that the Line of object relationships, which overlaps other Lines, also shows substantial interference. More narrowly, the diagnostician would look for some disturbance, if only in terms of associated mental content, on the Line that leads from wetting and soiling to bladder and bowel control.

How, then, might a diagnostic formulation of this case run? It would surely include the following points. The boy was clearly bright, with intellectually stimulating and caring parents who nonetheless overvalued the intellect and whose own obsessional traits were to some extent reflected in their child as his development unfolded. That development soon received a significant setback. Under the impact of rather strict toilet training, early signs of compliance were just beginning to reveal themselves in a "good," "clean," little boy when he fell victim to severe diarrhea. His wishes impelled him in one direction, but his body imposed on him another. Once recovery had set in, the usual processes of reaction formation were fortified, anality was excessively dreaded, and ensuing character traits were laid down which, from that time forward, became an integral part of his makeup. The body, as a source of loss of control, was feared and mistrusted, but it also had to be protected, assuaged, and, almost like a willful child, preserved from the consequences of its own acts. It could not be welcomed as an integral part of the self. The mind, on the other hand, which had never willingly betrayed its owner, was prized to the point of excess. In this it was at one with the parents whose admiration of the mind and censoriousness of the body could be shared.

It is of interest that, too early, the mother was allowed no part in his bodily care or in the alleviation of hypochondriacal concerns, and in this and in other respects the boy maintained a premature self-reliance and willful independence. We lack the details of the oedipal phase, but if the latter is seen as an integrating force for pregenital trends, then the persistence of such characteristics without adequate modification hardly suggests a successful negotiation of this stage. The consequences for later genital development could have been severe. However, the boy entered a period of what looked like near-normal latency, and it was not until the drive upsurge of puberty that defenses began to crack and regression to anal fixations was set in train. The earlier taming of drive expression, which had lent to latency a certain tranquillity, indicated the attainment of a fairly high level on the "Anxiety Line," but with the threat of renewed drive intrusion anxiety became more pervasive, and defensive attempts at phobic formation were revealed in the fear of dog dirt. These measures proved inadequate, and a compulsive disorder, in which anxiety could only be contained in washing rituals, supervened.

I hope this brief example illustrates how the contributions of Anna Freud to systematized and scientific diagnosis could lead to a unique personal formulation in each and every case. It was fascinating to discuss these many issues with her, and to experience her willingness to consider suggestions for modifications or fresh applications of her ideas whenever she thought these might be useful. But her work never ceased to evolve, and a fuller account of her contributions to nosology would call for a much more extended discussion, and include such important contributions as her later survey of symptoms in childhood (1970), written over a single weekend, and the concept of developmental disharmony (1979), of which she was particularly proud.

Anna Freud was a director who did not direct in any conventional sense. She set an example with an adult effectiveness reinforced by an unusual and almost childlike charm. She rarely told her staff what to do or how to do it. That was not her way. She believed that people gave their best when pursuing lines of investigation in which they themselves had a special interest. But she recognized special talents and often introduced her staff to gifts of which they themselves were unaware, and she sometimes surprised them with their own accomplishments. At the same time, all retained their autonomy. Anna Freud did not interfere once they set out on their chosen course. But she was always available to them whenever they wanted her.

Anna Freud was the unobtrusive but unifying agent for the Clinic's diverse activities. She read the minutes of every study group and followed their deliberations closely. She read every weekly report on the progress of children in treatment, the vast majority of whom she had never seen, and none of their achievements or setbacks escaped her. The minutes of every diagnostic or clinical discussion contain references to past or present cases, permanently stored in an extraordinary memory and available for instant recall whenever they were needed to exemplify important points at issue.

Clinical discussions were frequently enlivened by her witty or ingenious comments. At a diagnostic conference the staff was considering an unhappy little boy whose parents had split up. He invented an imaginary companion called "Turwump" who helped assuage his misery. Analysis was recommended, but the trouble was that the parents were not able to give him adequate support in the enterprise, and he himself was diffident. Anna Freud said to the diagnostician: "Perhaps you should tell Billy that Turwump needs treatment, but that Billy would have to bring him."

When a little Arab boy who displayed all sorts of defenses against unacceptable impulses was under discussion, he was said to have dismissed his wish to become a nautical engineer as "just a dream." After a little prompting he confided his ambition to become Defense Minister of the Arabs. Kalim's insistence that he was in favor of peace appeared at odds with his support of what he called the Palestine Liberation Army. Anna Freud remarked that in the meantime—until he became Arab Defense Minister—Kalim was looking to his own defenses.

It should be added that Anna Freud never considered psychoanalysis a therapeutic panacea. When the young daughter of a very fraught mother appeared to be in difficulties, she said that one ought to ask: "Does this child need analysis or does the mother need a housekeeper?"

Anna Freud was aware of her own intellectual value. In spite of her modesty, she never doubted the quality of her thinking.

In some ways this assurance was striking, since her self-esteem was not particularly high in certain other respects. Her confidence in her thinking was of a kind that inspired confidence in her colleagues: it was never arrogant, never cock-sure, and rarely bred antagonism. She welcomed disagreement based on clear thinking, and was once particularly distressed when she learned that certain members of the staff had been disquieted when she and I publicly expressed our differences on an important issue. "How can it be," she said in a shocked voice, "that people get *upset* about disagreement? How *can* there be any progress without it?"

In the same vein, she did not hesitate to change her opinions when fresh evidence obliged her to do so. When two of her colleagues read a paper that called into serious question certain accepted views on female sexual development, she opened the discussion by saying, a little tongue-in-cheek: "Well! to think we have been so wrong for so many years!" But she changed her opinions thereafter.

There were important, even basic, elements in Anna Freud's thinking that sometimes went unrecognized, in spite of her own clear statements in her writings. Just as her father took the view that people were programmed for the Oedipus complex, Anna Freud always acknowledged the importance of inborn propensities in child development. But unlike some psychologists, she never believed that development could be understood in the comparatively simple terms of nature and nurture. For her, *interactions* were all-important, but it was in the nature of things that the interacting forces were themselves changing at every step. This may seem a simple statement, but it is one that many find difficult to grasp. The problem is not necessarily resolved by the use of Freud's tripartite model of the mind—of id, ego, and superego—and of the ways they react with each other and with the outside world. From the perspective of the child analyst, the nature and quality of these interacting forces change with a changing world, and change with the internal development of maturational forces.

If this added to the complexities of Anna Freud's psychological thinking, it also gave it strength. She was never surprised when children from the most disturbing backgrounds drew on a few good experiences and went on to develop astonishingly well.

Equally, she recognized that many children who enjoyed the most favorable upbringing were surprisingly affected by the few adversities that befell them. At a time when it was fashionable to believe that everything that went wrong with children could be laid at the door of their parents, she knew that such a view was always attractively simple, frequently flawed, and often unfair. She neatly expressed this with calculated exaggeration when she said: "Babies are born themselves."

Anna Freud enjoyed the company of men. She sometimes regretted that child psychoanalysis was a profession that attracted far more women than men, and she used to say that the Clinic would function better if more men could be brought into it. She enjoyed working with men, and always looked forward to the visits of Professors Solnit and Goldstein with whom she wrote three books on family law. Certainly, she needed a man with whom to share her concerns about psychoanalysis and her thoughts and feelings about those ostensible friends in the discipline who she thought were undermining it. After the death of Willy Hoffer, her friend and colleague who had also come to this country from Vienna, I found myself gradually drawn into what was sometimes a difficult role. Whenever she had composed a paper, it was always a fascinating experience to be her first audience and to be asked for criticisms of something that did not invite them. But she was often pleased with what she had written and wanted to share that pleasure, to see it reflected and to enjoy the response. She also enjoyed sharing her pleasure in the writings of others when they had made a fresh contribution that seemed to her valuable. In later years, she would sometimes wonder whether or not she were too intolerant of someone else's work. Occasionally a manuscript would arrive, with a brief note: "Please read the enclosed paper. I think it's horrible. But please tell me whether you think I'm wrong."

Some day it will be necessary to delineate Anna Freud's place in the history of scientific psychology and its applications, including her contributions to psychiatric nosology, pediatrics, education, and family law in relation to such issues as fostering, custody, and adoption. When that time comes, attention will have to be paid to her approach to the psychoanalytic treatment and study of adults. My own acquaintance with her approach came about in a number of ways. One of these was through carrying medical responsibility for her adult patients. She never regarded this as a purely nominal matter. She always called attention to clinical phenomena that puzzled her and that she thought might have an organic basis, and she was uncommonly perceptive about them.

Her interest in conceptual problems of adult psychosis and, later, of general psychoanalytic psychiatry had its roots in Vienna. It was there, during her frequent visits to the Psychiatric Clinic, under the tutelage of Paul Schilder, that she acquired her considerable knowledge of the phenomenology of adult mental illness. She sometimes disclaimed this knowledge, saying that she was not a psychiatrist, but she nonetheless loved to discuss it.

But it was her view that child analysis brought a special and indispensable developmental perspective to our understanding of adult mental phenomena, normal and abnormal. She repeatedly searched for childhood forerunners of adult strengths and weaknesses, or of pathological phenomena. In the search, she was mindful of the fact that what was normal at one stage of development was abnormal at another.

The decision to revisit her native land, though in the end taken wholeheartedly, had not been reached without difficulty and hesitation. But it was a moving occasion when, in 1971, Anna Freud returned to Vienna to take part in the International Congress of Psycho-Analysis. None of us will forget the prolonged standing ovation she received for her summary of the proceedings of the Congress, the subject of which, ironically, had been "aggression." The summary was masterly, but the ovation was clearly not accorded solely on that account. There was a sense of exhilaration at a wrong symbolically righted; a reparation for her father, for herself, and for psychoanalysis. A year later, when she received one of the most treasured of her honorary doctorates—an M.D. from the University of Vienna—the event, to which she had invited one or two friends and colleagues from London, was no less moving. In the intervening time, the rapprochement with Vienna had become even closer. She spent some very full days, increasingly relaxed, with Viennese colleagues and friends. For the first time since the *Anschluss* she visited and addressed the Viennese Psychoanalytic Society. She spoke in German, discussing at some length the work at Hampstead. Perhaps a little carried away by the occasion, she forgot that I was not German-speaking, when she turned to me and asked me to support one of her contentions. I was obliged to reply that I never thought the time would come when I would listen to Anna Freud without understanding a word of what she said.

Anna Freud's personality was itself an instrument of a life and work that were closely interrelated. The tireless and rigorous investigator could never be wholly separated from the lover of thrillers and detective stories, or the adventurous thinker from the lover of explorations in the English and Irish countryside. Her love of life included the physical pleasures of swimming and horseback-riding. But although she was anything but self-destructive, her car-driving could be hair-raising. But she was aware of quirks in herself and others: perhaps this was why this meticulous diagnostician would simply say, when told of some unusual conduct, that "people are funny." In her view, human nature was essentially flawed. As a human being, she did not count herself an exception.

In spite of her interest in everyone around her, she remained a private person. For everyone who knew her—each, perhaps, in a different way—her personality and its impact were both personal and collective, but she set clear limits to relationships, beyond which few ventured to trespass. But something must be added: there was, about her, a quality that was timeless. Her ideas changed, expanded, and ceaselessly developed, but at their center there was a stability that encompassed more than strength of purpose. It informed her natural leadership and authority. It was a cornerstone of confidence for those who worked with her or whose work was influenced by her. It was the "still center" at the heart of her creativity.

In trying for this Festschrift to put together a coherent picture of Anna Freud and her work, I have sometimes used by way of illustration material variously discussed more fully elsewhere. I hope the Anna Freud that emerges is one that her colleagues and friends, and in particular Leo Rangell, will recognize.

REFERENCES

Freeman, T. (1976), *Childhood Psychopathology and Adult Psychosis.* New York: International Universities Press.

Freud, A. (1962), Assessment of childhood disturbance. *The Psychoanalytic Study of the Child,* 17:149–158. New York: International Universities Press.

——— (1963), The concept of developmental lines. *The Psychoanalytic Study of the Child,* 18:245–265. New York: International Universities Press.

——— (1965), *Normality and Pathology in Childhood.* New York: International Universities Press.

——— (1970), The symptomatology of childhood: a preliminary attempt at classification. In: *Collected Writings,* 7:157–188. New York: International Universities Press.

——— (1974), Child analysis as the study of mental growth: normal and abnormal. In: *Collected Writings,* 8:119–136. New York: International Universities Press.

——— (1979), Mental health and illness in terms of internal harmony and disharmony. In: *Collected Writings,* 8:110–118. New York: International Universities Press.

Hartmann, H. (1939), *Ego Psychology and the Problem of Adaptation.* New York: International Universities Press, 1958.

Nagera, H. (1966), Early childhood disturbances, the infantile neuroses, and the adulthood disturbances. *The Psychoanalytic Study of the Child,* Monogr. 2. New York: International Universities Press.

Rangell, L. (1984), The Anna Freud experience. *The Psychoanalytic Study of the Child,* 39:29–43. New Haven, CT: Yale University Press.

Yorke, C. (1980), The contributions of the diagnostic profile and the assessment of developmental lines to child psychiatry. *Psychiat. Clin. N. Amer.,* 3:593–603.

——— (1983a), Clinical notes on developmental pathology. *The Psychoanalytic Study of the Child,* 38:389–402. New Haven, CT: Yale University Press.

——— (1983b), Anna Freud and the psychoanalytic study and treatment of adults. *Internat. J. Psycho-Anal.,* 64:391–400.

——— Wiseberg, S. (1976), A developmental view of anxiety. Some clinical and theoretical considerations. *The Psychoanalytic Study of the Child,* 31:107–135. New Haven, CT: Yale University Press.

18

ON BEING A PSYCHOANALYST: INTEGRITY AND VULNERABILITY IN PSYCHOANALYTIC ORGANIZATIONS

PEARL H. M. KING, B.A. HONS.

On a huge hill,
Cragged, and steep, Truth stands, and he that will
Reach her, about must, and about must go;
And what the hill's suddenness resists, win so;

Keep the truth which thou hast found

John Donne

These words by the seventeenth-century English poet John Donne that appear in his poem "Satire III" (1931) made a profound impression on me when I first came across them as an undergraduate in the 1930s. I was keen to oppose the growing power of the Nazis, and frustrated that the British authorities did not seem to see the truth of what was happening in Germany, or if they were aware of what was taking place there, they were doing little to oppose or impede it. With the enthusiasm of youth, truth seemed so simple, and I felt right was on the side of my own version of truth. But the lines quoted above pointed in another direction. They confronted me with the necessity to struggle to discover truth, and to the painful fact that this discovery of the truth does not come easily.

Since then, and especially in my work as a psychoanalyst, I have realized the importance of Donne's words. To discover what is true, one has to see an issue from many vantage points, each of which may add to or change one's perception of it, until one can reach the apex of the "huge hill, cragged, and steep" where "truth stands." Only then can one integrate all facets of that truth for which one searches, and feel it match an inner core of rightness. Then, to keep the truth that we have found is to be true to our own inner sense of integrity.

In *The Mind of Watergate: An Exploration of the Compromise of Integrity*, Leo Rangell (1980) delineated the events that took place in the United States that led eventually to the resignation of President Nixon. Using his psychoanalytic understanding, he described some of the conscious and unconscious individual and group dynamics that facilitated the evolution of the behavior of those involved.

Discussing the subject of the leader and the led, Rangell (1980) wrote:

> A central aspect of the basic pathology is the relationship of man to the group and the influence of the group on the individual mind. . . . the subjugation of individual judgment to the will of the leader and the group is the psychological atmosphere in which choices are made. Here is where the issue of individual courage becomes important, not in the sense of heroism but in the ability to retain one's integrity against the pressures of the surrounding group. The group at whose behest the individual forms his conscience is, under certain conditions, a force which influences him to compromise it. . . .
>
> I gave the disease a new name, the syndrome of the compromise of integrity. . . . I was concerned with the chronic everyday erosions of integrity. Besides being conscious and accountable, they are as automatic and unconscious, as much an outcome of internal conflicts—and as camouflaged into everyday life—as any other emotional symptoms or traits [pp. 11–12].

It was not possible to read Rangell's comments on this period in his country's history without considering the extent to which the dynamics and the pathology that he describes could operate in one's own country, more relevantly within the groups of one's own profession —psychoanalysis.

In his presidential address to the Paris Congress in 1973, given prior to the publication of this book, but while he was working on it, Rangell pointed out that the mechanisms that he described did not fail to have their counterpart in psychoanalytic societies where the presence of internal conflicts of interests may result in issues being "resolved in favor of narcissism at the expense of principles."

> Psychoanalysts in training capacities, or in administrative positions of responsibility, dealing as they do in the evaluation of others, are frequently in tight and delicate situations, subject to crises of character of their own. Caught in conflicts between independent judgement and group pressures, attachments to charismatic or even just dominant figures, with the variety of attendant gains, or the same need 'to be a member of the team' as in the public situations noted above, may often cast the deciding influence [Rangell, 1974, p. 1].

He emphasized that the goal of psychoanalysis was the development of intrapsychic integrity, for the analytic attitude should be in its very essence a model of "relentless incorruptibility."

> To maintain this is its core; there is no analyst, subject to the daily spectrum of transference displacements, who does not know and feel the range of pressures to which this is put, from sexual to material to narcissistic. Basic trust is rightly tested and has to be earned. The capacity to use rather than to abuse transference cannot be taken for granted. Nor once achieved can it automatically continue for life. It needs to be worked at and constantly reaffirmed [Rangell, 1974, p. 11].

It seems to me that Rangell has opened up this topic as it applies to psychoanalysts and their organizations from two points of view: the first deals with the pressures of the leader and the group on the individual, while the second emphasizes the individual's responsibility for himself and especially for his own intrapsychic integrity—both very important for the healthy functioning of a psychoanalytic society and its members. I feel that the implications of the issues he raises should be better understood and discussed among psychoanalysts, and this I proposed to do in this paper.

PRESSURES OF THE GROUP AND THE LEADER ON THE INDIVIDUAL MEMBER

While members of most societies, organizations, and institutions are to some extent exposed to these pressures, members of psychoanalytic societies and institutes are particularly vulnerble to them.

Most professions rely on other training institutions and universities, outside their own professional organizations, to train their new members. The psychoanalysts, however, undertake this task for themselves for quite understandable reasons, as it could not easily by its very nature be delegated outside the psychoanalytic organization. The responsibility for the training of new members of the profession is delegated to a small committee of senior and experienced psychoanalysts.

This does mean that a small group of senior members of the same organization is responsible for selecting candidates for their personal psychoanalysis, for planning and supervising their theoretical and clinical training, for the assessment of their progress and their readiness for qualification, and with that the granting of professional status. While the election of those trained, to membership of the psychoanalytic society, is finally dependent on all full members, even their preparation for full membership is still under the auspices of an education committee in some psychoanalytic organizations. Hence throughout their training, students of psychoanalytic organizations are dependent on and vulnerable to the decisions of those with whom they will later have to work as colleagues. What hazards could one predict arising from this arrangement for training new members of our profession, for the future relationships of colleagues in a psychoanalytic society, and for the needs of individuals to develop their own creative identity? Would it not lead to a special vulnerability to the opinions of senior colleagues?

However, psychoanalysts are vulnerable for personal as well as organizational reasons. Their training involves the exploration of their total personality, conscious and unconscious, in the context of their past life and problems as experienced in the present of the analytic relationship, with all the painful affects that are aroused and the narcissistic wounds that can be revived. Also, in their work as psychoanalysts they have to be aware of and to use those aspects of themselves and their feelings that are brought to their awareness by their patients. To do their work well, they have to be able to remain vulnerable and not to cut themselves off from their feelings. But they also have to be able to tolerate long periods of "unknowing" or to live in what Keats (1952) called "negative capability . . . when a man is capable of being in uncertainties, mysteries, doubts without any irritable reaching after fact or reason" at a time when both they and their patients yearn for certainty.

One source of certainty is to be attached to a group from which it is possible to gain confirmation of one's theories, technique, or clinical understanding. There must be few psychoanalytic societies in which there is a genuine confluence of opinion in relation to the theory and practice of psychoanalysis. Therefore the majority of societies must contain groups of analysts, whether they are organized or unorganized, who share differing points of view from the majority and whose members are eventually elected into positions of authority with a chance of implementing their policies. If these policies are worked out and supported by the groups, there may be a danger of a split in the society. When these groups are led by significant senior psychoanalysts, what happens to the integrity of a psychoanalytic society will depend partly at least on the tolerance and understanding of these senior psychoanalysts.

If psychoanalysts, as I have suggested, are more vulnerable than members of other professions, they have a strong need to experience the security and sense of support that a group can provide. They can therefore more easily be drawn into a group that offers to share its identity with them, and the conformity demanded of them may seem but a small price for membership of the group, particularly as they may actually share most of the points of view held by members of that group.

There are, however, advantages as well as disadvantages to the societies as well as to the individual when such groups develop. In the context of our societies becoming larger, they offer, particularly to newly qualified psychoanalysts, the chance to belong to a smaller group. They develop a "feeling of belongingness" by supporting this group, patients are sent to them, and by sharing the identity of the group they get a pseudoidentity via the group. If they are unable to feel, "I am a psychoanalyst who has done this on my own," at least they can say, "I am an analyst who belongs to this group."

Thus, for psychoanalysts who are unsure of themselves the best defense against anxiety is to feel that they and their group have the "truth" and are "right," while the nonmembers of the group are "wrong." In other words, a "good-bad object" not only welds the group together, but it also protects its members from having to be too concerned about their own shortcomings and anxieties. As the Pharisee said in the New Testament, "Thank God I am not as other men are." But belonging to a group is important, and sometimes these factions grow up because younger members do not have enough positive support in the early stages of their career. They are therefore "fair game" for any older established colleagues (whose self-esteem is bound up with their group) to recruit to their group.

There are, however, several disadvantages attached to being a member of a group. First, conformity with group norms may be increasingly demanded, and no discoveries or formulations outside the theoretical platform or position on which group identity depends can then easily be tolerated. This can result in a sacrifice of integrity and creativity, which individuals tolerate in spite of the conflicts involved because of the advantages of belonging to a group. A second disadvantage is that this conformity is reinforced by various unverbalized sanctions such as fear of rejection by the group, or fear of hurting friends and colleagues to whom one is also grateful. A third disadvantage is that because of the group togetherness and the degree to which its members do in very many ways help and support one another, they get isolated from other groups within a particular society, and they then tend to build up stereotyped images of those other groups and stereotyped versions of their points of view. These stereotypes are seldom subjected to reality testing, and on investigation they are usually based on experience or opinion relevant to past situations and often not currently appropriate. But the reality testing of actual theoretical and clinical differences between two groups is hampered by the fact that when anything is said that would undermine the stereotype that one group has of another group, and on which they could be said to base their "negative identity," anything that would undermine that stereotype is felt to threaten the first group's identity and therefore the individual's rationale for belonging to this group. For this reason they seldom read or quote work done by members of a rival group.

THE PSYCHOANALYST'S RESPONSIBILITY FOR HIS OWN INTEGRITY

As Rangell has indicated, the goal of psychoanalysis should be the development of "intrapsychic integrity" and "relentless incorruptibility." But considering the pressures on the analyst, which I have already described, arising from their training and group membership requirements, the demands for "loyalty" from significant senior analysts and the gratifying of narcissistic needs, this is not always easy to achieve. Much may depend upon the extent to which an analyst has managed to achieve a stable and age-appropriate sense of his own worth and of his own identity as a person.

I first started thinking seriously about the lack of a sense of identity and consequent feelings of alienation in relation to the expectations aroused by psychoanalytic training after reading "The Quest for Identity" by Allen Wheelis (1959). I thought that he was describing a problem that psychoanalysts ought to take seriously. His complaint appeared to be that it was possible to go through many years of analysis and psychoanalytic training, and to end up without any feeling of being a person who has his own core of inner experience and who is able to contact an inner source of creativeness, often enough, over a period of time to feel that he is a viable human being, enriched by his relationships and activities, and not alienated from any inner source of replenishment. This complaint of alienation from oneself and the fruits of one's actions has become an increasingly frequent reason why many people seek analysis. It is as though they can only live in the present, and they have cut themselves off from their past and their inner roots, so that they cannot perceive a future for themselves.

I have observed that over the period of their analyses, patients often change quite dramatically *in their attitude to themselves* and *their own identity*. Most patients when they first come to analysis seem to me to have an impaired sense of their own identity, if any feeling of identity at all. Some patients only seem to feel themselves alive or to be a person when they are interacting with someone else, either in physical external reality or else in their own minds in their fantasy. Other patients seem to experience themselves as split between their minds and their bodies and feel *themselves* as situated only in their own mind. This "I" that they identify themselves with seems only very tenuously related to their body. Their body is felt as "alien," and it may even become a rival or enemy to the safety and peace of "themselves" which they experience as situated in their mind.

Every human being is confronted with crises related to his perception of his identity as he passes through different phases of his life cycle. Such crises are partly related to the processes of growth and aging and partly related to the acquisition of skills and achievements of goals as we take on various positions in society and learn to operate new roles in the social structure. Through the roles that we occupy we relate to each other in groups, in our social networks and social institutions, and we gradually acquire the appropriate knowledge and skills to operate these roles more or less effectively, particularly in our work situations. Our success in operating a professional or work role is of particular importance to us in our culture as our success in our work is usually assumed to be reflected in our earning power. But however seemingly important financial reward is with most professional people, the esteem and approval of our colleagues or peer group are often more important, though not unlinked with them, because this reflects on and enhances our self-esteem and our view of our own identity and work as human beings. In the course of our professional life as psychoanalysts, we too can be faced with the need to reassess ourselves, our view of ourselves, and how we are perceived by others. If we are unable to do so at the critical moment, we may find that we face what I call an *identity crisis*, when our perception of ourselves does not match how we are perceived by others in relation to the context within which we are working. Establishing an identity for oneself becomes difficult if people with whom we are in an emotional or subservient relationship define us in a way that is now compatible with our perception of ourselves. This is when we are tempted to operate on the basis of a *false self*.

Winnicott (1965) describes the false self as follows: "The concept of the false self . . . is not a difficult one. The false self is built up on the basis of compliance. It can have a defensive function, which is the protection of the true self" (p. 133). He states that only the true self can feel real, but it must never be forced to comply with external reality. It is the false self that adapts or alters itself in response to forced environmental pressures, but the individual retains some awareness of the "not-me" quality of this compliance. But "when the false self becomes exploited [either by the individual himself or by the environment] and treated as real there is a growing sense in the individual of futility and despair" (p. 133). Winnicott goes on to describe how the "false self develops when the mother fails to meet the infant's gestures, i.e., when she cannot sense her infant's needs and thus *the infant has to comply with hers to survive*. Thus the infant gets seduced into compliance, and a 'false self' results, and reacts to environmental demands, builds up a false set of relationships, and may even attempt to relate to people by imitating or copying them *instead of becoming himself*" (King, 1968).

I suggest that the way psychoanalytic training is organized can be unconsciously responded to by some psychoanalysts whose false self "adapts and alters itself in response to forced environmental pressures," as an experience that alienates them from their true selves, and their own identity, though they do retain some awareness of this "not-me" quality of the compliance, and hence a deep feeling of dissatisfaction. Such people are particularly vulnerable to the group pressures described earlier.

It is sometimes important to consider whether or not the way that we organize our training and administration in our psychoanalytic organizations facilitates a healthy development of the members within them, so that they can develop a strong sense of their own worth and professional identity. Or do they evoke conforming and placating behavior, the strengthening of false self defenses?

INTEGRITY AND A SENSE OF IDENTITY

It is one of my hypotheses that a psychoanalyst who has a secure sense of his own identity and of his own worth, based on a real appraisal of himself and not on narcissistic wishful thinking, is more able to contain his vulnerability and to act with integrity when confronted with the pressures of a senior colleague or a group of colleagues, against his better judgment. This capacity for integrity I link with an individual's sense of his own identity, which is rooted in a feeling of responsibility for himself as a whole person, for his mind and his body.

In 1976 the International Psychoanalytical Association held a symposium on "The Identity of a Psychoanalyst," and I discussed these problems at some length in the published version of my contribution to the proceedings (King, 1983). Then I considered the impact of life events on the psychoanalyst's sense of identity and the consequent crises that could develop in the analyst's sense of his own identity and worth. Now I would like to consider the various threats to their identity and view of themselves that confront analysts at different stages of their professional life-span and the extent to which their attempts to deal with these threats involve them in situations in which their integrity could be compromised.

As we pass through our professional lives, we undergo various changes in our capacities. There are, for example, a number of critical phases in the professional life cycle of psychoanalysts when they are faced with the need to reassess and accept changes in their own view of themselves, their identity, and the view of themselves taken by significant others, i.e., colleagues and members of their particular "reference group." Each of these phases is characterized by a *transition* from one stage of professional skill to another. They often involve a change in status from that which is *known* to that which is at least partially *unknown* and the loss of the past role and the identity associated with it.

Five critical phases will be considered. They have been selected because during these critical phases in an analyst's professional life, some psychoanalysts experience difficulties and have what might be called an "identity crisis" when they are confronted with the need to redefine themselves, their goals, their expectations, and their view of themselves.

On Being a Student of Psychoanalysis

Applicants for training in the profession of psychoanalysis, unlike applicants for most other professional trainings, must have already acquired proficiency in another relevant profession such as medicine, psychiatry, psychology, sociology, social work. This means that they will come to psychoanalytic training having acquired some professional identity. But they will discover that while it gives them an entrée into that profession, it is of limited help to them as psychoanalysts (except to enable them to earn a living while training), because many of the skills necessary for operating successfully in their original profession may be antithetical to the skills necessary for working as a psychoanalyst. Many psychoanalytic students experience their training as a process of de-tribalization in the course of which they feel they are having to give up their previous professional identity and the expectations and assumptions linked with it, before they have achieved a new professional identity as a psychoanalyst, and this in the context of the possibility that they might not be considered competent enough to be qualified as psychoanalysts on the completion of their training. This identity crisis usually comes to a head in the second last year of the training period and it may be accompanied by periods of depression.

In psychological and learning theory terms, it would appear as the "plateau" of the learning curve. It is important that education committees be mindful of this phenomenon as there is sometimes a tendency to assess students negatively during this phase with insufficient attention being given to the possibility that students are attempting to come to terms with an identity crisis imposed on them at least partly by the training system and the structure of the profession they are attempting to enter, rather than their difficulties arising from problems in their own psychopathology.

On Being a Newly Qualified Psychoanalyst

When the student has at last achieved his ambition to be a psychoanalyst—an ambition that will have cost him so much in terms of personal suffering, time, and money—he is faced with the task of coming to terms with the discrepancy between his fantasy of what being a psychoanalyst involves and the reality of being a newly qualified psychoanalyst. From being a senior student he becomes one of the most junior analysts—in most societies an associate member and not a full member—and therefore not yet considered experienced enough to be entrusted with the government of psychoanalytic affairs. From being a member of the student group he is now on his own with responsibility for his own future among colleagues, many of whom he does not know and some of whom he has only known as teachers.

If he gives up his previous profession and embarks on attempting to become a full-time psychoanalyst, his hopes of being quickly sent rich patients by senior analysts are seldom realized and he often finds himself in continuing financial difficulties. Many psychoanalysts continue to work part time in hospitals, clinics, or other organizations where they can have some financial security. Others continue to work part time in their previous profession from choice, for to work full time as a psychoanalyst would, they feel, cut them off from the real satisfaction that they gained from working as part of a team in an institution. They do, however, often feel a split sense of professional identity, and believe that those who work full time as psychoanalysts regard them as "second class" or "uncommitted" psychoanalysts, in spite of the fact that they may be making important links with those in other therapeutic professions and be acting as important "gatekeepers" for future members of the profession.

The most serious disillusion that often occurs is when the newly qualified psychoanalyst realizes that his personal psychoanalysis has not achieved all he had expected it to achieve and that he is still subject to anxiety, apprehension, and occasional depressions. Many young analysts wisely continue with their personal analysis until they have managed to work through their disappointment that the attainment of a psychoanalytic identity does not guarantee either an anxiety-free existence or the automatic attainment of a professional reputation, the latter only being achieved by much hard work. But some newly qualified psychoanalysts are unable to continue with their personal analysis for financial or psychological reasons and are often faced with an ongoing identity crisis about being a psychoanalyst. They may then carry a "chip" on their shoulder for much of their professional psychoanalytic career.

On Becoming a Full Member of a Psychoanalytic Organization

After two or three years as an associate member, they may well experience increasing pressure to take steps to gain election to full membership of their psychoanalytic society and therefore of the I.P.A. In order to achieve this they usually have to report their work to senior colleagues, either through writing a paper or through a regular assessment of their clinical work in seminars and consultations. This confronts them with another identity crisis. After years of supervision during their training, some analysts prefer to remain associate members and therefore ineligible to take on certain positions in the administration of their psychoanalytic organization or in the training process. They are, however, protected from the pressures and changes in role that confront those who feel able to complete the requirements for election to full membership of the society, the achievement of which opens the door to new sources of self-esteem and, some think, of financial reward.

Those who are thought highly of by their group find that they are especially encouraged and supported at this stage of their career, as they will be more valuable once they have obtained their membership. From their own point of view, they may realize that they will be able to make a more creative contribution to psychoanalysis once they are eligible to serve on the committees of the organization and to share in developing its policy.

But where committees have to operate in organizations that contain a number of different groups, owing allegiance to charismatic or dominant leaders who have attached the new member to their "convoy system," the associate member is indeed faced with an identity crisis and a temptation to compromise his integrity in return for the support he receives. To avoid this he has to be willing to reassess his identity as someone who has something to give to his colleagues as well as someone who needs to receive from them. What sort of psychoanalyst does he feel himself to be? Can he choose without undue looking over his shoulder to check that he is still "keeping in line" or still being approved of? This is not easy for there is still another hurdle for him to cross before he can potentially be in a situation in which he could feel free from the temptation of a neurotic dependence on the opinions of his superiors and mentors.

On Becoming a Training Analyst

After becoming a member it is only a matter of time before he is eligible to be selected or appointed as a training analyst. This is the zenith of most psychoanalysts' aspirations, but it is also a position that is carefully guarded in all psychoanalytic organizations. Access to it is restricted to the "cream" of members as it is felt that the future of analysis in that particular country will depend on their training analysts. Because of this there is usually much soul searching before a member dare apply to take part in the training activities as a training analyst. Most psychoanalytic societies have instituted selection procedures. Potential training analysts usually have to be supported by senior analysts who know their work. Members who have been picked out by their group do not have difficulty in obtaining this support, provided that they are felt to be reliable promoters of the group ethos and psychoanalytic standpoint. But where members have been isolated and have not attached themselves to a particular group, they have difficulty in obtaining such support, unless colleagues have read their papers and heard their contributions at scientific meetings. Most of those who never become training analysts also make few contributions to the scientific life of a society, for ability to communicate analytic ideas surely is central to the task of a training analyst!

Members who reach this point in their professional career and become training analysts have then to face the change in their role, from being a clinical practitioner to being an evaluator of their colleagues. As well as being responsible for their patients, they are also responsible in some degree for the future of their psychoanalytic society. They thus find themselves faced with a dual responsibility, and these interests may seem to clash. Some members find this very difficult and feel that the judgmental aspect of the training analyst's role is antithetical to psychoanalysis. This causes a serious identity crisis for some training analysts, which they never seem to resolve. Others respond to this identity crisis by becoming "Bolshie" and a "law unto themselves," refusing to work within training procedures and eventually breaking away from the psychoanalytic society.

On Becoming an Aging Psychoanalyst

A fifth critical phase in the professional life cycle of a psychoanalyst occurs when he becomes aware of his own aging, the depletion of his skills, capacities, and abilities, and his possible retirement from professional work. Psychoanalysts tend to work much longer and to retire later than people in other professions, with the possible exception of politics, the arts, or religion. They often only reach their full potentiality as psychoanalysts in the second half of life when the long training and period of apprenticeship start to bear fruit, so that they may attain positions of maximum professional responsibility at an age when their friends in other professions are preparing for retirement. Indeed, many analysts do their most creative work between the ages of 45 and 65, creative work that earns them the approval and gratitude of their colleagues. While attempts are made in some societies to encourage psychoanalysts to retire, at least from training activities, at an agreed age (this varies between 65 and 75 years of age), it has been difficult in most societies to obtain any general agreement or, where a policy has been agreed, to implement it as people are affected very differently by the aging process. In addition, the process of aging is also complicated by illnesses that exacerbate the depletion of abilities and undermine the capacities of an analyst prematurely.

Nevertheless, whatever date is given to the onset of this process, every psychoanalyst is inevitably confronted with its impact on the view he takes of himself, his capabilities, his expectations of what is possible, and finally of his identity and how he is therefore currently viewed by colleagues and close collaborators. But when psychoanalysts are overdependent or even parasitical on their role as psychoanalysts, using their patients and their professional activities as extensions of themselves, the main sources of their identity as a human being, then the process of retirement or withdrawal from overmuch professional activity can threaten the stability of their personalities and lead to their inability to face their aging and their own identity crisis in a creative and constructive way.

REACTIONS TO IDENTITY CRISES

Our first realization of an identity crisis may be in the perception of a discrepancy between our ego ideal or how we expect ourselves to function and to be responded to by others and what is actually the case. It may be accompanied by feelings of failure, alienation, and a questioning of the value of what we do, the goals of our work, and even the purpose of life itself. These are the "symptoms" that many psychoanalysts experience as they go through any of these critical phases described above. It is as though the individual has come to a "T" junction in his life. He can no longer continue in the direction he has been following up to that point in time, and therefore he has to decide to turn either to the left or to the right, that is, he has to make a choice. This choice is between an adaptive reaction (he can accept the changing situation in a creative way) and a maladaptive one (he can try to ignore the problems arising from his aging). It is when he chooses the latter that he exposes himself to pressures which could lead him to compromise his integrity.

It is at such times in our professional life as psychoanalysts that we need to seek the security of a group or a water-tight theory to compensate for our inner insecurity. This is when we are vulnerable to the innuendos or demands for loyalty from past teachers, colleagues, supervisors, or even our former training analysts. When this happens, we may find that by giving way to these pressures, we have taken up a position in relation to some important issue concerning an individual or a policy decision which on independent reflection we felt was wrong or unfair, and we realize that thereby we have compromised our integrity. In such a case we may even have been aware of the undercurrents, and felt that it was not worth risking the disapproval of colleagues by taking a different point of view.

But this can also happen at a more unconscious level, especially to those psychoanalysts who have avoided facing their own identity crises by abrogating their rights and handing over to the establishment their need to assess themselves or their situation, becoming overconformist and unable to tolerate the insecurity of evaluating the goals and functioning of the institution which shelters them. They oppose any change in its procedures or theoretical assumptions, fearing that any change might undermine their ontological security. The institution thus becomes an extension of themselves, and their ego structures become parasitical on it, their sense of right and wrong or their superego functions being handed over to the institution, so that they are absolved from responsibility for the effects of their actions. They were only carrying out orders.

The reaction of other psychoanalysts to an identity crisis is, however, of a more paranoid nature. They tend to blame psychoanalysis or the authority figures in their particular society for what is happening to them and for their affective responses to it. Some of them respond to the situation by leaving psychoanalytic work altogether or by working as very isolated individuals with "chips" on their shoulders. Other psychoanalysts join together with those who react to identity crises by "blaming others." Initially they may be an unorganized group, but later they may become a political force in a society, a force that is later identified and made acceptable by certain theoretical or technical disagreements with the "establishment." These disagreements may form the core of the group's identity, and members of the group can share in this identity even when they feel they have not one of their own. This maladaptive reaction is a very tempting one because it offers a *pseudopositive identity* based on and defined by negative images of other people, rather than on a *positive reevaluation of oneself*. Instead of aiding the growth of inner security and a professional identity, such people become *dependent on the negative identity of others* in order to define themselves (Erikson, 1968).

In a healthy reaction to this situation, the analyst perceives and consciously owns his feelings concerning what is happening to himself and responds to his understanding of himself by reviewing how he perceives himself, by redefining his goals, his lifestyle, and his expectations in relation to what is possible as well as what is still potential for himself. This involves the capacity to accept and mourn what had been possible or hoped for in the past and what is now no longer appropriate or available. For the psychoanalyst this may involve reassessing where he stands in relation to certain theoretical controversies, as a result of integrating what he has learned during his apprenticeship and training with his own independent experience as a practicing clinician. This process may result in disagreement with senior analysts from whom the psychoanalyst has learned much or who may take this differing point of view as ingratitude or disloyalty, rather than being able to appreciate that he has worked through another identity crisis and is concerned to assert what seems right for him for that phase of his life. Such reevaluations are especially painful in psychoanalytic circles as clinical concepts and insights are often felt to be the "property" of those who first formulated them. Although a similar situation also prevails in other branches of science, psychoanalysis is an especially lonely and anxiety-arousing profession, and the support of one's colleagues is therefore very important. However, the psychoanalyst who feels secure in his own professional identity sometimes has to stand on his own as well as to work with colleagues with whom he disagrees or who disagree with him.

OTHER PRESSURES TO COMPROMISE INTEGRITY

Finally, I would like to consider other situations in which psychoanalysts are or could be faced with making decisions that would lead them to feel later that they had compromised their integrity as human beings in order to fit in with group or institutional pressures.

Psychoanalysts are seldom in situations where there is a clear right or wrong course of action. Every day in their work as analysts they have to make choices; sometimes whichever choice they make, they are wrong in relation to the option that they rejected, and they are then left with the feeling of having let themselves or their patients down in some way. These issues become more important for those who become training analysts, for they take on a dual responsibility that some find hard to encompass within themselves. Most psychoanalysts would like to think of themselves as fair and unbiased in their judgments and assessments of people or situations. In fact, even if they had been drawn into agreeing with decisions that involved their compromising their integrity, most of them would be able to give a competent rationale (at least to themselves) for the point of view that they had supported, that would satisfy them at least until it was challenged from another vantage point outside their accepted frame of reference.

But what happens in so many committees, especially those connected with the education and training of psychoanalysts, is that a group or committee develops what I would call its own "ethos," which exerts a subtle pressure on all members of the group. This ethos may cover acceptable standards of behavior, expectations of conformity in relation to certain goals, and even shared "objects of disapproval."

What I have described will happen to some extent in all groups that have an ongoing task to perform for an institution, but it seems to be more apparent in those committees responsible for making decisions that involve judging and assessing, accepting or rejecting individuals about whom other colleagues in a psychoanalytic society have strong feelings. It may have developed as a protection from the group and other pressures previously described, but in its own way it can become impenetrable to external questioning. It has even been argued, when a decision of a committee was questioned as unfair, that because the committee's decision was unanimous, it must be fair and correct and therefore it cannot be challenged.

A committee ethos grows out of mutual trust between colleagues. Issues do not need to be spelled out each time, so that when a member gives his opinion or makes a clinical evaluation, it is taken as valid. From the point of view of a member of the committee, this state of affairs would indicate a good and effective committee, but as judged by outsiders it could also be seen and experienced as an oligarchy, often appearing to be self-perpetuating, replacing its members by those judged to share or to be prepared to adopt its own ethos.

However, in most psychoanalytic societies, the ethos of a group or committee is usually contained and operates within generally accepted policies concerning agreed methods of conducting the affairs of that society. If there are adequate facilities for members to comment on the behavior of those running their affairs, the processes I have been describing need not become pathological or malignant.

It is not an easy task to be a practicing psychoanalyst whose clinical task is to maintain, as far as possible, free-floating attention in response to whatever our patients tell us, without judging it or taking sides, keeping an open mind, and being aware of their problems at many levels and from many points of view, and yet in our relations with each other to have to take part in committees and to make decisions that affect our colleagues and the future of psychoanalysis. To feel that one has done so without compromising one's integrity and without losing touch with one's vulnerability would indeed be a worthwhile achievement. I think that Leo Rangell has inspired us to try to achieve this goal.

REFERENCES

Donne, J. (1931), Satire III in *Poems*, ed. H. L'Anson Fausset. London: Everyman's Library, pp. 114–116.

Erikson, E. H. (1968), *Identity: Youth and Crisis*. New York: Norton.

Keats, J. (1952), *Letters*, ed. M. B. Foreman. London: Oxford University Press.

King, P. H. M. (1968), Alienation and the individual. *Brit. J. Soc. Clin. Psychol.*, 7:81–92.

——— (1983), Identity crises: Splits or compromise: Adaptive or maladaptive. In: *The Identity of a Psychoanalyst*, ed. E. D. Joseph & D. Widlöcher. New York: International Universities Press, pp. 181–194.

Rangell, L. (1974), A psychoanalytic perspective leading currently to the syndrome of the compromise of integrity. *Internat. J. Psycho-Anal.*, 55:3–12.

——— (1980), *The Mind of Watergate: An Exploration of the Compromise of Integrity*. New York: Norton.

Wheelis, A. (1959), *The Quest for Identity*. London: Victor Gollancz.

Winnicott, D. W. (1965), *The Maturational Processes and the Facilitating Environment*. London: Hogarth Press.

19

INTEGRITY AND ETHICS IN "BECOMING A PSYCHOANALYST"

LEÓN GRINBERG, M.D.

I

The identity of the psychoanalyst is the result of a succession of introjective identifications emanating from the image of the analyst himself, his supervisors, seminar professors, and especially from Freud himself. These "analytic" introjective identifications are indispensable for shaping the "psychoanalytic ego" of the analyst and reinforcing "the psychoanalytic function of the personality."

Nevertheless, as Goethe said, "You must acquire what you have inherited from your parents with the purpose of possessing it." Thus, "the psychoanalytic function of the personality" can be operative only when it has been nurtured by mature identifications and assimilated by a positive disposition and a genuine vocation, in addition to the capacity for understanding psychic reality.

Together, these identifications make up the structural basis for "becoming a psychoanalyst" (Bion, 1974). It has been said that in order to achieve this "becoming" it is indispensable to have undergone the experience of "rediscovering" the Oedipus complex, the existence of the unconscious, the latent meaning of the complex web of a dream, the unmistakable value of a parapraxis, and the astonishing impact of a particular transferential link. In my opinion, however, the term *rediscover* is not appropriate here. I believe that, for the profound living experience of the individual, the process of "becoming a psychoanalyst" can only be experienced as a constant and continual discovery of everything I have mentioned above. It is in this process of identification with Freud that we feel we must *discover* the totality of analysis for ourselves. Naturally, I am referring to partial and "selective" identifications with Freud's image, as Rangell (1985) has pointed out, not to his entire image.

But even these partial and selective identifications of the analyst with Freud's image sometimes transcend the limits of the psychoanalytic session and influence the way in which his psyche is expressed, the modality of his object relations, his way of reacting and functioning in the face of problems that arise, and his conflictive or nonconflictive relations with colleagues, especially in situations involving ethics, morals, and truth.

In order to achieve our goal of "becoming a psychoanalyst" we must attain a genuine *conviction* in our basic theories and in psychoanalytic procedure. Our identification with Freud undoubtedly plays a fundamental role in the achievement of that psychoanalytic conviction. In some cases, however, it is rather a matter of pseudoidentification, or very precarious identifications, which are unable to withstand the test of the daily stimuli of the analytic task, as Rodríguez Pérez (1985) has pointed out. He adds that this may occur when what was acquired in personal analysis or in the various identifications "has not been assimilated, metabolized and become a part of one's own flesh." For Rodríguez, "our work consists in bringing meaning to something that should but does not exist, where it has been destroyed or where a false meaning has been imposed in order to block the emergence of the true meaning."

Once again we are faced with the problem of truth and the "psychoanalytic attitude." This attitude refers to a very important aspect of the psychoanalyst's identity. The following characteristics stand out among the specific traits that shape this identity (Grinberg, 1983): a particular type of curiosity about given aspects of the human being, about the way his mind functions and his psychic reality, a curiosity that extends itself to the analyst's own psychic functioning; a capacity for intuition, introspection, and self-analysis; a creative capacity, the ability to search for truth, to think under adverse conditions, in the middle of the storm, so to speak; a capacity for discretion, reserve, and ethical behavior in the relationship with patients, avoiding acting out and the enticements arising from transference and countertransference; a tolerance of a certain type of frustration such as those give rise to by the lack of immediate results and the occasional inability to understand or cure, and so on; a capacity for waiting and maintaining "floating" attention; and, to use an expression of Keats (1931), a "negative capability"; in other words, he must have the ability to cope with uncertainties, mysteries, doubts, and half-truths without feeling compelled to the irritating search for reasons and certainty regarding facts.

In enumerating these characteristics of the analyst's identity, I find several conditions—integrity, ethics, and the search for truth—which, given their importance, deserve to be developed in more depth and breadth. I could argue that it is difficult, if not impossible, to conceive of the professional identity of a psychoanalyst without the existence of these qualities in his personality. In Rangell's words (1974), the analytic attitude is essentially a model of "inexorable incorruptibility."

Freud's image would correspond to an ego ideal with those characteristics. Racker (1966) pointed out that psychoanalysis is, in the first place, a science, and as such it shares the ethics of science in general, its highest value or, in other words, the "good that rules it," which resides "in the knowledge of truth, or more precisely, in the search for and discovery of truth, its affirmation and defense" (p. 7). Freud (1937) held that "we should not forget that *the analytic relation is based on a love of truth*; in other words, on a recognition of reality, and that it excludes any kind of slander or deception" (p. 248; my italics).

For Bion (1970), a healthy mental development depends on truth in the same way that a living organism depends on nourishment. Without truth the mind cannot develop and will die of starvation.

II

In his well-known studies and in his excellent book on Watergate, Rangell (1974, 1976, 1980) especially emphasized the importance of the concept of integrity and what he called "the compromise of integrity." He arrived at the conviction that what had happened overtly on the highest level of government was a reflection of what was latent and widespread in the entire country. He pointed out that this problem was intimately connected to neuroses, and that "integrity" is gradually becoming the central problem of human character. He also referred to the value of being able to live in accordance with one's own principles, without having to give in to the impositions of falsehood and hypocrisy of other influential individuals surrounding him.

Rangell described a sick society on the basis of his observations during the course of the Watergate scandal that had centered on the influence of its leader Nixon and his group and the influence, in turn, of that group on the minds of many individuals. He then defined this illness as a "compromise of integrity," emphasizing its underlying pathological conditions. It was not merely a question of facing up to the lies and corruption of Nixon and his collaborators; it was also the day-by-day erosion of integrity.

Rangell's theory points out that this problem is due to an identification with the leader based on a universal desire to triumph over the superego. According to this theory, the struggle between the ego and the id leads to neurosis, while the conflict between the ego and the superego leads to "the syndrome of the compromise of integrity." For Rangell (1974), "The compromises of integrity indicate an absence of normal behavior and a lack of control over the id" (p. 7). He clarifies this by saying that many syndromes which are diagnosed as neurotic are frequently a mixture of neurosis and "the compromise of integrity." The stimulus that leads to this compromise is often uncontrollable and insatiable narcissism.

On the other hand, Rangell points out that these mechanisms also appear in a psychoanalytic community with conflicts of interests "resolved in favor of narcissism and in detriment to principles" (p. 10). He mentions, among other points, the crime of silence, the sin of omission, "deteriorated morals," rancor and corruptibility. He adds that those psychoanalysts who occupy positions of responsibility in institutions often find themselves cornered between their own independent judgment and group pressures and attachments to charismatic or dominating personalities, with all the benefits that they reap for them. Every analyst cannot help but feel the wide-reaching consequences of pressures, whether they be of a sexual, material, or narcissistic nature.

Rangell (1976) says that an analyst should be aware that "the analytic method aims at attaining psychic integrity" (p. 58), which is the inner aim of analysis, just as the prerequisite for interpersonal integrity is the outer objective. I believe that Rangell's extension of the Watergate syndrome to analysts and to the relations between them is correct and valid. Moreover, since it coincides with the specific theme of this chapter, I shall develop these aspects more fully in section four.

III

I should now like to include some references related to the concepts of "integrity" and "ethics."

According to Marjorie Brierley (1949), "The higher the degree of personal integrity attained, the stronger and richer the reality-ego will be, and the more capable of life-fulfilling adaptation even in the face of adverse circumstances" (p. 188).

M. Klein (1942) regards the infant's anxiety and love-promoted reaction against his own aggression as the root of morality and considers that "our first longings to preserve and save our parents and to reconcile ourselves with them persist in the depths of our mind," and that "whenever we have a feeling of moral goodness, this primary longing for reconciliation with the original objects of our love and hatred is fulfilled in our unconscious mind" (p. 323). I believe that, in this context, the word *morality* is used in the sense of *integrity*.

Psychoanalysis has shown that personal morality is the result of superego development through which certain cultural standards are individualized and operate as mental controls of instinct. The basic organization of the superego is completed at the end of the oedipal phase. Thus, the individual's ethics are based on values acquired in infancy, and his moral attitudes, however much they may be elaborated and modified in later life, will be rooted in attitudes developed in infancy.

Erikson (1964) says that *identity* and *fidelity* are necessary for ethical strength, but that they alone do not provide it. His baseline is the golden rule, which advocates that one should do (or not do) to others as he would have others do (or not do) to him. He distinguishes variations in moral and ethical sensitivity in accordance with stages in the development of man's conscience. He also adds an ethical dimension to psychoanalytic theory, and his conceptualizations of the distinctions between "morality," "ideology," and "ethics" are really excellent. According to Erikson, the dictionary defines morals and ethics as synonyms and antonyms of each other. Nevertheless, he proposes to consider moral rules of conduct as based on the fear of threats to be forestalled. They may be threats of abandonment, punishment, or a menacing inner sense of guilt. In other words, it is the threat that counts. On the other hand, he believes that ethical rules are based on ideals to be striven for with a high degree of rational assent and with a ready consent to a formulated good, a definition of perfection, and some promise of self-realization.

Money-Kyrle (1952) has dealt with the transference of ethical problems from a philosophical plane to a scientific level. Thus, we may reopen the old question in a new form and ask ourselves how our morals are affected as we become conscious of ourselves. Psychoanalysis is the technique that enables us to widen the boundaries of our consciousness. Its effect on our emotions and desires is solely the result of the *knowledge* it conveys, not of some other influence. The important thing is to help the patient discover the truth about himself. Bion (1962) points out that any attempt to know something necessarily involves a painful feeling inherent in the very emotional experience of that knowledge. K link (knowledge) is one of the three links that Bion considers essential in object relationships; the other two links are L (love) and H (hate).

As the patient gradually learns the truth about himself, changes appear in his ethical attitude. The discovery of the superego was one of the major achievements of analysis. In Freud's view, the superego is the necessary guardian of morality. Nevertheless, the superego he described is predominantly a morality of fear. In 1930, Freud stated that the cultural superego established certain ideal demands which, if unfulfilled, will be punished by a "conscience anxiety." There must, however, be another aspect of morality based on love, not fear, and what we have now learned about them we owe to M. Klein's (1952) discovery of early persecutory and depressive states.

Taking as a basis my classification of the two qualities of guilt (Grinberg, 1964), we could say that "persecutory guilt" is more closely related to morality, whereas "depressive guilt" is related to ethics. Persecutory guilt appears at an early state in life and corresponds to the functioning of a weak ego and a severe superego. This kind of guilt is characterized by intense anxiety, fear of retaliation, and destructive and self-destructive behavior that Freud (1923) had in mind when he linked the guilt feeling to the death instinct and when he stated that the superego was a pure culture of the death instinct. On the other hand, depressive guilt emerges later on in a more mature and better integrated ego, giving way to sorrow, responsibility, and a genuine desire of object reparation.

In my opinion, the feeling of persecutory guilt is one of the most important elements underlying those personalities with a tendency to develop the "Watergate syndrome." Thus, in manic or hypomanic personalities, the way of attempting to counteract persecutory guilt reveals itself through a complete denial of that guilt, which is in turn accompanied by strong feelings of omnipotence. These persons usually feel triumphant, very self-assured, and exaggeratedly optimistic, and tend to establish multiple relationships, albeit of a precarious and superficial nature. They constantly deny their guilt and project it onto others. They cannot admit their responsibility and try to manipulate their omnipotence in the attempt to use it to control everything and everyone. In reality, their superego is as stern and cruel as the melancholic superego. What happens is that they utilize their denial in such an extreme way as to try to diminish the danger of their persecutors. Furthermore, they sometimes exhibit psychopathic attitudes and function with a versatile behavior characterized by a search for an urgent and immediate satisfaction of their desires without being able to stand any postponement of their wishes. They are notably lacking in responsibility and a sense of ethics, and they are flagrantly inconsiderate of the norms of people around them.

One of the problems that has perplexed historians of ethics is how to pinpoint the exact moment in antiquity when Western thought arrived at the concept of human responsibility. Pasquali (1949, quoted in Mondolfo, 1962) pointed out, as the first discovery, a passage in Book 1 of the *Odyssey*, in which Zeus, as a result of Aegisthus' crime, angrily rails out against those men who refuse to assume responsibility for their own actions. The passage is as follows: "See now, how men lay blame upon us gods for what is after all nothing but their own folly. Look at Aegisthus; he must needs make love to Agamemnon's wife unrighteously and then kill Agamemnon, though he knew it would be the death of him; for I sent Hermes to warn him not to do either of these things, inasmuch as Orestes would be sure to take his revenge when he grew up and wanted to return home. Hermes told him this in all good will, but he would not listen, and now he has paid for everything in full" (Homer, 1948, p. 4).

We can deduce from this example that it is man's own free will that is responsible, or man himself who is responsible, for his acts. He is the maker of his own destiny. The transformation of moral judgments from the exterior to the interior is gradually being prepared through a modification of the concept of divine punishment.

As Racker (1966) pointed out, virtually a whole new era in human ethics began with psychoanalysis. He refers to the recognition of the instinctual impulses, on a conscious level, after a long period characterized by their denial. This recognition and awareness of man's instinctual impulses mark unmistakable progress, in an ethical sense, toward abandoning a hypocritical and negative attitude supported by rationalizations of a pseudoscientific, religious, and social origin.

At the moment when psychoanalysis provided an approach to truth based on a knowledge of psychic reality, the way was open for the investigation of those deep-seated motivations underlying unconscious fantasies and human conduct. Thus, the analyst could study man's morality without having to adopt a moralistic attitude. His primary objective was always to help his patient overcome his resistance to bringing the unconscious to the level of consciousness, even though this revelation might elicit anxiety and pain.

IV

In this section I shall discuss factors dependent on the specific nature of the analytic task which, in my opinion, elicits many tense and conflictive situations between analysts (Grinberg, 1963), or which may give rise to the reactivation of unconscious narcissistic feelings and fantasies that make up the "compromise of integrity" syndrome described by Rangell. In this sense, I should first like to mention some of Moses's ideas (1985) that lend support to the universality of the "Watergate syndrome." He says that there are two ways to bribe the superego and subvert the ego's ideal. One is inherent in the "Watergate syndrome"; here ideals, ideology, and ethical values are inverted, and unjustifiable means are used to obtain alleged lofty ends, albeit with the real and elusive goal of serving the personal interests of the leader and the tiny group surrounding him. The other modality often appears in individuals who have developed a strict and sometimes punitive conscience. They can go so far as to create extremist movements that do not hesitate to violate moral and ethical values by resorting to violent aggressive demonstrations which they feel are justified by the fanatical use of their ideologies.

I agree with Moses's hypothesis on the universality of the "Watergate syndrome" and the various ways to bribe the superego and subvert the ego ideal. As I mentioned above, I believe that something similar can also occur in the field of psychoanalysis in which some analysts can arrive at extreme attitudes by violating moral and ethical values in order narcissistically to satisfy their own desires and goals. Ultimately, this is one of the major factors in the "Watergate syndrome." It would be useful, however, to know the motivations related to psychoanalytic practice itself which may, in some cases, contribute to the reason why this syndrome could overstep the boundaries between reality and fantasy and turn into true acting out.

In the course of his tasks, the analyst may be exposed to the pressures and influence of the most unhealthy and corrupt part of some of his patients. In such cases, he would need the ability to maintain his integrity without falling into a corrupt alliance with those aspects of his patient that are due to the effects of a projective counteridentification reaction (Grinberg, 1956, 1979). On the other hand, we cannot disregard the notion that, because of their own unresolved conflicts and as a result of diverse circumstances, some therapists can exacerbate their ambition, desire for power, and opportunism in what Rangell (1980) termed those "three horses" of the "compromise of integrity" syndrome. I believe that, in doing so, they seek to satisfy their deepest narcissistic and omnipotent needs.

We know that the primary function of the analyst is to fulfill a role whose basic characteristics he cannot stray from and to which he must adhere as strictly as possible. In other words, he must confine himself exclusively to interpreting the material contributed by the analysand. He cannot enter into a dialogue with him to discuss events, ideas, or feelings concerning his private or professional life that are alien to the patient's sphere of interest. Nor can he transmit his countertransference reactions. Inevitably, his communication will necessarily be partial.

As a consequence of this isolation, his persecutory anxieties are reinforced and his reactions of rivalry, envy, and competition become more acute. In order to neutralize and compensate for his exclusion fantasies, he uses narcissistic defenses with an omnipotent content which arise as power fantasies and manic triumphs and which sometimes produce acting-out behavior. Isolation and a lack of communication occasionally will determine a particular greed for the supply of stimuli coming from external sources. This can explain why this type of analyst tries to take advantage of supervisions with candidates, since these sessions are used as true escape valves to give him his desired social contact. Nevertheless, this is not the most important problem. Sometimes, because of the reactivation of pathological characteristics within their personality, some analysts tend to see their supervisees as representatives of rival analysts or groups and fall into the acting out of dealing with them aggressively or trying to coax information from them in order to confirm their own paranoid fantasies. At other times, they use reaction formations and try to be idealized by the candidate through a seductive and psychopathic attitude.

This may even occur in analytic sessions in which the analyst actively interrogates his own candidates or elicits detailed information about external events. He does so because he is motivated by his own anxiety or for narcissistic reasons, not because he wants to have a greater amount of associative material at his disposal in order to understand the unconscious fantasies of the analysand. In accordance with the content of his anxiety, he will be interested in knowing what is happening "outside" with respect to him, if he is appreciated or criticized, and so on. Sometimes he will resort to denial or omnipotence fantasies. He sees himself as a powerful leader who has no need to move around or connect with the outside world or to know and inquire about the issues. He can feel as if he were a god or king, since, without moving from his throne (chair), he can be everywhere through his analysands who, as if they were some kind of pseudopods or antennas, can communicate the news from "outside," informing him of everything that goes on.

Occasionally, in order to fight off his anxieties and sense of loneliness, the analyst feels compelled to become a part of a group with whom he shares a mutual ideology or political position within the heart of the institution. What he is really looking for, however, is support and protection. At other times, he himself will form his own group, made up of his own analysands whom he will convert into acolytes and faithful followers of his theories, thus making a mockery of one of the basic principles of the psychoanalytic relationship: distance and neutrality.

These examples, together with many others, make up a sampling of how analysts may tend to bribe their professional superego, utilize all kinds of rationalizations to exploit the transference, and take advantage of their patients in a corrupt way. Unfortunately, there are cases of analysts—belonging to the societies of various countries—who have gone to extremes in regard to corruption and exploitation of the transference. Some of them, acting with a total lack of integrity and ethics, have not hesitated to take advantage of the affective dependence of an idealized transference in order to attain, for example, economic benefits in business transactions involving their own patients or, in other cases, through seduction and sexual misconduct in relation to their patients, causing enormous—and occasionally irreparable—harm to their psychic health. We might ask ourselves what is the extent of the analysand's participation, conscious or unconscious, in order to be able to tolerate or induce this "corrupt alliance" type of conduct and, in doing so, generate a situation similar to the "Watergate syndrome."

Those analysts who function primarily with this syndrome can reveal themselves through extreme and opposing attitudes: they tend to appear as fervent partisans of a more flexible and "humanistic" technique or, on the contrary, as "analytic apostles" and fanatical defenders of a rigid orthodoxy in regard to technique and theoretical concepts. In both cases, of course, they use disguises to conceal their narcissistic and omnipotent tendencies in order to gain power over others.

I have previously referred to selective identifications with Freud. I did so to emphasize in particular the identification with those positive aspects that can contribute to the formation of an analytic identity in full control over the issues of integrity and ethics. But there are also what we might call "pathological identifications" with Freud. These traits usually appear in analysts who were founders or pioneers of a psychoanalytic movement in specific areas. They behave like omnipotent leaders who attempt to exercise absolute power over a group of analysts whom they treat as subordinates in a relationship of total dependency, in an association that they consider as a fief under their exclusive domain. The same thing can happen to analysts who were not pioneers but who, nevertheless, harbor excessive ambitions to command.

Rangell (1980) also referred to the dangers inherent in the position of leadership which, in some way, is held by the analyst, and in which the transference, positive and negative, can attain grotesque proportions. Orgel (1987), in turn, points out the possible abuses inherent in the exercise of "real" power emanating from the transference and countertransference desires of the analyst. He refers to the reaction formations as opposed to the aggressive impulses that intervene in the intention to heal others. He describes the intense conflicts with analysands who wish to become analysts themselves: "Their success is tantamount to putting our immortality and our death in their hands. . . . They would replace us, and one day, perhaps, they will bury us, literally" (p. 13). In this unusual way Orgel warns us against our oedipal fantasies. These fantasies, together with the hidden forms of sadistic countertransference, can seriously come to hinder those analyses.

There are analysts who, under the influence of certain unconscious motivations, try to hold the analysand back by prolonging analysis indefinitely. They act as fathers or mothers who cannot accept the fact that some day they must let go of their children. For analogous motives they will try to sustain their candidate's idealization of them or will need to have their candidates firmly anchored to their own ideology or theories as a form of reassurance. Unfortunately, they are far from exercising proper discrimination and do not understand that, in these cases, instead of educating adult individuals with mature judgment, they are merely forming followers to satisfy their own narcissistic needs or placate their deep-seated feelings of insecurity and precarious identity.

In order not to fall into these attitudes of the "Watergate syndrome," the analyst would be advised to acquire an awareness of his countertransference fantasies or those unresolved conflicts in his own personality that may lead to the acting out of those fantasies.

If ethics means knowledge and implies the acquisition of truth, it leads to the need to confront and accept all those truths that, because they were painful, were denied and eliminated from the sphere of conscience. Naturally, there are no ideal solutions. I am convinced, however, that the decision to reenter analysis would be extremely helpful in approaching these truths. Without trying to be overly optimistic, perhaps this reanalysis might show, for example, that those fantasies were not so omnipotently sadistic after all. This would possibly lead to an appreciable change in the nature of guilt feelings, which, in turn, would become less persecutory and more depressive, thus allowing the analyst to assume full responsibility for his own acts and the function they perform, with a more genuine reparatory attitude.

Lastly, I believe that integrity and ethical sense would allow every analyst to accomplish his aim of admitting, with humility, his limitations in the complex task of understanding and helping another human being to know his own truth. At the same time, these qualities would contribute to affirming his professional identity by broadening his communication with himself and others and advancing in the process of "becoming a psychoanalyst."

REFERENCES

Bion, W. R. (1962), *Learning from Experience*. London: Heinemann.

——— (1970), *Attention and Interpretation*. London: Tavistock.

——— (1974), *Bion's Brazilian Lectures*. Rio de Janeiro: Imago Editora.

Brierley, M. (1949), *Trends in Psychoanalysis*. London: Hogarth Press.

Erikson, E. H. (1964), *Insight and Responsibility*. New York: Norton.

Freud, S. (1923), The ego and the id. *Standard Edition*, 19:3–66. London: Hogarth Press, 1961.

——— (1930), Civilization and its discontents. *Standard Edition*, 21:59–145. London: Hogarth Press, 1961.

——— (1937), Analysis terminable and interminable. *Standard Edition*, 23:209–253. London: Hogarth Press, 1964.

Grinberg, L. (1956), Sobre algunos problemas de técnica psicoanalítica determinados por la identificación y contraidentificación proyectivas. *Rev. Psicoanál.*, 13:507–511.

——— (1962), On a specific aspect of countertransference due to the patient's projective identification. *Internat. J. Psycho-Anal.*, 43:436–440.

——— (1963), *Culpa y depresión*. Buenos Aires: Paidós; Madrid: Alianza, 1983.

——— (1964), On two kinds of guilt: Their relation with normal and pathological aspects of mourning. *Internat. J. Psycho-Anal.*, 45:366–371.

——— (1979), Countertransference and projective counteridentification. *Contemp. Psychoanal.*, 15:226–247.

——— (1983), The identity of the psychoanalyst: A discussion of Joseph's and Widlöcher's papers. In: *The Identity of the Psychoanalyst*, ed. E. D. Joseph & D. Widlöcher. New York: International Universities Press.

Homer (1948), *La Odyssey*. Buenos Aires: Janes.

Keats, J. (1931), *Letters*, 4th ed., ed. M. B. Forman. London: Oxford University Press.

Klein, M. (1942), Some psychological considerations: A comment. In: *The Writings of Melanie Klein*, 3. London: Hogarth Press.

——— (1952), Some theoretical conclusions regarding the emotional life of the infant. In: *The Writings of Melanie Klein*, Vol. 3. London: Hogarth Press, pp. 198–236.

Mondolfo, R. (1962), *La Concienca Moral de Homero a Demócrito y Epicuro*. Buenos Aires: Editorial Universitaria.

Money-Kyrle, R. (1952), Psychoanalysis and ethics. *Internat. J. Psycho-Anal.*, 33:225–234.

Moses, R. (1985), Watergate as a universal phenomenon. Unpublished.

Orgel, S. (1987), Dilemmas of a training analyst. Pre-circulated paper for the Third I.P.A. Conference on Training Analysts, Montreal.

Racker, H. (1966), Ethics and psychoanalysis and the psychoanalysis of ethics. *Internat. J. Psycho-Anal.*, 47:62–80.

Rangell, L. (1974), Presidential address: A psychoanalytic perspective leading currently to the syndrome of the compromise of integrity. *Internat. J. Psycho-Anal.*, 55:3–12.

——— (1976), Lessons from Watergate: A derivative for psychoanalysis. *Psychoanal. Quart.*, 45:37–61.

——— (1980), *The Mind of Watergate: An Exploration of the Compromise of Integrity*. New York: Norton.

——— (1985), Our identification with Freud. Read at the 34th International Psychoanalytic Congress, Hamburg.

Rodríguez Pérez, J. F. (1985), Bases para una convicción psicoanalítica. Read at the Madrid Psychoanalytical Association.

20

ON INTERPRETATION AND ITS TESTING

R. HORACIO ETCHEGOYEN, M.D.

THE SCIENTIFIC SITUATION OF PSYCHOANALYSIS

During his entire scientific career, Freud believed that psychoanalysis had the status of a natural science and that its basic hypothesis, the existence of the unconscious, made a scientific explanation of the psychological (and psychopathological) phenomena possible. This statement has been disputed inside and outside our discipline and we all know that many distinguished psychoanalysts believe that psychoanalysis is another type of knowledge entirely, valuable, certainly, but which does not belong to science, or at least not to the natural sciences. Some even go to such lengths as to affirm that the young Freud who worked for Brücke, "who carried more weight with me than any one else in my whole life" (Freud, 1926, p. 253), found himself unable to shed a certain residual scientism, which constantly reappears in his works and at times even leads him astray.

This chapter is decidedly in favor of the way Freud places psychoanalysis within the philosophy of the sciences. I will deal especially with psychoanalytic interpretation, hoping to show that, when this is rigorously applied, following the demands imposed by our technique, it responds fully to the exigencies of the sci-

This chapter was originally presented at a conference held on September 17, 1987, by the Asociación Argentina de Epistemología del Psicoanálisis (ADEP).

entific method. This is, indeed, a difficult undertaking, but it is possible that this chapter may make some small contribution to a subject of the foremost importance, and one over which philosophers of the sciences and logicians are no less concerned than the psychoanalysts themselves.

The serious, patient study of the epistemology of psychoanalysis is only in its beginnings, and everything seems to point to its being slow and strenuous. Real progress in this field must contemplate, to my mind, an interdisciplinary task between epistemologists and psychoanalysts, since the former find it difficult to obtain a real picture of the analytic work in a consulting room; we analysts very rarely reach the philosophical learning to permit us to function entirely autonomously in this field. It becomes necessary, therefore, to work together, in the manner essayed by the Asociación Argentina de Epistemología del Psicoanálisis (ADEP), founded by Gregorio Klimovsky in 1979, where epistemologists, psychoanalysts, and clinical psychologists come together to consider and to discuss—heatedly, at times—this interesting subject.

THE ANALYTIC SITUATION AND THE ANALYTIC PROCESS

Various circumstances contribute to hinder progress in this area and to hamper the organization of the work. One of these is that, in general, psychoanalysis is studied as a whole; thus we run the risk of taking on too many problems and biting off more than we can chew. There is, perhaps, only one psychoanalysis, but undoubtedly there are various *schools* and many psychoanalytic *theories*. It follows, then, that epistemological studies should specify which part of psychoanalysis they are referring to, separating the essential from the merely accessory, as Lakatos (1975) proposes when he states that every theory has a strong nucleus that contains the basic hypotheses, and a safety belt, outside the nucleus, where the hypotheses are able to enjoy a much greater mobility.

Another circumstance that conspires against this work is that, perhaps due to the aforementioned tendency to generalize, the several fields in which the psychoanalytic theories may and should be studied are seldom discriminated. There are two that are decisive and that are hardly ever separated, the analytic situation and the analytic process. For the purposes of this chapter I shall call *situation* a cross-section of the treatment, a synchronic moment that does not carry beyond the session, the hour, and in which the dialogue between analyst and analysand is inserted; *process*, on the contrary, is diachronic and longitudinal; it has consistency and duration. It is not easy for us practicing analysts to understand that they may not be accounted for by the same principles. The analytic process entails slow changes and to it we may legitimately apply the ideas of those who, like Jones (1929), Reich (1933), and Racker (1957), believe in the stratification of the phenomena operating in the unconscious. These stratigraphic configurations that are defined by their consistency and duration do not appear during the session, or, rather, they do appear but move very rapidly and are apt to change from one minute to the next. If we wish to operate during the session with the assumptions of the process, we shall always find ourselves way behind the developments.

As I wish to transmit not only what I have read but also what I have learned from my clinical experience, I should like to say it took me years to realize that when I attempted to apply to a session what was crystal-clear to me from the process, I proceeded in an awkward and highly prejudiced manner. To express it in more concrete and personal terms, I found it hard to unite the precept of interpreting the first transferential resistance in a systematic, orderly, and consequential way (Reich, 1927), with the turmoil of rapidly and impartially interpreting the material at the point of urgency, in the way proposed by Klein (1926, 1932). It is only in the course of the last few years that I have been able to come to synthesize both attitudes, separating what occurs in the session from what transpires in the process.

TWO FORMS OF STUDYING THE ANALYTIC SITUATION

Once the difference between situation and process has been established, and in order to lend precision to the epistemic studies, we must establish one more difference within the very situation itself. When we take the psychoanalytic situation as the field of our observations, we tend to superimpose two methodological attitudes that must be discriminated with care: the session may be studied while it is going on or after its completion. Most authors who consider the session as the most privileged field of their investigation maintain that it is only pertinent to study it *after* it has happened and never while it is going on, a sort of meditation on the praxis which is incompatible with the practice itself. Those who adhere to this line of thought believe that in order to reflect on the session *during* the session itself, we must necessarily operate with a predetermined scheme and thus make it lose its freshness. Moreover, in setting aside our candor, our indispensable ignorance, we are violating a fundamental postulate of our technique, the evenly suspended attention (Freud, 1912b). This is what authors such as Bion (1963), Meltzer (1967), and Liberman (1970–1972) have stated in one way or another. When Bion introduces his celebrated grid in *Elements of Psychoanalysis*, he unceasingly warns us that this instrument can only be applied after the session is over. This methodology is naturally legitimate, unquestionably so; but I mean to study the session in the present tense because we set out from the assumption that it is possible to do so without impairing the basic psychoanalytic attitude, which must include, and which does indeed include, the search of truth, and moreover because we maintain as its fundamental thesis that the analysand's response to the interpretation contains the objective data necessary to decide upon its validity. On the contrary, when an analyst studies the session *a posteriori*, alone or in the company of other colleagues, he can only refer to a dialogue that is already past: his conjectures cannot be contrasted with what the patient says. In this I am following Wisdom's (1967) steps, though from a different perspective and with a different concept of what is contributed by the analysand.

INTERPRETATION AND CONSTRUCTION

From all that has been said, it should be clear that the extensive problem of psychoanalytic epistemology has been greatly limited, and that all my reflections concern interpretation and its testing. It behooves us here to add another demarcation which is that when I speak of interpretation, I am setting aside all other instruments of psychotherapy, in particular, constructions. In one of his last papers, Freud (1937) studied and prized this element, to the point of considering it his foremost psychotherapeutic instrument. In fact, constructions pose a completely different series of epistemological problems and thus require to be studied apart. To my mind, from an epistemological point of view, the value of constructions consists in that they can sometimes afford us a convincing objective confirmation that reaches us from outside, from another field, and herein resides their glory and their poverty. All of us analysts have recorded certain examples of constructions that fill us with pride. I will always remember the patient who at the start of his analysis so intensely expressed shame at being analyzed by me after having been under treatment for several years with a woman analyst. Backed by extremely eloquent material, I said to him on one occasion that, as a child, he had probably not felt himself the son of his own father. He then vividly remembered something he had always known and had always forgotten: his father had abandoned his family; and his mother, who was living with another man at that time, had enrolled him in kindergarden with her surname. The parents later reconciled, his father came back home, and his surname at school was changed back to his legitimate one. Although he did not give the correctness of my construction much importance, the fact is that from that moment on he did not again feel anxiety or shame at being analyzed by me, at least not above what any analysand might feel. Neither did he, from this time on, again feel that his real analyst was his previous one, and thus his analysis became noticeably more stable.

Constructions, however, are not exempt from logical and epistemological complications, and chief among these is the difficulty of conceptually discriminating between material truth and historical truth (Freud, 1937), a subject I dealt with in detail elsewhere (Etchegoyen, 1986, chaps. 27 and 28). By way of another example, quite the opposite to the previous one, in which this type of difficulty can be appreciated clearly, I recall a construction—basically correct, to my mind—which I made to a man of about 40, who had been exiled at the age of two and had arrived here with his mother at the outbreak of World War II. His father joined them some time later and he had then felt terribly displaced from his mother's side. From this stemmed a series of character traits and above all his megalomania of wanting to direct everything. This construction, which in fact was more precise and more detailed than what I have recorded here, impressed him greatly, and to begin with he accepted it fully. A short time later, however, he began to question it and to seek proofs that would confirm or refute it, and thus his analysis moved into a truly chaotic situation that lasted for an appreciable time.

ANALYTIC WORK AND THE SCIENTIFIC METHOD

When, with a view to making them more effective and more rigorous, the defining characteristics of the psychoanalytic interpretation are studied carefully, logical and epistemological considerations inescapably make themselves felt and with them, always arise, and forcibly, ethical problems of the highest order. What occurs is that theory, practice, and ethics are perhaps more indissolubly joined in psychoanalysis than in any other science.

This chapter attempts to demonstrate not only that the psychoanalytic interpretation can in fact be tested but that, in addition, our clinical work greatly benefits when it is carried out within the framework of the scientific method. This statement is perhaps surprising because one of the basic premises of our technique is that if an analyst wishes to avoid falling into the mortal sin of intellectualization, he must never impart his reasons or his reasoning. The analyst must be like Cassandra the slave, offering her prophecies without ever explaining them. To express it in a more personal vein, at one point in the course of my development as an analyst, which was long and complex, I realized that, without intending to do so, I was working in the sessions with the model of the scientific method that I had learned from nearly 20 years of studying with Gregorio Klimovsky. It is not simply that the *way* I interpret gradually became more conjectural and less authoritarian, but that concurrently the *content* of my interpretations began to be centered increasingly on what I believed was happening inside the analysand's mind at that precise moment, without worrying whether this coincided with my theories, my presumptions, or my prejudices. In this way I came to concede the analysand a privileged position for testing what I said. It may be unnecessary to stress that this was a slow, imperceptible, and spontaneous process, but undoubtedly it is worthwhile stating that these changes in me can also be validly described from the opposite pole by saying that the analysand's opinion about what I had said—in general very precise opinions and, moreover, altogether unconscious to him—gradually made me pay them more attention.

I have taken some time over this point because these statements in principle contradict Grünbaum (1984) and I shall come back to them later, but I should like to say now that in recognizing the high standard of the analysand's critical judgment, I am not led by any simplicity or naïveté on my part. I have learned it, and I am still learning it, day in and day out, through the harsh reality of my work in the consulting room (and naturally, also through the supervision). Nor am I suggesting that an interpretation should be evasive or ambiguous. On the contrary, it must be direct and concrete, because psychic reality admits of no potential verb modes, but it must be phrased as a hypothesis and never in oracular form. At the risk of being overmeticulous I should like to say that I am referring more to the attitude with which the analyst interprets than to the form taken by the interpretation.

Freud once captivatingly said that the voice of reason is weak but finally imposes itself. The technique I have come to evolve, and which I learned not only from my analysands but above all from my teachers, consists precisely in finding out how one should lift the voice of reason in order that the analysand may finally hear it. Insistence alone is not enough, however soundly we bet on the process of working through, because sometimes the only thing we achieve by this is to increase the resistances, when not imperceptibly walking into the blind alley of impasse.

As we all know, the psychoanalytic method conditions a singular dialogue in which the analysand associates freely; that is to say, he says whatever he wishes and whatever he feels like, without omitting, of course, what he would have preferred not to have thought of, while the analyst speaks exclusively about the analysand, keeping to certain rules that make up the act of interpreting. I shall not now stop over the problem of whether the analyst only interprets or whether he does other things as well, because this is an alternative that does not in essence vary what I have just said; moreover, it has been studied extensively (Bibring, 1954; Rangell, 1954). Even within the most rigorous technique other instruments may be used, but what is distinctive to psychoanalysis is that the analyst speaks *about* the analysand and not about himself or third parties and always from the material offered by his patient. Within these limits, which are indeed narrow, when the analyst says something which the analysand ignores about himself, we say he interprets. Many analysts believe they interpret when they refer to third parties; but to my mind this is a technical and methodological error, as well as a breach of ethics. The analyst can only speak of what the analysand thinks of himself, of others, and, in particular, of the analyst (transference), but never of what *others* think, because the analyst neither knows this nor, obviously, can this be tested in the analytic setting. An interpretation can only refer to whom it is destined, to the person who has the right to a reply. It has never been good form to speak of others behind their backs. This is a further example of ethics and scientific method always going hand in hand in psychoanalysis. I remember here the arresting words of Leo Rangell (1974): "The analytic attitude is in its very essence the model—I hope not the last bastion—of relentless incorruptibility" (p. 11).

SOME DEFINING CHARACTERISTICS OF PSYCHOANALYTIC INTERPRETATION

We may say that an interpretation tells the analysand something about himself that he does not know, that is unconscious to him. In this rather long-winded way, I have come to say that the psychoanalytic method consists in making conscious what is unconscious! However, this way of defining an interpretation is useful because it highlights two essential facts: that it is a hypothesis and that only the analysand, because it is about him, can provide, nearly always unconsciously, the data necessary to back or refute it. The analyst must therefore give up interpreting in a context in which his words cannot be tested, that is, outside the analytic dialogue, outside the analytic situation. I am not saying the analyst may not *assume* what is happening to others involved; what I am saying is that this inference should never reach the interpretation, or, to judge it uncompromisingly, it will be merely a wild interpretation (Freud, 1910). I wish to add that these assumptions generally arise from the unresolved problems of the countertransference, since the analyst is concerning himself about others and not about his analysand, i.e., his work.

What I have just explained is quite clear and logical, although there are not many analysts disposed to limit the scope of their instruments to the restricted field of the analytic situation. We frequently find, for example, that an analyst "interprets" to his patient that in his infancy his mother wanted to dominate him, when all one can truthfully say is that the patient felt it to be so and still goes on feeling it, or, on the contrary, that he denies having thought so. This is the gap that exists between interpreting and voicing an opinion. A matrimonial conflict often finds an iatrogenic reinforcement in this technique that interprets the spouse instead of the analysand. It is precisely due to the doubtfulness of these assumptions made from a distance that it is always safer to reach the actual conflict or the infantile conflict from the transference (Freud, 1912a; Klein, 1927, 1952; Strachey, 1934, 1937; Heimann, 1956; Gill, 1982; Cooper, 1987)—the transference is the only conflict of the analysand's of which the analyst is an eyewitness. Incidentally, this does not imply that the analyst must "seek" the transference, as he would then cease to be neutral and would be committing a technical error: "Attention to the transference neurosis alone, without a relentless establishment of its links to the past, is a technical error of many analyses today" (Rangell, 1985, pp. 87–88). The fact is that the less one seeks the transference, the more strongly and spontaneously it occurs. The principle of the technique we are proposing here is, precisely, to maintain an open mind toward the material, avoiding theoretical prejudices as far as possible, in the way we were instructed by Freud and all the other great masters of psychoanalysis.

Another defining characteristic of an interpretation, which in a certain way follows from the previous one, is that the analyst does not speak about the events but about what the analysand believes these events are. Bion (1962) has pointed this out with great accuracy, and before him we may trace it to Strachey's (1934) memorable words when he said an analyst must omit all references to reality so that the analysand can come into contact with it. This is the equivalent of saying that the analyst concerns himself with the analysand's *unconscious fantasy*, as defined by Susan Isaacs (1948), or with his *imagination*, if we prefer to use Edelson's (1984) term. As the process advances and the analysand distorts things less, his estimation of reality changes without the analyst needing to speak about it directly. If he does so, the psychoanalytic dialogue will inevitably become an indoctrination.

The analyst must always respect what the analysand thinks: our task does not consist in contradicting or convincing him but in seeing why he thinks in a certain way. Thus our technique must not only avoid suggestion and indoctrination but must also be directed toward discovering the misunderstandings that can lead the analysand to feel we are influencing him. This issue, of a high epistemological value, is not easily understood by those who do not practice psychoanalysis. If we are careful not to be intrusive and set aside all active techniques (Ferenczi, 1919, 1921; Freud, 1919), we will find, to our surprise, how unshakable many of the analysand's ideas are, and how far they belong to an overvalued or even to a delusional category. Experience has taught me it is when these serious conflicts are mobilized, and with them the transference becomes extremely intense, that the analyst is tempted to have recourse to certain visible or disguised forms of active technique or to its most exposed and naïve shape—suggestion. A strict psychoanalytic technique, such as we conceive today and such as we in fact put into practice, completely dispenses with suggestion, that is, with all ideological components. Freud never came to conceive it thus, and he always said that suggestion operated in analysis—though indirectly—to overcome resistances by means of the positive transference. Later, when I mention Grünbaum's (1984) objections to psychoanalysis, I shall return to this subject; but let us now just say that suggestion does exist but that it is avoidable. To a great extent, the psychoanalytic method consists in uncovering and then denouncing it.

INTERPRETING VERSUS EXPRESSING AN OPINION

To understand not only what I have just said but also my main thesis, I now wish to establish a clear-cut difference between interpretation and expressing an opinion. It is obvious that opinion is a more extensive term which may include interpretation; in fact, interpretation differs from all other opinions. Accordingly, I think it will be better to define both terms.[1]

Strictly speaking, interpretation is a hypothesis about the material that the analyst proposes to the analysand. It never refers to events, as other opinions do. It may also be said that an interpretation is directed toward psychic reality (fantasy) and not toward objective or material reality. It is the analysand who will have to accomplish the inalienable task of connecting the newly acquired psychic reality with the material reality of his surroundings. To express it in more technical terms, psychoanalysis deals with object relations, not with interpersonal relations, which belong to social psychology. Lawyers hold that a judge expresses an opinion solely by his verdict. I should like to say that the analyst's only valid opinion is his interpretation of the material. Every other opinion is out of place, since it will lend itself to agreement or disagreement, but not to being tested. To put it more precisely: to express an opinion is to say what one thinks about something, to interpret is to suggest (tentatively) what *the other* thinks about something. This being so, it becomes immediately obvious that no one is in a better position than the analysand to decide upon what was interpreted. To say it in a form that pleased Liberman: *I* (the analyst) *think that* you (the analysand) *think that. . . .* An opinion is always something advanced

[1] What I am about to propose bears some relation to Aristotles' distinction between *episteme* and *doxa*.

for the other to share or to question; an interpretation, if it is in truth an interpretation, only awaits a decision about its truth or falsehood. If the analyst operates with a minimum of conflict in the countertransference, he will not be hoping that the analysand will agree with him, but rather that he will reflect upon what has been said. I am aware this is an extremely hard attitude to adopt, but it is not one that is impossible for an analyst with a certain amount of experience who feels more bound to the method and the search for truth than to the gratification contingent to a moment of praxis. In this way, the analyst's attitude coincides with the scientific method and with the ethics that the practice of his profession requires.

However assertive the form of the interpretation—and there are moments when it may be justified for it to be so—insofar as it refers to something that occurs inside the analysand, it can hardly be more than a hypothesis, a proposal about what is happening to him. Should this be otherwise, should we be affirming something, we would be incurring in omniscience. To express it more graphically, only by means of projective identification could we *get inside* the analysand in order to know "for sure" what is happening to him. This is why the analysand's response has such a high epistemic value for me: in fact, the interpretation always poses an implicit question which the analysand has to answer, even though he may not do so and even if often neither he nor the analyst understands the answer. Although it is obvious, it may be worthwhile to stress once more: this implicit question is directed to the unconscious and has nothing to do with the manifest thoughts.

From this perspective one could say that the interpretation has a certain metalinguistic character in that it does not speak of the facts (objects) but about what the patient thinks about the facts. An opinion is a statement about things: an interpretation is a statement about what someone thinks about things.

WAELDER'S PRINCIPLE

If the analyst must impose upon himself so many restrictions when he interprets, it is not only due to what I have said above but also because he must take into account a basic rule of our discipline—that psychic acts are overdetermined. Freud always said this about symptoms, and Robert Waelder (1936) stated it as the principle of multiple function.

We are touching on a truly important point here. The principle of multiple function affords us, apparently, a great theoretical advantage: just by knowing something of psychoanalysis and putting our ideas in the shape of an interpretation, we can say anything without being afraid of being mistaken. This is the Achilles heel of psychoanalysis which, for example, made Popper (1953, 1962) remark that psychoanalytic theories, like astrological and homeopathic theories, are irrefutable. If we treat a patient harshly imagining he is refuting our interpretations "due to resistance" and at the same time treat ourselves leniently by finding something that will prove us right, it is because we do not wish to recognize the extreme complexity of the analytic dialogue and we are trampling over Waelder's principle. If we took it into account, we should have to believe, more cautiously, that the analysand never refutes something *only* due to resistance and that besides the reason we wield to back our interpretation, there are, without any doubt, others that dispute it.

For the analyst's sayings to reach the level of an interpretation, therefore, it is not enough for these to refer to the analysand and to his material; they must also refer to a concrete and defined segment of the emerging conflict, be this a transferential, actual, infantile, or an early conflict (Etchegoyen, 1982). The ever present effects of Waelder's principle oblige us, then, to be more precise and not to disperse our efforts. As Strachey (1934) liked to say, an interpretation will only be mutative when it is directed to a conflict that is alive and present, to an impulse that is taking on the state of a cathexis. When we manage to operate in this way, our interpretation will offer the analysand just one hypothesis, and he will then have the opportunity of pronouncing upon its validity. This is why I am against long interpretations that join up various hypotheses, since the analysand's testing is then hampered; moreover, one runs the risk of overburdening him with information he will not always be able to process. Once the analyst has been able to imagine an extensive interpretation, he will do better to communicate a part of it to the patient and then, according to the reply, the rest of it, step by step. If the analysand rejects the first part of an interpretation, it is no use adding the second; if he accepts it, the next may go a little further, it may be "deeper." Through the years I have become opposed to complex interpretations and much more so to brilliant ones. The former become more and more irrefutable as more hypotheses are added to them, hypotheses that sometimes end up contradicting each other; the latter appeal to the emotional adhesion of the listener instead of inviting him to think or to reason about them.

INTERPRETATION AND THE CONTEXT OF DISCOVERY

If the material our patient offers us is complex and manifold and if we always have an enormous desire to influence him (suggestion), how will we be able to choose what is most adequate for constructing our interpretation? From the point of view of the method, this is a fundamental problem. If we do not hit upon the right solution, all our technique will be left up in the air and we will not be able to lift the charge, often aimed at us, of indoctrinating our analysands.

As many snares may be found here to lead us down mistaken paths, there are also elements to direct us toward choosing with an acceptable degree of rationality. Many authors have dealt with this subject, and it was to this that López (1972) referred when he explained his ideas about the way in which an interpretation is *invented*. As this author says, following Liberman (1970–1972), an interpretation will have that much greater a possibility of being right if it pays as much attention to the verbal signifier as to the paraverbal and nonverbal signifiers—and, I may add, if it consults the information that at that moment is being received from the countertransference.

One cannot deny that intuition, which Reik prized so much, can often orient us in the complex material offered by the patient, and we all know that there are many great analysts with outstanding powers in this direction, but to trust in intuition beyond the context of discovery most certainly entails a countertransferential involvement that is good neither for psychoanalysis nor for the patient. To follow this path is rapidly to reach certainty, always a form of omnipotence (omniscience).

The proposal we offer as an interpretation to the analysand, therefore, must not issue merely from a sudden inspiration or from what we knew previously (theories) but from a reflexive appreciation of all the variables present at the time, among which, of course, will be the analyst's fantasies, his countertransference.

In the '30s, a celebrated controversy arose between Theodor Reik and Wilhelm Reich. Reik (1933) maintained that psychoanalytic technique, far from being systematic, had to start with surprising the analysand with an act of intuition; Reich (1933), for his part, advocated orderly, systematic, and consequential work on the characterological resistances which would uncover the material in layers. This discussion could not be resolved satisfactorily with the theoretical instruments that were then available, though the majority of scholars, and among them principally Fenichel (1935, 1941), were inclined to favor a systematic technique as proposed by Reich.[2]

After the revolutionary papers by Heinrich Racker (1948, 1960) and by Paula Heimann (1950, 1960) on the countertransference, the problem could be posed on much surer ground, since what Reik called intuition is above all a countertransferential phenomenon—"countertransference thoughts," as Racker (1953) accurately called them. The singular phenomenon of projective counteridentification described by Grinberg (1956, 1963, 1976, 1982) is also a sensitive element in choosing the context of discovery of interpretation, as the intensity of the projective identification forces an almost automatic response into the analyst.

As a rule, an adequate interpretation emerges from what at one and the same time we are informed by the patient's material, taken in its most ample sense, and by our countertransference. If both coincide, the possibilities that it will be correct are greater. The great methodological value of Racker's countertransferential thoughts is precisely that it appears suddenly and without any direct relation to the material, which nevertheless confirms them

[2] Recently Rangell (1985) returned to this subject in order to recall Reik's emphasis on intuition as being a way of moving away from the theory and from reflexive thought.

a short time later. If the countertransference emits no obvious signals, it is legitimate to interpret exclusively on the basis of the material, seeking out the points of urgency, that is, the anxiety, as Melanie Klein (1932) taught us, and tying up the loose threads the material leaves, above all when the same signifier or subject is repeated in different contexts.

As opposed to the majority of analysts, I am not in favor of including in the interpretation material from other sessions, because we run the risk of making a mistake in our selection, or to add things that are out of the analysand's reach. Having said we can make mistakes in selecting from the present material, what confidence can we have on that which we add? The greatest difficulty in choosing an interpretation lies in the fact that the material offered us is always vast; it is never prudent, therefore, to extend it even further. Perhaps no error is more pathetic in psychoanalytic teaching than that of the candidate interpreting in the next session what his supervisor has pointed out in the previous one, and always failing. In short, when we open up the field in this way, we lose accuracy and are more exposed to an arbitrary selection, that is, one promoted by countertransferential conflicts. To state it in even stronger terms, if we abandon the session's material, we also abandon the method since we may then be able to justify any interpretative hypothesis: we shall always find something to support us in the previous sessions, just as we could also find something in them to contradict us.

A recent supervision accorded me a very clear example in this respect. The analysand related a very similar situation to others of her analysis, and her analyst reiterated the interpretation she had offered on previous occasions. I asked my intelligent colleague why she had made that interpretation which in no way emerged from the material, and she answered that it was something she knew only too well due to the history of the analysis. The patient immediately asked whether she was condemned to repeat the same thing, adding bitterly that in that case there was no way out for her. A genius at putting people in the wrong, she was right on this occasion: she took advantage of the analyst's hasty interpretation to disqualify it unmercifully.

It is a different thing altogether when, after the interpretation has been supported by the analysand's material and above all if insight has taken place, we then complete it recalling things from previous sessions, which under these circumstances the patient often alludes to himself. In this case one is carrying out the natural process of working through (Freud, 1914; Richfield, 1954; Etchegoyen, 1986).

If it is not legitimate to lay hands on material of other sessions to form our interpretative hypothesis, much less so is it to interpret exclusively from the countertransference. One can only use the countertransference when the material authorizes it. On its own it exposes us to arbitrariness and bewilderment. Here one can apply with all precision the aphorism Hanna Segal (1981) is so fond of: "Countertransference is the best of servants but the worst of masters" (p. 86). The interpretations that begin with "I feel" are, in fact, irrefutable because neither the analysand nor anyone else can say anything about what the other person "feels." Here again we observe how a technical error and an ethical failing come together, since the analyst should not expose his feelings that are not to the point.

A lot more could be added to the subject of how an interpretation is chosen, but I trust I have given a few reasons to uphold the fact that it can be done by scientific and rational means, without thereby omitting either emotions (countertransference) or experience or one's clinical métier (intuition).

INTERPRETATION AND KNOWLEDGE

From a noseological point of view, an interpretation attempts to reach knowledge with which the analyst endeavors to find out what is going on in the analysand's unconscious. Klimovsky (1986) made a decisive contribution to this subject when he distinguished two types of interpretation: by reading and by explanation.

An interpretation always tries to link the observable material A to the unobservable or conjectural material B, or what amounts to the same thing, the manifest content to the latent content. Sometimes the observable A is linked to the conjectural B through a law that says *if A then B;* in this case it may be said that the analyst "reads" B thanks to the theory linking it to A. This is the case of a *reading interpretation,* where the manifest A is a *sufficient condition* for the latent B, and, simultaneously, B is a *necessary condition* for A. In other words, A cannot occur without the presence of B.

The most well-known type of interpretation, however, links the manifest A content with the latent B content in a way opposite to the previous case: *if B then A,* where the manifest content is the *necessary condition* and the latent ideas are the *sufficient condition,* so that if B is in the unconscious, then A must be apparent, A must occur, without gainsaying the fact that another cause C can also provoke A. In this case we have the *explanation interpretation,* where from a manifest material A we may *suppose* that B (and not C) is in the unconscious. Here an explanatory pattern is applied, Hempel's (1965) model, which allows us to give reasons why the manifest material A appears in a certain clinical situation. To achieve this we have no other option but to frame a hypothesis on the latent material and to articulate it with the manifest material by means of a law. This law says that when the supposed latent material actually exists, A must necessarily occur. In this way *one explains* why this or that manifest element has emerged. According to these considerations, psychoanalysis contributes a model of psychic apparatus functioning from which certain consequences susceptible to observation are deduced. In other words, the interpretation formulates a hypothesis and awaits the analysand's confirmation or refutation through his associations.

THE CONTEXT OF JUSTIFICATION

The knowledge the analyst arrives at when he reads or explains the material always refers to the other, to the analysand, who will have to be the one to corroborate or refute his interpretation. Naturally, as we have already seen, there are other ways of doing so, studying the report of a session, for example, or recurring to different extraclinical observational resources, but the incontestable test of the interpretation must, by definition, be the analysand's response. Freud undoubtedly concurred with this idea which was later set forth rigorously by Kubie (1952) and then by Wisdom (1967) in a now classic paper. This statement should neither cause surprise nor give rise to dispute since it does no more than to apply to psychoanalysis what no one questions in any other field of science. In the same way as Mendel's laws can only be answered by the sweet peas because they are their subject matter, who, if not whom they concern—the analysand—can account for the analyst's hypotheses?

The difference between the sweet peas and the analysand is certainly very great, because the former cannot intend to deceive us and we do not influence the color they acquire. However, there is an evident likeness: in the same way that the answer of the peas to Mendel's cross-breeding is the indispensable element of the empirical basis to test the laws of heredity, the patient's answer to an interpretation also is an indispensable element of the empirical basis for the analyst. Whoever denies this is stating, over and above what psychoanalysis affirms, that the study of the human mind is logically impossible.

Not only do I affirm that the interpretation is a scientific hypothesis that, like any other, is tested from the observational events it promotes, but also that if it is stated according to art, it promotes a reply in the analysand, which when purged of the distortions that in fact accompany it, bears a very close relation to the degree of its accuracy. In other words, clinical experience teaches us that the unconscious judgments of the analysand on the interpretations have great epistemical value.

The real problem lies in how to correct the distortion, since problems of suggestion (and of countersuggestion!) always impinge upon the analysand's reply and these can transform the interpretation in a *self-predictive hypothesis* and also in a *suicidal hypothesis*. It is only by overcoming these two difficult obstacles that a solution may be found to the problem I am discussing. To those with no clinical experience suggestion will always appear to be the greater hazard, but the practicing analyst knows that countersuggestion is just as dangerous.

SUGGESTION (AND COUNTERSUGGESTION)

In *The Foundations of Psychoanalysis* (1984), a most thoughtful and rigorous book that spares no efforts in studying the scientific credentials of psychoanalysis, Adolf Grünbaum comes to the conclusion that one cannot trust the epistemic value of our clinical data because they are always irreparably contaminated by suggestion. Grünbaum does not believe, as Popper does, that psychoanalytic hypotheses are irrefutable, and reminds us that Freud himself rejected more than one theory during the course of his investigations, precisely because he realized it had been refuted by the clinical facts; what Grünbaum thinks is that "the epistemic decontamination of the bulk of the patient's productions on the couch from the suggestive effects of the analyst's communications appears to be quite utopian" (p. 128). In Grünbaum's opinion, the clinical data put forward by Freud and his followers in order to prove their hypotheses are extremely scanty. Clinical confirmations of psychoanalysis, Grünbaum states severely, insofar as they are always an artifact of positive transference, are spurious, fatally spurious.

It is true that Freud, as Grünbaum says—and we all know—never came to separate entirely, in a clear-cut way, transference from suggestion, most probably, I think, because he did not interpret the negative transference thoroughly and unconditionally.[3] Moreover, Freud sometimes forgot the advice he gave in 1912 and tried to convince his analysand of the truth of his hypotheses (constructions), believing, with generous simplicity, that the health and freedom of the person under his care depended on this consent. It was this same Freud (1912b), however, who warned us against our *furor curandis* and recommended we become like mirrors, only recording and reflecting the projected image (p. 118). He also advised giving the interpretation with the spiritual attitude of that wise French surgeon—Ambroise Paré, perhaps—who said: "Je le pansai, Dieu le guérit" (p. 115).

As Freud often said, though not always perhaps with the most accurate words, the key to our method lies precisely in the cir-

[3] It is easy to find confirmations of what I have just said throughout Freud's work (Mahony, 1986).

cumstance that by resolving the transference we restore to the analysand, through insight, the capacity to think for himself. Backed by some ambiguous statements made by Freud, Grünbaum "does not believe" this, without taking into account that this (dis)belief of his may proceed from his ignorance of the method and—why not?—from ideological, that is, suggestive, factors that are impinging upon his reasoning. As far as I am concerned, I "believe" that the analysand, the analyst, and Grünbaum himself can all equally be victims of suggestion and of countersuggestion, and equally, too, they may all rise above them. What occurs is that Grünbaum denies psychoanalysis what on principle no thinking being should be denied, the capacity to reflect upon and to correct his errors.[4]

I recall an anecdote from more than 20 years ago when I was a psychiatry professor in Mendoza and was training a group of students who, under the direction of Dr. Clara Ruiz Garasino, would later form the present Psychoanalytic Society. A philosophy professor of the university, a very well-known and respected man, consulted me, suffering from a crippling obsessional neurosis. In the first interview he warned me that due to what he had read (Popper, Bunge), he had many misgivings about psychoanalysis, though he did not for a moment doubt my professional capacity. He added that he did not say this "due to resistances" and I conceded without any trimmings that, like him, the great majority of philosophers of the sciences questioned the psychoanalytic method. Slightly reassured, in a second interview he told me things about his mother and his childhood while reiterating his critical attitude to psychoanalysis. I listened to him pleasantly and said that notwithstanding his objections, psychoanalysis was the treatment best suited to his complaint. Could a treatment, he asked, be effective although he did not believe in it? I answered it could; analysis did not operate with trust since it restricts itself to finding out what happens in the unconscious. With all respect he disagreed with me over this: a psychological treatment that is carried out without faith could not be viable. He

[4] Most valid remarks on Grünbaum's paper and on the epistemology of psychoanalysis in general may be found in Wallerstein (1986), Spruiell (1987), and Pinto Ribeiro (1987).

went on speaking about his problems and left saying he would consider my indication.

He returned to the third interview and told me a dream of the night before, about his parents, whom he criticized over some of the norms they had for bringing him up, and so on. Unfortunately I do not recall the text of that dream and I am really sorry I did not record it scrupulously. It was evident to me, by the defiant and hopeful tone with which he told me the dream, clear and naïve—as Freud used to say—as are those of the first interviews, that this cultured and tormented man was well disposed to the treatment. I rapidly measured the risks and certain as I was that if I went on respecting his resistances, I would not find the way to show them to him, I told him with the utmost possible candor that his dream not only referred to his childhood and to his objections to the upbringing he received, but to me, represented by his father, explaining the sound reasons that led me to think so. I also pointed out that his attitude toward his father in the dream authorized one to imagine a conflict relating to childhood jealousies. He looked at me with surprise and in his eyes I seemed to discern the approval of the thinking man toward a correct piece of reasoning. Over and above his philosophical objections, his doubts also had to do with those that, as a professional, I awoke in him—also quite legitimate, in fact. The interpretation obviously reached him, and all he said by way of a comment was that he did not know analysis worked that way. In the fourth interview he told me he agreed to the treatment. The fact is, one can never discuss the epistemological foundations of a branch of science if one does not understand its *modus operandi*.

WISDOM'S CRITERIA

By way of the exception that proves the rule, Wisdom is one of the few philosophers of the sciences who has direct contact with the theory and practice of psychoanalysis. In his outstanding works (1956, 1967) he maintains that the test of an interpretation must proceed from the analysand, from the latter's reply.

Once one accepts that an interpretation must be tested by the analysand's response, the real problem emerges: How does one decide whether the reply confirms or refutes it? This is always a problematic decision because, in order to make it, the analyst is obliged, more often than not, to interpret the patient's reply. This is serious from a logical point of view because one is exposed to the danger of circular reasoning: an interpretation is validated by means of another.

To break this vicious circle, Wisdom proposes this validation criterion: an interpretation is considered corroborated if the reply it produces can be interpreted by means of the same clinical hypothesis applied to the previous material. Let us recall Wisdom's example of a patient who to a transferential interpretation about his oedipal rivalry replies he has no hostility toward the father-analyst, but he does have some toward his boss at the office. Since the latter is clearly a subrogate of the former, the patient's response may again be interpreted with the same hypothesis—the Oedipus complex. If we allowed ourselves to interpret the patient's reply with just any other theory whatever, we would then find ourselves always able to do so and we would be proving right those who state that the theories of psychoanalysis are irrefutable. In fact, were the patient's reply to have a different structure from the first set of associations, we should conclude that the interpretation has been falsified. For Wisdom, this is the way Popper's refutability requisite is fulfilled, though it is necessary to bear in mind a fundamental objection, the influence of suggestion, which Wisdom discusses in the last part of his essay.

Wisdom's corroboration and refutation criteria are useful, although slightly too general. They do not sufficiently take into account the speed with which the analytic situation sometimes changes or the pitfalls of misunderstandings, perhaps because Wisdom, like the majority of epistemologists, thinks that the only danger to the psychoanalytic dialogue derives from suggestion. As we shall see immediately, the problem—at least for me—is much more complex.

THE ANALYSAND'S EVALUATION

The idea that an interpretation may be tested *within* the analytic situation opens up the road toward establishing a more accurate and concrete basis of an epistemology of psychoanalysis, insofar as it may address itself straight to the clinical facts and receive there its validation or refutation. It is necessary to point out that an interpretation always remits us to something that is happening to the analysand, and in this sense it is always near the empirical basis. The testing of high-level hypotheses deserves a different approach. In this, as over many other points, I coincide with Edelson's book (1984), which is a relevant contribution to the epistemology of our discipline. "An interpretation, properly speaking, is an inference or hypothesis about the analysand (not necessarily a psychoanalytic hypothesis) which follows logically or with some degree of probability from what the analysand has (or has not) said in conjunction with a general and perhaps probabilistic psychoanalytic hypothesis" (pp. 130–131).

These characteristics of the interpretation explain why I previously insisted on discriminating two ways of studying the session. When one considers the session after it is over, what we are really doing is studying a report and, however valuable this may be, we do not then have the analysand's response. It is the same difference there is between a study *in vivo* and *in vitro*. Personally, I believe the study of the report of a session is of enormous importance and, in fact, the whole praxis of supervision is based on it, but it is only during a session that we can propose an interpretation so that it can be tested.

Moreover, as I said before, the study of the session *in vivo* is a basic principle of my activity in my consulting room, as I believe the analysand not only can evaluate the work of the analyst but that, in addition, he is fitted to do so and in fact does do so continuously. This is perhaps the most daring thesis of my essay: the analysand permanently evaluates the analyst's work and he does so with surprising, not to say diabolical, accuracy.

It takes years of patience and of pain to recognize that our patient, that same individual who came to ask us to help him understand himself, is at the same time our best critic, benevolent at times and, in general, implacable. This fact repeats itself daily with such assiduity that finally one can do no less than to accept it. I first learned it from the analysands of the colleagues who came to supervise with me, because there it is less painful to admit it; but later on I was able to listen to my own analysands and to see to what extent they read me correctly.

I have previously (1988) dealt with this subject and given an example that I think is convincing. Here I only wish to insist upon an experience that daily recurs in supervision: when I pass judgment on the work of my colleague and for some reason I keep my opinion to myself, it frequently appears expressed in the next material, without, of course, the analysand realizing that he is passing judgment on the analyst's work. Experiences such as these provide the best grounds for the idea that the analytic work is testable and, therefore, scientific. As soon as we accept that this is so, we have no option but to concede the analysand a much more important place than that which he has had in the context of the justification of our interpretation, recognizing he evaluates us and that he is fitted to do so, however much this may hurt our professional pride and bring home to us how far we depend upon our patients.

COMMUNICATION AND MISUNDERSTANDING

As a dialogue, the psychoanalytic situation is a communication process that has its starting point in the free association of the analysand, to which the analyst responds with an interpretation and the analysand in turn with new associations. The psychoanalytic dialogue, as Enrique Pichon Rivière liked saying, is spiral in form.

This spiraling dialogue is indeed very complicated, not only on account of the numerous variables involved but also because *misunderstandings* pierce it through and through. All of Liberman's work (1962, 1970–1972) is an attempt to systematize the communication difficulties in the psychoanalytic dialogue. Roger Money-Kyrle's (1968, 1971) last years in his fruitful life were directed toward understanding cognitive development and to clarifying misunderstandings. Contrary to these authors, Lacan (1966) is skeptical and maintains that misunderstandings are the essence of human communications. Accordingly he believes that the analyst is the one who bestows meaning, that he is the lord of the truth. From the moment he introduces the fundamental rule, the analyst, from the patient's point of view, occupies the place of the one who knows. This *sujet supposé savoir* is for Lacan (1953, 1964) the pivot of the transference.

A misunderstanding is born of the most varied sources. In effect, it may be a kind of logical response to the great complexity of the psychoanalytic dialogue (see Waelder's principle) and it may also be legitimate to the analyst's ambiguity. The analyst must not be ambiguous; he will contribute to the development of the dialogue if he avoids introducing elements that do not belong to it, and, of course, he must keep away from all suggestive attitudes and from discussion (see what was said about the opinions of the analyst).

At other times the misunderstanding proceeds from a biased evaluation of the analyst's work made by the analysand, but even knowing that the analysand does not always act in good faith, it is only from what he says that we will be able to obtain the observational consequences in order to discern whether we are correct. After acknowledging this, our work in our consulting rooms becomes defined as a singular, problematic dialogue in which misunderstanding and ambiguity are both at the core of our work and at the same time continually interfere with it, because in this evaluation, the cooperation and rivalry, love and hatred, and admiration and envy that we must analyze will all come together.

The decisive part of the analyst's work is the moment in which he must evaluate this evaluation made by the analysand. In this evaluation he must find the deep, unconscious response to his interpretation, which rarely coincides with what is said consciously and must always be sorted out from innumerable misunderstandings which turn our interpretative hypothesis into a self-predictive hypothesis (complacency, positive transference) or into a suicidal hypothesis (aggression, negative transference). This is an extremely difficult decision and yet, to a large extent, whether the dialogue continues or is broken off depends on its correctness as exhibited in the new interpretation.

REFERENCES

Bibring, E. (1954), Psychoanalysis and the dynamic psychotherapies. *J. Amer. Psychoanal. Assn.*, 2:745–770.

Bion, W. R. (1962), *Learning from Experience*. London: Heinemann.

——— (1963), *Elements of Psychoanalysis*. New York: Basic Books.

Cooper, A. (1987), Changes in psychoanalytic ideas. *J. Amer. Psychoanal. Assn.*, 35:77–98.

Edelson, M. (1984), *Hypothesis and Evidence in Psychoanalysis*. Chicago: University of Chicago Press.

Etchegoyen, R. H. (1982), The relevance of the 'here and now' transference interpretation for the reconstruction of early psychic development. *Internat. J. Psycho-Anal.*, 63:65–75.

——— (1986), *Los Fundamentos de la Técnica Psicoanalítica*. Buenos Aires: Amorrortu Editores.

——— (1988), Der psychoanalytische Dialog. In: *Die psychoanalitische Haltung*, ed. P. Kutter, R. Páramo-Ortega, & P. Zagermann. Munich: Verlag Internationale Psychoanalyse, pp. 115–139.

Fenichel, O. (1935), Concerning the theory of psychoanalytic technique. In: *Collected Papers*, Vol. 21, first series. New York: Norton, 1953, pp. 332–348.

——— (1941), *Problems of Psychoanalytic Technique*. New York: Psychoanalytic Quarterly.

Ferenczi, S. (1919), Technical difficulties in the analysis of a case of hysteria. In: *Further Contributions to the Theory and Technique of Psychoanalysis*. New York: Brunner/Mazel, 1980, pp. 189–197.

——— (1921), The further development of an active therapy in psychoanalysis. In: *Further Contributions to the Theory and Technique of Psychoanalysis*. New York: Brunner/Mazel, 1980, pp. 198–217.

Freud, S. (1910), 'Wild' psycho-analysis. *Standard Edition*, 11:219–227. London: Hogarth Press, 1957.

——— (1912a), The dynamics of transference. *Standard Edition*, 12:97–108. London: Hogarth Press, 1958.

——— (1912b), Recommendations to physicians practicing psycho-analysis. *Standard Edition*, 12:109–120. London: Hogarth Press, 1958.

——— (1914), Remembering, repeating and working-through. *Standard Edition*, 12:145–156. London: Hogarth Press, 1958.

——— (1919), Lines of advance in psycho-analytic therapy. *Standard Edition*, 17:157–168. London: Hogarth Press, 1957.

——— (1926), The question of lay analysis. *Standard Edition*, 20:177–258. London: Hogarth Press, 1959.

——— (1937), Constructions in analysis. *Standard Edition,* 23:255–269. London: Hogarth Press, 1964.

Gill, M. M. (1982), *Analysis of Transference,* Vol. 1. New York: International Universities Press.

Grinberg, L. (1956), Sobre algunos problemas de técnica psicoanalítica determinados por la identificación y la contraidentificación proyectivas. *Rev. Psicoanál.,* 13:507–511.

——— (1963), Psicopatología de la identificación y contraidentificación proyectivas y de la contratransferencia. *Rev. Psicoanál.,* 20:113–123.

——— (1976), *Teoría de la Identificación.* Buenos Aires: Paidós.

——— (1982), Los afectos en la contratransferencia. XIV Congreso Latinoamericano de Psicoanálisis. FEPAL, Garamond. *Actas,* pp. 205–209.

Grünbaum, A. (1984), *The Foundations of Psychoanalysis.* Berkeley: University of California Press.

Heimann, P. (1950), On counter-transference. *Internat. J. Psycho-Anal.,* 31:81–84.

——— (1956), Dynamics of transference interpretations. *Internat. J. Psycho-Anal.,* 37:303–310.

——— (1960), Countertransference. *Brit. J. Med. Psychol.,* 33:9–15.

Hempel, C. G. (1965), *Aspects of Scientific Explanation and Other Essays in the Philosophy of Science.* New York: Free Press.

Isaacs, S. (1948), The nature and function of phantasy. *Internat. J. Psycho-Anal.,* 29:73–97.

Jones, E. (1929), Fear, guilt and hate. *Internat. J. Psycho-Anal.,* 10:383–397.

Klein, M. (1926), The psychological principles of early analysis. In: *Love, Guilt and Reparation and Other Works.* London: Hogarth Press, 1975, pp. 128–138.

——— (1927), Symposium on child-analysis. In: *Love, Guilt and Reparation and Other Works.* London: Hogarth Press, 1975, pp. 139–169.

——— (1932), *The Psychoanalysis of Children.* London: Hogarth Press, 1975.

——— (1952), The origins of transference. In: *Envy and Gratitude and Other Works.* London: Hogarth Press, 1975, pp. 48–56.

Klimovsky, G. (1986), Aspectos epistemológicos de la interpretación psicoanalítica. In: *Los Fundamentos de la Técnica Psicoanalítica,* ed. R. H. Etchegoyen. Buenos Aires: Amorrortu Editores, pp. 433–456.

Kubie, L. S. (1952), Problems and techniques of psychoanalytic validation and progress. In: *Psychoanalysis as Science,* ed. E. Pumpian-Mindlin. Stanford: Stanford University Press.

Lacan, J. (1953), Fonction et champ de la parole et du langage en psychanalyse. In: *Écrits.* Paris: Editions du Seuil, pp. 237–322.

——— (1964), *Les Quatre Concepts Fondamentaux de la Psychanalyse: Le Seminaire*, Livre 11. Paris: Editions du Seuil.

——— (1966), *Écrits*. Paris: Editions du Seuil.

Lakatos, I. (1975), La falsación y la metodología de los programas de investigación científica. In: *La Crítica y el Desarrollo del Conocimiento*, ed. I. Lakatos & A. Musgrave. Barcelona: Ediciones Grijalbo.

Liberman, D. (1962), *La Comunicación en Terapéutica Psicoanalítica*, 2nd ed. Buenos Aires: EUDEBA, 1966.

——— (1970–1972), *Lingüística, Interacción Comunicativa y Proceso Psicoanalítico*. Buenos Aires: Galerna.

López, B. M. (1972), Descubrimiento de la fantasía e invención de la interpretación en el abordaje técnico de los trastornos de carácter. *Rev. Psicoanál.*, 29:189–215.

Mahony, P. J. (1986), *Freud and the Rat Man*. New Haven, CT: Yale University Press.

Meltzer, D. (1967), *The Psychoanalytical Process*. London: Heinemann.

Money-Kyrle, R. E. (1968), Cognitive development. *Internat. J. Psycho-Anal.*, 49:691–698.

——— (1971), The aim of psychoanalysis. *Internat. J. Psycho-Anal.*, 52:103–107.

Pinto Ribeiro, R. (1987), Conferência inaugural: psiquiatria e psicanálise. *Rev. Psiquiatria*, 9:6–14.

Popper, K. R. (1953), La ciencia. In: *El Desarrollo del Conocimiento Científico*. Buenos Aires: Paidós, 1967, pp. 43–79.

——— (1962), *Conjectures and Refutations*. London: Routledge & Kegan Paul.

Racker, H. (1948), A contribution to the problem of counter-transference. *Internat. J. Psycho-Anal.*, 34:313–324.

——— (1953), The meanings and uses of countertransference. *Psychoanal. Quart.*, 24:303–357.

——— (1957), Contribution to the problem of psychopathological stratification. *Internat. J. Psycho-Anal.*, 38:223–239.

——— (1960), *Estudios sobre Técnica Psicoanalítica*. Buenos Aires: Paidós.

Rangell, L. (1954), Similarities and differences between psychoanalysis and dynamic psychotherapy. *J. Amer. Psychoanal. Assn.*, 2:734–744.

——— (1974), A psychoanalytic perspective leading currently to the syndrome of the compromise of integrity. *Internat. J. Psycho-Anal.*, 55:3–12.

——— (1985), On the theory of theory in psychoanalysis and the relation of theory to psychoanalytic therapy. *J. Amer. Psychoanal. Assn.*, 33:59–92.

Reich, W. (1927), Zur Technik der Deutung und der Widerstandsanalyse. *Internat. Z. Psychoanal.*, 13:142–159.

——— (1933), *Análisis del Carácter*. Buenos Aires: Paidós, 1957.

Reik, T. (1933), New ways in psychoanalytic technique. *Internat. J. Psycho-Anal.*, 14:321–334.

Richfield, J. (1954), An analysis of the concept of insight. *Psychoanal. Quart.*, 23:398–408.

Segal, H. (1981), Countertransference. In: *The Work of Hanna Segal*. New York: Aronson, pp. 81–87.

Spruiell, V. (1987), The foundations of psychoanalysis. An essay on a philosophical book by Adolf Grünbaum. *Internat. Rev. Psychoanal.*, 14:169–183.

Strachey, J. (1934), The nature of the therapeutic action of psychoanalysis. *Internat. J. Psycho-Anal.*, 15:127–159.

——— (1937), Symposium on the theory of the therapeutic results of psychoanalysis. *Internat. J. Psycho-Anal.*, 18:139–145.

Waelder, R. (1936), The principle of multiple function: Observations on over-determination. *Psychoanal. Quart.*, 5:45–62.

Wallerstein, R. S. (1986), Psychoanalysis as a science: A response to the new challenges. *Psychoanal. Quart.*, 55:414–451.

Wisdom, J. O. (1956), Psychoanalytic technology. In: *Psychoanalytic Clinical Interpretation*, ed. L. Paul. London: Collier-Macmillan, 1963, pp. 143–161.

——— (1967), Testing an interpretation within a session. *Internat. J. Psycho-Anal.*, 48:44–52.

21

ON HAVING AND GIVING VALUE

Nikolaas Treurniet, M.D.

During the 1970s Rangell studied the syndrome of the compromise of integrity (1974, 1976, 1980). His patient was America in distress: Watergate. Since then this syndrome was found to be ubiquitous. All Western countries appeared to have their "-gates." Rangell (1980) believed this to be the consequence of a "sensitivity and weakness of the moral fiber, an absence of resistance against the effects of these and a resulting deficiency in the realm of integrity" (p. 210) in our civilization. Emphasizing the problem of integrity as an important area for psychoanalytic consideration, he thought the question of courage in group situations to be the most pressing problem of human character in civilized man: to say no when all others say yes. He also noted a collective triumph over the superego (1982). This was recently again visible as "Olliemania," the stormy popular worship of Colonel Oliver North during the Irangate hearings. This aroused my interest in how we come to value our values, remembering Eissler's statement (1965) that "we do not yet know for certain why human life can develop only within the framework of value-positing, but it is an indisputable fact that the necessity of positing values is as inherent to human life as the existence of the drives" (p. 28). How we make and give value, i.e., "valuing," is the subject of this chapter.

Synonymous with valuing are not only "estimate," "assess," "appraise," "rate," but also "prize," "appreciate," "esteem," "treasure." To value, then, has both a knowing and a feeling aspect. Valuing is different from loving. Not only can we sometimes not value what we love, it is also possible to value what we hate. It has more to do with friendship (Leupold Löwenthal, 1980). To give value, or valuing, resembles to "give meaning" but is not the same. Valuing has a stronger affective quality, but there is considerable overlap. It is also not congruent with pleasure. We can value painful experiences, or work, or even our destiny. It also seems to be connected with the ego and its interests. It is "ego-related" (Winnicott, 1965). The capacity to be alone and the capacity for concern are part of giving value. It has to do with giving something a *personal* quality, an "ego quality." I do not think we ever "love" truth; in fact, we rarely even like it. What we do value or like, however, is someone, a *person*, who is willing to face the truth, which makes him or her reliable. Valuing personalizes our world and determines the "ego-ness" or "me-ness" of it, which is the opposite of depersonalization and derealization. It is an essential motivating force in conflict and defense. Valuing also precedes every choice. Choosing is valuing translated into action. Valuing is also a central motivating force in the process of decision making, which Rangell (1969, 1971) identifies as *the* central function of the ego. A function, however, is always a function of something else. Valuing, it seems to me, might even be not a function at all, but the core of the ego, the ego's "I." These thoughts—and one may well call them fantasies—need some reflection. Therefore I invite the reader to join me in looking at some considerations concerning development, technique, and theory, followed by considerations concerning environment, culture, and civilization.

DEVELOPMENT

Recent infant research has produced massive evidence indicating that affective bonding is not simply a derivative of libidinal energies, but an independent force establishing affective links between a baby and his objects. Contrary to classical psychoanalytic developmental theory, the need for "holding" responses from the mother forms an independent basis for the development of attachment and object relations and is not secondary, or anaclitic, to the satisfaction of oral drives. So-called primary object love (Balint, 1937) is claiming at least an equal footing for our psychological beginnings as Freud's primary narcissism. The capacity to gratify sexual needs and to use aggression in healthy self-assertion is strongly influenced by early attachment behavior. The more secure the healthy attachment between mother and child, the greater is the likelihood of independent and exploratory behavior. A baby needs an experience like: "How lovely for you all that I exist." It needs, in other words, the feeling of having value, which is *not* a feeling of omnipotence (*vide infra*).

In a recent paper Stechler and Halton (1987) put the question whether "all efforts by the infant aimed at making something happen in the outside world derive from the primordial aggressive instinct, or . . . from a totally different source" (p. 822). They see the child's active moves toward the world and the many functions that are not responses to a threat as emanating from sources totally removed from aggression. "The blocking of assertion can . . . be perceived by the child as just that kind of threat to the self that will elicit a self-protective, possibly angry, and ultimately aggressive reaction. . . . If the child is not permitted to refuse, and if the child's plans are continually blocked by the caretakers, . . . the integrity of the emerging self is threatened" (p. 827–829). A vicious circle can be established with chronic rage about anticipated devaluation, which has all the appearance of aggression as defined in classical drive theory, but which is really a desperate attempt of the child to preserve his feeling of having value from total destruction. I shall not enter the often political and *ad hominem* discussion of aggressive behavior as deneutralization of secondary ego autonomy, as a disintegration product of a badly mirrored self, or as frustration of self-assertion, nor on the question of which satisfactions are more central, those of destruction, of self-love, or of power. Stechler and Halton implicitly show how metaphors of a theory can unintentionally support a mother who labels every sign of self-assertion as aggressive. A baby's refusal to have his diapers changed, a toddler's forcefully saying no, a child's feeling that living is also hating—all these test the playful resources of parents to acknowledge the value of independent existence. Every child needs acknowledgment, appropriation, or recapture of his aggression. Reductionism in theoretical metaphors is intimately correlated with reductionism in clinical and technical qualifications. Characterizations like omnipotence or grandeur imply adult standards, often have the effect if not the aim of humiliation, and are not always free of envy.

The father of a one-year-old watched his son making his very first leap in imitation of his mother's joyful frolicking. Having watched the TV sports news, the father reported that the expression on his son's face was exactly like the expression on the face of the athlete, who had just improved the world record in high jumping. Exuberant joy of mastery was common to both. Fortunately for the boy he could have experiences like this nearly every day, while the athlete had to work for years to recapture this lost paradise. Such feeling states are often called omnipotent. The delightful, even ecstatic, elation of both, however, has nothing to do with omnipotence. Omnipotence knows no joy, only triumph, and is a normal revengeful reaction to and compensation for destruction of the value of the self in the feeling of being powerless, which is reality for every child.

Eagle (1982) points to what he calls metapsychological infantilizing. The concept of the "fragmented self," for instance, is a metaphor for feeling fragmented. Many believe that this is an explanation. Having a feeling of defect, however, is not synonymous with being defective. Naming it a defect is a humiliation, is value destruction.

In closing this section I shall give an observation of Lampl-de Groot (1985):

> Francis is four years old, a clever town kid in the country with his grandparents. He observes with great interest the various birds pecking for food but afterwards flying up to trees and far away. Francis found himself a walking path to a farm and one day he wanted to take his grandfather there. This was arranged and they watched the various animals intensely. There were chickens and granddad used the word birds for chickens. Francis: "But Granddaddy, chickens are not birds!" Granddad tried to explain to Francis but the little boy insisted: "Chickens are no birds." Granddad: "Well, Francis, when we come home we will call daddy to ask him whether it is true or not." Francis: "No, Granddaddy, do not ask

> daddy." Granddad: "But whom shall we ask then?" Francis (with quiet conviction): "Me" [pp. 335–336].

In the way of thinking of a four-year-old complete logic reigns: birds fly high in the sky, chickens walk on the ground to peck seeds and can therefore not be birds. This is not grandeur. Granddad had not asked him indeed. This is a claim for recognition of the value of his logic. The boy is entitled to value, not omnipotence. But if you treat his entitlement to value as if it is omnipotence, then he really claims omnipotence, because his sense of value is destroyed.

Returning now to our starting point we can summarize with Basch (1983) that our present view "suggests that the human infant is not essentially asocial, that maturation is not based on an adversary relationship but on a co-operative one and, furthermore, that development is not based in the first instance on instinctual frustration and conflict, but rather on the anticipation of a harmonious interplay between instinctually potentiated genetic patterns . . . [and the] care giver's empathic response to the infant's affective communications" (p. 700). In other words, a developing child needs a sense of having value for others. This seems a truism, but is not. How often do we hear from adults: "Don't pay attention, it is only a child." Being small in comparison to others is a permanent humiliation *sui generis*. Sometimes the self-assertion of every two-year-old is murder.

TECHNIQUE

In 1960 analysis was still held to be a value-free enterprise (Hartmann). Since then analysts have realized that their purist view is an outdated myth that has lost plausibility. However neutral and reserved an analyst strives to be, his silences, his questions, his selections, and his "music" give the patient access to what the analyst values and what he does not. And reversely, there is nothing neutral in the assumption that whatever the patient may say or do, at bottom he is invariably seeking the gratifications of forbidden, repressed, instinctual wishes. These official convictions are in striking contrast to the picture of Freud as it has been painted by a number of his analysands as "humorous, warm and friendly but also irritable, contemptuous and angry when he felt the occasion called for it" (Basch, 1983, p. 701). A significant number of influential analysts, among which Gitelson, Greenson, Kanzer, Kohut, Lampl-de Groot, Loewald, Modell, and of course Winnicott, have stressed the influence of the analyst's attitude. The emphasis is on his contribution to the working alliance. The analyst's counterpart to Freud's "unobjectionable transference," Lampl-de Groot's "narcissistic tie," and Kohut's "selfobject transference"is his tender respect, his "unobjectionable countertransference," his "holding," his "free-floating responsiveness" (Sandler, 1976). Neutrality, then, is not restricted to not taking sides with one side of a conflict versus another, but has to include a non-intruding, but definitely affirmative, attitude with respect to the whole person. Basically, the analyst must be experienced by the patient as being on his side in whatever he faces in his inner life. Many analysts show theoretical agreement on technical admonitions against concerning themselves with objective, external truths. Their psychoanalytic listening, however, "betrays a stance in which they adhere to a reality other than that of the patient's inner world, assuming the position of arbiter—even if a silent one—of what is or is not 'distorted' in the patient's perceptual experience" (Albrecht Schwaber, 1986, p. 911).

The important thing about these technical developments is that they offer the best possible chance for psychoanalysis to develop its finest potential: to create value (not values!). They do so by giving meaning to psychic content which is experienced by the patient as worthless, "bad," meaningless, or chaotic. Even the most objectionable thoughts, feelings, or enactments appear to be the best possible solution in the context of that situation at that moment, which may be either or both cumulative and a very long time ago. The affect is always "right" but concerns a different context. I do not mean morally right, but contextually right. And antisocial impulses, i.e., envy, murderous rage, greed, omnipotence, triumph, sadistic lust, fit into the context of a normal, healthy, and vigorous drive development, if we know the experiential world of the child. An affect is also "right," of course, in case of a disruptive influence from the analyst. Then the context is the actual, here and now, transference-countertransference interaction, and this in turn is very often again a reenactment of a past relationship, a practically daily occurrence in every good-enough analysis. Countertransference responses only need recognition to become involved in the same meaning creating and thereby value-creating process.

This process of making and giving value to our patient's inner life, and so to his sense of self-value, is what Loewald (1960) meant by communicating to the patient an image of the person he could become. This "integrative experience" is the experience of wholeness instead of totality, indicating that good enough is better than perfect. This is also what Lionel Trilling (1955) meant when he pointed to the "willing suspension of disbelief" as an organizing principle, creating meaning and value in literature as well as in psychoanalysis. By not being disbelieved a patient can eventually tolerate to renounce his self-deception.

THEORY

In an interesting chapter ("Id-Ego Revisited") in his recent book, Eagle (1984) distinguishes two meanings of the ego-id polarity. The ego can be viewed as being only apparatus, an energyless controlling structure, while the id is a structureless reservoir of energy, a "seething cauldron." This meaning is a consequence of Freud's system psychology: there are two different systems of mental functioning, primary process, the id, and secondary process, the ego.

The other meaning of ego-id is closer to the German "Wo Es war, soll Ich werden." According to this version, the ego's conquest concerns not only a greater control over the inherently chaotic, but also a transformation of the impersonal, thinglike "it" into the personal realm of "I desire, I want, I claim," and so on. This view of the ego can be understood to mean that which was impersonal and disowned before is now appropriated and experienced as part of the self, of a "me." It is possible to view an ego-self-"me"-"I" continuum as a complementary series: from abstract to concrete and from reflective to experiential. The German language has all these meanings condensed in the word *Ich*. In French, it is differentiated into *le moi* and *le je*. We can also call the two poles functional ego and personal ego (or "self"), but we should not confuse them. It is essential, however, to realize that this continuum expresses a measure of reflective objectivization, which if driven too far can result in a "depersonalized" use of metapsychology. Structural theory is metaphor.

The concept of drive is also first of all a *metaphor*. Freud replaced the concept of force by that of drive (van der Leeuw, 1969). In clinical theory drive signifies the totality of sexual, aggressive, self-assertive, narcissistic impulses, wishes, demands, needs, satisfactions, anxieties, and object ties developing in the child from birth on through childhood and adolescence into adulthood. What we observe in daily practice is temperament, lust, gusto, affect, emotion, passion, i.e., forces and intensities, their movements and "distributions," from the most stubborn resistances to the most expressive enactments. An id cannot be substituted by drive and vice versa. An id is a system with a specific way of functioning, i.e., primary process; a drive is an experiential world with specific affective qualities. Ego, superego, and id are metaphors, on an abstract level, for different systems of functioning; and on an experiential level for emotional needs for safety, value, and pleasure. When safety, value, and pleasure coincide, we have happiness. The two levels, however, must not be confused. Ego, superego, and id also cannot be identified with sides of a conflict. Conflict *always* involves splitting of an ego (Coultre, 1967). Reification of ego, superego, and id metaphors, however, is in itself an expression of a splitting process, is in other words a sign of disavowal and depersonalization, a failure to integrate, to appropriate, to make it into a personal, i.e., a valued, possession. Then it is used as a defense against the affective impact of clinical reality. That is to say, an ego-id view positing a *primary* antagonism between the two is *not* an adequate description of the human mind but an emotional qualification.

Loss of the intimate relationship between psyche and soma is pathological. When id becomes ego again, value has been restored to a drive. We can also expand an ego, or rather an I, however, from the side of its other boundaries: superego and reality. As we all know, conflicts at the boundaries of our conquering I-ego, our personal ego, also pertain to the ruthless persecutors of the childhood hells of guilt-ridden and compulsive patients, the repressed superego. Here sometimes ego should become more id instead of the other way around. This is also valid for a child's conflicts with reality, especially those private and public social realities we call object relations. These external realities can become so threatening, especially to the child's sense of value, that they call for defensive measures, i.e., so-called object relational defenses. The reality principle *differentiates* outside from inside, which is a very painful affair. To make this bearable we need an intermediate area between inside and outside, where at least some *reintegration* between inside and outside can take place, where objective reality can be imbued with personal value: the potential space of cultural experience.

ENVIRONMENT, CULTURE, CIVILIZATION

"Cultural experience starts as play and leads us to the whole area of man's inheritance, including the arts, the myths of history, the slow march of philosophical thought and the mysteries of mathematics and of group management and of religion . . . it starts in the potential space between a child and the mother, when experience has produced in this child a high degree of confidence in the mother, that she will not fail to be there if suddenly needed" (Winnicott, 1986, p. 36). In the meantime, however, just to be sure and because mothers are fortunately not perfect, the child creates a transitional object, i.e., transitional or intermediate between me and not-me. "Of the transitional object it can be said that it is a matter of agreement between us and the baby that we will never ask the question: Did you conceive of this or was it presented to you from without? The question is not to be formulated" (Winnicott, 1958, pp. 239–240). Asking the question, of course, would mean utter destruction of value, either of the object or of the self. It would amount to a mother who prevents a child from playing, or enjoying fairy tales "because it isn't real." By not asking, i.e., by not making inside or outside into an either/or verdict, we give value to a third world, neither real nor unreal, a world of play, imagination, and creativity, in short, a world of culture. As the child becomes older, the reality principle is introduced in careful and complex manners, while at the same time the child is given back to the child. In that way it can tolerate the not-me by its creativity, i.e., the retention throughout life of something that belongs properly to infant experience: the ability to create the world, to make one's own not-me, to personalize reality, to be "at home" in the world. In short, to give it value.

The value of a civilization is a function of its ability to offer its members an opportunity for the creation of personal value. In our Western world this is not a static fact. There is a mutual influence of society and its members. A free civilization, an "open" society, is more dependent on its members than the other way round. In a closed society the situation is reversed. Its members are more dependent on the sociocultural environment than the other way round. The problem of Watergate, then, and of all other "-gates" for that matter, is typically a problem of open societies. As such it is a sign of hope. It is *not only* an integrity problem, it is also a result of the unmasking activities of our media. One example: Gary Hart's incipient campaign came to naught over one stupid "affair." Nobody mentioned President Kennedy's numerous escapades. His affairs were just not perceived by the media, because their attitude was different. It just was not news. Of course, this does not excuse Hart's misjudgment of the public interest, but it was a serious failure, rather than a "crime." Our open society also forces politicians into sham performances. Presidents now have to be actors, which incidentally might be preferable to actors being presidents. If the cloud of denial could be lifted, political history before the 1968 revolution would reveal the same, the difference being that nobody in power needed to be very careful. Now we all are witness, which increases our political awareness, maturity, independence, involvement, sense of ownership, and responsibility. Like anything of value, however, it has a price: the breakthrough of our defense of denial. If information threatens our well-being and sense of value in a sufficient degree, it has to be denied. Melvin Lasky (1985), that master critic, put it this way:

> This critical spirit [of our journalists] has become an increasingly relentless one. In the past it helped to open up windows in a fairly closed society. Is it, in its systematic devotion to airing every issue, blowing a wild wind into every nook and corner, still opening windows or smashing them? . . . As a result we have had throughout the 20th century in the democratic communities an unending cascade of devastating criticism. We know about the horrors of mounting crime; the dirt in hospitals; the child abuse in schools; the corruption of the police; the wastage of millions in the military establishment; bribery in high and low government places; the monstrous hypocrisy of Northern affluence in a world of Southern poverty; the swindles of financiers and the greed of doctors and lawyers; the miseries of prison life in our jails; the mugging in our parks and the gang warfare in our streets. And my point is that it is a wonder of our lives, almost a psychosocial miracle, that we can get up each day and survive yet another round of doom and despair. . . . We are justifiably proud of what has gone wrong. . . . But I have also come to the unhappy feeling that we in the West all too easily say, of course we are relentlessly critical—therefore ours is a healthy society—. Writers have made a fetish of "swimming against the tide," but there is also a danger of drowning. . . . As in certain doctor-patient relations, the result of careless and blunt truth telling does not reinforce the will to live but induces despair [pp. 75–76].

Lasky then reminds us of Lionel Trilling's statement that modern culture is "adversarial."

> Has there ever been, in all recorded history, a civilization whose culture was at odds with the values and ideals of that culture itself? All social forms and human arrangements must be unmasked; all myths demythologized; all politicians exposed and all present politics rejected. Our culture is adversary toward the ideals of its commercial, bourgeois civilization itself [p. 77].

So far this is Melvin Lasky criticizing the critics and our media culture. He then calls for a historic reconsideration and asks if there is not

> some virtue in a balanced overview which corrects the distortions of thousands of scraps of bad news. Neo-Nazis [he continues] are not always "on the march again" in Germany; and when a peaceful

> constitutional order stabilizes itself over three decades, as in the Bonn Republic, then it should be registered, even at the expense of ferreting out a group of young Bavarians wearing swastikas on their sleeves in a Munich suburb or digging up the graves of SS-men in a Bitburg cemetery. A few facts, sometimes even a great many are being confounded with the whole truth [p. 76].

He is, of course, right. There is a bombardment of selective information, which makes it sometimes difficult to give our pluriformity the value it deserves, because selective information produces selective valuing. In trying to understand this phenomenon interpretations have been offered: the 1968 revolution was a successful attempt of the "second" generation, which had only experienced the great war through the dramatizing and glorifying eyes of their parents, in order to have their own "drama," their own war, their own "underground culture," their own ideology. In the meantime, however, ideologies have been unmasked. Habermas (1971, 1973) described ideology as motivated false consciousness of social classes; Althusser (1976) characterized it as an unconsciously determined system of illusory representations of reality. It is indeed possible to relate the present "selective valuing" as signaled by Lasky, for instance, to an angry disappointment in the ideology of the 1960s, a furious nostalgia for the lost paradise of an imagination having the power to forbid all forbidding. In 1980 van der Leeuw advised us: "Contemporary society needs a renewal of social ideals. Testing out such ideals is part of the psychoanalyst's task in our time. To be able to live in the world of reality, it is necessary to find out whether you are motivated by an illusion or an attainable ideal" (p. 144). Moreover, is an attainable ideal really "ideal"?

According to these theories, then, our present culture is adrift because too many ideals have been found to be illusions. It is possible that nostalgia for lost illusions plays a role in the selective indignation of our media. There is an analogy, however, between an open society struggling for the balanced emancipation of its members and a regressed patient in advanced stages of his analysis. Analysts have revised their generally critical attitude toward regression. The ego is viewed more and more as an organization *encompassing* the irrational instead of replacing it. Enactment is telling a story nonverbally instead of "only" a stubborn defense (Loewald, 1981). This change in valuing also reflects a change in functioning of the analyst. An analyst functions by listening, feeling, containing, understanding, and interpreting. A regressed patient can endure, contain, and understand his many painful discoveries, i.e., changes in what he gives and does not give value, because his analyst can. The whole analytic process, then, can also be described as a process of change in valuing. Patients are only able to renounce their entitlement to a lost paradise of perfection because it is replaced by an increased meaning and mastery of his inner world.

A comparable process is going on in society. An analysand can expose and explore his inner world because of the safety created by his analyst's "holding," which enables him to tolerate the irrational storms evoked by free association. Our society can expose and explore its own world because of the safety of its democratic institutions and the independence of its media, a free press. Both are absolutely indispensable: democracy and a free press for society, just as much as "holding" and free association for analysis. And just as a patient experiences sequences of different selective valuing in his analysis, so is our Western world caught in storms of selective valuing on a parochial as well as on a global scale. Europeans are usually more critical of the United States than of the Soviet Union, not only because the organized mendacity—as Lester Kolakowsky calls it—of the Soviets gives them the privilege to be idealized, but also because America is more "our own," more "our—not us," more personalized. Any piece of selective information can be corrected by new information provided the press is really competent and independent. Lasky's criticism exactly criticized the critics. His tolerance for insight, his giving preferred value to information, gave our regressed patient the feeling that his inner world is full of contradictions, conflicts, emotions, perceptual distortions, childishness, and so on—in short, a hardly bearable compilation of imperfections. For an analyst this is a sign of hope. Correspondingly the stream of uncovering information in our society could be a sign of hope, even though it puts our capacity to bear disillusion to a severe test. That, however, could be the price we pay to imbue pluriformity with the value it deserves, the value of maturity. It could be, but is it really? Or rather, is it only a sign of hope?

Before I go into that question I first want to give an example of a not yet mentioned plague: the hooligan culture. I am drawing on an essay by Jeffrey Richards (1985), published in the same issue of *Encounter* as Melvin Lasky's critique. It concerns British hooligans, but they are probably not very different from Dutch hooligans. Hooligans tend to be well dressed and employed, some of them even with such ordinary burdens as mortgages. They are well organized and, outside the stadium, not affected by excessive drinking. They are not notable for being socially deprived; only a minority of them is unemployed. They spend the week planning the campaign for the weekend match. The aim is to ambush the hooligans of the opposing team and engage them in battle. If it cannot be done at the football field because of police intervention, it will be done somewhere else. They fight "because fighting is human nature. Tribal ain't it," said one of them. To a certain extent they are interracial. Although there may be serious tensions between blacks and whites, they willingly come together for the greater cause of common hooliganism. "I loved me parents," one black youth confessed, "but West-Ham became like a family." In Holland the hooligans of four major cities made a pact to bury their hatchet temporarily for the bigger cause of a forthcoming match between Holland and England. A nearly spotlessly typed "declaration of war" announced that they should unite to fight the common enemy, British football fans.

Romanticizing this into a continuing Westside story is sympathetic but of course very dangerous. What this conduct amounts to is a form of crowd savagery and irrational mob violence not so different from that of the fascist mobs in prewar Germany or the lynch parties in the old South. Hooliganism, fascism—or those religious mafia called fundamentalists—have in common a psychotic defense against unbearable anxieties concerning estrangement, abandonment, loss of intimacy, and loss of structure. Aston Villa's hymn of hate is illuminating: "We hate Nottingham Forest, we hate Albion too, we hate Birmingham City, but Villa we love you."

There is, however, also a big difference. If hooliganism is a substitute for "fascist movement" or even war, it is perhaps not such a bad substitute, with which I am not defending hooliganism but our open society exposing it. Thanks to that open society, our media and the unmasking—could we say Freudian?—nature of our culture, fascist movements are exposed immediately. Since the war they all disintegrated sooner or later after their inception. The "Revolt of the Hordes" has been canceled. In our Western world masses have crumbled into many small crowds (van Doorn, 1988). This value of what hooliganism is not, i.e., fascism, must not blind us, however, to what it is: a desperate cry for intimacy and belonging, for value really. But calling it a psychotic defense is too easy.

Now a look at what we have got. Good parenting implies giving back the child to the child by valuing and protecting his intermediate, transitional area, his play, his imagination. For adults this intermediate playground is culture. A good civilization offers its members an opportunity to create value through culture. The value of a good civilization is a measure of giving its members this opportunity. To judge the value of our civilization, then, is to put the question: After having destroyed so many existing social ideals, what value have our open societies left for us to create?

The uncovering potential of our culture has unmasked all ideologies as illusory and dangerous, as "false consciousness" and "illusory representations of reality," in short, as false narcissistic systems of thought and as an excuse for aggression. It left us to make, not another ideology, but what Raymond Aron has called an *ideothèque*, a kind of library of ideas about the world, a set of principles, a particular philosophy of life (Grunberger, 1987). It enabled us to incorporate in our ideals the nonideal, the good enough which is always better than the perfect. It changed, moreover, our emotional housekeeping from socially commanding to negotiating, thereby strictly limiting the satisfaction of our aggressive impulses. This has resulted in a culture of reasonableness (not reason).

Since the decline of our last ideology, that of the 1960s, there has not been a decrease in permissiveness but an increase in tolerance. Permissiveness delivers freedom by indifference, in the end leading to the transmission of irreality and chaos. During the 1968 revolution and for quite some time thereafter, permissiveness was an ideology, a command. This ideology paraded as tolerant but was not. It was simply not permitted to be nonpermissive. In preaching permissiveness the New Left was extremely intolerant. Tolerance, on the other hand, breeds freedom by concern, transmitting a reality both bearable and reasonable. In a tolerant society, what is bearable and what is reasonable at a given time can only be decided by its members and only when they are maximally informed, i.e., when there is complete and independent news gathering. In short, it is democratic and has independent media.

There has been a change in the content of that part of our culture which has its roots in the French revolution. The tensions between liberty, equality, and brotherhood have been tried out by reality resulting in a far-reaching integration. Liberals have discovered the devouring greed of free enterprise, Democratic Socialism has become "organized liberalism," as a prominent Dutch socialist party ideologue has recently called it, and Christian Democrats finally have discovered that brotherhood also includes the story of Cain and Abel, of which the last can be considered the first victim of inequality. All this is the result of increased openness and of the de-ideologizing process. It is a very fine collection of values indeed: reasonableness, democratic openness, tolerance, together with their derivatives of emancipation of women, minorities, and so on. It looks too good to be true. And it is.

We have, of course, the threats of nuclear war and environmental disaster and the very serious consequences of massive unemployment. In principle, however, these problems have technical solutions attainable by negotiations. There is, however, a much more serious problem: our loss of past and future while drowning in the present.

In Freud's time man escaped from his drives by taking refuge in a Victorian world. Now the situation seems reversed: man escapes from the world by taking refuge in his drives and narcissism. One example out of many, many others: the upsurge of film titles including the word *dirty* in an admiring sense: *The Dirty*

Dozen, Dirty Harry, Play Dirty, Dirty Dingus Magee, Dirty Little Billy, and the latest, *Dirty Dancing*—a triumph over the superego (Rangell, 1982). As argued before, narcissism is value perverted by rape. The rape by technological thinking, seeing processes only as a totally controllable pattern of cause and effect without any historicity. "World" has changed into objective reality *pur sang,* into pure matter, while man himself wanes into being an official functionary of his own subjectivity, a bureaucratic robot of his own destiny, a nonperson having mechanized even his own hate. I do not attack technology. That would be as nonsensical as wanting to abolish the bicycle. I only criticize the use our culture makes of it. Our civilization, then, has created a degree of rationality, affectlessness, and indifference, so devoid of concrete and parochial *Menschlichkeit* that it has turned around on our culture itself, which has become a form of madness. Again, one example out of many others: calling on our medical services often entails being split-up into many separate functions, attended to by many expert connoisseurs each passionately exploring their own square inch and disregarding the person as a whole.

Man's society treats him as a depersonalized set of functions, a sum of fragments. At the same time while sitting before the tube he is expected to personalize the whole world which tumbles daily on a global scale into his living room. His potential space has been stretched over the globe, while his ego's "substance" has become thinner and thinner. When an ego creates the world, this includes the creation of limits, but in this expanded universe every limit produces envy and the feeling of not belonging. Expansion in breadth, moreover, occurs at the expense of depth, of the value of the past, of our roots. This depth is likewise fragmented when we put away our babies in crèches and our parents in nursing homes, cutting off roots as well as branches. The child and its family, the cornerstone of *every* civilization, are really our seriously discriminated against minorities now. There always has to be a strong connection with the matrix of childhood. In the words of Eagle (1984),

> The adult who has become capable of a true universal spirit was once an infant embedded in a biological-affective libidinal matrix of a quality unique to him—parochial in its very essence. If his

> universalism is truly human, it will have emerged organically from this early matrix and will, in very subtle ways, reflect its early roots and ties. The relationship between mother and child is always concrete and parochial and so is, I believe, any human relationship between man and man. Any universalism which overlooks this fact has permitted ideology to dominate flesh and bone and usually leads to the treatment of man as an object and his subjection as a means to an end [p. 212].

And as Winnicott (1986) has worded it, "The most valuable support (of democratic tendency) is given in a negative way by organized non-interference with the ordinary good mother-infant relationship, and with the ordinary good home" (p. 251). "There is special significance in the devotion of the ordinary good mother to her infant, the capacity for eventual emotional maturity being founded as a result of the devotion. Mass interference at this point, in a society, would quickly and effectually lessen the democratic potential of that society, just as it would diminish the richness of its culture" (p. 259). Flaubert has put it into one sentence: *le bon Dieu est dans le détail*.

We do need the past, then, for the value of the present. Past-present-future form in health a coherent continuum, personalized, owned, appropriated. It is "our" life. Owning the past is indispensable for a sense of identity, wholeness, integrity. As important as the past is for the value of our present, so vital is the present, being our future past, for the value of our future. Destruction of the past, which is tradition and memory, is destruction of the future. Our technology cannot do with time what it can do with space, i.e., to promise unlimited movement, because time is irreversible. Every memory is an irretrievably lost perception, every move in time is approaching death. One way not to feel the pain of that loss is to ridicule the past as worthless, queer, and trivial. When our past and consequently our future are destroyed, only a timeless "immortality" remains in the compulsive immediacy of instant satisfactions. Nonacceptance of limits implies defective separation, impaired individuation, and ego damage.

The ego, then, is imprisoned in a crushing catch. Our culture demands of its participants that they personalize a tremendously expanded world without allowing ideologies with their escape into clear-cut causes. At the same time, however, modern civilization depersonalizes its members by affectless rationality and fragmentation, both of potential space and of personal roots. Our culture demands affect and returns indifference, demonstrating an uncanny resemblance with bad parenting. Both inflated by TV in its global, its universal, aspect, and fragmented by bureaucracy in its parochial, its homely, aspect, potential space has lost transitional quality by a collective double bind. If a culture has no concern for its participating individuals, they in turn can have no concern for their own culture. All this sounds like a sermon—and it is.

CONCLUSION

Making and giving value are the core of any ego and a function of having received value, first by our parents, later by our culture. In our civilization, the lost child and his family need be given back to both adult and child in order to be saved from the present and its overwhelming immediacy. For this Freud's work is indispensable, especially what I would call the Cassandra function of psychoanalysis. Cassandra, Priamus' daughter, was convicted to a very special hell: always to tell the truth and never be believed. An ultimate priority of sincerity, not succumbing to the wish to be believed, is an ultimate test of one's integrity (Rangell, 1974). When truths of drive *and* trauma (Grubrich-Simitis, 1988) are too often disbelieved, a child is robbed of value and splits his self into true and false. If he cannot receive value by telling the truth, he has to do so by compliance. Belonging to a false self, however, this value is false value.

Freud has redeemed Cassandra by willingly not disbelieving her, which calls for our protection and concern. Then, as the poet Lucebert remarked, all things of value are defenseless.

REFERENCES

Albrecht Schwaber, E. (1986), Reconstruction and perceptual experience: Further thoughts on psychoanalytic listening. *J. Amer. Psychoanal. Assn.*, 34:911–933.

Althusser, L. (1976), *Positions*. Paris: Editions Sociales.
Balint, M. (1937), Early developmental states of the ego. In: *Primary Love and Psychoanalytic Technique*. New York: Liveright, 1965.
Basch, M. F. (1983), Affect and the analyst. *Psychoanal. Inq.*, 3:691–703.
Coultre, R. le (1967), Splijting van het Ik als centraal neuroseverschijnsel. In: *Hedendaagse Hoofdstukken uit de Psychoanalyse*. Arnhem: Van Loghum Slaterus.
Eagle, M. N. (1982), Essay review of "Object and self: A developmental approach." *Rev. Psychoanalytic Books*.
——— (1984), *Recent Developments in Psychoanalysis: A Critical Evaluation*. New York: McGraw-Hill.
Eissler, K. R. (1965), *Medical Orthodoxy and the Future of Psychoanalysis*. New York: International Universities Press.
Grubrich-Simitis, I. (1988), Trauma or drive—drive and trauma. *The Psychoanalytic Study of the Child*, 43:3–35. New Haven, CT: Yale University Press.
Grunberger, B. (1987), Discussion remark on p. 93 in *Maintenance of the Psychoanalytic Identity and Functioning in a World of Flux*. I.P.A. Monogr. 6, ed. J. Chasseguet-Smirgel.
Habermas, J. (1971), *Knowledge and Human Interests*. Boston: Beacon Press.
——— (1973), *Theory and Practice*. Boston: Beacon Press.
Hartmann, H. (1960), *Psychoanalysis and Moral Values*. New York: International Universities Press.
Kohut, H. (1977), *The Restoration of the Self*. New York: International Universities Press.
Lampl-de Groot, J. (1985), *Collected Papers of Jeanne Lampl-de Groot*. New York: International Universities Press.
Lasky, M. (1985), Towards a theory of journalistic malpractice. *Encounter*, 65:74–78.
Leupold Löwenthal, H. (1980), Psychoanalysis and friendship. In: *Psychoanalytici aan het Woord*. Deventer: van Loghum Slaterus.
Loewald, H. W. (1960), On the therapeutic action of psychoanalysis. *Internat. J. Psycho-Anal.*, 41:16–33.
——— (1981), Regression: Some general considerations. *Psychoanal. Quart.*, 50:22–43.
Rangell, L. (1969), Choice-conflict and the decision-making function of the ego: A psychoanalytic contribution to decision theory. *Internat. J. Psycho-Anal.*, 50:599–602.
——— (1971), The decision-making process: A contribution from psychoanalysis. *The Psychoanalytic Study of the Child*, 26:425–452.
——— (1974), A psychoanalytic perspective leading currently to the

syndrome of the compromise of integrity. *Internat. J. Psycho-Anal.*, 55:3–12.
——— (1976), Lessons from Watergate: A derivative for psychoanalysis. *Psychoanal. Quart.*, 45:37–61.
——— (1980), *The Mind of Watergate: An Exploration of the Compromise of Integrity*. New York: Norton.
——— (1982), The self in psychoanalytic theory. *J. Amer. Psychoanal. Assn.*, 39:863–892.
Richards, J. (1985), The Hooligan culture: Violence and the ethic of the undermass. *Encounter*, 65(4):15–23.
Sandler, J. (1976), Countertransference and role-responsiveness. *Internat. Rev. Psychoanal.*, 3:43–47.
Stechler, G., & Halton, A. (1987), The emergence of assertion and aggression during infancy: A psychoanalytic systems approach. *J. Amer. Psychoanal. Assn.*, 35:821–838.
Trilling, L. (1955), *Freud and the Crisis of Our Culture*. Boston: Beacon Press.
van der Leeuw, P. J. (1969), On Freud's theory formation. *Internat. J. Psycho-Anal.*, 50:573–581.
——— (1980), 'Modern times' and the psychoanalyst today. *Internat. Rev. Psychoanal.*, 7:137–145.
van Doorn, J. A. A. (1988), De opstand der horden is afgelast. *N.R.C.-Handelsblad*, Nov. 2.
Winnicott, D. W. (1958), *Through Paediatrics to Psychoanalysis*. London: Hogarth Press.
——— (1965), *The Maturational Processes and the Facilitating Environment*. London: Hogarth Press.
——— (1986), *Home Is Where We Start From*. Hammondsworth, UK: Penguin.

22

PRECOCIOUS ASPECTS OF THE FORMATION OF MORALITY

SERGE LEBOVICI, M.D.

This respectable woman is a doctor. Her husband has a religious occupation. One day she relates that she has just been summoned by the police because one of her prescriptions had been found on the corpse of a young man. The deceased had been romantically involved with her daughter, who had had a child by him, but had left him. My patient nevertheless remained in contact with the boyfriend; he had had a car accident of an evidently suicidal nature, and subsequently suffered cranial trauma requiring regular dosages of antiepileptic medication. She sent him prescriptions, however, without seeing him. Now she feels guilty because she had not wanted to receive his calls when he requested a new prescription.

She does not insist on this subject and tells me that she feels ashamed of the demands of her little ego. The previous night she had had to host her daughter, whose boyfriend was the deceased. My patient had anticipated letting her daughter take her bedroom, which she conveyed to her husband when asked how she had resolved the problem of accommodations. The husband then followed with the question, "And you, where will you sleep?" She replied, "With you," meaning in the conjugal bed, which had been abandoned several years prior. My patient then sensed her husband's mockery: she left no doubt about the annoyance and disgust that this arrangement stirred in him.

She wondered how she could dare to admit to me that her

"little ego" was preoccupied with such frivolities in face of the distress caused by the death and her possible responsibility in its occurrence.

This brief clinical report has apologic and allegorical value regarding the compared effects of guilt and shame. The patient spoke eloquently about her little ego, which, more precocious and archaic, quietly allowed its demands to be understood, but in so doing aggravated the guilt that the lack of demands by her superego and ego ideal aroused.

Otherwise stated, shame precedes and reinforces guilt. This chapter will attempt to demonstrate and examine the clinical experiment of the psychoanalyst researching the archaic and precocious bases of moral demands. It will accord only cursory treatment to the most well-known aspects of this question, which primarily concerns the origins and functioning of the superego, as set forth by Freud while elaborating his topic descriptions.

MORAL DEMANDS ACCORDING TO FREUD

In Freud's writings the issue of censorship, which is predominantly social, takes precedence, as argued in *The Interpretation of Dreams* (1900). Noteworthy is the outline of chapter 7, which addresses the first topic and places the censorship barriers between the preconscious system and the perception-consciousness system. Repressed desires are described as the product of the derivative of the unconscious, aroused by internal or external stimulation, but passing through the channel of thoughts turned latent in the preconscious system, and of which censorship demands figurability.

In other words, the repressed desires of childhood are only expressed if they revolve around educative, social, and cultural exigencies. It is only when repression represents the essential and very potent agent of the anti-impulse struggle and of counterinvestment that morality becomes an issue of mental functioning, relatively independent of parental reality. For it is their images that cause morality to be respected, since they reign by terror.

This evolution, which governed the history of psychoanalysis, henceforth stressed the imaginary and the fantastic.

Morality was then seen as projections onto exterior reality after tremendous repressive effort. Subsequently, Freud integrated the theoretical advances of Abraham on cannibalism and incorporation as well as Ferenci's work on oral sadism, the avatars of introjection at the edges of the ego. Thus he linked the demands of morality and respect with the anxiety of loosing the love of the object. In other words, respecting the demands of the object of love consisted in avoiding the risk of finding oneself confronted by its loss and in not knowing the condition of the melancholic, in whom the shadow of the lost object invaded the ego (Freud, 1914). It is worth noting that Freud was soon to describe the superego. The same rule would be applied: the shadow of the superego invades the ego.

This reorientation of Freudian theory, which went from the description of the demands of parental reality to that of the rigors of their internal representations, spanned a few years.

This evolution transformed punitive threats made by the parents into those of internal reality. It did not prevent recommending the avoidance of castration threats, in particular vis-à-vis masturbation. It was then hoped that a real prophylaxis of neurosis would be achieved, by recommending that parents be less severe and avoid making such threats (Bonaparte, 1930). The experiment showed the failure of these educative methods, even though they were still popularized after World War II.

Nonetheless it had to be recognized that infantile sexuality was of a perverse nature (Freud, 1905) and that the evolution of the Oedipus complex was structural. This point of view is beyond the scope of this chapter. For our purpose it suffices to note that the desire of the object results from its deprivation and that it is the fruit of the reactivation of the traces of experiences associated with the satisfaction of needs. It is hominized, meaning quickly independent of its chronobiology. It is perverse because it uses mental representations to its liking.

The appearance of defense mechanisms in the wake of efforts of counterinvestment and of the organization of reaction formations, and subsequently the immense effort of repression opportunely reintroduces educative demands of parents and *the effects of what would be described as the superego*. Thus a certain homeostasis would be maintained or reestablished between libidinal demands and both those of society and parents on the one hand and of the superego on the other (A. Freud, 1936).

The structure of conflictual mechanisms that preside at the evolution of the Oedipus complex thus depends less on each individual history than on structural mechanisms. Freud (1913) would present it as the phylogenetic heritage of murder of the father of the primitive horde. Today one would attempt to inscribe these rules in the necessities of interfamilial exchange which define all familial classifications. This concerns the incest prohibition and the prescription of the exogamy obligation (Levi-Strauss, 1949).

Elsewhere the focus of the debate is on genetic programs, such as among primatologists who observe the prohibition of incest among the simian hordes. Whatever the case, the establishent of infantile neurosis, model of the transference neurosis (Lebovici, 1980), prompted Freud to demonstrate how one could consider it as the negative of partially polymorphic impulses. This notion stems from the photographic technique and reflects the fact that on a negative the darks are light. The analogy is that the psychoanalyst works on the negative of the negative and that he resurrects desires recurrent in their intentionality (sadism is expressed in the form of masochism) and in their meaning (violence against the object boomerangs back to the "I").

This very schematic recapitulation of Freudian theory allows me to make several comments:

1. The causes of guilt that affect oedipal desires of infantile sexuality are not only their prescribed prohibition, but also their ambivalence and deadly violence, sustained by what one will later call their pregenitality. In this context it is important to recall the significance attached by Freud to the control of impulse (*Bemächtigungtrieb*). Impulse is characterized by the will to seize the object cruelly and without remorse.

2. In the Freudian description of pregenital moments of childhood sexuality, sacrifice of desire and control of impulse were considered as the means of assuring oneself of the persistence of parental love. This struggle against violence may be considered

as a prelude to the internalization of moral rules. It is also the basis of the renunciation of ano-urethral freedom, which justifies the model of the sphincteral rudiments of morality.

3. Morality and cleanliness are thus linked: the cultural bases of the establishment of moral rules can be traced here. Daily life shows that mothers, when they want to forbid, often say, "Don't touch, it's dirty."

4. The violence of condemned desires can be imagined, fantasized, or projected, but the child can always tell himself that his imagination is unattainable. Oedipal and secondary identification is delayed. The child feels impotent before the power of his father whom he admires, and can tell himself that he will postpone his parricidal exploits: his shame protects him from guilt.

5. Prior to the formulation of the second Freudian topic, which dealt with the instance of the superego, idealization of the loved, yet hated, object dictated that the narcissistic investment of the object—deployed with autoerotic and primary narcissistic activities—conduce to the merging of self-esteem and object idealization. Put differently, in the examination of the precocious foundations of moral establishment, the vicissitudes of narcissistic investments cannot be overlooked.

THE DEATH IMPULSE AND THE SUPEREGO

It may be recalled that structural links were a unifying theme in Freud's (1921) analysis of mental functioning "beyond the pleasure principle," and that he linked the death impulse and the harshness of the superego. Now the role of parents in early child development were played down even more. The demands of the superego were deemed to be on a par with deep-seated masochism; based on the view of the paternal superego as the projection of this savagery on its representation, it was concluded that the real dimension of aggression was masochism (or submission to the superego). An example of this was the fantasy described by Freud (1919) as "a child is being beaten."

Another way of situating the birth of sexual desire and its attendant guilt would stem from the premise that the hallucination of pleasure cannot quantitatively compensate for the loss of the object. The child must learn to temporalize his desire and hallucinatory satisfaction. He has then to exercise his violence against the self and to transform his intrinsic masochism, which is a conversion of his aggressive impulses into erogenous and sexualized masochism (Rosenberg, 1982). When Freud (1924) wrote that "masochism is the protector of life," he affirmed that the child can feel himself continuing to exist only by the painful restrictions that he imposes on himself.

Freud's use of these theoretical-clinical references attest to the structural depth of his argument. That he was able to fathom as he did was not without having borrowed from the psychoanalytic work of the narrowest circle of his disciples. Likewise, mention must be made here in the post-Freudian contributions to the establishment of these themes. My discussion will take a critical approach.

POST-FREUDIAN WORKS

The theoretical movement, which has removed Freud from the reconstructive positions concerning the lifting of infantile amnesia in psychoanalytic practice, was largely followed by the Kleinian and post-Kleinian school. Freud, in describing the rigor of the superego as the product of the projective figuration of death and/or aggressive impulses, was inevitably led to propose the existence of two simultaneous and contradictory states of the ego: at birth, the child wanted to incorporate, introject his good experiences, which conformed to the demands of hallucinated pleasure. But at the boundaries of the ego, he projects his aggressive parts onto the outside world. External reality is bad and made of the bad part of the ego which is thus split, whereas this undesirable part is denied. Melanie Klein, in defining projective identification as a projection of the bad—formerly aggressively desirous—into the internal object describes the splitting of the object and sees in this universal mechanism the roots of a primitive morality. The splitting of the object reproduces the opposition of life and death instincts, of love and hate, of the desired, cannibalized, and envied object and of the rejected, torn despised object. This struggle is, according to her, the basis of precocious schizoparanoid positions, a time of projective identification, and of reparative desires of the total object, toward its established permanence as well as the depressive position.

Post-Kleinian authors were to stress these metaphoric descriptions, as exemplified by D. Metzer's attempts to show that the "aesthetic dance" of the fetus ceases when it finds itself narrowly lodged in its prison, the uterine "claustrum," and that delivery leads it to confront the rigors of a breast which dislodges and rends the mouth with its cutting nipple. Previously, Bion had described the "mother's capacity for reverie," and had endeavored to describe how the mother could or could not "detoxicate," by her reveries, what he called this anxiety of the baby's death.

It is of course impossible to consider these allegorical versions of the first relational moments as scientific accounts of development. Yet, their metaphoric power appears very usable for empathizing with the wild excesses of certain autistic children who are incapable of renouncing their aggressive or self-sensory and/or self-mutilating behavior.

Winnicott has always focused on the confines of fantasy construction and the reality of experience. Specifically, he describes the rage of the sated child, which he sees as the source of the child's concern, as well as of his depressive condition which leads him to separate himself from his mother and to organize his continuity of experience of life. This he terms the "self." Thus the baby can, according to Winnicott, organize a zone of experience that is neither self nor mother, a zone of illusion and of culture as well as of play, unless an overindulgent mother obligates the child to engage exclusively in making amends to her by dissimulating the cries of his "self, behind the perfect conduct of his pseudo-self." This is what Alice Miller (1979) terms "the drama of the talented child."

For his part, Spitz (1965) had described the third of his proposed organizers as a preliminary of moral injunctions with which the baby identifies during the beginning of his second year. It is then that he imitates by nodding movements the interdictions posed by the mother. This does not involve identification with the aggressor, but rather identification with the frustrating and forbidding agent. According to Spitz, by taking on the maternal gesture, the child regressively reactivates the initial experience of "rooting" of the head along the lines of burrowing behavior, such as the baby effects since birth.

Many additional references could be cited of post-Freudian works on the genesis of forbidding behavior. However, my purposes here have been rather to demonstrate a double, seemingly contradictory, evolution. I have recounted how Freud apparently distanced himself from event-oriented narrative in favor of structural accounts of the genesis of moral behavior. The moral behavior to which he referred caused the individual to repudiate his impulsive violence, which is associated with the preoedipal period of his destiny. For their part, Kleinian writers are attached to the description of pregenital oedipal organization, thus of the existence of a precocious, rigid, and cruel superego. The post-Freudian authors cited above have been concerned with the reconstruction of the very early stages of the infant's mental life. Interested in this perspective, they have attempted to show the genesis of the infant's submissive behavior toward his parents. The following discussion will attempt to show how the psychoanalytic study of first interactions provides another approach to the understanding of the genesis of submission among very young children to the demands of morality.

CONTRIBUTION BASED ON THE STUDY OF EARLY INTERACTIONS

The importance placed on the superego in the second topic leads students of Freud to assume that psychoanalysis regards it as the sole basis of morality. The forbidding and idealized role of the father in the central development of the child reinforces this conviction. In France, owing to the legacy of Lacan, it is taken for granted that "the Law of the Father" is included in the debate. Yet, on the other hand, this oedipal reference leaves somewhat ambiguous the description of the oedipal superego of the daughter who logically should be maternal, but who also remains paternal.

Moreover, one must not forget the literature linking anxiety to loss; this has been previously alluded to above. Here we must recall that the threat of loss leads the child—and the adult—to control the demands of his desires. This is another way of examining the demands of moral conduct, meant here to preserve the object of investment and his love. This conception is at the heart of Freudian theory, as expressed in *Inhibition, Symptoms and Anxiety* (Freud, 1926). It will be recalled that the thesis presented in this work is that uncontrolled excitation and the aggression which sustains it are the source of anxiety, which now appeared as a warning signal of the danger described in its increasingly regressive patterns, i.e., a threat of castration, of the loss of the object's love, and of the loss of the object itself. This leads one to relocate the demand of self-control at the origins of what may be called morality and its mental expressions, themselves intended to avoid separation and the anxiety which its fear causes in the infant from the moment he is aware of the maternal object's continuity of existence.

This last theory of Freud regarding the nature of anxiety naturally leads us to focus on the dawn of life and to attempt to use contemporary works concerning first interactions to give meaning to the infant's initial attempts at control while in his mother's arms. This serves to link attachment and loss in the rudiments of psychic life observed in the interactive mode.

From this point of view, psychoanalysts must at least concede that infant attachment behavior is constantly interpreted by the mother by virtue of what we have proposed to call "her creative anticipation," which includes her unconscious psychic life, her desires, and eventual condemnation of them. Maternal care is not stripped of ambivalence, as daily experience shows. Our point of reference here is not abusive mothers, but rather those who are impatient and aggressive in intent, sustained by their potential for hate. It suffices to observe a woman washing her baby and pleasantly insulting its dirtiness. The term *pig* is attenuated by the fact that the mother calls her baby "little pig" and that she modulates her tone, thus adding to the pleasure manifested by the baby.

The violence projected onto the father who represents the superego thus transfers the maternal violence which Freud seldom addresses. Numerous works have observed this, trying with varying degrees of success to find reasons in Freud's personal past. Bergeret (1987) remarks, like many others, that Freud, during his only encounter with Little Hans, proposed to him a central interpretation of his phobia, which he linked to his father. He told the child that he "knew that one day a Little Hans would be born who would be afraid of his father, because he would want to have his mother for himself." This prophetic and efficacious interpretation was based on the following: on the one hand, on the intuitive resemblance proven by Freud between the image of the horse of the phobia and the face of the father who sported a beard and glasses; on the other hand, on the theory of the oedipal bases of the superego which condemned the aggressive wishes of the little boy. Nonetheless, Freud knew, if only by reading Little Hans's journal which his parents kept daily, that his mother had not ceased to harrass her son and to threaten him in the event of his continued "foolishness." Bergeret also recalls that Freud no doubt knew more about the young woman who had been his analysand and suggests what he described as a preconflictual "fundamental violence" which the child encounters, according to him, in maternal care.

One hypothesis of this genre is still endorsed by Laplanche in his description of the mother. He introduces his own translation of the nonindicative excitation of the baby in the face of seductive maternal care. This he proposes to call "enigmatic indications" of the traducing mother. Representing culture and the outside world here, the mother plays a role that is both violent and seductive. This thesis permits Laplanche to propose a radical modification of psychoanalytic theory; he feels that object investment can no longer be described through the libido; rather, he advocates speaking in terms of the object as the "source of impulsive life," largely infused with psychic significance.

For my part (Lebovici, 1983), in describing fantasy interactions, I believe I made a certain contribution to the understanding of the role of parents, concerning their parenting functions, in transmitting values, in the transgenerational mode (Lebovici, 1988). It is sufficient to keep in mind that I propose to describe a child as three children in their mother's arms:

(1) The one she is carrying.

(2) The imaginary child representing her desire for pregnancy; representing her thoughts rendered latent, preconscious; representing what she no doubt saw on the echographic screen and which she and the male procreator have named—in sum, the one that she has already come to know during pregnancy. The richness of fetal sensorality which reinforces the preexisting power of this imaginary child is well appeciated.

(3) The fantasy child, who is the product of oedipal wishes of giving a child to his maternal grandfather, the desire of which is thus affected by guilt vis-à-vis the two future grandparents. The mother's ancient desire for maternity leads her to find in her baby the support of paternal transference, engendering a debt of life (Bydlowski, 1988) with regard to the maternal grandmother.

The immense seductive power exerted by the infant on his mother must also not be overlooked. He gives her satisfaction and has the power to make her a real mother. From this perspective, it must be underscored that interactive exchanges are remarkably synchronized. They are charged with affectations, as shown in vocal and tonal mimicry exchanges. The two protagonists swim in a bath of affects which are attuned (Stern, 1985). The affects, initiated by the baby, are "in hunger" of representations (Pinot-Douriez, 1984).

This dyad, including its reality and the unconscious of the procreator mother, is equally vulnerable to everything that could depress one or the other of its protagonists. Discomfort or illness on the part of the baby depresses the mother, of course more so when the baby suffers an infirmity. The mother's depression prevents her from adequately interacting with the affective demands of her baby, who is incapable of proclaiming her as mother due to the impoverishment of the interactive exchanges.

On the other hand, certain events may affect maternal capacities, such as deaths and funerals, secrets which the baby bears because he is marked, as evidenced by the intergenerational transmission. In the research in progress, which concerns the study of interactions between the mother and her baby when the latter is born after the sudden and unexpected death of a prior baby, a recurrent phenomenon is that the future of the "replacement" child is affected by the guilt released by the young woman in the light of the preceding child. She had not watched over him during the night when the death occurred because she had gone out for amusement. She had had an abortion in preceding years. Of course, these events would not have weighed upon her mental life had the drama not occurred. These observations confirm the Freudian theory concerning the need to refer to the theory of the aftermath in order to enlist them in the context of their epigenetic value. In any case, it is thus that the past life of parents helps feed the child's guilt feelings.

These factors constitute a fairly composite whole, consisting in reconstructions and constructions while also in the results of psychoanalytic observation of the early interactions between mother and newborn. The weight of early life is certainly discernible in behavior and affects, in representations and thought, and in fantasies that imply, through violence and seduction, the weight of archaic patterns of guilt, of anxiety, and of loss and separation. All of these factors, I believe, contribute in regulating behavior and in preparing for acceptance of postoedipal secondary identification which give the superego its efficiency.

MORALITY AND GUILT

That moral behavior expresses our feelings of guilt cannot be doubted. However, the superego is also the vehicle of our moral masochism, quickly eroticized or annexed to our erogenous masochism, as shown above. Consequently, the weight of the superego and its precursors risks resulting in diverse forms of depression. The loss of love exercises its effects very precociously. But when it is justified by the weight of experienced events or by the organization of the mental life of the mother, it stresses moral masochism and becomes a source of acting—acting against its body or against others—as if the adult had thus to pay the consequences of being represented in the guilt and punitive mental life of its mother.

These considerations are no doubt added to those that psychoanalysts develop concerning unconscious feelings of guilt and their role. In any case they contribute to Leo Rangell's (1974) work, which shows the heavy consequences of the individual and collective range of what he called the "compromise of integrity."

SUMMARY

Freud's work, which concludes with the description of the structural theory and the superego, is preceded by a long discussion linking guilt with existence and the development of infantile sexuality. This body of work aims to grasp the first moment in the interactive exchanges of the infant and his parents, in particular the mother. Exchanges of violence and seduction indicate to the baby his powers as well as their limits, which are called in the interior life of the child and the adult fear of separation and loss. On the other hand, the link between moral masochism and erogenous masochism can explain acting which goes against individual and collective morality. In these cases shame can protect against the effects of guilt.

REFERENCES

Bergeret, J. (1987), *Le Petit Hans et la Réalité*. Paris: Presses Universitaires de France.

Bonaparte, M. (1930), La prophylaxie infantile des névroses. *Rev. Franc. Psychanal.*, 31:85–135.

Bydlowski, M. (1989), *Dettes de Vie*. Paris: Presses Universitaires de France.

Freud, A. (1936), *The Ego and the Mechanisms of Defense*. New York: International Universities Press, 1946.

Freud, S. (1900), The Interpretation of Dreams. *Standard Edition*, 4 & 5. London: Hogarth Press, 1953.

——— (1905), Three essays on the theory of sexuality. *Standard Edition*, 7:125–243. London: Hogarth Press, 1953.

——— (1913), Totem and Taboo. *Standard Edition*, 13:1–162. London: Hogarth Press, 1955.

——— (1914), Instincts and their vicissitudes. *Standard Edition*, 14:109–140. London: Hogarth Press, 1952.

——— (1919), 'A child is being beaten.' *Standard Edition*, 17:175–204. London: Hogarth Press, 1955.

——— (1921), Beyond the pleasure principle. *Standard Edition*, 18:3–64. London: Hogarth Press, 1955.

——— (1924), The economic problem of masochism. *Standard Edition*, 19:157–170. London: Hogarth Press, 1961.

——— (1926), Inhibitions, symptoms and anxiety. *Standard Edition*, 20:77–175. London: Hogarth Press, 1959.

Lebovici, S. (1980), Névrose infantile, névrose de transfert. *Rev. Franc. Psychanal.*, 44:733–857.

——— (1983), *Le Nourrison, la Mère at la Psychanalyste*. Paris: Le Centurion.

——— (1988), Fantasmatic interactions and intergenerational transmission. *Infant Mental Health J.*, 6(1):10–19.

Levi-Strauss, C. (1949), *Les Structures Élémentaires de la Parenté*. Paris: Presses Universitaires de France.

Miller, A. (1979), *Le Drame de l'Enfant Doué*. Paris: Presses Universitaires de France, 1983.

Pinot-Douriez, M. (1984), *Bébé Agi, Bébé Actif*. Paris: Presses Universitaires de France.

Rangell, L. (1974), A psychoanalytic perspective leading currently to the syndrome of the compromise of integrity. *Internat. J. Psycho-Anal.*, 55:3–12.

Rosenberg, B. (1982), Masochisme mortifié et masochisme gardien de la vie. *Les Cahiers du XIII*[e], 5:41–97.

Spitz, R. A. (1965), *The First Year of Life*. New York: International Universities Press.

Stern, D. (1985), Affect attunement. In: *Frontiers of Infant Psychiatry*, ed. J. Call, E. Galenson, & R. Tyson. New York: Basic Books.

23

AGGRESSION, SEXUALITY, AND THE DEATH INSTINCT

ADAM LIMENTANI, M.D., FRCPsych

The title of this chapter was suggested to me as the basis for a talk to a professional audience interested in psychoanalysis. I accepted the task as I felt it was both intriguing and challenging. My initial response, though, was that if I were to stress the position of aggression within the drive theory, those more familiar with psychoanalysis would think that nothing much was truly settled about the drives and that object relations were slowly displacing them in theoretical discussions; others would say that the understanding of sexuality still defies us, and the death instinct—that was a controversial subject which has divided the psychoanalytic scene for over half a century.

1. Faced with the task of discussing matters utterly central to our mental functioning in less than an hour, I thought of attempting a brief overview of what I personally felt was of theoretical relevance to the topic rather than embarking on a review of the literature that would inevitably be unsatisfactory and incomplete.

In his presidential address presented at the opening of the 27th International Psychoanalytical Congress in Vienna in 1971, when the main topic was "Aggression," Leo Rangell had this to say: "As hard as man has fought against an uncovering of the forbidden components of his love instincts, he may be pitted in an even more primitive and tenacious sense against the exposure of his aggressive proclivities. Perhaps he is basically only ashamed of the one but afraid of the other. Is not anxiety over sexual transgression due basically to the fear of aggressive retaliation?" (Rangell, 1972, p. 4). Viewed in such simple terms we might assume that the topic to be discussed in this chapter would present fewer problems than expected. But in the next paragraph, Rangell goes on to say: "The problems to be subsumed in studying aggression are kaleidoscopic, and we can expect no more than a modest advance towards their solution from the discussions to be held this week" (p. 4). That was a fairly accurate forecast as the Vienna discussions turned out to be somewhat disappointing, as we shall see in due course.

Since 1971, little has been added to our notions of the drives. Green (1987) has given us an admirable summary of what he calls our current alternatives: (1) *Those who radically reject the concept of instinct,* such as Fairbairn and Guntrip, for whom the concept of object relations replaces that of instinct. Or the views of some American psychoanalysts such as Gill who favors the adoption of more manifestly psychological concepts; or the specific approach (action language) of R. Schafer. (2) *Those who relativize the concept of instinct,* such as Melanie Klein, finally stressing object relations, archaic anxieties, and primitive defenses. On the other hand, in Green's view, American ego psychology, "in replacing the death instinct by the concept of aggression on a par with erotic libido, tampered with the radicalism of Freud's last theory of instincts" (p. 153). Green also believes that when Kohut postulated "an opposition between instincts on the one hand, and the self and vicissitudes of narcissism on the other," he drastically distanced himself from Freud. (3) *Those who retain the essentials of the concept of instinct but introduce changes of detail,* which includes most of the French writers who have not basically altered Freud's fundamental formulations, even if they have often expressed them differently.

Be that as it may, Freud's observations after the publication of "Instincts and Their Vicissitudes" in 1915 are still of momentous significance to psychoanalysts.

Hate and love as affects and attitudes in the ego had come under scrutiny, and it was soon apparent to Freud that hate could be directed at the object with the intention of destroying it, while love became fixated on sexual objects. Thus, in this earlier formulation, we can see how the sexual instincts, with their immediate urge for satisfaction, are wholly dominated by the pleasure principle, while the ego instincts are more ready to conform to the reality principle which is wholly devoted to matters of self-preservation and a capacity for postponement.

Although in the early '20s psychoanalysts could not have been satisfied with the state of the drive theory, they were hardly prepared for the upheaval resulting from Freud's introduction of the life and death instincts.

Many suggestions have been put forward to account for Freud's shift from his earlier position. The most cogent reason, perhaps, is the one that accounts for the fact that by the mid-20s, foremost in his mind was the awareness of a tendency shown by many individuals to repeat painful experiences in their lives. This, he thought, was older than the tendency toward pleasure or avoidance of pain. The repetition compulsion was now seen as a way to reduce instinctual tensions and was eventually defined as a tendency innate in living organic matters, compelling it into reinstatement of an earlier condition, the inorganic or death, a statement that is still unacceptable to many contemporary analysts. On the other hand, the new theory was now able to account for that inexorable clinical challenge of the negative therapeutic reaction which is alleged to be the source of some psychoanalytic failures.

With the dichotomy of Eros and Thanatos, oral libido and aggression, a critical position had been reached (Laplanche and Pontalis, 1973). According to this proposition, the instincts tend to revert to an early state of inactivity, just as in biology things tend to return to the inorganic state. The Nirvana principle was introduced into psychoanalytic thinking. The libido is there to unify, bind together, and preserve Eros; the sexual instincts neutralize the destructiveness. The death instinct is not felt or noticeable internally, but it does become apparent when it is deflected outwardly as destructiveness, or simply aggressiveness. Once a defusion of the two instincts has occurred, it is possible for the death instinct to be once more taken back from the object into the self. We note here the subtle change on the views on sexuality brought about by the new theory and not least the fact that aggression is now given the status of an instinct, a fact that is in some doubt even today.

But let us sum up Freud's views in his own words: "The dangerous death instincts are dealt with in the individual in various ways: in part they are rendered harmless by being fused with erotic components, in part they are diverted towards the external world in the form of aggression, while to a large extent they undoubtedly continue their internal work unhindered" (Freud, 1923, p. 54). He gave an example of this in melancholia when the superego becomes the reservoir of the death instinct; the aggressiveness is turned upon the self as a result of desperate attempts to control it.

The next inexorable jolt to psychoanalytic theory came from the development of an object relation theory which was inevitable, insofar as sooner or later the interaction of the individual with his environment had to be taken into account. We should bear in mind, though, that by relation we actually mean interrelationship (Laplanche and Pontalis, 1973, p. 277). Also, by "object" we mean object as a choice, or as an object of love. For example, in the baby's fantasy, the breast feeds it, calms it, or bites it, as the case may be. The concept, therefore, does not evoke only instinctual life but also various defense mechanisms, the development of the ego, its structure, and so on: in summary, the concept of object relationship emerges as comprehensive and typological, when applied to the development of personality. Different types of relationships will be noted (and we are not talking of real ones), and we shall seldom think in terms of different stages of development. With the interest in object relations, the psychoanalysis of affects and anxiety in particular becomes an overall preoccupation, especially under the influence of the Kleinian school.

In an early formulation, M. Klein (1951) wrote: "The infant is faced at the very beginning of development with the task of mobilizing the libido against the death instinct; a division of the fused instincts takes place in the id (at the instinctual level)" (p. 250). Thus the superego is formed and no wonder it will at times be very aggressive, or extremely destructive. The child will think of the parents as monsters and, indeed, the fear of the object will be proportional to the child's sadistic impulses. According to Klein, the anxiety (the direct representative of the death instinct) generated in the infant in response to the creation of hostile objects in the environment through projection ends up by increasing sadistic impulses.

In both Freudian and Kleinian approaches, the interplay of libido and aggression is therefore basic to mental economy. Freud saw the oral phase as cannibalistic (insofar as it stimulates the desire for incorporation) as well as sadistic. In the case of sadism, impulses consist of libido plus aggression resulting from frustration or as a primary instinct (death instinct) which is externalized through projection. The instinctual impulses condition external dangers by regulating each instinct, while the repression of aggressive components creates a sense of guilt. In fact, excessive destructiveness always leads to psychological helplessness in the face of instinctual dangers. For example, a mother in a state of postnatal depression is totally helpless in dealing with her child because she sees it as the source of her problems and wishes to destroy it.

Klein goes much further in proposing that the frustration at the breast promotes oral sadism. The biting that goes with feeding provokes further similar stimuli, as will weaning. In other words, sadistic tendencies flow from every source, oral, urethral, and anal impulses, all directed at the primary object, the breast, as an object of ambivalence and envy.

The interaction of life and death drives, as described in later Kleinian writings, is expressed in love and hate. With the decline of the sadistic impulses expected to occur in the sixth month of life, there is a switch from part object to whole object relations. Genital impulses are released, facilitating the promotion of oedipal feelings with related conflicts (much earlier than envisaged by Freud). The parents are now loved, and there is a strong wish to preserve them. Love and sexual desire are closely linked with aggressive fantasies and impulses. As the latter are addressed to love objects, they will cause guilt and fear; as a result of it, the sexual desire becomes disconnected, or even repressed, so that people can be quite simply loved. The fixation on libidinal organization at an early stage will inevitably prevent the establishment of genitality, which I shall consider when I discuss sexuality.

Some of these ideas have not gone unchallenged. Brierley (1951), for instance, has noted how the early object relations proposed by Klein imply a too early endopsychic coordination of instinctual drives. Be that as it may, Klein's formulation about the life and death drives goes well beyond anything envisaged by Freud. Perhaps the most outstanding differences of approach between Freud and Klein are to be seen in relation to anxiety. Castration anxiety is still central to his thinking, insofar as he regards it as being truly represented in fear of death.

For Klein, the latter is another form of anxiety, as all anxieties contain a fear of annihilation of life. But a cornerstone of Kleinian theory is that it is the fusion and the interaction of the libido and aggression that cause anxiety and guilt.

2. How can we reconcile all this with our views on sexuality? As Rycroft (1968) has pointed out, psychoanalysts use the terms *sex, sexual,* and *sexuality* interchangeably, so much so that Jones recommends that we should use the term *sex* in the restricted, more popular sense, and sexuality for the more general categories of phenomena. To borrow Laplanche and Pontalis's definition (1973), "sexuality embraces a whole range of excitations and activities observable from infancy which procure pleasure" (p. 418). Such activities cannot be accounted for on the basis of physiological need; they reemerge as component factors in what is generally referred to as sexual love. If psychoanalysts are no more and no less clear than the general public about adult sexuality, it must be due to our justifiable refusal to speak of normal sexuality, and also to the fact that we know much more about its pathology than about the mechanisms at work in the ordinary manifestations of sexual love involving two adults. We know, for instance, that for adolescents, making love is another word for getting rid of sexual tension, a valuable outlet, unfortunately more so for the boy than the girl. In this case, love-making has all the qualities of masturbation, rather than that of a two-person relationship. If it should not improve, the adult male may be less than aware that something is amiss. The girl may also develop into an adult with little belief in her right to have pleasure and satisfaction.

How should adults then reach some reasonable degree of satisfactory sexuality? We do know that this is only possible with the resolution and the successful outcome of childhood developmental phases, and that the understanding of those early processes can indirectly lead us to what contributes to happier, easier forms of adult sexuality.

A study of sexuality forces us to examine the interrelationship of the sexual and the destructive (aggressive) instincts which, when they are fused, are turned into sadomasochism. In this area, Klein has expanded on the start made by Freud in describing the sexual theories of children, showing how these theories are the basis for the most sadistic, primitive fantasies. In a paper on criminal tendencies in normal children (1927), she describes how early fantasies and sexuality in later life are interrelated. Fantasies of parental intercourse in the guise of eating, cutting, beating, and so on (so often found in adult perversions) are gone over and over again. While some criminal acting out may occur, most children can switch from sadistic fantasies and activities to loving ones in a flash. Empathy with the loved object will prevent reenactment, but at times projective identification processes are too strong to be resisted (see sexual murders, rapes, burglary).

Klein considers that gratification at the breast is an essential part of the child's sexuality. With the advent of loving feelings and the onset of the oedipal situation, the sexual impulses take up a different connotation, as they are associated with efforts directed at repairing the damage caused by fantasies during the pregenital stages.

This will be important for all future sexuality, a view to which I adhere wholeheartedly. I should add here that Klein stresses that, in order to establish a good and healthy sexuality, the child must develop a good attitude toward father and his genitals, this being valid for both boys and girls. But let us briefly compare Freud's and Klein's views on the sexualization of aggression which leads to sadism.

In 1905 Freud stated: "The sexuality of most male human beings contains an element of *aggressiveness*—a desire to subjugate; the biological significance of it seems to lie in the [male's] need for overcoming the resistance of the sexual object. . . . Thus sadism . . . [becomes] an aggressive component of the sexual instinct which has become independent and exaggerated" (pp. 157–158).

The future of sexuality then rests on an attenuation of the sadism, so that it is compatible with good functioning, and acceptability by a partner. This statement has caused some difficulty for some psychoanalysts who hold the view that aggression can be (1) sexualized, as just described; and (2) that it can exist in its own right, in a pure state, so to speak, at the service of the self-preservative instinct (Glasser, 1979).

My own view is that Freud's assertion that sadism is a component of the sexual instincts is too extreme. The reference to its biological significance is too vague and, in my view, hard to prove. The statement also implies that all women are (more or less) masochistic in their sexual disposition. This is scientifically untenable and, to my knowledge, unconfirmed by psychoanalytic investigation. I should add, female masochism as a perversion has its own well-defined pathology.

Klein, on the other hand, stresses the fact that sadism will be corrected by the introjection of a good object, leading to better object relations and adaptation to reality. Thus erotic development, the foundation of sexuality, is stimulated by anxiety and love impulses. Attractive as this theory may be, the contention that it is anxiety that is a spur to development, with maximal sadism and introjective processes during the first year of life, is often difficult to prove. If we leave aside such considerations, it must be clear that modifications of these early sadistic impulses cannot be all that is required for the establishment of a conflict-free adult sex life. We must also expect a fair resolution of the oedipal situation, peaceful internal object relations, and a successful development of identifications, so hard to pinpoint at times but so vital in facilitating masculine and feminine drives and attitudes. Such optimal conditions do not always materialize, as is shown by those instances where bisexual elements are very pronounced in a man and a woman, when their relationship thrives on the reciprocal exploitation of masculine and feminine strivings through projective identifications. The considerable gratification to be derived from such situations can conceal its inadequacies for remarkably long periods, only becoming apparent in the course of extensive psychoanalytic investigation.

These remarks will not be surprising to those who are familiar with Freud's (1905) cryptic statement: "the exclusive sexual interest felt by men for women is also a problem that needs elucidating" (p. 146n.). It would have been an even more astonishing flash of insight if it had referred to women as well. In this respect I shall confine myself to noting that, in the establishment of a satisfactory sexual life, biological, instinctual, and sociocultural factors are to some extent more important in women than in men.

I shall also say in passing that social factors may well contain many of the answers still needed to unravel the mystery of human sexuality. Consider, for instance, the case of Indians in Peru who are openly homosexual, whereas the Canadian Indians are very limited and restricted in their sexual behavior (Panoff, 1984).

In my opinion, all discussions about sex are too concerned with the role of aggression, at the expense of the importance of "the whole range of excitations," to quote Laplanche and Pontalis, who ignore aggression as a component of the sexual instincts in their definition of sexuality.

In another context (Limentani, 1984) I noted how "excitement [a term I have come to use interchangeably with excitation] is something that we all know about and can recognize in others and ourselves, but it might be difficult to state precisely what it really is, as it often is more mental than physical, or vice versa or both at the same time. Heightened affective intensity in response to external or internal stimuli will produce excitement" (p. 393). As Alexander (1971) has pointed out, sexual excitement can prepare for action, but if it is too intense and is linked with fear, it can disrupt and cause panic, recklessness, and despair. This author also suggests that desire arouses impulses from instinctual needs that are ego-syntonic, and the question is how they will be regarded by the superego. He further underlines the fact that the psychic apparatus contains an immense amount of excitement with little or no conscious awareness due to repressions.

Thus excitement is the essence of sex. Its maximal expression is in the orgasm, when for a fleeting moment there is a loss of contact with the self and the environment. Although it does not amount to unconsciousness, it is conceivable that it could be comparable to the little death so often spoken of. The intensity of the excitement is frightening as it is incapable of being regulated by the ego, without taking recourse to very drastic defensive mechanisms: dissociation, splitting, denial, projective identification with a partner, often expressed as "thinking more of the other one." It should be noted that the absence of orgasm, or of any sense of gratification, is often found in hypochondriacal individuals, or in association with psychosomatic disturbance. These cases must be distinguished from those where the dominant fear is loss of control, invariably associated with excessive sadism and aggressiveness.

Is the fantasy of dying, with the implicit risk element, an additional factor in sexual excitement? Is overcoming the fear of death what ensures peace of mind, which Glasser (1979) believes to be the main reason for seeking sexual gratification?

Anxiety about death, of course, is not the same as what is implied by the concept of the death drive.

From what has preceded, it will be apparent that it is possible to discuss the roles of aggression and sex without taking recourse to the death drive. In a very thoughtful summing up of the IPA Vienna Congress of 1971, Anna Freud (1972) pointed out (with some regret, I thought) that her father's introduction of the dualistic drive theory in the 1920s had divided the analytic world into two factions; those bitterly against the death drive, and those utterly in favor of it. What was interesting, though, was that she pointed out that Freud had never implied that the life drive was the source of sexual urges, and that these were always acknowledged as being either hormonal or anatomical. She also stressed the twin roles played by the two drives, sex and aggression, in psychical conflict. Both needed to be reduced in quantity and changed in quality for an acceptable life in a community. She added that some aggression is needed in any sexual activity, while unmodified aggression leads to disaster. In Anna Freud's view, we are prejudiced in overlooking the differences, rather than the similarities between the two drives, possibly, she thought, because a number of major defenses are the same and equally effective in both the sexual and the aggressive drives. (She was referring here to denial, repression, identification, projections.)

Thus, as predicted by Rangell, the Vienna Congress did nothing to resolve our doubts and uncertainties about the role of aggression in the drive theory.

Undoubtedly there are occasions when our theoretical constructs do not meet some clinical challenges. We have all encountered massive outbreaks of anxiety in response to loss of sexual power in males, demonstrating beyond all doubt how something of a sexual nature is needed to counteract the emergence of destructive and sadistic impulses against the self or a partner. Yet it is often impossible to dismiss the hypothesis that an inherent excess of destructiveness and sadism as well as fear of death (at a superficial level presenting as castration anxiety) associated with extreme excitation was responsible for the loss of sexual power which brought about the outbreak of anxiety. Is Joyce McDougall (1983) then right in saying that "death anxiety is in all things sexual"? This is, of course, not too far removed from a literary cliché which would represent sex as an act of violence on a person, which is close to death, and so on.

My own view is that we could well dispense with the concept of the death drive, not because death should be denied. On the contrary, life can hardly be appreciated without some awareness of death, but the concept creates more problems rather than solves them. I believe we could account for some of the worst and at times unthinkable anxieties that can affect both infants and adults by giving due weight to that primitive, original anxiety of the loss of the self; or to the anxiety of fragmentation and annihilation associated with utterly catastrophic feelings resulting from the first separation from the primary object. As Gaddini (1972) has pointed out, such primitive experiences do tend to reappear in dreams in a most vivid fashion and as such are infinitely more accessible to a patient and analyst.

Perhaps our preoccupation with the death instinct makes us overlook the force of the life instinct. In recent times there has been much renewed interest in biological issues, among them those autoregulatory mechanisms that control aggressivity, which is a prerogative of human behavior.

In the midst of much scientific uncertainty, it is relevant to mention some investigations that have been carried out around the stress of journeying along the birth canal which, in general, is not harmful to most infants. Recent work has shown that the surge of "stress" hormones it releases can be important for the neonate's survival outside the womb. In the event of serious hypoxia and pressure on the head, the fetus produces abnormally high levels of stress hormones, adrenaline and noradrenaline—higher than in such severely taxed adults as a woman giving birth, or a person having a heart attack. The catecholamines (adrenaline and noradrenaline) typically spur the body to fight or flee from a threat of survival (stress); high concentration of these hormones indicates that the organism is in danger. It would seem that the resulting surge of hormones prepares the infant to survive outside the womb. These hormones also ensure that a rich supply of blood goes to the heart and brain and may even promote attachment between mother and baby (Lagercrantz and Slotkin, 1986).

3. In 1985, Rangell wrote: "theory begets therapy; therapy is intrinsic to psychoanalytic theory" (p. 66). It would therefore seem appropriate to devote this final section to a brief clinical presentation concerning a patient whose multiform symptomatology kept intruding into my mind as I was writing the above theoretical overview.

Mr. A. was referred to me at the age of 60 by an experienced colleague who assured me of the patient's faith in the psychoanalytic method, although his attempts to engage in an analysis with five eminent colleagues had not been very successful. Each attempt had come to grief, either because the patient felt a lack of rapport, or because the analyst did not feel Mr. A. could be helped. The patient had indeed had a reasonably successful analysis at the age of 27, which was brought to an end after three years by his marriage to a woman who had helped him to overcome his sexual impotence.

At the start of this new attempt, Mr. A. was in despair, as his marriage was failing as a result of a recurrence of sexual impotence and reciprocal hostility between himself and his wife. His unhappiness was aggravated by his children turning against him. There was a long history of ill health, consisting of a variety of somatic disturbances but, more seriously, a long-standing mucous colitis which had led him to consult physicians in many countries.

We agreed to have a few exploratory interviews which were both alarming and fruitful. Mr. A. was a fairly heavily built man who looked older than his years and was obviously under considerable mental stress. His behavior as he sat down and began to talk was nothing short of grotesque. He would stammer and make a variety of grunting noises, inhaling a vast quantity of air, which he would then forcibly expel, while his arms and legs would violently jerk in all directions. He informed me that these symptoms had appeared in the course of his second attempt at analysis and had become a regular pattern of the early part of each session. I soon noticed, though, how being understood, or having given vent to some frustrated feeling, would result in a cessation of this odd behavior.

After we agreed to make a start, it became clear that the previous premature interruptions of therapy had been due to acts of sabotage on his part. Even his first analysis had been terminated shortly after he was able to express his homosexual fantasies and impulses which provoked uncontrollable anxieties. Mr. A.'s current sexual impotence was readily understood as being linked with his increasing hostility toward his wife. That he was very threatened by his aggressiveness was also shown by a rapidly developing positive transference with much idealization of myself as a cure-all analyst. It was also very apparent that Mr. A. could turn his hatred and hostility into a host of hypochondriacal and somatic disturbances. Countertransference problems were not far away, as I heard myself saying to him rather aggressively that all he wanted was another analytic scalp to add to his collection. The patient's reaction, though, was nothing short of alarming, as he seemed to relish the thought that I had acknowledged his triumph over so many distinguished analytic experts and that I could see myself as his victim. Yet, after those early skirmishes, a fruitful analytic relationship ensued, which was to last for many years, with reasonably good results.

Mr. A.'s early life throws some light on his later development, although in some ways it poses more theoretical questions than it solves. He had been breast-fed, which he admitted with reluctance as his overall memories of his infancy were of "absolute unhappiness and misery." He came from a comfortable middle-class family whose many children required the employment of nurses. He particularly hated a young nurse who had been on the receiving end of his fury when he had been put on solid food. He could not stand his older brother and sister, but it was a younger sister, born when he was just three years old, who was the source of his inconsolable misery. The true battleground with mother and the nurses, though, was about his constipation which he felt no one seemed to tolerate. But he was grateful to one nurse who was very understanding and sympathetic about his enuresis, which continued until he was 13 years old. He was, in fact, very fond of this nurse, to the point of asking her to undress herself for him, and could never understand why she had refused to do so. This was well in keeping with his current imperious manner, which led him to expect people to fall in with his wishes. His relationship to his father was extremely ambivalent. He enjoyed being idolized by him but "hated his wet kisses" which made him feel "like a little girl." There were few sexual games with boys of his own age, but there was a memory of his having been excited when he was still a small child by a young man fighting with a policeman.

Mr. A. reached puberty unhappy, frustrated, and worried about masturbation, but there were no school problems. He refused to go to university and soon became involved in a business life which brought him success, fame, and riches. He readily acknowledged his hatred of women, but he was little, if at all, aware of some basic homosexual impulses which were responsible for some difficulties he had encountered with colleagues, and his utter ruthlessness.

As his analysis started to move, there was a steady improvement, with the disappearance of his mucous colitis and the many somatic disturbances. As his latent homosexuality was coming to light through the transference, he was compelled to seek a heterosexual outlet. His association with a sexually insatiable woman led to the recovery of his potency but, more often than not, he was unable to ejaculate, while maintaining an erection indefinitely. He was equally shattered to discover that he had no difficulty in ejaculating when he was uncontrollably angry with this woman, or following a dream in which he was able to express his sadistic fantasies.

He finally divorced his wife, but the proceedings caused him considerable anguish, to the point of his suffering several coronary spasms which threatened his life. This had occurred during an inevitably fairly long interruption in the analysis, owing to his many commitments, but on his return he appeared to be full of vigor and almost rejuvenated. Having rid himself of his mistress as well, he thought there would be no further need for analysis. The first serious attempt to fix a date for termination was marked by a severe negative therapeutic reaction (Limentani, 1981). The stammer and the violent jerking movements which had almost totally disappeared were again much in evidence. Grunting like a wounded lion, he felt extremely aggressive toward the analyst. Under the threat of termination, he took steps to ensure that there would be a suitable replacement for the analyst. Mr. A. now fell deeply in love with a woman who seemed to answer all his possible desires, except that soon after they had married, she revealed herself to be basically depressed and less than interested in frequent sexual exploits. Mr. A. responded by developing an absolute state of sexual impotence which brought him back to analysis. My patient was now in an almost permanent state of seething rage against both his wife for rejecting him, and the analyst for not having performed a miraculous cure. He insisted that all would be well if his wife would see eye to eye with him about his sexual needs. On the other hand, he could not understand that there was something deeply wrong with his way of relating to this woman, which needed correction. As Mr. A. could now talk about nothing else other than his sexual frustration, I began to feel at the end of my tether. Something of this must have got across to the patient who suddenly in one of his more explosive moments shouted at me that I simply did not understand why he was so "obsessed" (his word) with sex. Only sex, and nothing else, could make him feel alive, he said. And, furthermore, that was his only way out, short of strangling his wife. This outburst and frank admission of his barely controlled aggressiveness seemed to clear the air. A period of very fruitful analytic work followed, leading to an improved relationship with his wife, the recovery of his potency, and the final termination of his analysis. This latter step was taken by mutual consent, but not before we had thoroughly analyzed his anxiety about mortality, and particularly his fear of death, which had been concealed by his more overt castration anxiety which had haunted him all his life.

I do not propose to offer a systematic conceptualization of the material presented. I also leave it to the reader to come to some conclusion about the theoretical considerations which preceded in relation to the clinical findings. I shall therefore confine myself to conveying some of my impressions, reactions, and feelings in relation to the patient's disordered instinctual anxieties.

I generally felt that, on reaching late middle age, this man had been confronted more and more by the disturbance of his sexuality, which bordered on perversion, while his aggressiveness was threatening his capacity to survive. There were times when it was difficult for me to keep a coherent picture of his mental state in my mind. However, the heart attack and the experience of being close to death, over and above the disastrous second marriage, had forced Mr. A. to come to terms with the fact that his latent homosexuality was something to be reckoned with. As his homosexual impulses were more and more focused on in the transference, analytic work of a deeper significance became possible. Until then the development and the evolution of his oedipal complex had emerged largely as intellectual discourse.

The interrelationship of his sexuality with aggressiveness and the role of his pregenital development in influencing the development of his personality and character became clearer and more meaningful to the patient, as the analysis slowly came to a close. I should add that the decrease of the tendency to somatize had gradually been replaced by conscious forcefulness about his capacity to control his aggression and, indeed, he had become aware of his fear of madness. It finally became apparent how this fear had been encapsulated into a variety of symptoms at different times in his life (see Rosenfeld, 1985).

In the paper previously quoted, Rangell (1985) insists that it is inevitable for us to approach our clinical work with some theoretical construction in our minds. In my estimation, there must be very few people who would not admit to some preconceived idea in formulating certain interpretations. Mistakes due to such preconceptions are more difficult to detect than countertransference mishaps. My approach to Mr. A.'s pathology was centered on the fact that in the course of his previous therapies, he had accumulated a fair amount of intellectual insight, coupled with a great deal of reconstructive work. I therefore decided to concentrate on the analysis of the affects as they emerged at various times, well in keeping with my preconceived belief that the analysis of the affects is more likely to bring reasonable results than anything else (Limentani, 1977).

Finally, I would say that this analysis did not inspire in me a desire to seek a fresh or new reformulation of some old theoretical constructs of disparate origins. On the other hand, I think it did show me, with considerable force, that modern Oedipus does not go to Colonus. Not only does he make the wrong choice of partner, in keeping with the myth, but he also has a heart attack, mucous colitis, crippling backaches, while toying with the prospect of a homosexual solution.

REFERENCES

Alexander, J. (1971), On excitement. *Bull. Phil. Assn. Psychoanal.*, 21:162–172.

Brierley, M. (1951), The work of Melanie Klein. In: *Trends in Psychoanalysis*. London: Hogarth Press.

Freud, A. (1972), Comments on aggression. *Internat. J. Psycho-Anal.*, 63:163–173.

Freud, S. (1905), Three essays on the theory of sexuality. *Standard Edition*, 7:125–231. London: Hogarth Press, 1953.

——— (1915), Instincts and their vicissitudes. *Standard Edition*, 14:117–141. London: Hogarth Press, 1957.

——— (1923), The ego and the id. *Standard Edition*, 19:3–63. London: Hogarth Press, 1961.

Gaddini, E. (1972), Aggression and the pleasure principle. *Internat. J. Psycho-Anal.*, 53:191–199.

Glasser, M. (1979), The role of aggression in the perversions. In: *Sexual Deviations*, ed. I. Rosen. Oxford: Oxford University Press.

Green, A. (1987), Instinct in the late works of Freud. In: *On Freud's Analysis Terminable and Interminable*. IPA Educ. Monogr., 1:149–171.

Klein, M. (1927), Criminal tendencies in normal children. In: *Love, Guilt and Reparation*, Vol. 1. London: Hogarth Press, pp. 170–186.

——— (1951), The effects of early anxiety situations on the sexual development of the boy. In: *Contributions to Psychoanalysis*, Vol. 2. London: Hogarth Press.

Lagercrantz, H., & Slotkin, T. (1986), The stress of being born. *Sci. Amer.*, 25:92–102.

Laplanche, J., & Pontalis, J.-B. (1973), *The Language of Psychoanalysis*. London: Hogarth Press.

Limentani, A. (1977), Affects and the psychoanalytic situation. *Internat. J. Psycho-Anal.*, 58:171–182.

——— (1981), On some positive aspects of the negative therapeutic reaction. *Internat. J. Psycho-Anal.*, 62:379–390.

——— (1984), Towards a unified conception of the origins of sexual and social deviancy in young persons. *Internat. J. Psychoanal. Psychother.*, 10:383–409.

McDougall, J. (1983), L'homosexualite dite inconscient. *Rev. Franc. Psychanal.*, 3:675–687.

Panoff, M. (1984), La sexualite des autres ou le jardin du voisin. *Nouvelle Rev. Psychanal.*, 29:123–136.

Rangell, L. (1972), Aggression, Oedipus, and historical perspective. *Internat. J. Psycho-Anal.*, 53:3–13.

——— (1985), On the theory of theory in psychoanalysis and the relation of theory to psychoanalytic therapy. *J. Amer. Psychoanal. Assn.*, 33:59–92.

Rosenfeld, H. (1985), Psychosomatic symptoms and latent psychotic states. In: *The Yearbook of Psychoanalysis and Psychotherapy*, 1:1381–1398. Emerson, NJ: New Concept Press.

Rycroft, C. (1968), *Critical Dictionary of Psychoanalysis*. London: T. Nelson.

24

SOME CONTROVERSIAL ISSUES IN HOLOCAUST STUDIES: PSYCHOANALYTIC REFLECTIONS

MILTON E. JUCOVY, M.D.

There is hardly an area in human life and thought that is not in some way involved in controversy. This is certainly true in the history of psychoanalysis, as it developed from the original concepts proposed by Sigmund Freud. Included are the loyalties in the psychoanalytic community to the structural or topographic theories and the attribution of pathogenesis to the various "villains" described by Arlow (1981). This has been dramatically illustrated by the recent skirmish involving fealty to the seduction theory, as opposed to conflict derived from infantile and childhood psychosexual development. Debates about the relative significance of developmental lags and the role of conflict and compromise formation in pathogenesis, as well as adherence to the single or dual instinct theory have also played a prominent role in scientific deliberations.

Despite the universal prevalence of controversy, we would expect that among people of general good will and objectivity, there would be a consensus about the impact of the terrible and awesome period of the Holocaust on the world in general and on survivors and their children in particular. Nevertheless, some significant differences of opinion have emerged in the course of psychoanalytic studies of this period of infamy. A number of these disagreements have been based on relatively objective scientific grounds. Some, however, have been influenced by the not unexpected passion which can be mobilized by any discussion of events of such magnitude and horror. A survey of some of these differences may be helpful in clarifying our feelings and defining our goals in this post-Holocaust world, using studies at the interface of individual and social pathology.

It might be appropriate to summarize the steps which led to psychoanalytic studies of the effects of the Holocaust on members of survivor families and the children of the persecutors as well. In a world characterized by Adorno's statement (1973), "No poetry after Auschwitz," it became clear that the concept employed in devising the "final solution" was primarily directed toward the Jewish people as a fulfillment of an ideology of hate and an apocalyptic end in itself. The death of six million and the agony of so many others transcend all previous ordeals which marked the Jewish historical experience. The sophisticated technology applied to the relentless destruction of a people consumed one-half of world Jewry in Eastern Europe and erased an entire civilization. The slaughter ended in mounds of ashes and skeletons and the disappearance of the rich and lively culture of European Jewish life.

The victory of the Allied military forces enabled the liberation of the death camps and those who remained alive were finally allowed to make their way to some semblance of safety. Large numbers of the stateless and impoverished were cared for in displaced persons' camps, waiting for visas to more hospitable places. Those who tried to return to their towns and villages of origin met with a hostile reception at best. Some managed to escape the British blockade and made their way to Palestine before 1948. A group of survivors was able to make contact with relatives in the United States, Canada, and South America and emigrate to the Western hemisphere.

During the first years after liberation, the energies of survivors were absorbed in finding a way back to an approximation of ordinary life. Most had to learn a new language, many had to acquire new skills, and they all had to meet the usual challenges posed by living in a foreign land. Many families clung together, hoping to re-create their original communities. This seemed particularly important when they felt surrounded by an alien culture which regarded them at best with awe and mistrust, the very embodiment of a past the survivors wished to forget. Because it was relatively rare for a family to have survived intact, new marital partners, frequently fellow survivors, were found and new families established. While life was safer and more bearable, adaptation was not easy.

The shock and drama of liberation and the need to deal on an emergency level with the plight of the victims of Nazi persecution helped to mobilize action and keep survivors in the eyes and conscience of the world for a time. Then, for powerful reasons, a curtain of silence descended. For close to a decade after liberation, intense individual and collective defenses functioned to ward off involvement with the past. The Jewish people, traditionally enjoined to remember and commemorate common trauma, were still not prepared to confront the ultimate horror of the Nazi plan for genocide. Another reason for the silence, apart from the need of the victims to forget, was the need of the world to forget. People did not listen, understand, or share and there was a division between those who had endured and those who had only read about the atrocities. The gap was too wide at first and a period of latency had to be traversed before the chasm was narrowed (Bergmann and Jucovy, 1982).

HOLOCAUST TRAUMA, INDEMNIFICATION, AND GENERATIONAL TRANSMISSION: CONFLICTING VIEWS

Mental health professionals were no exception to the general rule, ignoring or minimizing psychological problems, when plans were formulated for the rehabilitation of those who survived the camps and were being implemented. An exception was Paul Friedman (1949), who paid special attention to the problems of children in surveying mental health among Jewish displaced persons. An event which helped to bridge temporal and emotional distance was the passage of a uniform law in 1953 by the German Federal Republic, which provided that people who were persecuted because of their nationality with contempt of human rights should receive appropriate compensation for permanent damage to their body. At first only physical injuries were considered for indemnification; it has only been since 1965 that psychiatric conditions were recognized as caused by persecution. Before that, according to traditional theories adhered to in Germany as far back as the end of World War I, any traumatic experience, no matter how severe, could have only a temporary effect on the individual. Late sequelae of trauma and so-called permanent disorders were considered genetic and thus unrelated to persecution. Milton Kestenberg (1982) has written about K. Kisker, an influential German psychiatrist, whose writing (1961) prompted the German courts to revise their usual view and rule in favor of restitution for psychiatric reasons. He cited the case of a five-year-old boy who was deported from Hungary in 1944 with his parents. He was in a group submitted to mass shooting, and he lay for days among the corpses. He was rescued by local people and hidden until liberation. After the war he was so disturbed that he hid under tables and benches and was afraid of all adults. Later he complained of imaginary agents and was hospitalized with the diagnosis of a paranoid illness. Kisker suggested that schizophrenia cannot be created by persecution, but that a traumatic experience may be the determining factor in eliciting a psychotic episode. The patient was declared disabled and a pension awarded, a case which turned out to be an exception. In the ensuing few years, recognition of the role of persecution became practically nonexistent.

In the meantime, several psychiatrists, Niederland (1964), Eissler (1960), and Wangh (1971) pressed for a change in the interpretation of the law so survivors could receive funds for psychiatric treatment. The courts finally ruled favorably in 1965, but other complications arose which perpetuated injustices. Many psychiatric clinicians who were authorized to examine survivors for the reparations program were classically Freudian in orientation with respect to their view of the definition of psychic trauma, a theoretical position which did not appear consistent with explaining the vast and bewildering array of late sequelae presented by the claimants they examined. Sigmund Freud (1920) had originally proposed an explanation, essentially economic in nature, which stressed a breaching of the stimulus barrier, which implied that response to a trauma was bound to be temporary and that a normal state would ensue following a state of shock and disorganization caused by overstimulation. Freud's contention had been based on his belief that it was highly unlikely that a neurosis could develop without the participation of deeper levels of the psychic apparatus. He had pointed out that there was nothing in unconscious mental life that could correspond with the idea of the complete annihilation of life, so that fear of death could more likely be regarded as analogous to the fear of castration (1926). These views, although later amended to include other pathogenic factors, rather than sexual ones alone, were difficult to reconcile with the observations of those who were grappling to understand, within the framework of then classical psychoanalytic theory, the continuing symptoms and the late sequelae seen in Holocaust survivors.

The problems that faced mental health professionals came to attention in a more focused way to the scientific community at the 1967 Congress of the International Psychoanalytical Association during a symposium entitled "Psychic Traumatization through Social Catastrophe." The general tone of the presentations and discussion suggested that the traditional way in which psychoanalysts had regarded the effects of what they had considered to be traumatic events lacked some important elements which might help them to understand and treat victims who had emerged from their experiences with some psychological impairment, particularly in instances where predisposing factors seemed to be minimal. A number of investigators have described aspects of the traumatic effects of Nazi persecution: among them are Leo Eitinger (1961), Paul Chodoff (1963), H. Z. Winnik (1967), and Martin Wangh (1969). Whether one agrees with the assertion that the previous personality plays but a minor role in the symptoms seen among survivors, or remains a proponent of the traditional theory of the pathogenicity of trauma, the group of symptoms described by William Niederland (1968), named the "survivor syndrome," was one landmark in the psychoanalytic study of Holocaust victims. The symptoms of this syndrome are multiple and varied, and the study done by Niederland was based almost exclusively on observations made in the course of seeing applicants for restitution. There was no intention of suggesting that the appearance of this conglomerate of symptoms was universal in survivors or that the symptoms themselves were unique or exclusive. While some have claimed that survivors of other man-made and natural disasters may show similar symptoms, there are no comparable psychological studies of the victims of a master plan for the deliberate extermination of a group whose members were regarded as unfit to inhabit the earth with other humans. It must also be emphasized that in recovery, many survivors have shown an unusual degree of resilience and have adapted to the renewal of their lives with much vitality. Many have achieved remarkable success, and because of their attention to continuity and life-affirming attitudes, have inspired their offspring to live a life of dedication and service.

Because the examining physicians for the reparations program had to struggle often enough with what constitutes a trauma, particularly in those instances where late sequelae appeared, it would be appropriate to examine further the question of what is traumatic and how it can be linked to the presumably causative stimulus. There is little disagreement that a sudden acute event can breach the stimulus barrier, overwhelm the psychic apparatus, and render the victim helpless for a time. In these instances the so-called traumatic event can have a different impact on different individuals, and it is important to understand what the stimulus means to an individual. The issue of how the traumatic event is related to the phase of the individual's development is also to be kept in mind. A little boy, for example, may be more apt to be traumatized during the height of his oedipal phase by a stimulus which has the meaning of castration. There does seem to be agreement among responsible investigators that survivors who have shown symptoms have sustained such massive and cumulative assault that powerful pathogenic effects can be detected, even if one can see little evidence of predisposition prior to persecution. Ilse Grubrich-Simitis (1981) has summed up this point of view in discussing extreme trauma, which can become cumulative trauma and thus cause permanent rather than only temporary changes in the psychic apparatus. The consideration of what constitutes trauma in members of the second generation is more complex. The children of survivors have been exposed to the Holocaust as filtered through the experience of their parents, and we have to be more careful in the assignment of pathogenicity.

Milton Kestenberg (1982) has written eloquently of some of the problems and abuses which attended the application of the reparations law passed by the German Federal Republic. Almost immediately there arose problems which were centered around the complicated procedures involved in making a claim and in the filing process. Under the now considered "infamous" paragraph 7 of the law, compensation can be refused for "inaccurate statements which were made merely for simplification in the presentation of evidence." Some of the problems resulted from the view of German psychiatrists that one whose first two or three years of life was spent in a concentration camp or in hiding will not remember the details of that suffering and cannot therefore be permanently damaged, a view certainly not supported by modern findings. Martin Wangh (1971) described the case of a young woman who spent two years of her early childhood in Theresienstadt. He quoted from a German examiner's report that damages in the neurological field were not probable and that permanent damage after the persecution was not supported by other findings. Also cited in this report were Anna Freud's Theresienstadt children who were separated from their parents. The disturbances these children developed were said to have disappeared after a time. In rebuttal, Wangh quoted Anna Freud's discussion (1960) of Bowlby's paper. She said that these children who had undergone repeated traumatic separation from birth or infancy onward, or from preadolescence onward, displayed almost without exception withdrawn, depressive, self-accusatory, or hostile moods. In a personal communication to Wangh, she also said that it never crossed her mind that anyone could doubt the harm created by such circumstances. These findings have also been confirmed by Hans Keilson's study (1979) of Dutch children who had been hidden or deported to concentration camps during the Nazi period. He discovered that not only the first traumatization, the separation from parents, was decisive for further development, but also later experiences such as changes of hiding places for fear of discovery.

Kestenberg's experience with clients was even more convincing to him than reading psychiatric reports. A young woman suffered from learning disabilities, fear of using public transportation, stranger anxiety, and depression. She had made several attempts at suicide. She was born in a concentration camp; her father had died there and her mother had been able to save her. Her claim for restitution was rejected on the basis of absence of causal relationship between her condition and her early experiences. Ultimately, her claim was sustained in the form of a lump sum settlement.

Another poignant example cited by Milton Kestenberg concerned his client, Moshe, who was seven when his mother was killed after his father had been taken to a labor camp. Moshe was sent with his twin brother to a camp where, in his presence, his twin was slaughtered. His application for a pension was rejected on the grounds that this seemed to be a classical instance where a childhood experience does not have to leave a traumatic mark on an individual. Moshe had graduated from a rabbinical school in a displaced persons' camp and was now employed as a clerk in a small company. He was married and had two children. During the discussion with his attorney he did not utter one word; his wife, who did the talking, said that he always acted this way. Moshe's routine consisted of being picked up by a co-worker and driven to work. Once there, he was directed to his immediate task where he performed like an automaton. His co-worker took him home after working hours. At home he did not talk to his family and after a period of staring at the ceiling following the evening meal, he retired to his bedroom. At night he screamed, probably as a result of terrifying nightmares. His wife claimed she had children with him only because he had raped her and that she could not take this life any longer. At the rabbinical school Moshe was said to have attended, he had clung to a particular teacher, but spoke to no one else, and never played with other children. Because of the additional information obtained, the decision about the pension was finally reversed. The irony is that most of this information had been available to the original examiner, but disregarded as not relevant.

An attempt has been made so far to review some of the background which characterized the genocidal program of the Nazis and its aftermath. For psychoanalysts, apart from their general human concern, a major interest has focused on the possible traumatic psychological effects on survivors and their children and how they might be dealt with therapeutically. The question of reparations for harm to mental health has been considered in some detail and some of the shortcomings and abuses of the laws dealing with compensation described. It is precisely this area which has probably stimulated the most contention and polemic exchange. One of the more passionate critics of what has been written about Holocaust survivor families is Jack Terry (1984), who writes that Holocaust literature has become increasingly exploitive, politicized, and trivializing. He feels that even those whose avowed purpose has been to aid survivors have been agents, however unwitting, of this exploitation. He also states that the early writers on the effects of the Holocaust, whose material was gathered from interviews rather than treatment sessions, are considered experts because they were pioneers. He deplores the fact that they have been given authority without question to draw conclusions without sufficient clinical data and that tentative original views are being repeatedly quoted, thus compounding what he regards as probable error and distortion. Terry further cites the fact that many examiners in the United States and other countries had escaped from Europe themselves and many still had remaining family members there. He feels that these examiners were themselves likely to suffer from survivor guilt as they were not the ones who paid so dearly for survival from persecution in the camps and could lose their objectivity and present skewed data sympathetic to victims. Another speculation offered was that psychiatrists who did not recommend restitution could be accused of hostility toward the survivor and left open to charges of being identified with the Nazi aggressor.

Relying on K. R. Eissler's discussion (1967) of the prevalence of contempt for the victim of persecution and humiliation and its possible roots in a mobilization of castration anxiety, as well as an intensification of superego conflicts, Terry argues that the feeling of contempt may have been present in those who were seemingly sympathetic toward the victim. This feeling may have played a role in what Terry says are the generalizations inherent in defining the "survivor syndrome." This definition, says Terry, shows no more distinguishing qualities among individuals than that shown by the Nazis, who lumped all Jews together by a yellow star and a tattooed number. In this connection I cannot help but recall a conference of Holocaust survivors and their children, where I was scheduled to make a presentation. I noted that many of the young people who were registering were getting badges of different colors, depending on whether they were a survivor, child of a survivor, concentration camp prisoner, partisan, or refugee. Some wore their badges on their wrists as if they were camp tattoos. Later, during one of the presentations by a distinguished psychiatrist, who spoke of the great amount of vulnerability to physical illness among survivors, he was roundly attacked by members of the audience for labeling and thus stigmatizing his listeners. This provided a dramatic object lesson in the part played by activity versus passivity in determining one's emotional response to an experience.

Terry questions whether external trauma must be pathogenic and asserts that it is only possible through analysis to trace an event or an aspect of an event which might be responsible for the pathogenic process to be initiated. Bergen (1958) is quoted as reporting the analysis of a girl whose mother was murdered by the girl's father in the presence of the child. As four fatal chest wounds were inflicted, the mother screamed out for the girl to "get out of here." It is stated that during the course of an analysis, it was established that the outstanding traumatic effect for the child was not the bloody murder, but the yelling of the mother, which was experienced by the girl as an exclusion and a rejection. Gyomroi (1963) is cited as having analyzed a young concentration camp survivor, where the pathogenic factor appeared to be the experience of object losses rather than the horror of the camp. Anna Freud (1958) is referred to as having said that we do not always know which element of an experience will be selected for cathexis and emotional involvement. She described a young boy who singled out the confiscation of his father's car, which meant the father being robbed of potency. These examples must be carefully scrutinized and we must not make the error of accepting at face value a designation of a consciously recalled trauma, when it may in fact be used in the service of screening out the emotional impact of even more dramatic events, like the horrors of violence, destruction, and death.

It has been strikingly convincing that one hears from one's patients and elsewhere rather infrequently about the details of a survivor's camp experiences. More often, we hear about events which seem more innocuous than we expect to learn about. One may speculate that the onslaught of trauma during life in a concentration camp or in other extreme circumstances makes it almost impossible to recall and retell the experience in a coherent and logical way. The tendency for regressive processes to affect a developing and presumably vulnerable psychic structure can extend to an already developed psychic structure and result in the impairment of formerly intact ego functions when the trauma is massive and cumulative. The results produced may be more akin to something like primary process thinking than the expected secondary process thinking that would characterize an ordinary autobiographical account. As many survivors may have attempted to narrate their histories to their children, what emerged can have resembled a waking nightmare more than a lucid memory, a nightmare which frequently had to be suppressed and substituted for by a more coherent, more acceptable, and even more trivial memory.

Anna Ornstein (1984) has directed her criticism more specifically to those clinicians she feels are being indiscriminate in explaining the symptoms of children of survivors as a consequence of growing up in the homes of parents who have been exposed to the trauma of Holocaust experiences. She apparently feels that the concept of "transmission of Holocaust trauma" is no longer even questioned, but taken for granted as an established fact. An example she cites deals with questioning the methodology of a group of analysts who have advised therapists who presented case material to the group to ask their patients if they had been named after a family member who died in the Holocaust. She designates the inquiry as suggested for follow-up visits and therefore not as an integral part of the analytic material. Actually, the suggestion was made in a spirit of inquiry during the analysis, much as a supervisor might indicate to a student that question asking is a perfectly appropriate part of analytic technique. It is, of course, true, as Ornstein points out, that naming children for deceased relatives is an ancient Jewish custom and that naming them for someone who died in the Holocaust maintains a generational continuity and is an appropriate memorialization. There may be, however, a particular meaning for a child to know that one is named after a dead child of a parent's first family, a half-sibling, for whom mourning may not have been adequately completed.

When a scientific question is considered over a period of time, differences are bound to arise and opinions change as new information is gathered. In the instance of studying, from a psychoanalytic point of view, the effects of the trauma inflicted on their victims by the Nazi persecutors, the pendulum seems to have swung. Several decades ago, those examiners who were negatively disposed to recommend compensation for survivors were considered hostile and insensitive. Those who pressed for a more lenient attitude concerning indemnities were regarded as humane and caring. Recently some voices have claimed that the entire indemnification process was a disservice to the survivor. Criticism has also been leveled at those who have appeared sympathetic to survivor claims in the form of suggesting that the examiners, many of whom were refugees who had managed to escape from Europe before being caught in the Nazi net, were warding off their own guilt and even showing contempt for victims. It is also possible that those mental health professionals who are now so critical are survivors who have a need to show that they have emerged from a situation of mortal ruin even better able to consolidate their intactness than those of us who have not been so crucially tested.

Sharp differences may be encountered during treatment in the way Holocaust material is recounted and how it is used by the therapist. An interesting analysis was reported by Freedman (1978), with a published discussion by Blum (1978). The patient was a survivor of the Warsaw ghetto and had developed an unusual perversion after the war. The analysis was conducted with hardly a reference to the events of the Holocaust and the patient's participation in the heroic and doomed ghetto uprising. The determinants of the perversion were accounted for and explained by the earlier life history of the patient and by intrapsychic conflicts developed during this early period. Although the patient lost his family in Europe, helping him to mourn his losses and to bear witness seemed to have played no significant role in the treatment, which was said to have terminated with relief of presenting symptoms. Blum, in his discussion, had some question about the omission of Holocaust material in the analytic work and stressed the likely importance of certain elements in the perversion which turned the patient's personal tragedy into triumph over the Nazi persecutors.

In contrast, we can consider the case of Susan, an intelligent and perceptive woman in her late 50s, who sought treatment for severe guilt feelings, anxiety, low self-esteem, and various somatic symptoms, referable to her gastrointestinal and cardiovascular systems, clearly not identifiable as organically determined. She was married to an American husband, who had some creative talent, but worked at a job he despised. His bitterness, disappointment, and uneven temperament contributed to marital discord. The couple had an older daughter who was a high achiever, but indicated signs of a larval bulemic syndrome and problems in relationships with men. A younger son seemed relatively healthy and showed promise in a business career.

Susan was born to a middle-class Jewish family in a Western European country that was invaded by the Nazis early in the war. When she was ten, her family, consisting of her parents, her brother, and herself, was captured by the Nazis and sent to a concentration camp, where they spent nearly five years before liberation. All survived, except her father, who contracted dysentery weeks before the camp was liberated. She rarely spoke to anyone about her experiences, but did so in the treatment. She recalled the horror of life in the camp, but no memories of fear or intense hatred of the guards. She was able to see her family, and one thing that sustained her was the thought that if life became totally unbearable, she could at least look forward to death. She recalled an incident when she was marching with her group in the yard; suddenly she saw a load of beets piled in a heap. Desperately hungry, she broke formation and ran to grab some food. A guard saw her, drew his gun, shot at her—and missed. It was likely he was drunk; at that distance it was almost certain she would have died.

All through the ordeal, Susan's relationship with her father, who was cheerful and optimistic, was a sustaining force. She recalled his last days with great sadness; exhausted by dysentery and pneumonia, he died in her arms and she knew she had not mourned him adequately. She could not go to the memorial service during the High Holy Days, because she could not pray with people who had lost less than she did. After liberation she returned to her native city, where her mother soon married a man the patient disliked. When he died, the family emigrated to the United States, where her brother became very successful in business. The patient had a constant feeling of guilt, worried about her mother, her children, her husband, and could not leave home for a vacation trip because she would not leave her dog with a stranger. Her only gratification was her work, which she performed skillfully and conscientiously. She also liked and admired her boss.

At first timid and cautious, she became increasingly trustful but continued to employ a cynical manner to ward off strong affects. She frequently made her own interpretations, because accepting something from her therapist would place her in his debt and put her at a disadvantage. She kept track of the time, called a halt to her sessions, and consistently paid her bill at the end of the month before she received it. When this vignette was first reported (Jucovy, 1982), it was suggested that Susan's early development did not indicate a potential for the sustained and chronic disability shown in her adult life. Her guilt, self-deprecation, tendency to somatization, and moderate xenophobia seemed to conform to the complex of symptoms seen and described in the literature as late sequelae of massive and cumulative Holocaust trauma. The relatively good adaptations made by her mother and brother made her difficutlies stand out in even bolder relief, but were not necessarily puzzling. It would not be rash to speculate that the age at which she suffered the trauma may have made her particularly vulnerable and placed her at greater risk. The complexities involved are highlighted by comparing this clinical experience, where it was well-nigh impossible to ignore the Holocaust, to the one reported by Freedman, where the entire analysis was hinged to pre-Holocaust experiences, although it was indicated that attention to the Warsaw ghetto experience may have enriched understanding of the symptoms.

THE HOLOCAUST: FAMILY SECRETS AND SUPEREGO PATHOLOGY

The nature of psychic structure, particularly the superego, as it appears in many who have been touched by the Holocaust, has received considerable attention. Helen Epstein (1979) has commented on the extremes which might be noted, stating that it was as if many felt that the Holocaust had created a kind of human mutant, intrinsically different from ordinary people. Novels, plays, and films have frequently presented polarized characterizations, portraying survivors either as saints and martyrs, people who had experienced the worst and could do no wrong, or as little more than shells of their former selves, near criminals at times, who must have stooped to inhuman measures to prolong their lives and have continued their misanthropic and deviant behavior and attitudes into the post-Holocaust world.

Some examples of creative literature which have painted this polarized picture might be mentioned. John Hersey's novel, *The Wall*, presented a dramatic account of the Warsaw ghetto uprising, as did *Mila 18,* in memorializing this courageous and doomed struggle. Leon Uris, the author of the latter novel, also wrote a stirring popular book, *Exodus*, later made into a film, about the attempts of survivors to reach Palestine during the British mandate. Claude Lanzmann, with passionate dedication, has conveyed something of the unknowable into our collective awareness in what many consider the greatest documentary film about contemporary history ever made. Without being idealized, the survivors interviewed in *Shoah* are impressive in their wholeness, their dignity, and courage. Intermediate in the range of presenting Holocaust survivors is a film called *The Pawnbroker,* a portrayal of a man in almost interminable mourning, closed off and psychologically numbed, whose redemption and "self-healing" occur through a touching relationship with his young Hispanic assistant. Lina Wertmuller's film *Seven Beauties* was about a non-Jewish, Italian man, a small-time sociopath, sent to a concentration camp after deserting his military unit. His section in the camp was commanded by a particularly sadistic woman. The survival of the anti-hero, as suggested by the film, is precisely a result of his lack of scruples and contrasted to the degradation and death of a courageous and altruistic fellow prisoner. *The Night Porter,* set in post–World War II Europe, described the accidental reunion of two former lovers, a young woman who had been a concentration camp prisoner and a man who had been a guard in the camp. Flashbacks depict explicit sadomasochistic sexual activity between the prisoner and her guard. The film, though skillfully made, was offensive to many, who felt its portrayal of the Holocaust victim an exploitation which did more than hint at collaboration and betrayal. *The Man in the Glass Booth,* by Robert Shaw, is a curious and ambiguous play in which the main character is a Jew who pretends to be a Nazi war criminal obviously modeled after Eichmann, who arranges to be tried in Jerusalem in order to highlight further Nazi crimes. These selected examples, while not reflecting complete polarization, nevertheless give some indication of the range of superego qualities attributed to survivors in current popular literature and theater.

Terence Des Pres (1976) provides a model for those who wish to turn from a total preoccupation with the horror of the camps and to attend to examples of life and decency, however dim and scattered, which can be seen as the existence of good in the midst of evil. He attempts to portray how even in the state of extremity in which the victims dwelled, documents and testimony indicate a connection between staying alive and staying human. He claims that life in the camps was intensely social and included the most essential qualities of humanness, an active sense of conscience and dignity, significant acts of help and sharing, and collective resistance to the Nazi tyranny.

Turning to the other side of the ledger, we must consider the contributions of Ilse Grubrich-Simitis (1981), who pointed out that the threat of narcissistic depletion was due not only to extended periods of deprivation of external narcissistic supplies, but also to changes in the superego as a result of massive assaults on the victims' psyche. These alterations consisted of regression to more archaic forms of superego functioning and led to grave changes in the ego ideal. The devalued image propagated by the persecutors established itself insidiously in the ideal self of the victims, thus transforming it and contributing, for defensive needs, paradoxically and tragically, an additional dimension to the mechanism of identification with the aggressor, originally utilized by the victims in an attempt to undo their sense of helplessness and to check the process of narcissistic depletion. A poignant example of how the perpetuation of this pattern of defense can affect the future was noted in the case of a young man who was hospitalized during a psychotic episode. He told his therapist how during his childhood, his mother, a concentration camp survivor, would place his head in the kitchen oven when he misbehaved and warn him that this was what the Nazis did to Jews in the camps.

Maria Bergmann (1982) found in her experience with survivor families that in a number of instances superego functions seemed more disturbed than ego functions. Although these individuals appeared to adapt normally in the external world, an understanding of people's motivations, certain value judgments, or some other environmental phenomena might often be confused. The superego of the survivor parent was often found to have undergone disorganization by the invasion of Nazi ideology. In many case histories, splitting of self and objects in superego representation was manifested, with the survivor parent at times identified with Nazi morality, but also at other times condemning it vigorously. Because of such splitting, parental messages to children were often confused.

Laub and Auerhahn (1984) emphasize similar themes they found regularly in the life of families damaged by the Holocaust. They report on the one hand the presence of a harsh superego, but also one which is featured by what they call "lacunae," which may develop in a superego which is adapting to an abnormal reality, one where all the usual rules are broken. The individual then comes to believe that customs, rules, or contractual agreements cannot be taken seriously in a world in which survival is at stake. The commitment to life, one's own, those close to one, and the lives of one's people overrides every other consideration.

Judith Kestenberg (1982) presented a metapsychological assessment or profile based on psychoanalytic observations of the daughter born to a survivor family. In describing her patient's superego, she noted that the girl's ego ideal was not easily distinguishable from the punitive superego and from her narcissistic omnipotence. The patient aspired to be a redeemer who would bring back all Jews in some magical way. She overvalued what her body could endure without suffering and also hoped to compensate for what she regarded as her physician father's unlawful escape from death during the Holocaust. She felt the escape was not lawful because most of her father's family had died and because he was paid by his patient, which meant a betrayal of his ideals. When her father provided money for her education, it appeared to her that this indulgence contradicted his injunctions that she must steel herself against the Nazis; money from the father and from the Nazis coddled Jews and made them weak. But money was also proof that her father was smarter than the Germans and could be more powerful and outwit the enemy. Her father had also taught her that knowledge was superior to money and could be used to sabotage plans of the persecutors. She formed the idea that to work for oppressors and to undermine them was the most valuable aim in life. To be both a redeemer and a victim and to serve her father through the workings of her body were all interwoven with Rachel's code which resembled the one the Nazis imposed upon the Jews. Rachel needed to be punished for her sexual fantasies. She had to become sexless through starvation, pregnant through being constipated, deprived of progeny through loss of menstruation, and also symbolically castrated. She had a need to be punished for eating when she was hungry and to train herself not to go to the bathroom. She saw the Nazis as aggressive jailers, but also so stupid that they could be outwitted. She frequently used totally gratuitous and devious tricks at school to destroy material entrusted to her care. These tricks were easily discovered, and she was reprimanded and threatened with expulsion from school. Being caught implied that she would be sent to a concentration camp and become a slave. One of her teachers, not knowing her background, but intuitively recognizing a possible source of her curious behavior, told her that the school was not a labor camp.

Additional support can be lent to a perception that superego functions may be subject to compromise and distortion in survivors and their children by the following clinical example. A young, married, professional man in his 30s came for analysis because of difficulties in his work and personal life. His parents had been born in Eastern Europe and had been in labor camps during the Nazi era. The parents had met and married in Europe after the war and eventually emigrated to the United States after the birth of the patient and his younger sister. During the analysis we learned that there was a marked discrepancy between his behavior as a devoted husband and father and his conscientious devotion to most of his responsibilities and his tendency to take certain short-cuts in his work which were easily detected and counterproductive to his professional advancement. He was extremely suspicious in his dealings with merchants and not always scrupulous in the usual commercial transactions which can occur in life. He thought me quaint and innocently impractical when I invited him to scrutinize these traits more closely. He insisted that one cheats in order not to be cheated until he recognized that his tendency to be less than diligent arose from the same conflicts as the traits he tended to dismiss with his typical cynicism. When this was related to his parents' struggle for survival in the hostile world of the Holocaust, important modifications occurred.

Turning our attention to a significant element in the development and function of the superego, the presence of family secrets, we might note that the issues of knowing and not knowing are at the very core of our psychoanalytic work as we attempt to help our patients resolve their unconscious conflicts. During these efforts, we are continually working with secrets the revelation of which we trust will result in changes consistent with greater adaptational capacities. Although encounters with secrets are ubiquitous in our work, their presence and impact may be more apparent in members of certain groups. In the families of both victims and persecutors of the Holocaust, important segments of a child's development may be influenced by parental withholding of information and even revelations of parental and family experiences may be shrouded in uncertainty, distortion, and mystery. The clinical example to be cited, one reported anonymously (1982), concerns the stepdaughter of a Nazi SS officer, who was killed during the war. The patient's mother continued to be an unregenerate and virulent anti-Semite. Frieda, the patient, whose early life was spent on the safer side of the barbed wire, was nevertheless as surely a victim of Nazi ideology as those who survived internment in the camps or as partisans in the woods. It may be considered improper and objectionable to link a child of persecutors with issues affecting the victims of persecution (which brings up yet another controversy in Holocaust studies), but while vast differences remain, unsuspected similarities have emerged, justifying the comparison. In this vignette, superego distortions which reflected inconsistent and uneven development were found, and the connection with family secrets will be stessed as an explanatory concept.

Frieda was an attractive and intelligent young woman who had emigrated after the end of World War II with her twice-widowed mother to a country where it was not popular to express anti-Semitic ideas openly. The symptoms which led her to seek analytic treatment included periods of anxiety and depression, difficulties in sustaining an involved and committed relationship with a suitable man, and a moderate degree of frigidity, with an inability to achieve orgasm. She also confessed, after treatment began, that she had a history of stealing small objects from stores, things she could easily have paid for. This behavior was in sharp contrast with her otherwise conscientious and responsible qualities. The patient was born just after the war began and later spent time in a displaced persons' camp with her mother, a place where some educational experience and indoctrination with democratic ideals must have occurred. She became rather strongly philo-Semitic in her adopted country, made many Jewish friends, and specifically requested a Jewish analyst when she sought treatment.

The patient's father died before she was born and when she was three, her mother remarried. The patient revered her stepfather, who was an officer in the German army and was killed in combat when she was five years old. During the analysis she learned that he had been an officer in the notorious SS and that he and other members of the family had participated in the extermination of Jews. Before she learned about this, her mother had continued to tell her that she herself knew nothing of what was going on during the period of the persecutions, although she did not condemn what had occurred. The patient told her analyst that her own knowledge about what had happened to Jews was acquired from the mass media after the war and she had been deeply shocked by what she read.

After her mother's remarriage when Frieda was three, the stepfather's activities were idealized by the little girl, who felt he must be the bravest man. She may have been exposed to some knowledge of the activities of the stepfather's unit when he was home on leave. It was among the most ferocious in the Nazi military machine, but a combination of defenses were utilized to preserve the idealization and ward off knowledge of the stepfather's complicity in murder.

A series of dreams and associations enabled the analyst to confront his patient with some reconstructions which brought further material to the surface. At one point she mused about Lady Macbeth and ruminated over whether she had actually killed Duncan or had merely been an accessory. These thoughts occurred as associations to a dream in which she was in a room with a dangerous homicidal man and saw that her hands were bloody. She wondered about feeling like an accessory in the murder of Jews and about her stepfather's part in it. She recalled that the man in the dream was someone she read about who was committed to a mental hospital for trying to kill his family with a gas oven. There was another dream about a fish tank with powder on the bottom which stuck to her hand like the blood in the other dream. There were stone slabs on the bottom of the tank and nothing was alive in it. The analyst pointed out the similarity to gas chambers, but the patient insisted this could not be so. She had no knowledge of what went on and her mother kept insisting to the patient that she had no knowledge either.

When recurring dreams about fish tanks ensued, the analyst felt the patient could be confronted with the possibility that on some level, during her childhood, she had some inkling about what was really happening and that she assumed her stepfather's guilt, but had to treat it as a secret, even from herself. She then reported persistent memories of playing in a basement which contained an abandoned pool with stagnant water and a series of tunnels. She and her playmates had believed that the pool was filled with the bodies of dead Jews and the tunnels were where the Jews had hidden before they were killed. She recalled that the word "Jew" had been an abstraction that meant the same thing as someone to hate. The patient had been told for years by her mother that the family knew nothing about the persecutions and the killings and had been certain she believed it. Now she could finally confront her mother and question her further to learn what was going on when she was a child. When the guilty identification with her stepfather was interpreted and worked through, her kleptomanic tendencies which appeared to be linked with this guilty identification cleared up and she was soon able to report to her analyst that she had reached orgasm for the first time. The analysis was successfully terminated not long thereafter. This clinical example seems to be of particular interest and significance because it appears related to Judith Kestenberg's discussion (1972) of the contribution of parents to the way in which screen memories can be structured in the child. She pointed out how a child organizes nonverbal memories under the guidance of parents who supply the words and the organization. During this process, certain deletions and distortions can occur, particularly when the parents are prone to deny and repress. When the child remembers something the parents have a need to forget, access may be lost to the verbal communication of the memory, and acting out is likely to occur.

The influence of family secrets may thus have an important effect on the child's developing personality and might particularly involve the function of memories which touch on the child's basic fears of object loss and loss of love. A number of others have commented on the importance of family secrets as they affect analytic work. In a communication about the issue of "knowing" about details of the Holocaust, Jucovy (1985) asserted that while the usual vicissitudes encountered in development are certainly important, Holocaust material can become a crucial organizing factor in pathogenesis and the importance of family secrets must be carefully considered in analytic work. Theodore Jacobs (1980) pointed out that the word *secret* comes from the same root as "secretion" and suggested that the idea of a secret may be associated with the private secretions of the body. Secrets may thus be associated with issues of control and power linked to sphincter control and also involved with precursors of superego development. The harboring of secrets may also promote additional guilt as a result of overstimulation of the drives, both libidinal and aggressive. In this context, family secrets about the Holocaust may be experienced in terms of the child's secrets, thus augmenting a connection between universal developmental conflicts and problems derived more specifically from Holocaust-related issues. Excessive drive stimulation may involve sexual and aggressive fantasies and the masturbatory practices associated with such fantasies. It is certainly not unreasonable to suspect that knowing or not knowing about the details of a secret which is suspected to exist may provide additional impetus to scoptophilic impulses, particularly those connected with primal scene fantasies. The use of words like "to know," when interpreted in a concrete, archaic, and "Biblical" sense, can suggest the possibility of a special coloring to phallic and oedipal fantasies in some instances. Guilt may be thus increased and pose additional problems for oedipal complex resolution and further maturation of a stable superego, freed of its primitive tyrannical features.

When one is excluded from sharing a secret or made partner to it, a burden is created. Increased tolerance for deceit and subterfuge may result from exposure to deception or collusion. This pattern may also result when communication about the Holocaust is excessively colored by a personal myth or distortion. A young man, whose mother had been in Auschwitz, consistently romanticized her memories, he told his therapist. It has been noted by those who gathered material for archival projects of Holocaust testimony that concentration camp prisoners often sustained themselves by the elaboration of halcyon fantasies of liberation, reunion with family members, and a future free of pain and torture. The energy and imagination required to construct such fantasies can serve an important adaptive function in warding off feelings of helplessness. However, when such fantasies are sustained through the years and told to a child as if they represented historical truth, considerable confusion can be created and potentiate later problems in reality testing. We may need to idealize some aspects of life in the camps, but we must also be aware, as examples indicate, that victims may be vulnerable to superego and also ego pathology. This must be confronted if we, as mental health professionals, are to help those who consult us for treatment.

MOURNING, REMEMBERING, AND COMMEMORATING THE HOLOCAUST

An extensive literature, mainly clinical, has developed about the Holocaust, once initial barriers were breached. The hands of the clock have indeed behaved metaphorically as a pendulum, and the passage of time has uncovered some important controversies in Holocaust studies which were not initially apparent. Luel and Marcus (1984), in the introduction to their book, have deplored the meager offerings about the broader ramifications extending beyond the clinical. Maintaining that psychoanalysis comes closest to conveying the turbulence of human behavior, and compellingly passionate in the sense of being involved with human suffering, they cite Erich Kahler's statement (1967) that the most frightening aspects of our present world are not the horrors and the atrocities themselves, but the fact that at the very root of it all is the fading of any human criterion. The question is posed whether psychoanalysis can aim only at circumscribed goals such as contributions to treating individual emotional problems, or whether it can be preventive in ameliorating the pathology of contemporary society. We apparently cannot escape the Furies, but may help in their being felicitously renamed the Eumenedies. It might, therefore, be appropriate to examine some of the statements and recommendations made about our responses to the Holocaust and how it might be seen in future generations. Divisions of opinion here are less intense and polarized than in the issues already described.

Mourning, remembering, and commemorating are foremost on our agendas in our ongoing struggle to prevent the occurrence of yet another Holocaust, whatever form it may take. After the long period of latency and silence, the active awakening has seen the increasing formation of groups of survivors, their children, large gatherings and conferences, gathering of testimony for important archival projects for further historical research and education. Memorials have been erected or planned and a day of remembrance, Yom Hashoa, has been declared and observed in many countries. Sheldon Roth (1988) has wisely and correctly reminded us that there are still remote places and preliterate peoples on earth where the Holocaust has never been heard about or ever will. Despite the efforts of a few, either to minimize it or deny it ever took place, the accessible world knows about the persecutions.

K. R. Eissler (1969) is among those who stand firmly against denial which he feels may be stimulated by the tragic comprehension that may be invited by psychoanalytic study. He said, "Truth, bitter as it is, may enlarge man's self—as it has so often in the past—and man, having shed one more denial, may enjoy the state of enlarged inner freedom despite the recognition of how merciless that reality is of which he is a part" (p. 312). Martin Wangh (1984) confronts the future by discussing defenses often employed by both victims and the outside world in the wake of the Holocaust, which have led to denial, numbing, and silence. He warns that the persistence and comforting protection provided by such defenses can be dangerous in the face of the grave threat of a nuclear holocaust, and that excessive complacency may result in plunging us all into the abyss. Just a little more than 25 years after the end of World War II, which uncovered, with the liberation of the camps, how society could murder its soul, events occurred in the United States which exposed once more how ambition, the obsession with power, and rampant arrogance and narcissism could nearly envelop a society. The exploration of this phenomenon by Leo Rangell (1980, 1984) is yet another scathing indictment of how the integrity of ordinary people could be surrendered to the will of a flawed leader and coterie.

Sheldon Roth (1988) feels that we are destined to remember,

as mourning is designed for loss, not catastrophe, and therefore for most victims, psychological processes do not contain a sector for fully integrating the Holocaust. Henry Krystal (1984) addressed the problems of the aging survivor and suggested that the achievement of serenity requires a successful completion of adequate mourning, a process denied during the persecutions. There is a great need, Krystal feels, that aging survivors relinquish their outrage in any self-healing process. This is very difficult to do, as many feel that this would grant the Nazi killers a posthumous and ultimate victory. Roth feels that when Krystal asks victims to complete their mourning and relinquish their rage, he is asking what most humans are incapable of doing.

Rafael Moses (1984) expressed the hope that remembrance of the Holocaust in Israel will not remain a decreed institutionalized event and that visits to Yad Vashem and other memorials will not always be regimented, demanded, or even expected. He feels that the mourning and remembering will be chosen by the individual as far as time, place, and manner, to commemorate the tragedy that befell the Jewish people and that such freedom would further the study of the aftereffects of the Holocaust, a project for which we have little time left. It is clear that the differences expressed are more delicate and related more to issues of form, rather than content, which characterized problems described earlier. Cohen and Moses (1988) called attention to the emotional closeness or distance we allow ourselves in our own reactions to the Holocaust and said it was important to pay attention to our intrapsychic processes and to what degree we are touched by the suffering, the grief, and the terrible choices which had to be made. Anna Freud (1936) had commented that identification in combination with other mechanisms can be a potent weapon in dealing with external objects which arouse anxiety. Moses and Cohen propose that a more mature defense can be nurtured, less primitive than identification with the aggressor, which involves acknowledging consciously identification with perpetrators of violence and locating and identifying the aggressor within ourselves. This awareness can allow distancing from the Holocaust in a way that would allow at least a modicum of internal peace and tranquillity.

As I conclude, it might be appropriate to return to something suggested by Roth (1988), for it resonates with some thoughts I have pondered for some time. Roth feels that those of us who were distant from the Holocaust must integrate the experience in some significant way. It would only be possible for the survivors to dilute their grief in bearable portions in future generations. The special task of those who were not directly involved is that we innoculate ourselves with a homeopathic dose of the experience, to feel the pain and the loss of dignity and humanity. Some windows into our childhood fantasy and terror may allow us to catch some glimpses of what others felt. In some ways this can be similar to the prism through which children of survivors have experienced their parents' ordeals. Here we may turn to our knowledge of the normal developmental process which takes place in adolescence and culminates in the attainment of autonomy as a mature adult. We have observed that one of the special tasks of being a survivor's child is the relinquishment of a redemptive need which binds the child to the parent in an excessive way and creates problems in the development of autonomy and individuation. The hoped-for result is that the mourning process can be reduced and diluted, so that it becomes no longer a pathological burden. In this way those who perished in the Holocaust can be memorialized, those who survived can be respected and honored, and the generations to come can maintain their historical identity and realize their potential as honorable and responsible members of society.

REFERENCES

Adorno, T. (1973), After Auschwitz. In: *Negative Dialectics*. New York: Seabury, pp. 366–367.

Anonymous (1982), Child of persecutors. In: *Generations of the Holocaust*, ed. M. S. Bergmann & M. E. Jucovy. New York: Basic Books, pp. 183–196.

Arlow, J. A. (1981), Theories of pathogenesis. *Psychoanal. Quart.*, 50:488–514.

Bergen, M. D. (1958), The effects of severe trauma on a four-year-old child. *The Psychoanalytic Study of the Child*, 13:407–429. New York: International Universities Press.

Bergmann, M. S., & Jucovy, M. E., eds. (1982), *Generations of the Holocaust*. New York: Basic Books.

Bergmann, M. V. (1982), Thoughts on superego pathology of survivors and their children. In: *Generations of the Holocaust*, ed. M. S. Bergmann & M. E. Jucovy. New York: Basic Books, pp. 287–309.

Blum, H. P. (1978), Discussion of psychoanalytic study of an unusual perversion by A. Freedman. *J. Amer. Psychoanal. Assn.*, 26:785–792.

Chodoff, P. (1963), Late effects of the concentration camp syndrome. *Arch. Gen. Psychiat.*, 8:323–333.

Cohen, Y., & Moses, R. (1988), The meaning of the Holocaust for those not directly affected. Read at the Fourth Conference of the Sigmund Freud Center of the Hebrew University of Jerusalem, May 24–26.

Des Pres, T. (1976), *The Survivor*. New York: Oxford University Press.

Eissler, K. R. (1960), Variationen in der psychoanalytischen Technique. *Psyche*, 13:609–624.

——— (1967), Perverted psychiatry. *Amer. J. Psychiat.*, 123:1352–1358.

——— (1969), *The Psychiatrist and the Dying Patient*. New York: International Universities Press.

Eitinger, L. (1961), Pathology of the concentration camp syndrome. *Arch. Gen. Psychiat.*, 5:371–379.

Epstein, H. (1979), *Children of the Holocaust*. New York: Putnam's.

Freedman, A. (1978), Psychoanalytic study of an unusual perversion. *J. Amer. Psychoanal. Assn.*, 26:749–777.

Freud, A. (1936), *The Ego and the Mechanisms of Defense*. New York: International Universities Press.

——— (1958), Child observation and prediction. *The Psychoanalytic Study of the Child*, 13:112–116. New York: International Universities Press.

——— (1960), Discussion of Dr. John Bowlby's paper. *The Psychoanalytic Study of the Child*, 15:53–62. New York: International Universities Press.

Freud, S. (1920), Beyond the pleasure principle. *Standard Edition*, 18:3–64. London: Hogarth Press, 1955.

——— (1926), Inhibitions, symptoms and anxiety. *Standard Edition*, 20:77–174. London: Hogarth Press, 1959.

Friedman, P. (1949), Some aspects of concentration camp psychology. *Amer. J. Psychiat.*, 105:602–605.

Grubrich-Simitis, I. G. (1981), Extreme traumatization as cumulative trauma. *The Psychoanalytic Study of the Child*, 36:415–450.

Gyomroi, E. L. (1963), The analysis of a young concentration camp victim. *The Psychoanalytic Study of the Child*, 13:484–510. New York: International Universities Press.

Jacobs, T. (1980), Secrets, alliances and family fictions. *J. Amer. Psychoanal. Assn.*, 28:21–42.

Jucovy, M. E. (1982), Prelude. In: *Generations of the Holocaust*, ed. M. S. Bergman & M. E. Jucovy. New York: Basic Books, pp. 3–29.

——— (1985), Telling the Holocaust story. *Psychoanal. Inq.*, 51:31–49.

Kahler, E. (1967), *The Tower and the Abyss*. New York: Viking.

Keilson, H. (1979), *Sequential Traumatization of Children*. Stuttgart: Ferdinand Enke.

Kestenberg, J. S. (1972), How children remember and parents forget. *Internat. J. Psychoanal. Psychother.*, 1(2):103–123.

——— (1982), A metapsychological assessment based on an analysis of a survivor's child. In: *Generations of the Holocaust*, ed. M. S. Bergmann & M. E. Jucovy. New York: Basic Books, pp. 137–158.

Kestenberg, M. (1982), Discriminatory aspects of the German indemnification policy. In: *Generations of the Holocaust*, ed. M. S. Bergmann & M. E. Jucovy. New York: Basic Books, pp. 62–79.

Kisker, K. P. (1961), Die psychiatrische Begutachtung der Opfer Nationalsozialistischer Verfolgung. In: *Psychiatria et Neurologia*. Dresden: Geselloch.

Krystal, H. (1984), Integration and self-healing in post-traumatic states. In: *Psychoanalytic Reflections on the Holocaust: Selected Essays*, ed. S. A. Luel & P. Marcus. New York: Ktav, pp. 113–133.

Laub, D., & Auerhahn, N. C. (1984), Reverberations of genocide. In: *Psychoanalytic Reflections on the Holocaust: Selected Essays*, ed. S. A. Luel & P. Marcus. New York: Ktav, pp. 151–167.

Luel, S. A., & Marcus, P., eds. (1984), *Psychoanalytic Reflections on the Holocaust: Selected Essays*. New York: Ktav.

Moses, R. (1984), An Israeli psychoanalyst looks back in 1983. In: *Psychoanalytic Reflections on the Holocaust: Selected Essays*, ed. S. A. Luel & P. Marcus. New York: Ktav, pp. 53–69.

Niederland, W. G. (1964), Psychiatric disorder among persecution victims. *J. Nerv. Ment. Dis.*, 139:458–474.

——— (1968), Clinical observations on the "survivor syndrome." *Internat. J. Psycho-Anal.*, 49:313–315.

Ornstein, A. (1984), Survival and recovery. Read at the American Psychoanalytic Association, November.

Rangell, L. (1980), *The Mind of Watergate: An Explanation of the Compromise of Integrity*. New York: Norton.

——— (1984), German psychoanalysis, the moral issue. *Amer. Psychoanal. Assn. Newsletter*, 18:1–6.

Roth, S. (1988), The shadow of the Holocaust. Read at the Fourth Conference of the Sigmund Freud Center of the Hebrew University of Jerusalem, May 24–26.

Terry, J. (1984), The damaging effects of the "survivor syndrome." In: *Psychoanalytic Reflections on the Holocaust: Selected Essays*, ed. S. A. Luel & P. Marcus. New York: Ktav, pp. 135–148.

Wangh, M. (1969), Workshop on children of survivors. International Psychoanalytical Congress, Rome, August.

——— (1971), Die Beurteilung von Wiedergutmachungsansprüchen der während der Nationalsozialistischen Verfolgung geborenen Kinder. In: *Spätschaden nach Extrembelastungen*. West Germany: Herberg, pp. 270–274.

——— (1984), On obstacles to the working-through of the Nazi Holocaust experience and on the consequences of failing to do so. In: *Psychoanalytic Reflections on the Holocaust: Selected Essays*, ed. S. A. Luel & P. Marcus. New York: Ktav, pp. 197–205.

Winnik, H. Z. (1967), Psychiatric disturbances of Holocaust survivors. *Israel Ann. Psychiat. Rel. Discip.*, 5:91–100.

25

SHAME AND ENTITLEMENT: THEIR RELATION TO POLITICAL PROCESS

RAFAEL MOSES, M.D.

In examining the appearance of shame and entitlement, their antecedents, and their structural aspects, I will lay the ground for the question: Do they play a part in the political process? Here the reader will already discern a connection to Leo Rangell's writings, particularly "The Mind of Watergate" (1980) and "A Psychoanalytic Perspective Leading Inevitably to the Syndrome of the Compromise of Integrity" (1974).

Both shame and entitlement have not been examined very much in psychoanalysis. More has been written about shame, especially in the last 15 years, than about entitlement. Yet even with regard to shame many authors complain that shame has not been sufficiently dealt with. Clearly this is much more true for entitlement about which I could not find more than about ten to 12 specific references (Blechner, 1987; Freud, 1916; Horowitz, 1981; Jacobson, 1959; Kriegman, 1983; Lax, 1975; Levin, 1970; Murray, 1964; Rothstein, 1977, 1980; Segel, 1981). Both Kernberg (1977) and Kohut (1971, 1972, 1977) deal with areas closely related to both phenomena. The British school of psychoanalysis and Kohut are probably most responsible for bringing shame into clinical psychoanalysis in the past ten to 15 years.

Why did I choose to put shame and entitlement together? I believe that there is a connection between the two. They are connected in that each of them is closely related to the self, to narcissistic proclivities. But further than that, it seems to me that shame and entitlement are in some way opposite sides of the same coin. A person who is full of conscious shame will usually not feel a conscious sense of entitlement. The converse is also true: a person brimming with a conscious sense of entitlement mostly does not consciously feel shame. Shame and a sense of entitlement do not consciously exist at the same time. However, repressed shame, particularly of past suffering perceived as shameful, at times serves as the basis for a sense of excessive entitlement which may be or become conscious (Moses-Hrushovski, 1987, personal communication). There may also be a link between entitlement and shamelessness (Lowenfeld, 1976).

We do not know very much about the development of shame. There is little information on the time at which shame is first observable in children. I could find no reference to shame in Mahler, Pine, and Bergman (1975). Freud (1905, 1916–1917) connects shame with exhibitionism and scoptophilia, which would place it somewhere in the phallic period. Yet some authors place these phenomena at an earlier period. Broucek (1982) places the appearance of shame, in Kohutian terms, at the age of 18 to 24 months, when objective self-awareness begins to lead to a shame crisis. Kohut does not give a specific age at which shame first appears. His formulation is that shame arises when the ego is unable to provide the proper discharge for the exhibitionistic demand of the narcissistic self (Ornstein, 1978). Elsewhere Kohut (1972) speaks of shame as "a disorganized mixture of massive discharge (tension decrease), and a blockage (tension increase) in the area of exhibitionistic libido that is experienced as shame." Kohut also speaks of shame as resulting from empathic failure by the parent or the analyst. Erikson (1950) relates shame to the anal period when the focus is on the child's reaching autonomy; if he does not do so, the danger is that he will become mired in shame and doubt.

Structurally shame has been defined as the discrepancy between the ego ideal and the assessment of the extent to which these goals have or have not been reached, i.e., "the real ego," or the ideal self and the real self. I would wonder, however, whether there are not signs of shame behavior in a child of a year to a year and a half. A relevant consideration would be when the parents feel that shaming can be used with a child. At what point does it happen that they use the specific, educational mechanism of shaming, in addition to forbidding an act, when they want the child to refrain from doing something?

The situation with regard to entitlement seems more complicated. A child behaves quite early in a way that indicates that he is indeed entitled to the total, undivided attention of the mother or the adults that take care of him. Feelings of entitlement are certainly an integral part of the toddler's early omnipotence. He ascribes the same omnipotence to the parents to whom the entitlement demands are addressed. The question here needs to be posed in the reverse form to that posed for shame: At what age do those children who are not narcissistically damaged give up their excessive sense of entitlement?

Levin (1967, 1971) was the first to indicate three quantitatively rough categories of attitudes of entitlement, namely, normal, excessive, and restricted entitlement. On this latter category, entitlement is being withheld and not expressed.

Mark Blechner (1987) similarly differentiates between entitlement that is expressed and entitlement that is withheld. He also differentiates between claims of entitlement which are issued in fact and attitudes of entitlement which are kept to oneself and suppressed or repressed. In other words, there can be a sense of underentitlement or overentitlement (see also Grey, 1987).

We will, of course, not forget that the original description of entitlement was given to us by Freud (1916) in his paper on the exceptions. He clearly tells us that each one of us tends to think of himself as an exception and will therefore make special demands. It is because we all want to be exceptions that a particular and special reasoning is needed for someone who wants to claim the rights of an exception and to behave as one. Freud tells us that the sense of entitlement to be considered an exception and therefore to have special rights may relate to experiences gone through most often in early childhood. For the person to be entitled, it is essential that such experiences or suffering should be known to come about without any fault of the person himself; it must therefore be perceived by him, as by others, as an unjust deprivation. Rothstein (1980), on the other hand, states that some people overcome early suffering or deprivation without a sense of entitlement; whereas others who do show excessive entitlement have a narcissistic personality without having undergone sufferings in the past.

Freud (1916) paraphrases Gloucester's opening soliloquy in *Richard III* as: "I may do wrong myself, since wrong has been done to me" (p. 315). Freud also makes a statement that I want to take out of the context in which it seems totally to disappear. He says, "Nor do I propose to go into the obvious analogy between deformities of character resulting from protracted sickliness in childhood and the behaviour of whole nations whose past history has been full of suffering" (p. 313). Through this sentence, Freud opens up a field which has not been investigated or dealt with, namely, the sense of entitlement as it affects nations. This would be one example of how a sense of entitlement might be active in the political process. We might wonder how easily discernible this sense of entitlement might be in nations (see also Moses, 1982). We will also ask ourselves whether the nation he had particularly in mind was the Jewish nation.

It is through focusing our attention on narcissistic phenomena that we psychoanalysts have in recent years become more aware of the importance of entitlement. We have met this phenomenon first and foremost in persons with severe narcissistic disturbances who megalomanically make demands which seem out of place, yet to them seem absolutely essential (Rothstein, 1977, 1980). It is much more difficult to become aware of a hidden sense of entitlement not directly discernible behind a cloak of marked modesty. In this case the sense of entitlement is often largely unconscious or at best preconscious; it will surface in analysis only after considerable work has been done. As in reaction formation, it will only strike us in extreme cases, or after a while, that something is out of kilter. Only since we have become more attuned to the existence of entitlement and its importance in dyadic relationships have we adapted our stance so as to enable us to pick out a minimal sense of entitlement. It is only subsequently, at the third stage of having become sensitized to intense demands of entitlement and also to attitudes of underentitlement (behind which entitlement often secretly lurks), that we can focus on what would or should be the normal range of entitlement. This normal range of entitlement consists of making demands which are appropriately one's right. They are due to one not because of special experiences or of being an exception in the sense in which Freud and Edith Jacobson (1959) describe it; rather, this sense of entitlement is within the normal range.

A sense of entitlement may not be conscious. It can be unconscious or preconscious. It makes sense to conceive of entitlement as existing on an unconscious level. To think of unconscious guilt similarly makes evident sense; this has been written about a great deal.[1] When we examine whether shame can also exist without being conscious, the situation is less clear. To conceive of unconscious shame is more difficult because shame is an affect. It seems reasonable to assume that once it makes its appearance on the stage of the self, shame does not come out of nowhere. Kohut (1971) speaks of "small shame signals" (p. 181). In shame, the person feels that he would sink into the earth, disappear, because he feels so ashamed of the failure or mishap which has taken place. Wurmser (1981) speaks of shame as existing in three forms: shame anxiety (as a signal), shame affect (as an affective state), and a shame attitude (as prevailing tendency). Shame emerging in a specific area must have lurked in the wings, so to speak. Shame may have existed as a precursor or with a readiness to come out. In that sense I think we can speak of feelings of shame which have not yet reached the shame threshold.

This distinction between unconscious and conscious shame became most clear to me in thinking about shame within the framework of the political process. Here it will be apparent—or probably have become apparent—that shame and entitlement, as they may show themselves in the political process, are closely connected with the work of Leo Rangell. His book on *The Mind of Watergate* (1980) and his work on the compromise of integrity (1974) deal with an area related to shame and entitlement. Clearly Richard Nixon had an enormous sense of entitlement. It was this sense of entitlement, this feeling of "l'etat c'est moi," which made him believe that he was entitled to break the law, entitled to do things

[1] It was dealt with for the first time in a serious way by Freud (1916) when he referred to "those who are wrecked by success."

which other, lesser people had no right to do. Whether his sense of being entitled derived from a feeling that he was an exception, or that he had undergone exceptional experiences or suffering, is a moot question. Perhaps he even felt he was special, having been hounded and mistreated more than any other leader (p. 213). Rangell alludes to the suffering Nixon experienced, but it does not relate to early childhood. He may have collected injustice (Bergler, 1952; quoted in Cooper, 1984). As regards shame, Richard Nixon could not be seen to show any signs of shame with regard to the long series of events before, during, or after Watergate. Those moments where one would have most expected him to display feelings of shame, e.g., when impeachment seemed around the corner, Nixon showed anger, rage (perhaps the righteous rage of entitlement), apparent a feeling of having been discriminated against—but no shame. One might say that his behavior was shameless, not only at that crucial moment when he was about to resign, but shameless throughout much of his life.

Nixon's sense of entitlement derived also from his august office. He clearly felt that because he was President, he was entitled to being treated differently from other persons. Indeed as President he received special treatment in a variety of ways, which must have enhanced his attitude of entitlement. One particular area of entitlement is the sense of having the right to use means that are not legitimate for other people. It is here that we come close to the area that was so beautifully described by Rangell in "The Compromise of Integrity" (1974). As Rangell points out, "Ambition, power and opportunism could be called the three horsemen of the syndrome of the compromise of integrity" (1980, p. 23). Rangell also states, "The chronic, everyday erosions of integrity, besides being conscious and accountable, are automatic and unconscious . . . and as camouflaged into everyday life—as in other emotional symptoms or traits" (p. 12).

I made a case for viewing the Watergate syndrome as a chain of events which could take place in any society (Moses, 1986). I thought it probably took place in a variety of societies, but was not being discovered, i.e., not brought up in public and therefore not dealt with openly. I pointed out that there were probably some countries, for example, France, where it was more likely that such events had taken place without coming to public attention. My thesis about the Watergate syndrome, therefore, is that this is a pattern of behavior which allows its instigators a conduct which in any other situation would be judged to be unacceptable, deviant, and illegal. The person or persons involved in a Watergate situation, however, convince themselves that they have the right, or even the duty, to use exceptional means in order to attain what they regard as their lofty goals. In order to convince themselves, a bribing of the superego and a subverting of the ego ideal need to take place (Moses, 1986). The person so involved holds tenaciously to the conviction that his behavior is correct, appropriate, and adequate. We do not know enough about whether such people have concurrent doubts or shame but relegate them to the background, i.e., deny them. The surface impression is that they do not entertain doubts or experience shame. These are shunted aside, if necessary, by their sense of entitlement.

Since Watergate we have had another chance to know about and look at persons involved in similar ways of behaving, once more in the United States. Let me state again, I am convinced that it is to the credit of the American society that such ways of behaving are brought out into the open, are divulged, and are dealt with in public for everyone to see. In Israel there are indications of similar ways of behaving, but here considerably less material is available to document the actions as well as the mental processes of the participants. In addition, the behavior on the America scene is by now public property.

I am of course referring to what has been termed the "Irangate scandal" and to the Irangate Congressional hearings. The public view of Lieutenant Colonel Oliver North, but also of National Security Adviser Admiral Poindexter, as well as the knowledge made public about the late CIA director William Casey, provide much further material for the examination of a sense of entitlement in the political process. No matter how much of an actor Oliver North might have been, it seems likely that he was convinced that he indeed had been behaving in ways he considered to be right and proper. Elsewhere I have talked about the narcissistic gratification, the narcissistic sustenance received by a person committing illegal acts through convincing himself of the rightness of the cause on behalf of which he perpetrated these acts (Moses, 1982). Such gratification and sustenance are provided in an important way through the in-group of which the person is a part. From its members he receives repeated confirmation by people with whom he is in close contact, usually socially as well as substantively—that indeed their joint course of action is legitimate, justified, and necessary.

It seems reasonable to assume that the sense of entitlement has two derivatives: the first pertaining to a personal aspect of one's own past history where there have perhaps been exceptional events or exceptional suffering, which Freud indicated. Or, alternatively, that the preoedipal and oedipal relations have been such that the sense of entitlement, related to narcissistic needs of one or both parents, could not be given up (Rothstein, 1980). Both of these are persons who "collect injustice" (Bergler, 1952; Cooper, 1984). But the entitlement can also derive from two other sources related to the political process: from the cause in which the person is engaged, usually represented by an ideology. In the case of Irangate, this was the cause of locating allies in the hostile Iranian administration and providing money for a good, worthwhile, democratic, anticommunist cause, namely, the Contras. The second source of this sense of entitlement relates to the locus of power in the head of the nation, the President of the administration. Through his exalted status, a sense of power and importance is passed down to those working for him and in his name. This seems even more striking when we find that the person working in the President's name acts to assure "deniability" for the President. In other words, both Admiral Poindexter and Lieutenant Colonel North acted in a way which, so they convinced themselves, was in the best interests of the country, of the President, and of his policies. At the same time, they either kept the President ignorant, or at least he could behave in a way which would allow him subsequently to deny awareness of the chain of actions which had been instituted. Their sense of entitlement thus derived from (1) serving the President and his policies, and (2) protecting the President from possible harm, both very lofty-sounding goals indeed.

Since Irangate is a chain of events in which Israelis were particularly involved, I feel remiss in not bringing out more details about the behavior of the Israeli actors in this drama. My assumption is that the various actors were, each one for himself and as a group, full participants in what I call a "Watergate situation." That is to say, they also regarded themselves as particularly entitled because of exceptional status (connection to the highest levels of the Israeli as well as the U.S. administrations), but entitled also because of the cause to the service of which they had thought they were dedicating themselves. Both the cause and their special status, the best of both countries' interests, so they assumed, provided them with entitlement and therefore with justification. They saw themselves as very special and as carrying out very special tasks.

There is at least one other affair in Israel which has a similar flavor, namely, the Pollard affair. Here, too, Israelis allowed themselves to slide into behaving in ways which, in retrospect, were not only illegal, not only unjustifiable in terms of the relations of Israel and the United States, but were also proving to be an enormous disservice to Israel. Here again we meet persons who convince themselves, because of ideological reasons, on the one hand, and because of the persons and the high authority which they serve, on the other, to have special rights of entitlement: hence the right to use means which in fact cannot be justified by any cause. However, a person in this situation convinces himself that such unjustifiable means can indeed be justified by the cause and by the authority in whose name he operates. The cause, through its ideology, bribes the person's superego and the authority on whose behalf the person believes himself to be righteously operating adds a further bribe to the person's superego, and both subvert his ego ideal: now the behavior can be countenanced. This is once more reinforced by the group atmosphere in which the person moves. Other members of the group support and strengthen his conviction that his behavior is morally right and appropriate. Viewing such behavior as morally right again and again reinforces the bribing of the superego and the subverting of the ego ideal that have taken place in part through narcissistic supplies thus provided.

A further area which promises to be fruitful for the study of an excessive sense of entitlement in the political process are extremists, fanaticists, and terrorists of whatever persuasion. We can here do no more than point out the connection. Self-righteousness and self-righteous rage are also connected to entitlement and shame (Lax, 1975; Horowitz, 1981; Segel, 1981). The narcissistic individual shows much righteousness and reacts with self-righteous rage in response to being blamed or feeling a sense of blame or when he adapts to what he considers to be indignity. Kohut, as quoted in Ornstein (1978), has connected shame and rage in a number of papers, most clearly in his paper on narcissistic rage (1972). Rothstein (1980) describes how a patient's narcissistic rage derives from her sense of entitlement (p. 200). Elsewhere (p. 80) he describes that the frustrations of entitlement are experienced as life-threatening assaults because they challenge "the integrity of the entitled self-as-agent." Morrison (1984) also speaks of "the interaction of shame, vulnerability, rage . . . and reactive narcissistic entitlement." Let us look at the political actor: Does he also show a phenomenon comparable to narcissistic rage? Does he show self-righteous indignation? If so, under what circumstances? Kohut (1972, 1976) describes narcissistic rage and then links it with the charismatic leader who, through his feelings of grandiosity, conveys his rightness and his righteousness to his followers.

Generally, self-righteous indignation is aroused whenever a person feels his entitlement is challenged in some major way. In the political actor self-righteous indignation wells up when his view of himself as someone with rights of special entitlement is challenged, doubted, or attacked. His behavior usually comes under attack when his use of means has become public and is challenged, or when any part of the seemingly coherent ideological edifice which he has built up is being seriously challenged. In Richard Nixon the self-righteous indignation could be seen during the Watergate period, but also earlier. One such occasion was when he lost the 1960 election and blamed the press. He acted as someone absolutely sure that he was being wronged. There was no doubt in his mind. The same can, I think, be said of some of the Irangate central figures. Even though there was little indication during the television hearing of rage in Oliver

North, there was discernible a marked moral self-righteousness and on occasion self-righteous indignation.

I would now like to show how the phenomenon of shame connects with the political process. It is true, I think, that persons in politics, i.e., on the public stage, do not seem to suffer much from conscious shame. Some others, as mentioned, show some aspects of shamelessness. I believe that shame is discernible in the political process in other ways. Shame, as has been indicated by a number of the authors who have written about it (Broucek, 1982; Bursten, 1977; Feldman, 1962; Kinston, 1983; Levin, 1967, 1971; Lewis, 1971; Lichtenstein, 1963; Lowenfeld, 1976; Lynd, 1950; Morrison, 1983, 1984; Piers and Singer, 1953; Thrane, 1979; Ward, 1972; Wurmser, 1981), is an affect that appears mainly in relation to acts of commission or omission, often in public or as seen by others. Feldman (1962) quotes Herman who said that shame is not related to separation from a person but rather to separation from the group; that it stems from a violation of the accepted customs of a collective group. Shame also appears, however, with regard to events pertaining to persons who are close to us, e.g., an adolescent who feels ashamed of the behavior of his mother or father because it does not conform to the norms of his peer group. "We are ashamed of him" or "her" is a statement we can hear in a number of situations when the person feeling the shame perceives the other to be representative of him in some way. In other words, the behavior or the external appearance manifested by the person to whom our actor is close will lead him to feel acutely embarrassed and painfully ashamed. It is as though he himself were being shamed in public; indeed, "in public" is often a central aspect of feeling shame.

It is my conviction that such shame is also felt for behavior carried out in the name of a person or a group. The member of that group then feels that this behavior disgraces him in some way (Thrane, 1979). It makes him appear both to himself and to others in a manner which he cannot accept or tolerate. It is thus, I believe, that shame can arise in a large group of individuals who will feel acutely ashamed because of certain acts committed by persons acting in the name of their group. It is in this way that I would understand the intense reaction of Israeli youth in the

'60s to their view of their parents' generation having "allowed themselves" to be led "like lambs to the slaughter."

I can demonstrate this principle with two examples: one relates to the situation in Israel in December to February of 1987–1988, which is where I first became aware of the intensity of painful feelings of shame that I felt within myself. When Palestinians who demonstrate or throw stones are being shot at by armed soldiers, no matter how much they are provoked, this arouses shame. When Israeli soldiers use wooden billy clubs to beat Palestinians, no matter whether it is a well-formulated official policy, or whether these are exceptional cases, even if it is in response to willful provocation, this arouses intense shame in me. There are many other examples.

It is my contention that such shame is latently present for a while. In other words, it does not become conscious until it reaches a certain threshold. Once the shame has become conscious, it relatively quickly becomes mixed with frustration and anger, and perhaps with other feelings. It is then, I believe, that shame, frustration, and anger can motivate individuals to participate in what becomes macropolitical behavior. This happened, I believe, at the time of the Vietnam war.

Here the American public was mobilized to feel revulsion and shame at the events that had taken place in Vietnam. Daily pictures on television detailing the gruesome events that took place, a report on the My Lai massacre, and the trial of Lt. Calley (Kelman and Hamilton, 1974) were all parts of the events which made Americans feel shame. The shame, I believe, resulted from acts being committed in their name in faraway lands. Conscious shame combined with frustration and anger to mobilize political action. That this political action was successful is now a fact of history.

A similar mobilization of shame probably also played a part in bringing about the demonstration of 400,000 Israelis in 1983 intended to press for the appointment of a government commission of inquiry into the responsibility for the massacres at Sabra and Shatilla in Lebanon, even though the massacres had not been carried out by Israelis. The phenomenon of shame is more easily identifiable in Israelis at the end of 1987 and in early 1988 when the behavior of Israeli soldiers in the administered territories produced shame in some, which in turn pushed toward political action. Shame can be similarly demonstrated to have operated in some other public issues brought up in Israel within recent years, notably the killing of two Arab terrorists after they were apprehended; and the methods used by the General Security Services which were made public. We must keep in mind that shame of this kind is triggered in some individuals and not in others. To understand this difference is a worthwhile task.

The point I wish to make is that shame is aroused in groups of individuals by public behavior in the name of the group. Such shame exists first in a prethreshold form. While the threshold of course differs in different people, there does seem to be a threshold at which the number of persons in the group who show shame is such that macropolitical activities begin to be mobilized.

In summary, both shame and entitlement are narcissistic phenomena of the individual. While excessive entitlement is a narcissistic phenomenon, shame is universal in all types of personalities. Shame and entitlement, along with self-righteousness and self-righteous rage, are related in a variety of ways: they both seem to be connected to discrepancies between the ego ideal and the ego; or the ideal self and the self. In some way they are the other side of the coin of each other. They are both psychic phenomena that we have only gradually come to know better.

Both shame and entitlement, I believe, allow us to move from the individual to the group. They both affect what happens in a society under certain very specific circumstances. There is much more to be looked at with regard to these phenomena. Leo Rangell has pioneered in work on the connection between the individual and political events, particularly in the important area of integrity. Clearly, both shame and entitlement relate directly to this area.

REFERENCES

Bergler, E. (1952), *The Superego*. New York: Grune & Stratton.

Blechner, M. (1987), Entitlement and narcissism. *Contemp. Psychoanal.*, 23:244–254.

Broucek, F. J. (1982), Shame and its relationship to early narcissistic development. *Internat. J. Psycho-Anal.*, 63:369–378.

Bursten, R. (1973), Some narcissistic personality types. *Internat. J. Psycho-Anal.*, 54:287–300.

——— (1977), The narcissistic course. In: *The Narcissistic Condition*, ed. C. M. Nelton. New York: Human Sciences Press.

Cooper, A. M. (1984), The unusually painful analysis: A group of narcissistic-masochistic characters. In: *Psychoanalysis: The Vital Issues*. New York: International Universities Press.

Erikson, E. H. (1950), *Childhood and Society*. New York: Norton.

Feldman, S. (1962), Blushing, fear of blushing and shame. *J. Amer. Psychoanal. Assn.*, 10:368–385.

Freud, S. (1905), Three essays on the theory of sexuality. *Standard Edition*, 7:125–243. London: Hogarth Press, 1955.

——— (1916), Some character-types met with in psychoanalytic work. *Standard Edition*, 14:309–331. London: Hogarth Press, 1957.

——— (1916–1917), Introductory Lectures in Psychoanalysis. *Standard Edition*, 15 & 16. London: Hogarth Press, 1963.

Grey, A. (1987), An interactional defense of self-esteem. *Contemp. Psychoanal.*, 23:255–263.

Horowitz, M. J. (1981), Self-righteous rage and the attribution of blame. *Arch. Gen. Psychiat.*, 38:1233–1238.

Jacobson, E. (1959), The exceptions: An elaboration of Freud's character study. *The Psychoanalytic Study of the Child*, 14:135–154. New York: International Universities Press.

Kelman, H. C., & Hamilton, V. L. (1974), Availability for violence. In: *The Future of Violence*, ed. J. D. Ben-Dak. Lund, Sweden: Student Litteratur.

Kernberg, O. F. (1977), *Borderline Conditions and Pathological Narcissism*. New York: Aronson.

Kinston, W. (1983), A theoretical context for shame. *Internat. J. Psycho-Anal.*, 64:213–226.

Kohut, H. (1971), *The Analysis of the Self*. New York: International Universities Press.

——— (1972), Thoughts on narcissism and narcissistic rage. *The Psychoanalytic Study of the Child*, 27:360–400. New York: Quadrangle.

——— (1976), Creativeness, charisma, group psychology. In: *Freud: The Fusion of Science and Humanism*, ed. J. E. Gedo & G. H. Pollock. *Psychol. Issues*, 34/35:379–425.

——— (1977), *The Restoration of the Self*. New York: International Universities Press.

Kriegman, G. (1983), Entitlement attitudes. *J. Amer. Acad. Psychoanal.*, 11:265–281.

Lax, R. F. (1975), Some comments on the narcissistic aspects of self-righteousness. *Internat. J. Psycho-Anal.*, 56:283–292.

Levin, S. (1967), Some metapsychological considerations on the differentiation between shame and guilt. *Internat. J. Psycho-Anal.*, 48:267–276.

——— (1970), On the psychoanalysis of attitudes of entitlement. *J. Phil. Assn. Psychoanal.*, 20:1–10.

——— (1971), The psychoanalysis of shame. *Internat. J. Psycho-Anal.*, 52:355–362.

Lewis, H. B. (1971), *Shame and Guilt in Neurosis*. New York: International Universities Press.

Lichtenstein, H. (1963), The dilemma of human identity. *J. Amer. Psychoanal. Assn.*, 11:173–223.

Lowenfeld, H. (1976), Notes on shamelessness. *Psychoanal. Quart.*, 45:62–72

Lynd, H. M. (1950), *On Shame and the Search for Identity*. London: Routledge & Kegan Paul.

Mahler, M. S., Pine, F., & Bergman, A. (1975), *The Psychological Birth of the Human Infant*. New York: Basic Books.

Morrison, A. P. (1983), Shame, the ideal self and narcissism. *Contemp. Psychoanal.*, 19:295–318.

——— (1984), Working on shame in psychoanalytic treatment. *J. Amer. Psychoanal. Assn.*, 32:479–505.

Moses, R. (1982), The group self and the Arab-Israeli conflict. *Internat. Rev. Psychoanal.*, 9:55–65.

——— (1986), Watergate as a universal phenomenon. In: *Psychoanalysis Today* (German), ed. H. Lobner. Vienna: Verlag Orac, pp. 185–204.

Murray, J. M. (1964), Narcissism and the ego ideal. *J. Amer. Psychoanal. Assn.*, 12:477–511.

Ornstein, P. H., ed. (1978), *The Search for the Self: Selected Writings of Heinz Kohut*, Vols. 1 & 2. New York: International Universities Press.

Piers, G., & Singer, M. B. (1953), *Guilt and Shame*. Springfield, IL: Charles C Thomas.

Rangell, L. (1974), A psychoanalytic perspective leading currently to the syndrome of the compromise of integrity. *Internat. J. Psycho-Anal.*, 5:3–12.

——— (1976), Lessons from Watergate. *Psychoanal. Quart.*, 45:37–61.

——— (1980), *The Mind of Watergate: An Exploration of the Compromise of Integrity*. New York: Norton.

Rothstein, A. (1977), The ego attitude of entitlement. *Internat. Rev. Psychoanal.*, 4:409–417.

——— (1980), *The Narcissistic Pursuit of Perfection*. New York: International Universities Press.

Segel, N. P. (1981), Narcissism and adaptation to indignity. *Internat. J. Psycho-Anal.*, 62:465–476.

Thrane, G. (1979), Shame and the construction of the self. *Ann. Psychoanal.*, 7:321–341.

Ward, H. (1972), Affects of shame in analysis. *Amer. J. Psychoanal.*, 32:62–73.

Wurmser, L. (1981), *The Mask of Shame*. Baltimore: Johns Hopkins University Press.

26

THE WRITINGS OF LEO RANGELL

1942 Cerebral air embolism. *J. Nerv. & Ment. Dis.*, 96:542–555.

1943 A psychosomatic study of "maladie des tics" (Gilles de la Tourette's disease) (with Mahler, M. S.). *Psychiat. Quart.*, 17:579–603.

1945 Acute spinal epidural abscess as a complication of lumbar puncture (with Glassman, F.). *J. Nerv. & Ment. Dis.*, 102:8–18.

1947 Peroneal palsy caused by crossing the legs (with Nagler, S. H.). *J. Amer. Med. Assn.*, 133:755–761.

1950 The ocular findings in multiple sclerosis (with Savitsky, N.). In: *Multiple Sclerosis and the Demyelinating Diseases*, 28:403–413. Published for the Association for Research in Nerv. and Ment. Dis.

On homonymous hemianopsia in multiple sclerosis (with Savitsky, N.). *J. Nerv. & Ment. Dis.*, 111:225–231.

A treatment of nightmares in a seven-year-old boy. *The Psychoanalytic Study of the Child*, 5:358–390. New York: International Universities Press. Reprinted in: *Dream Reader: Psychoanalytic Articles on Dreams*, ed. T. M. Alston, R. C. Calogeras, & H. Deserno. Madison, CT: International Universities Press (in press).

1951 The role of emotions in cardiovascular disorders. *Ann. West. Med. Surg.*, 5:610–618.

1952 The analysis of a doll phobia. *Internat. J. Psycho-Anal.*, 33:43–53. Reprinted in: *The Yearbook of Psychoanalysis*, ed. S. Lorand, 9:178–198. New York: International Universities Press, 1953. Also reprinted in: *Psychoanalytic Case Studies*, ed. G. P. Sholevar. New York: International Universities Press, (in press).

Macroscopic transmission and the macroscopic point of view. *J. Hillside Hosp.*, 1:228–233.

Report of Panel on "The Theory of Affects." *Bull. Amer. Psychoanal. Assn.*, 8:300–315.

Book Abstract, E. B. Brody and F. C. Redlich, "Psychotherapy with Schizophrenics." *Annu. Surv. Psychoanal.*, 3:564–579.

1953 Psychiatric aspects of pain. *Psychosom. Med.*, 15:22–37.

The interchangeability of phallus and female genital. *J. Amer. Psychoanal. Assn.*, 1:504–509.

Critique and methodology. Chapter 2 in: *Annu. Surv. Psychoanal.*, 4:23–51. New York: International Universities Press.

1954 Report of Panel on "Psychoanalysis and dynamic psychotherapy: Similarities and differences." *J. Amer. Psychoanal. Assn.*, 2:152–166.

Psychoanalysis and dynamic psychotherapy: Similarities and differences. Abstracted in Rangell, L., report of Panel on "Psychoanalysis and dynamic psychotherapy: Similarities and differences." *J. Amer. Psychoanal. Assn.*, 2:152–166.

Similarities and differences between psychoanalysis and dynamic psychotherapy. *J. Amer. Psychoanal. Assn.*, 2:734–744.

The psychology of poise: With a special elaboration on the psychic significance of the snout or perioral region. *Internat. J. Psycho-Anal.*, 35:313–333.

Television and young children. In: *The Family Goes to Nursery School*, 7th Annual Education Conference, Los Angeles Council of Coop. Nursery Schools, UCLA.

Critique. Chapter 2 in: *Annu. Surv. Psychoanal.*, 5:14–30. New York: International Universities Press.

"A tertiary gain of symptoms." Presented to the Meeting of American Psychoanalytic Association, New York, December 3.

1955 The role of the parent in the Oedipus complex. *Bull. Menn. Clin.*, 19:9–15.

Report of Panel on "The borderline case." *J. Amer. Psychoanal. Assn.*, 3:285–298.

Discussion of "The borderline case." Abstracted in: Rangell, L., Report of Panel on "The borderline case." *J. Amer. Psychoanal. Assn.*, 3:285–298.

On the psychoanalytic theory of anxiety: A statement of a unitary theory. *J. Amer. Psychoanal. Assn.*, 3:389–414.

Critique. Chapter 2 in: *Annu. Surv. Psychoanal.*, 6:15–54. New York: International Universities Press.

"The quest for ground in human motivation." Address to the first Western Divisional Meeting of the American Psychiatric

Association and the West Coast Psychoanalytic Societies, October 29.

1956 Report of Panel on "The dream in the practice of psychoanalysis." *J. Amer. Psychoanal. Assn.*, 4:122–137.

Some historical patterns in the place of the dream in psychoanalysis. Abstracted in Rangell, L., Report of Panel on "The dream in the practice of psychoanalysis." *J. Amer. Psychoanal. Assn.*, 4:122–137.

Chairman's introductory address on "The borderline case." Abstracted in Robbins, L. L., Report of Panel on "The borderline case." *J. Amer. Psychoanal. Assn.*, 4:550–562.

The borderline state and the analytic attitude. Abstracted in Robbins, L. L., Report of Panel on "The borderline case." *J. Amer. Psychoanal. Assn.*, 4:550–562.

1957 Discussion of Kubie, L. S., "The use of psychoanalysis as a research tool." In: *Applications of Basic Science Techniques to Psychiatric Research*, ed. R. Cleghorn. Washington: American Psychiatric Association, pp. 143–150.

1958 Chairman's introductory address on the "Psychoanalytic theory of thinking." Abstracted in Arlow, J. A., Report of Panel on "The psychoanalytic theory of thinking." *J. Amer. Psychoanal. Assn.*, 6:143–153.

Psychosomatic medicine. *Calif. Med.*, 88:357–364.

1959 The role of conversion in psychopathology. Abstracted in Fox, H. M., Report of Panel on "The theory of the conversion process." *J. Amer. Psychoanal. Assn.*, 7:173–181.

Discussion of Schur, M. Metapsychological aspects of phobias. Abstracted in Report by Tausend, H. *Bull. Phil. Assn. Psychoanal.*, 9:44–45.

Chairman's address on "The role of early psychic functioning in psychoanalysis." Abstracted in Rubinfine, D. L., Report of Panel on "Some theoretical aspects of early psychic functioning. *J. Amer. Psychoanal. Assn.*, 7:561–576.

Reconstruction and theory formation (with Ekstein, R.). Abstracted in Rubinfine, D. L., Report of Panel on "Some theoretical aspects of early psychic functioning." *J. Amer. Psychoanal. Assn.*, 7:561–576.

The nature of conversion. *J. Amer. Psychoanal. Assn.*, 7:632–662.

Discussion of Freud, A. "The nature of the therapeutic process." Abstracted in Report by Tausend, H. *Bull. Phil. Assn. Psychoanal.*, 9:111–112.

1960 Discussion remarks on "Psychosomatic diseases in children and adolescents." Abstracted in Gosliner, B. J., Report of Panel on "Psychosomatic diseases in children and adolescents." *J. Amer. Psychoanal. Assn.*, 8:152–158.

Discussion of Miller, S. "Metapsychology." Abstracted in Report by Tausend, H., *Bull. Phil. Assn. Psychoanal.*, 10:25–29.

Discussion remarks in Panel on "The psychology of imagination." Abstacted in Kohut, H., Report of Panel on "The Psychology of imagination." *J. Amer. Psychoanal. Assn.*, 8:159–166.

They are entrusted to your care. *J. Nursery Ed.*, 15:120–122.

Some re-thinking on our psychoanalytic nosology. Abstracted in Report by Hayman, M. *Bull. Phil. Assn. Psychoanal.*, 10:158–160.

Chairman's introductory address on "Problems of nosology from the psychoanalytic standpoint." Abstracted in Ross, N., Report of Panel on "An examination of nosology according to psychoanalytic concepts." *J. Amer. Psychoanal. Assn.*, 8:535–551.

1961 Presidential Newsletter. Amer. Psychoanal. Assn. vol. 2, no. 1. June.

The role of early psychic functioning in psychoanalysis. *J. Amer. Psychoanal. Assn.*, 9:595–609.

Reconstruction and theory formation (with Ekstein, R.). *J. Amer. Psychoanal. Assn.*, 9:684–697.

Chairman's address "Towards an improved psychoanalytic nosology." Presented to Symposium on "A re-classification of psychopathological states." 22nd International Psychoanalytic Congress, Edinburgh, Scotland, August 2.

Presidential Newsletter. Amer. Psychoanal. Assn. vol. 2, no. 2, November.

1962 Chairman's address on "The role of object relations in psychoanalysis." Abstracted in Ritvo, S., Report of Panel on "Object relations." *J. Amer. Psychoanal. Assn.*, 10:102–117.

Presidential Newsletter. Amer. Psychoanal. Assn. vol. 2, no. 3. February.

The New York society and American psychoanalysis. In: *The Fruition of an Idea: Fifty Years of Psychoanalysis in New York*, ed. M. Wangh. New York: International Universities Press, pp. 57–62.

Prospect and retrospect: An interim report by the President. *J. Amer. Psychoanal. Assn.*, 10:227–257.

Presidential Newsletter. Amer. Psychoanal. Assn. vol. 2, no. 4. April-May.

1963 On friendship [presidential address]. *J. Amer. Psychoanal. Assn.*, 11:3–54.

Our face towards the behavioral sciences: Some reflections. Abstracted in *Bull Med. Staff Westwood Hosp.*, vol. 1, no. 1, September.

Beyond and between the no and the yes: A tribute to Dr. Rene A. Spitz. In: *Counterpoint: Libidinal Object and Subject*, ed. H. S. Gaskill. New York: International Universities Press, pp. 29–74.

The scope of intrapsychic conflict: Microscopic and macroscopic considerations. Abstracted in Nemiah, J. C., Report of Panel on "The significance of intrapsychic conflict." *J. Amer. Psychoanal. Assn.*, 11:619–627.

The scope of intrapsychic conflict: Microscopic and macroscopic considerations. *The Psychoanalytic Study of the Child*, 18:75–102. New York: International Universities Press.

Structural problems in intrapsychic conflict. *The Psychoanalytic Study of the Child*, 18:103–138. New York: International Universities Press.

Die frühen psychischen Funktionen im Lichte der Psychoanalyse. *Psyche*, 17:401–413.

Rekonstruktion und Theoriebildung (with Ekstein, R.). *Psyche*, 17:414–425.

1964 Book Review of Greenacre, P., *The Quest for the Father: A Study of the Darwin-Butler Controversy, as a Contribution to the Understanding of the Creative Individual. Psychoanal. Quart.*, 33:575–578.

President's Bulletin No. 1, Los Angeles Psychoanalytic Society, July 23.

Discussion of Zetzel, E. R. "Depression and the incapacity to bear it." Abstracted in Report by Zaitlin, R. *Bull. Phil. Assn. Psychoanal.*, 14:177–179.

Discussion of Bird, B. "Mother-daughter vexation: A study of the phallic phase of female development." Abstracted in Report by Zaitlin, R. *Bull. Los Angeles Psychoanal. Soc. & Inst.*, 1:4–5. Also in: *Bull. Phil. Assn. Psychoanal.*, 14:238–240.

1965 The scope of Heinz Hartmann: Some selected comments on his *Essays on Ego Psychology*. An appreciative survey on the occasion of his seventieth birthday. *Internat. J. Psycho-Anal.*, 46:5–30.

Discussion of Little, M. "Transference in borderline states." Abstracted in Report by Zaitlin, R. *Bull. Los Angeles Psychoanal. Soc. & Inst.*, 2:3–5.

Chairman's address, "The relationship between child analysis and the theory and practice of adult psychoanalysis." Abstracted in Casuso, G., Report of Panel. *J. Amer. Psychoanal. Assn.*, 13:159–171.

Discussion of Horowitz, W. S. "Toward a unifying conception of narcissism." Abstracted in Report by Zaitlin, R. *Bull. Los Angeles Psychoanal. Soc. & Inst.*, 2:3–4. Also in: *Bull. Phil. Assn. Psychoanal.*, 15:180–183.

Discussion of Brunswick, D. "The drives and the affects." Abstracted in Report by Zaitlin, R. *Bull. Los Angeles Psychoanal. Soc. & Inst.*, 2:4–5. Also in: *Bull. Phil. Assn. Psychoanal.*, 15:244–246.

Profile by Pumpian-Mindlin, E. In: *S. Calif. Psychiat. Soc. News*, 12:1–5, June 24.

Report of the President. Los Angeles Psychoanalytic Society, June 17.

Some comments on psychoanalytic nosology: With recommendation for improvement. In: *Drives, Affects, Behavior*, ed. M. Schur. New York: International Universities Press, Vol. 2, pp. 128–157.

Discussion of Beres, D. "Structure and function in psychoanalysis." Abstracted in Report by Zaitlin, R. *Bull. Los Angeles Psychoanal. Soc. & Inst.*, 2:4. Also in: *Bull. Phil. Assn. Psychoanal.*, 16:47–50, 1966.

Discussion of Stoller, R. "The analysis of the mother of a transvestite boy." Abstracted in Report by Zaitlin, R. *Bull. Los Angeles Psychoanal. Soc. & Inst.*, 3:5–7. Also in: *Bull. Phil. Assn. Psychoanal.*, 16:50–54, 1966.

1966 Dedication (to Dr. Maxwell Gitelson). In: *Psychoanalysis in the Americas*, ed. R. E. Litman. New York: International Universities Press, pp. 5–6.

Recent history of the Pan-American Psychoanalytic Congress. In: *Psychoanalysis in the Americas*, ed. R. E. Litman. New York: International Universities Press, pp. 9–15.

An overview of the ending of an analysis. In: *Psychoanalysis in the Americas*, ed. R. E. Litman. New York: International Universities Press, pp. 141–165.

Man facing the unknown: Some reflections by a psychoanalyst. Address abstracted in Marjorie D. Kern. *J. Amer. Soc. Psychol. Res.*, 60:63–73.

Psychoanalysis and the problem of schizophrenia. Academic address to the Annual Meeting of the Southern California Psychiatric Society. Abstracted in *S. Calif. Psychiat. Soc. News*, Vol. 13, no. 9, May.

Discussion of Hays, C. A. "Clinical aspects of homosexuality." Abstracted in Report by Shane, M. *Bull. Phil. Assn. Psychoanal.*, 16:99–101.

Discussion of Berenson, M. H. "Introjection in the countertransference." Abstracted in Report by Shane, M. *Bull. Los Angeles Psychoanal. Soc. & Inst.*, 3:8–10. Also in: *Bull. Phil. Assn. Psychoanal.*, 17:118–121, 1967.

Presidential Newsletter. Amer. Psychoanal. Assn., Vol. 7, no. 1, October.

Discussion at Panel on "Transference and countertransference." Abstracted in Report by Shane, M. *Bull. Los Angeles Psychoanal. Soc. & Inst.*, 4:3–6. Also in: *Bull. Phil. Assn. Psychoanal.*, 17:56–58, 1967.

1967 A message from the President. Amer. Psychoanal. Assn. Newsletter, Vol. 1, no. 1, New York, February.

Psychoanalysis, affects, and the "Human Core": On the relationship of psychoanalysis to the behavioral sciences. *Psychoanal. Quart.*, 36:172–202.

The metapsychology of psychic trauma. In: *Psychic Trauma*, ed. S. S. Furst. New York & London: Basic Books, pp. 51–84.

Discussion at Panel on "The Psychoanalyst and the training of psychiatrists." Reported by Schrut, A. *Bull. S. Calif. Psychoanal. Soc. & Inst.*, no. 18, p. 5.

Psychoanalysis: A current look. *J. Amer. Psychoanal. Assn.*, 15:423–431.

Discussion of Tausend, H. "Identification, identity, and sexuality." Abstracted in Report by Shane, M. *Bull. Phil. Assn. Psychoanal.*, 17:121–123.

Discussion of Bion, W. R. "Reverence and awe." Abstracted in Report by Wixen, B. *Bull. S. Calif. Psychoanal. Soc. & Inst.*, no. 19, pp. 3–5.

Discussion at Panel on "The application of psychoanalytic method and theory to social problems." Abstracted in Brodsky, B., Report of Panel. *J. Amer. Psychoanal. Assn.*, 15:686–694.

Presidential Address. Business Meeting of Members, Amer. Psychoanal. Assn., May 7. Reported in *J. Amer. Psychoanal. Assn.*, 15:887.

In memoriam: William C. Menninger. *J. Amer. Psychoanal. Assn.*, 15:923–929. Also in: Memorial for William C. Menninger. New York Academy of Medicine. Hosack Hall, Dec. 14, 1966. New York: Clarke & Way, Inc.

The concept of psychic trauma. In Report by Shane, M. *Bull. Los Angeles Psychoanal. Soc. & Inst.*, 4:3–6.

1968 Psychoanalysis: Its present stance. Guest Editorial in: *Medical Tribune*, February 1.

The psychoanalytic process. *Internat. J. Psycho-Anal.*, 49:19–26.

Reflections on a visit to Buenos Aires: On crossing the psychoanalytic equator. Reported by Wixen, B. *Bull. S. Calif. Psychoanal. Soc. & Inst.*, no. 22.

The Inside Story. Broadcast 7934—U.E. 2047, The University Explorer, University of California, CBS Radio, Armed Forces Radio, Voice of America, Los Angeles, CA. October 20.

A point of view on acting out. *Internat. J. Psycho-Anal.*, 49:195–201.

A further attempt to resolve the "problem of anxiety." *J. Amer. Psychoanal. Assn.*, 16:371–404.

Prefacio. In: *Psicoanalisis en las Americas*, ed. L. Grinberg, M. Langer, & E. Rodrigue. Buenos Aires: Editorial Paidos, pp. 12–14.

El proceso psicoanalitico. In: *Psicoanalisis en las Americas*, ed. L. Grinberg, M. Langer, & E. Rodrigue. Buenos Aires: Editorial Paidos, pp. 23–26.

1969 Die Konversion. *Psyche*, 23:121–147.

The intrapsychic process and its analysis: A recent line of thought and its current implications. *Internat. J. Psycho-Anal.*, 50:65–77.

Zur Analyse des intrapsychischen Prozesses: Neue Überlegungen zur psychoanalytischen Theorie und Praxis. *Psyche*, 23:438–460.

Il processo intrapsichico e la sua analisi: Una recente linea di pensiero e le sue attuali applicazioni. *Rivista de psicoanalisi*, 15:119–141.

Abstract of "The intrapsychic process and its analysis: A recent line of thought and its current implications." *Dig. Neurol. Psychiat.*, series no. 37, August, p. 244. Hartford: Institute of Living.

Discussion of termination of analysis. Abstracted in Firestein, S. K., Report of Panel on "Problems of termination in the analysis of adults." *J. Amer. Psychoanal. Assn.*, 17:222–237.

Extracts of "Beyond and between the no and the yes." In: *Reading Notes*, by Karl Menninger. *Bull. Menn. Clin.*, 33:315–316.

Reflexiones sobre mi visita a Buenos Aires: Al cruzar el Ecuador psicoanalitico. Comentarios Finales. *Revista de Psicoanalisis*, 26:443–462.

Chairman's Introductory Address on "Nonverbal communication in the analysis of adults." Abstracted in Suslick, A., Report of Panel on "Nonverbal communication in the analysis of adults." *J. Amer. Psychoanal. Assn.*, 17:955–967.

Choice-conflict and the decision-making function of the ego: A psychoanalytic contribution to decision theory. *Internat. J. Psycho-Anal.*, 50:599–602.

Discussion of Rascovsky, A. and M. "On Filicide." Abstracted in Report by Wallace, L. *Bull. Phil. Assn. Psychoanal.*, 19:248–252.

1970 A further attempt to resolve "the problem of anxiety." Abstracted by Applebaum, A. Transactions of the Topeka Psychoanalytic Society. *Bull. Menn. Clin.*, 34:35–36.

Perspective, Rome: The "viewpoint" of the psychoanalyst: Remarks of the incoming President. *Internat. J. Psycho-Anal.*, 51:55–57.

The return of the repressed "Oedipus." In: *Parenthood: Its Psychology and Psychopathology*, ed. E. J. Anthony & T. Benedek. Boston: Little, Brown, pp. 325–334.

Discussion of "The intrapsychic process and its analysis: A recent line of thought and its current implications." *Internat. J. Psycho-Anal.*, 51:195–209.

Leo Rangell, M.D. Midway in his journey. Profile by Jacoby, William D. In: *S. Calif. Psychiat. Soc. News*, 17:4–6, June.

Psychoanalysis and neuropsychiatry: A look at their interface. *Amer. J. Psychiat.*, 127:125–131. Reprinted in: *Neurologia —Neurocirugia—Psiquitria (Mexico)*, 11:125–131 (1970).

President's Newsletter. *Internat. Psychoanal. Assn.*, Vol. 3, no. 1, March.

Obituary, Dr. Heinz Hartmann. *Internat. J. Psycho-Anal.*, 51:567.

The intrapsychic process and its analysis: A recent line of thought and its current implications. Address to the Phil. Assn. Psychoanal. Reported by Beskind, H. *Bull. Phil. Assn. Psychoanal.*, 20:257–260.

Discussion of Rascovsky, A. Towards the understanding of the unconscious motivations of war. Abstracted in Report by Compton, A. *Bull. Phil. Assn. Psychoanal.*, 20:261–262.

Discussion of Wallace, L. Apparent influence by psychoanalysis on a case of multiple sclerosis. Abstracted in Report by Compton, A. *Bull. Los Angeles Psychoanal. Soc. & Inst.*, 6:8. Also in: *Bull. Phil. Assn. Psychoanal.*, 21:197–198 (1971).

Reflections on issues in psychoanalysis: 1970. Abstracted in Report by Compton, A. *Bull. Phil. Assn. Psychoanal.*, 20:346–348.

The decision-making process: A contribution from psychoanalysis. Fifth Annual Freud Lecture of the Psychoanalytic Association of New York. Reported by Langs, R. J. *Bull. Psychoanal. Assn. New York*, 10:5–6.

1971 Nouvel essai pour resoudre le "probleme de l'angoisse." *Rev. Franc. Psychanal.*, 35:161–189.

Reply to Beecher, L. H. Letter to the Editor on "Integrating psychoanalysis." *Amer. J. Psychiat.*, 127:976.

President's Newsletter. *Internat. Psychoanal. Assn.*, Vol. 3, no. 2, April.

Discussion of Wangh, M. Some thoughts on the psychogenesis of present-day student rebellion. Abstracted in Report by Compton, A. *Bull. Phil. Assn. Psychoanal.*, 21:46–47.

Psychoanalysis and neuropsychiatry: A look at their interface. Abstracted in: *Psychiat. Dig.*, 32:35.

The decision-making process: A contribution from psychoanalysis (Annual Freud Lecture). Reported by Langs, R. J. *Psychoanal. Quart.*, 40:546–547.

Agressao, Edipo e perspectiva historica. *Revista Brasileira de Psicanalise*, 5:284–302.

Psicoanalisis y psicoterapia dinamica: Similtudes y diferencias (Relatos de mesas redondas de la Asociacion Psicoanalitica Americana). *Revista de Psicoanalisis*, 28:73–89.

Obituary, Dr. Elizabeth R. Zetzel. *Internat. J. Psychoanal.*, 2:229–231.

Psychoanalyse in Berlin. Meisenheim am Glan: Anton Hain.

Toward a cool look at burning issues. Book Review Essay on: Waelder, R., *Progress and Revolution. Psychoanal. Quart.*, 40:663–677.

The dilemmas of psychiatry in changing times. Academic Address to Annual Fall Meeting of the Southern California Psychiatric Society. Reported in: *S. Calif. Psychiat. Soc. News*, 19:1–11. Reprinted in: *Newsletter, N. Calif. Psychiat. Soc.*, 16:11.

Discussion (Comentario) of Etchegoyen, H. La primera sesion de analisis. *Revista de Psicoanalisis*, 28:520–527.

The decision-making process: A contribution from psychoanalysis. *The Psychoanalytic Study of the Child*, 26:425–452. New York: Quadrangle.

1972 President's Newsletter. *Internat. Psychoanal. Assn.*, Vol. 4, no. 1, January.

Aggression, Oedipus, and historical perspective (Presidential address to the 27th International Psychoanalytical Congress, Vienna, Austria, July 26, 1971). *Internat. J. Psycho-Anal.*, 53:3–11.

La agresion, Edipo y la perspectiva historica. *Revista de Psicoanalisis*, 29:63–83.

Address to the Opening Plenary Session, 9th Latin-American Psychoanalytic Congress, Caracas, July 16, 1972. In: *Discursos: IX Congreso Latinoamericano do Psicoanalisis, 17/21 Julio, 1972.* Publicacion del Instituto Venezolano delos Seguros Sociales.

On the cacophony of human relations (A report of the April 18, 1972, Scientific Meeting of the Association). Reported by Silvert, R., *Bull. Assn. Psychoanal. Med.*, 12:7–10.

1973 Discussion of "The fate of the transference after the termination of analysis." In Hurn, H. T., Report of Panel "On the fate of the transference after the termination of analysis." *J. Amer. Psychoanal. Assn.*, 21:182–192.

President's Newsletter. *Internat. Psychoanal. Assn.*, vol. 5, no. 1, April. (Also: Translations in French, Spanish, and German.)

Die Aggression und der Odipuskomplex (Aus der Eröffnungsansprache des Präsidenten der IPV auf dem 27. Psychoanalytischen Kongress in Wien am 26. Juli 1971). *Psyche*, 3–27:193–204.

On the cacophony of human relations. *Psychoanal. Quart.*, 42:325–348.

Connections of psychoanalysis with other medical fields. *Nosokomiaka Chronika (Hospitals Chronicle)*, 35:297–302 (Athens, Greece).

1974 A psychoanalytic perspective leading currently to the syndrome of the compromise of integrity. *Internat. J. Psycho-Anal.*, 55:3–12.

Message presidentiel, Juillet 1973: Une perspective psychanalytique menant au syndrome du compromis d'integrite. *Rev. Franc. Psychanal.*, 38:385–404.

Perspektiven der Psychoanalyse: Bemerkungen zum drohenden Verfall der Integrität. *Psyche*, 28:933–950.

Uma perspectiva psicoanalitica a conduzir ao sindrome de conciliacao da integridade. *Revista Brasileira de Psicanalise*, 8(3):367–386.

Uma perspectiva psicoanalitica de la cual se deduce y expone el sindrome del compromiso de integridad. *Revista de Psicoanalisis*, 31(3):517–540.

Chairman's Opening Address on "Affects and the signal process." Abstracted in Castelnuovo-Tedesco, P., Report of Panel on "Toward a theory of affects." *J. Amer. Psychoanal. Assn.*, 22:612–625.

Letter to the Editor. *The Academy*, 18:4.

Chairman, "Open forum: An exchange on psychoanalytic issues." Reported by Adatto, C. *Internat. J. Psycho-Anal.*, 55:323–332.

Chairman, Business meeting, International Psychoanalytic Association. Abstracted in 139th Bulletin of the International Psychoanalytic Association Report of the 28th International Psychoanalytical Congress, ed. D. Widlöcher. *Internat. J. Psycho-Anal.*, 55:89–166.

1975 Psychoanalytic contributions to the theories of sexuality. Presented at the Milton S. Eisenhower Symposium, 1974. "New perspectives on human sexuality." Abstracted in: *Johns Hopkins Magazine*, 26:31–34.

Psychoanalysis and the process of change: An essay on the past, present and future. *Internat. J. Psycho-Anal.*, 56:87–98.

Psychoanalyse und Veränderung: Ein Versuch über Vergangenheit, Gegenwart und Zukunft. *Psyche*, 29:481–502.

Psychanalyse et changement: Essai sur le passe, le present et l'avenir. *Rev. Franc. Psychanal.*, 39:315–338.

El psicoanalisis y el proceso de cambio: Un ensayo sobre el pasado, el presente y el futuro. *Revista de Psicoanalisis*, 32(1):5–32.

Lessons from the Watergate: A Derivative for psychoanalysis. Freud Anniversary Lecture, N.Y. Psa. Inst. Reported by Wyman, H. M., Newsletter, *N.Y. Psychoanal. Soc. & Inst.*, 12(3):22–23, July.

Watergate and analytic theory. News article by Herrington, B. S. *Psychiat. News*, Vol. 10, no. 16, August 20.

Book review of the Freud/Jung Letters, ed. W. McGuire. Bollingen Series 94, translated by Ralph Manheim and R. F. C. Hull, *Amer. J. Psychiat.*, 132:980, September.

"Man in a group." Address to the Third Robert Waelder Memorial Lecture. To the Philadelphia Association for Psychoanalysis, October 17.

1976 Lessons from Watergate: A derivative for psychoanalysis. *Psychoanal. Quart.*, 45:37–61.

Discussion of the Buffalo Creek Disaster: The course of psychic trauma. *Amer. J. Psychiat.*, 133:313–316.

Gelassenheit und andere menschliche Möglichkeiten. Frankfurt am Main: Suhrkamp Verlag.

Psychoanalysis and the process of change: An essay on the past, present, and future. Abstracted in: *Psychiat. Dig.*, December, p. 31.

1977 Different types of anxiety and their handling in the psychoanalytic situation. Precis of paper for forthcoming dialogue at 30th Int. Psychoanal. Congress in Jerusalem. President's Newsletter. *I.P.A.*, 9(1):17–20.

Discussion remarks to panel "The psychoanalytic treatment of male homosexuality." In: Payne, E. C., Report of Panel on "The psychoanalytic treatment of male homosexuality." *J. Amer. Psychoanal. Assn.*, 25:183–199.

El analisis de una fobia a las munecas. In: *Practicas Psicoanaliticas Comparadas en las Neurosis*. ed. L. Grinberg. Buenos Aires: Editorial Paedos, 53:209–228.

1978 Response to Osman, M. P. "Reflections upon hearing Dr. Leo Rangell's talk." *Bull. S. Calif. Psychoanal. Soc. & Inst.*, no. 52, spring, pp. 11–14.

On understanding and treating anxiety and its derivatives. *Internat. J. Psycho-Anal.*, 59:229–236.

On understanding and treating anxiety and its derivatives. Abstracted in Gaddini, E., and Kuchenbuch, A. "Dialogue on 'different types of anxiety and their handling in the psychoanalytic situation.' " *Internat. J. Psycho-Anal.*, 59:237–244.

The creative thrust: A psychoanalytic theory. *Amer. Imago*, 35:27–44. Also in: *Myth, Creativity, Psychoanalysis* ed. M. Solomon. Detroit: Wayne State University Press, 1979, pp. 27–44.

Bridges: Psychoanalytic essays in honor of Leo Rangell, M.D. Annual Fall Meeting of the Southern California Psychiatric Society. Reported by Fintzy, R. T., *S. Calif. Psychiat. Soc. News*, 26(3):4–8.

1979 The "dynamic" of dynamic psychiatry: The role of psychoanalytic theory in the future of psychiatry. Reported by Johnson, R. G. *Bull. S. Calif. Psychoanal. Soc. & Inst.*, 55:11–12.

Bridging bridges. Reported by Friedman, R. J. *Bull. S. Calif. Psychoanal. Soc. & Inst.*, 55:13–14.

Book review of Loewald, H. W. Psychoanalysis and the history of the individual. *Psychoanal. Quart.*, 48:116–121.

Psychoanalysis and dynamic psychiatry. *Hillside J. Clin. Psychiat.*, 1(1):5–38.

Contemporary issues in the theory of therapy. *J. Amer. Psychoanal. Assn.*, 27:81–112. Reprinted in: *Psychoanalytic Explorations of Technique: Discourse on the Theory of Therapy*, ed. H. P.

Blum. New York: International Universities Press, pp. 81–113 (1980). Also reprinted in: "A Decade of Psychoanalysis in the United States," Spanish Ed., 1984. Also reprinted in "Japanese Anthology Collection. *J. Amer. Psychoanal. Assn. 1973–1982,*" ed. H. P. Blum, 1984.

On understanding and treating anxiety and its derivatives. Abstract in: *Digest/Psychiatry*, October, p. 96.

1980 *The Mind of Watergate: An Exploration of the Compromise of Integrity*. New York: Norton.

What's happening to American integrity? *Amer. Med. News Impact*, pp. 1–4, November 28.

A neglected classic X: Otto Fenichel's "Problems of psychoanalytic technique." *J. Phil. Assn. Psychoanal.*, 7:93–103.

"The self and others: Narcissism and object relations in total psychoanalytic theory." The Bernhard Berliner Memorial Lecture. Address to the San Francisco Psychoanalytic Institute, December 6.

1980 Aggression: Theoretical and clinical aspects. Address to the Baltimore Psychoanalytic Institute, February 16

1980–81 Some notes on the post-analytic phase: Discussion paper to Borenstein, D. B., & Fintzy, R. T. "Post-analytic encounters." *Internat. J. Psycho-Anal. Psychother.*, 8:165–170.

1981 Leaders and led: From official politics to psychoanalytic group life. Congress summary: Statements by leaders of special discussion groups. 32nd Internat. Psychoanal. Cong., Helsinki, July 30, 1981, p. 51.

From insight to change. *J. Amer. Psychoanal. Assn.*, 29:119–141.

Discussion of Sandler, J. "Transference and defense." Los Angeles Psychoanalytic Society, April 20, 1981. Reported by Wilson, S. L. *Newsletter of the S. Calif. Psychiat. Soc.*, 28:14–16.

Nouvel essai pour resoudre le "probleme de l'angoisse": Dix ans de psychanalyse en Amerique. *Anthologie du J. Amer. Psychoanal. Assn.*, ed. H. P. Blum, S. Lebovici, & D. Widlöcher. Paris: Presses Universitaires de France, pp. 179–212.

David Brunswick, Ph.D., 1897–1981. *Newsletter of the Amer. Psychoanal. Assn.*, 15:8.

Chairman and discussant: Hampstead Scientific Forum on "The Superego: Its early roots and the road from outer to inner conflict as seen in psychoanalysis." *Bull. Hampstead Clin.*, 4:101–103, 112–117.

The self in psychoanalytic theory: Content and controversy. Joan Fleming Memorial Lecture. Address to the Denver Psy-

choanalytic Society, February 27, 1981. Reported by Jacobson, J. G. *Newsletter of the Denver Psychoanal. Soc.*
From insight to change. Abstracted in Report of Panel by Simon, R. C. "Contemporary problems of psychoanalytic technique." *J. Amer. Psychoanal. Assn.*, 29:643–658.
A view on John Gedo's Revision of Psychoanalytic Theory. *Psychoanal. Inq.*, 1:249–265.
Psychoanalysis and dynamic psychotherapy: Similarities and differences twenty-five years later. *Psychoanal. Quart.*, 50:665–693.
The psychology of pain. Address to Vista Hill Foundation Symposium, Coronado, CA, February.
1982 Book review of Leavy, S. A. *The Psychoanalytic Dialogue. Psychoanal. Quart.*, 51:127–132.
Psychoanalysis and dynamic psychotherapy: Similarities and differences 25 years later. Reported by Wilson, S. *Los Angeles Psychoanal. Bull.*, 1:15–19, January–March.
The self in psychoanalytic theory. Abstracted in Richards, A. D., Report of Panel on "Psychoanalytic theories of the self." *J. Amer. Psychoanal. Assn.*, 30:717–733.
The self in psychoanalytic theory. *J. Amer. Psychoanal. Assn.*, 30:863–891.
Transference to theory: The relationship of psychoanalytic education to the analyst's relationship to psychoanalysis. *Annu. Psychoanal.*, 10:29–56.
Discussion of Gediman, H. K. Actual neurosis and psychoneurosis. American Psychoanalytic Association, New York, December 17.
Some thoughts on termination. *Psychoanal. Inq.*, 2:367–392.
1983 SCPS Spotlight—Leo Rangell, M.D. (Part I) by Lebe, D. *Newsletter of the Southern California Psychiatry Society*, vol. 30, no. 5, pp. 1, 5–7, 12. January. Part II, vol. 30, no. 6, pp. 11–12, 15 February.
Book review of Klauber, J. *Difficulties in the Analytic Encounter. Psychoanal. Quart.*, 52:99–104.
The problem of integrity. Address to Meeting of the Oregon Psychoanalytic Foundation and Oregon Psychiatric Association, April 23, 1982. Abstracted by Berthelsdorf, S. In: "Notes." *Psychoanal. Quart.*, 52:155.
The legacy of Anna Freud. Address to Memorial Meeting for Anna Freud, San Diego Psychoanalytic Society, La Jolla, CA, February 18.
The enduring armature of psychoanalytic theory and method.

Address to The Psychoanalytic Forum, American Psychoanalytic Association, Philadelphia, PA, April 28.

Defense and resistance in psychoanalysis and life. *J. Amer. Psychoanal. Assn. (Suppl.)*, 31:147–174. Reprinted in: *Defense and Resistance: Historical Perspectives and Current Concepts*, ed. H. P. Blum, 1984.

Some thoughts on Barry Siegel's thoughts on "Thoughts on Termination," by Leo Rangell. *Psychoanalytic Inq.*, 3(4):705–714.

Psyche and soma: Leaps and continuities. Address to German Psychoanal. Assn., Wiesbaden, Germany, December 1.

Book Review of *The Meaning of Hitler*, by Sebastian Haffner. *J. Amer. Psychoanal. Assn.*, 31:790–793.

Obituary, David Leach, M.D. Newsletter, The Michigan Psychoanalytic Society-Institute, Vol. 13, no. 1, November, p. 5.

Structure, somatic and psychic. Abstracted in Report by Martin, J. "Infancy in a changing world." *Bull. S. Calif. Psychoanal. Inst. & Soc.*, no. 67, fall, p. 28.

Criterios contemporaneos en la teoria de la terapia. In: *Diez Anos de Psicoanalisis en los Estados Unidos (1973–1982)*. Compilacion de Harold P. Blum. Madrid: Alianza Universidad, pp. 221–244.

1984 The analyst at work. The Madrid Congress. Synthesis and critique. *Internat. J. Psycho-Anal.*, 65:125–140.

The analyst at work. Madrid Congress. Reported by Pomer, S. L. *Bull. S. Calif. Psychoanal. Inst. & Soc.*, spring, 68:15–16.

The Anna Freud experience. *The Psychoanalytic Study of the Child*, 39:29–43. New Haven, CT: Yale University Press.

The roots of power in psychoanalytic theory. Address to Symposium of the Sigmund Freud Gesellschaft, Vienna, Austria, September 22.

Discussion remarks in Panel Report by Halpert, E., on "The value of extratransference interpretation." *J. Amer. Psychoanal. Assn.*, 32:137–146, p. 144.

Discussion remarks in Panel Report by Lytton, S. M., on "Value judgments in psychoanalytic theory and practice." *J. Amer. Psychoanal. Assn.*, 32:147–156.

German psychoanalysis: The moral issue. *Amer. Psychoanal. Assn. Newsletter*, 18(4):1–6.

On the theory of theory in psychoanalysis: The relationship of theory to psychoanalytic therapy. In Report of Panel by Richards, A. D., on "The relation between psychoanalytic theory and psychoanalytic technique." *J. Amer. Psychoanal. Assn.*, 32:587–602.

Structure: Somatic and psychic—the biopsychological base of infancy. In: *Frontiers of Infant Psychiatry*, vol. 2, ed. E. Galenson, J. D. Call, & R. L. Tyson. New York: Basic Books, pp. 70–81.

Criticism and enactment: The matter of Masson. Address to Los Angeles Psychoanalytic Society, March 13.

1985 The object in psychoanalytic theory. Abstracted in Goldberg, D. A., Panel Report "A reexamination of the concept 'object' in psychoanalysis." *J. Amer. Psychoanal. Assn.*, 33:167–185.

On the theory of theory in psychoanalysis and the relation of theory to psychoanalytic therapy. *J. Amer. Psychoanal. Assn.*, 33:59–92.

The object in psychoanalytic theory. *J. Amer. Psychoanal. Assn.*, 33:301–334.

Anna Freud: 1895–1982. In: *The Social Science Encyclopedia*, ed. A. Kuper & J. Kuper. London, Boston and Henley: Routledge & Kegan, pp. 316–317.

Discussion to "Anorexia Nervosa and the Rapprochement Phase," by N. Fischer. International Symposium on Separation-Individuation, Paris, France, November 2–4.

Historical perspectives and current status. Opening address to two-day workshop on "The Significance of the Interpretation of Dreams in Clinical Work," Amer. Psychoanal. Assn., New York, November 23–24. Presented again in San Francisco, March 15–16, 1986.

Discussion remarks to Panel "Perspectives on the Superego." In Report of Panel by Tyson, P. *J. Amer. Psychoanal. Assn.*, 33:217–231.

Book review of Pontalis, J.-B., *Frontiers in Psychoanalysis: Between the Dream and Psychic Pain*. *J. Amer. Psychoanal. Assn.*, 33 (*Suppl.*):153 158.

1986 Seventeen: A developmental view. Plenary Address to Week-end Meeting of Chicago Soc. Adolesc. Psych., Fontana, Wisc., February 22–23.

The Century of Freud. Opening Address to UCLA Extension Division Symposium, Los Angeles, CA, April 11.

A Psychoanalytic Saturday with Leo Rangell. The Intrapsychic Process: The Human Core. An Organizing Concept of Behavior. Week-end Symposium of Los Angeles Psychoanalytic Society and Institute and Southern California Psychoanalytic Institute, Los Angeles, CA, April 11.

Discussion remarks in Panel Report by Friedman, R. C., on "Toward a further understanding of homosexual men." *J. Amer. Psychoanal. Assn.*, 34:193–206.

The enduring armature of psychoanalytic theory and method. In: *Psychoanalysis—The Science of Mental Conflict: Essays in Honor of Charles Brenner*, ed. A. D. Richards & M. Willick. Hillsdale, NJ: Analytic Press, pp. 89–106.

The executive functions of the ego: An extension of the concept of ego autonomy. *The Psychoanalytic Study of the Child*, 41:1–37. New Haven, CT: Yale University Press.

Von der Einsicht zur Veränderung. In: Festschrift for Harald Leopold-Loewenthal. *Sigmund Freud House Bull.*, Vol. 10/special issue, winter, pp. 237–249.

Discussion remarks to symposium "Repeating: Enactment and verbalization in different stages of development," held at the Anna Freud Centre Colloquium, Hampstead Clinic, London, England. November 8–9, 1985. In: *Bull. Hampstead Clin.*

Psyche und soma: Sprünge und Kontinuitäten, tr. into German by Ursula und Alois Palzer. In: *Deutsche Psychoanalytische Vereinigung: Arbeitstagung. Psychoanalytische Psychosomatik und aktuelle Probleme der Psychoanalyse.* Hofheim/Wiesbaden, pp. 35–59.

1987 The roots of evil in everyday life: A psychoanalytic perspective. To: The Anatomy of Evil: Confronting the Dark Side, UCLA Extension, Los Angeles, CA, February 5.

A core process in psychoanalytic treatment. *Psychoanal. Quart., Psychoanalytic Technique: 1914–1984*, 56:222–249.

Structural and inter-structural changes in psychoanalytic treatment. To: The Potential for Structural Change in Psychoanalytic Psychotherapy. Conference of: The Adolescent Day Treatment Center of the Psychiatric Service of Children's Hospital of San Francisco, CA. February 28–March 1.

A presentation of the work of Dr. Leo Rangell. Pt. I, Reported by W. H. Holyoak. *Bull. S. Calif. Psychoanal. Inst. & Soc.*, no. 78, summer, pp. 15–17, 31. Pt. II, reported by R. N. Anshin. *Bull. S. Calif. Psychoanal. Inst. & Soc.*, no. 77, winter, pp. 22–25.

Discussion remarks to film *Your Neighbor's Son*, Walter Briehl Human Rights Foundation Conference. Official Terror: Psychological Causes, Consequences, and Remedies. Reported by R. Brooks, *Bull. S. Calif. Psychoanal. Inst. & Soc.*, no. 78, summer, pp. 18–19.

Psychoanalysis: Where next? The Bottom Line. The Role and

Responsibility of the American. Part I. *Amer. Psychoanal. Assn. Newsletter*, 21(1):6–7. Part II. 21(2):6–7.
Introduction to Harold P. Blum, Plenary Session, American Psychoanalytic Association, Chicago, IL, May 8.
The decision to terminate one's life: Psychoanalytic thoughts on suicide. Plenary Address to: First Combined Meeting, American Association of Suicidology and the International Association for Suicide Prevention, on "Suicide and Cultural Values: National and International Aspects," San Francisco, May 25–30. In: *Suicide and Life-Threatening Behavior*, 18(1):28–46, 1988.
Discussion remarks, and Report of Discussion Group I, on "Sexual and Gender Identity in Childhood, Adolescence and Adulthood." Anna Freud Centre Colloquium, Hampstead Clinic, London, England. Nov. 7–8, 1986. *Bull. Anna Freud Centre*, 10(3):181–184, 229–230, 215–218.
Historical perspectives and current status of the interpretation of Dreams in Clinical Work. Chapter 1. In: *The Interpretation of Dreams in Clinical Work*, The Workshop Series of the American Psychoanalytic Association, Monogr. 3, ed. A. Rothstein. Madison, CT: International Universities Press, pp. 3–24.
1988 A look around. *Los Angeles Psychoanalytic Bulletin*, Special Issue Honoring Leo Rangell, M.D., winter, pp. 55–60.
In Memoriam: Helen Tausend 1906–1988. In: *Bulletin of the S. Calif. Psychoanal. Inst. and Soc.*, no. 80, spring, pp. 3–4.
The future of psychoanalysis: The scientific crossroads. *Psychoanal. Quart.*, 57:313–340.
Book review of G. Herdt, *Rituals of Manhood: Male Initiation in Papua New Guinea. J. Amer. Psychoanal. Assn.*, 36:833–839.
Roots and derivatives of unconscious fantasy. In: *Fantasy, Myth, and Reality: Essays in Honor of Jacob A. Arlow*, ed. H. P. Blum, Y. Kramer, A. Richards, & A. D. Richards. Madison, CT: International Universities Press, pp. 61–78.
A tribute to Ernst Lewy. *L. A. Psychoanal. Bull.*, Summer, pp. 41–44.
1989 Structural and interstructural change in psychoanalytic treatment. In: Change and Therapeutic Effectiveness in Psychoanalysis and Psychotherapy. *Psychoanal. Inq.*, 9:45–66.
Book Review of *The Analysis of Defense: The Ego and the Mechanisms of Defense Revisited*, by J. Sandler with A. Freud. *J. Amer. Psychoanal Assn.*, 37:245–251.
Synopsis of a treatment of nightmares in a seven-year-old boy.

(1950) In: *Instinctual Stimulation of Children: From Common Practice to Child Abuse*, vol. 2, *Clinical Cases*, ed. J. L. Weil. Madison: CT: International Universities Press, pp. 6–9.
Rapprochement and other crises: The specific and nonspecific in analytic reconstruction. *Psychoanal. Study Child*, 44.
Seventeen: A development view. In: *Adolescent Psychiatry*, vol. 16, ed. S. C. Feinstein. Chicago, IL: The University of Chicago Press.
Action within the structural view. In: *Internat. J. Psycho-Anal.*, 70:189–203.

Papers Delivered and in press:

The roots of power in psychoanalytic theory. Address to Symposium of the Sigmund Freud Gesellschaft, Vienna, Austria, September 22, 1984. *Bull. Sigmund Freud Soc.* (in press).
Choice and responsibility: An extension of psychoanalytic theory. Scientific Address to American Psychoanalytic Association, Chicago, IL. May 9, 1987.
Unconscious choice: An extension of psychoanalytic theory. Scientific Address to International Psychoanalytic Congress, Montreal, Canada. July 27, 1987.
Seventeen: A developmental node. In: *Frontiers of Adult Development*, ed. R. A. Nemiroff & C. A. Colarusso. Basic Books (in press).
The psychoanalytic theory of affects. In: *Compendium on Psychoanalytic Terms and Concepts*, ed. B. D. Fine & B. E. Moore (in press).
Introduction and overview. In: *Psychoanalytic Case Studies*, ed. G. P. Sholevar. Madison, CT: International Universities Press (in press).
From anxiety to integrity. The psychoanalytic journey. Address to Barcelona Psychoanalytic Society, October 8, 1987. Also: Plenary Address to 30th Anniversary Celebration of the Mexican Psychoanalytic Assn., Puebla, Mexico, December 3. Also: The O. Eugene Baum Lecture, 50th Anniversary Meeting, Philadelphia Psychoanalytic Institute, April 20, 1988. Also: Academic Lecture to The New Orleans Psychoanalytic Society, April 15, 1988. Also: Israel Psychoanalytic Society, Jerusalem, Israel, April 23, 1988.
Welcoming address to the 30th Anniversary Celebration of the

Mexican Psychoanalytic Assn., Puebla, Mexico, December 3, 1987.

From the work of Leo Rangell. The Human Core. The intrapsychic basis of behavior. Three Plenary Addresses to 30th Anniversary Celebration of the Mexican Psychoanalytic Assn., Puebla, Mexico, December 3.

How analysis works. Visiting Teacher Conference to Candidates of the San Francisco Psychoanalytic Institute. January 9, 1988

The Human Core: The Intrapsychic Base of Behavior, vols. I and II. Madison, CT: International Universities Press (in press).

Discussion, "The Significance of the Data of Infant Observational Research for Clinical Work with Children, Adolescents and Adults," Amer. Psychoanal. Assn., Seattle, WA, March 12–13, 1988. In: *The Significance of Infant Observational Research for Clinical Work with Children, Adolescents, and Adults,* Workshop Series of the Amer. Psychoanal. Assn., Monograph 5, ed. S. Dowling and A. Rothstein. Madison, CT: International Universities Press (in press).

Rapprochement and other crises: Infantile trauma in adult life. And a reminiscence of Margaret Mahler. Paper in honor of Margaret Mahler. Presented at the International Symposium on "Separation-Individuation and the Roots of Internalization and Identification," Paris, November 3, 1985.

The Human Core. The Intrapsychic Base of Behavior. Two Lectures. Visiting Scholar, Sigmund Freud Chair, Hebrew University, Jerusalem, Israel, April 24–25, 1988.

Discussion remarks: International Scientific Colloquium of the Anna Freud Centre on "Self-esteem and Shame: A Psychoanalytic Approach," Hampstead Clinic, London, England. October, 28–29, 1988. *Bull. Anna Freud Centre,* (in press).

Discussant of "The Need to Have Enemies: From Clinical Practice to International Relationships," by Vamik D. Volkan, M.D., Meet-The-Author Panel. Amer. Psychoanal. Assn., San Francisco, CA, May 6, 1989.

NAME INDEX

SUBJECT INDEX